On Rainy Days the Monk Ryokan
Feels Sorry For Himself

Ron Throop

Preface to second edition

I have always wanted to have a preface to a second edition. Here it is. There are very few changes from the original publication, besides a better proofread. This was meant to be a book of *feel*. A very rare find eleven years ago. Even moreso today. I remember sending copies off at my own expense to obscure bookshops in cities across America, hoping to be read by anyone, by chance. I would sneak them on the shelf at my local Barnes and Noble time and again, until I was threatened by a representative in New Jersey. I cannot recall the particulars of the threat, but it must have been good. I got scared and stopped the practice. I shelved it at the college library next door after the librarian refused to circulate it. Every couple of weeks I'd go back and find it gone, to which I would put another in its place (right beside Thoreau).It must have made her crazy angry.

"...*The present time disgusts me, even to describe. It is sufficient merely to endure it. I wanted to make a book with new mountains, a new river, a country, forest, snow, and men all new. The most consoling thing is that I have not had to invent anything at all, not even the people. They all exist. That is what I want to say here. At this very time when Paris flourishes—and that is nothing to be proud of—there are people in the world who know nothing of the horrible mediocrity into which civilization, philosophers, public speakers and gossips have plunged the human race. Men who are healthy, clean and strong. They live their lives of adventure. They alone know the world's joy and sorrow. And this is as it should be. The others deserve neither the joy nor the sorrow. They know nothing of what they are losing. They think only of adding to their comfort, heedless that one day true men will come up from the river and down from the mountain, more implacable and more bitter than the grass of the apocalypse.*"

—Jean Giono

"*Most of the young men of talent whom I have met in this country give one the impression of being somewhat demented. Why shouldn't they? They are living amidst spiritual gorillas, living with food and drink maniacs, success mongers, gadget innovators, publicity hounds. God, if I were a young man today, if I were faced with a world such as we have created, I would blow my brains out. Or, perhaps like Socrates, I would walk into the market place and spill my seed on the ground. I would certainly never think to write a book or paint a picture or compose a piece of music. For whom? Who beside a handful of desperate souls can recognize a work of art? What can you do with yourself if your life is dedicated to beauty? Do you want to face the prospect of spending the rest of your life in a straight-jacket?*"

—Henry Miller

Freeflow Publishing
Second Printing
Copyright© 2002, 2014 by Ron Throop
Library of Congress Catalog Card Number: No, Congress is stacked
with lawyers, which makes the whole lot very, very bad.
ISBN: 9781499532333

This book is dedicated to

Rose with her dinner plate.

She continues to separate the tiny pieces of sautéed onion from the buttered brown rice. I could leave the onion out, but then she would have nothing to never complain about.

(Keep reading. It's a purposeful double negative.)

Mr. President,

My dog is driving me absolutely crazy this morning! Trying to ignore the incessant barking and chewing up of his sheet rock cage is impossible. Yet I have to ignore him if I want to get these letters polished and sent. Who am I? I am a Frenchman. I write this letter to you in English because you know only one language. I know a hundred. I even know dog talk. He's quieted down now. I think all puppies are crazy!

These letters are open ones that I send to you from my country farm in southern France. Open for anyone to read so my name is not chosen by your secret service as a name to eradicate. I do not want American fighter jets spraying my farm. I am told that if I publish my letters to you, without actually addressing and sending them, then I won't be extradited and sent to one of your luxury prisons to watch TV. I like it in France. I want to stay here and sow lentils and beans. I am not dangerous. I am quiet, but lately I have been losing sleep. I cannot sleep at night, and my wife was wondering if it's asthma. No, it is not that. I am very disturbed over the recent history of your country. How do I mean, "recent?" I would say from your revolution until the present day. I am nervous and losing sleep and French farmers are not supposed to get nervous, nor lose sleep. My face is red and hot, and I keep waking up to find the moon in a different window. My wife snores softly. She is a woman. How could she possibly understand? That is why I have been writing these letters to you, *in secret*. You are a man, and the President. We have a President of France, but nobody cares. He comes to your bank often, and ends up leaving with a McDonald's. That pleases enough of us not to make any difference. But I cannot lose any more sleep. I am upsetting the farm. Just yesterday morning I forgot to milk

Aubrey the cow.

During these nights of insomnia I have been sitting down at the kitchen table scribbling my thoughts to you. I write with my pencil, a loaf of bread, and strong coffee. I am a native of France, and a patriot. My family has worked this land since before the days of our revolution. I am a peasant farmer. I made this table myself. Yesterday my wife got out our horse and cart and drove to town. I knew something was wrong, for she never left the farm before without me. I had time to make a yeast dough, look over our accounts, clean the barn, feed the dog, insulate the house, change the water, and sweep the floor. When she returned, her dinner and I were waiting at the table. She wasn't hungry. She had a bean crepe at the Taco Bell in Manosque. I asked her what is a "Taco Bell". She laughed a long time, and then asked me to sign her separation papers. I asked her what were "separation papers?" She did not laugh. She told me. Then I put her in the root cellar.

I want my wife back. I do not expect her to survive our winter at a constant two degrees centigrade. So this morning I got out all my scribblings to you. I must hurry and put them in order. If I can convince her that you are a monster and I am a human being, then I might get her to stop this foolishness. If she remains firm, and refuses to change back into a French woman, I will have to hire Antonio's wife to do the sewing and cooking. And, I will have to build another root cellar.

Sincerely,

Monsieur Throop

A New Baby In America

September 9

Our gifts

Why Democracy doesn't work.

The same everywhere

Last week I wanted to try prison. Now I don't know.

All too often I am having flights of daydream that take me to the essence of life. I see the light so to speak, and promise myself to get to it. Always later. I can have news radio turned on while driving up my street and hope that by the time of my death, I possess nothing besides a small cabin in the woods and a bushel of ripe apples resting in the autumn sun. There is too much stuff. It is difficult to remain aloof of things. But a single smell can show me the truth. Stuff doesn't have a smell comparable to the washing of dead leaves. Yet, when the right smell comes, stuff overwhelms it, and so many things get in the way. Is that not true despair?

It's a feeling of ripping your clothes off and running, or staying dressed but keeping nothing. You want a world of people, but you want them to be exactly like you. Nobody cares. You begin believing in squirrels.

Last week I would not mind going to prison. I welcomed the thought with an open mind. That was last week. Then I watched a movie about a man in prison. If he wanted visitors, he had to stand in line naked with other prisoners, while uniformed guards sat at the front of the line forcing each man to turn around, bend over, and spread his butt cheeks apart. If that is what prison is like, then I won't go. If that is prison, then I agree one hundred percent with murder. Any man who gets paid to inspect assholes cannot possibly respect his own human heart. So who should care if his heart stopped beating? We kill our food for standing in a field. We slaughter, chop, slice, dredge the meat in flour, splash it with wine over high heat, and call that dinner. We have no respect for hearts outside our own species. Armed robbery or asshole inspection? You tell me which man is more proud. Prison is a nice place to sit alone for hours and wonder.

These foggy mornings at the start of Indian Summer... Oh, my inspiration! My most natural lust! The first leaves to color are dead and stripped naked along the roadside. Three crows stand in the shape of a triangle, waiting. They must be witches. Squirrels forage. Life moves. The wind blows the leaves off the curb. They swirl around the bird's tiny feet. In the morning haze this scene appears ethereal, so much better than human. Whatever the crows are thinking will not be profound. They are positively not whispering the song "Reunited" by Peaches and Herb. Each might wish that she was a very big crow and that I was a worm. You would think autumn could make us hungry. By 7 a.m. I should have scrounged enough nuts and pears for the week. I could fill up the rest of this journal with "Ha, ha, ha, etcetera." I am six feet tall. My spine is straight enough. My big hands could easily wrap around a crow's throat; maybe even an eagle's. I can count. My brain is tremendously active. I can speak. I am so ashamed of my careless waste of manhood.

September 19

My Ford is Lord (to the tune of "Empty As a Frog's Stool")

Daddy's got a big truck, big truck, big truck
Daddy's got a big truck,
He's sad, he's fat, he's old
I'm gonna drive his big truck, big truck
I'm gonna drive it
to the Ford truck store
They're gonna loan me thirty grand, thirty grand
They're gonna loan me
My Daddy won't disown me
My wife will be so lonely

My dog will even bone me
My kids will always stone me
for a big truck, big truck
My kids will always stone me
I wish somebody'd kill me
in my big truck, big truck
I wish somebody'd kill me
in my depreciating Ford.

I am reading to Rachelle about the European explorers. Bartholomew Diaz, Amerigo Vespucci, Christofo Columbo, Balboa, Cabot, Cabral... What names! Great, brave, potentially consumptive men who really knew how to murder. The book might read, "...and the stark naked natives showered Columbus with exotic fruits and flowers, brilliantly plumed birds, and golden arrows. He and his men were in awe. This might be the lost Garden of Eden. The beauty was spectacular, the inhabitants peaceful and happy, food and drink plentiful. Europe was such a hard place to live in with all its disease, poverty and ruthlessness. It would be difficult to think of this new found world as anything but a paradise."

What the book might hint at but refuse to show in detail is the sardonic look on Columbus' sweaty face while he rapes a young island girl. She came aboard to deliver an armful of flowers. No mention of the chief's disgust of Columbus for emptying his shitbucket overboard. No words about the offensive smell of the Europeans, nor the slaughter of any man over fourteen who could not deliver his bell of gold every three months. Did it matter that there wasn't enough gold on the island to fill four bells? No. These were Tainos, naked and stupid. Put on this planet to wait forty thousand years for an anus-scented mad man to arrive on their beach demanding the impossible. And of course, to rape, plunder, and murder with the kind of obsession which only the most serious religious persons can muster.

So teach them. Instruct our little Columbus'-to-be on the virtues of fear. Give our future explorers and murderers of the soul an early education on what happens when a man kills because he will not understand. Why not create a holiday in his name? A day to Columbus, to Washington and Lincoln, to veterans of foreign wars, why not to Hitler, de Gama, Popes throughout the ages, tomorrow's American president, the serial killer who boils bones?

This morning I will ask her which stars in the night sky she would search for in the event that she became lost on a sea voyage to Greenland. Moments ago I was out in the dark marveling at the moonlight shining through the autumn leaves. I saw Orion the Hunter and gave to it my silent admiration. This will be my patron constellation. It must be so tired of men who look to it for gold. I will always give my wonder and praise to the mystery of the unknown. The simple question of a star. What is it?

Now where do the dead creeps of old Europe go after discovering what has already been discovered? To obscurity? One would hope so. But that isn't the case. Today their flesh rotting disease blows into my living room via the Illusion Winds. Into my home? How come? What do Columbus' twisted, sick thoughts have to do with our pancakes and maple syrup for breakfast?

"Today we went ashore and met with a band of natives. They had a strange habit of clasping their nostrils shut and making sour grimaces at my men. Fernando offered their leader an iron ball. The chief smiled, but did not appear sincere. Then, after a dramatic display of nose holding and hopping up and down, waving a hand back and forth under his nose, their chief vomited at Fernando. I had the entire band arrested immediately, attempted to convert their heathen souls overnight, and killed every last one upon discovering they could mutter only a 'goo-goo' in the name of Jesus Christ.

Still no strait to the Indies."

Before dawn I am an explorer too. There is a part of your brain that instructs itself to stop where it is, and search for the moonlight through the leaves. At this simple moment in time it accepts the wet grass, the soft breeze, the zillion stars in the pre-dawn sky as the starkest reality. I want her and everyone to be a poet. People have got to bury history in a deep hole. Cover it with dirt that is ancient but never mentioned in books. Love and superstition must regain their rightful thrones. Fifth graders know all about the European explorers. They have listened long enough to your candy-coating of arrogance and prejudice. Homework for Rachelle next week: A pre-dawn exploration through the woods. Listen for running water. Sit on a rock in the water and wait. What do you see?

That is a proper lesson plan for exploration. Bury the Spanish, Portuguese, English, and French. Their forefathers do not deserve a respectful heritage. Cross off their history. Make it a blank, a blotto. We are

devoting too much time to death.
Angst this week. Heavy without explanation. Stress.

September 20

The wind is a fierce lion. Watch out for the old trees! It might be their simple pleasure to drop a limb and crack open a human head.

Got a phone call from Tony last night. He let it ring twenty times like he used to when we were friends. Friends. Ha! Now I couldn't tell you who that condescending freak show is. In five short years he has destroyed our friendship. One that I swore would last a lifetime. He talked about my books like my mother used to... "What's this about having sex with cats Ronnie?" I felt so quiet. The most quiet man on earth. An aborigine holding tightly to my blow dart, tiptoeing across a wide open plain hunting nervous kangaroo.

"You must be in love with me. I never knew. I'm quite flattered."

No Tony. Once you occupied a kindred spirit log blocking my path to peace and happiness. I thought you were an artist, a gentle soul, a man. I stopped at the log to eat from my loaf of bread. You talked with me like we understood each other perfectly. I was easily fooled. I put all my faith in you. I finished my bread and rose to leave after watching two playful squirrels run past our log and up a tree. "Would you like to come with me my friend? No? Fine. I hope to meet up with you soon. So long and farewell!" Five years pass and I am sitting in the tall grass of an autumn day. Where are you? What are you? How dare you call and upset my constant! O God I got a life so rich and supreme! I am a humble pilgrim with holes in my shoe and the Russian winter rapidly approaching. My idea of happiness is the urban man crapping his pants at the fearful thought of it. I got up from the log eager to pursue the sameness of my dream. Why didn't you tell the truth? Why, after so much energy spent covering up white lie upon lie, why do you still call and expect me to talk back carefully? Are you that stupid? Is sophistication that naive to assume everyone else is a phony too?

I was your best friend. I was the calm center of your insanity. I was the reason to live in a world where no one cared about you. I accepted every deviation and never questioned your sincerity. Now I admit I am no longer able to give. But you can watch me and learn. Oh you expensive piece of shit! That is condescension, shot at you from a knowing heart. I won't play humble anymore to a sophisticated hamster. I know that I know I am a man. I have a sameness and a simplicity that balances on a log over rapture and ecstasy. I, my old friend, am perfectly sane.

Who am I writing for?
Maybe just one man. Someone will get this book by chance, or mistake it for a murder mystery to read on a windy day, by the lakeside, near a tree, in a barn. I write for the aspiring poet. Not the word-picker, but the feeler. I write for the man and the daughter he loves. For the working man who uses his nose, ears, and eyes, as well as his hands, to feel. I write for dogs and cats and only the unknown human masters of life, who would never waste their precious time reading a single word I wrote.

I write for the woman who lays in bed content and overflowing. I write for the cook who can expand his heart with just a small exertion of his will. He drops a cardamom into his shirt pocket, and works the rest of the night in India, oblivious to the imprisoned monkeys surrounding him. I write to prove that the world is wrong. I write not of hope but of truth. My mission statement: "Humble your ass now Jimmy. Not to men. To animals. To birds in the air. To the small innocent children. (Not all of them are innocent. Some will grow up to be a president.)" I write because I have to. Because I paint sloppy and will not kill. I write for the memory of poets. I write to perpetuate freedom's hope. What does that mean? I write to be clear, to be understood, but seldom am I either of these things. I write knowing everything I write is useless to the useful.

Goodness me, "teach them about anger." Finally I sit down to rest and dream, comfortably, with music swirling leaves in the air. A windy afternoon. The door wide open. Leaves running without legs or arms. I am an angry man. But I say this without guilt or repentance. I am glad to be angry. I am fortunate to be on this road. Such a glorious day to be at war with men. The forest road is long. The day is done. I stop at an inn to request a bed. *The Boiling Cauldron.* Oh, look around this room! There are some very shady characters casting mean looks my way. That guy has no teeth and grasps and ax handle, ready to strike. The one by the fire sharpens his knife on a stone. Everyone takes turns spitting on the dirt floor after giving me their hardest look. I have no fear. One loud snarly "Boo!", some frantic confusion, the big door slams, and the room is emptied. I've been recognized. They know me.

The jokers are afraid. I tell the keeper, "Forget the bed, I'll sleep under the stars." By now the whole world must know my honest, very dangerous intentions.

I hate you. I love you. But first I must hate you. And hating you is no light affair. I am standing still with my eyes fixed, watching your every move.

September 22

A beautiful morning! I love the fake dying of nature. The wrought iron fence, the dark before dawn, the cold moon... A temperate autumn in the Northern Hemisphere. Today I feel like a runaway pilgrim, a converted infidel. I left the hand-folders and head-bowers to follow the partridge and the stag. No more imaginary wildness! No refinement. I need to kill.

At work I read cookbooks to pass the time. One that I am particularly interested in is the *Joy of Cooking* by Rombauer and Rombauer Becker. These women are old world homemakers who know how to cook their catch. Jesus, they still strangle their ducks for aesthetic purposes. Strict meat eaters, with vegetables used to aid in digestion. The book was first published in 1931 and shows everything. How to skin squirrel, can hearts, prepare the woodchuck and the bear for roasting...

Women who cook for their men. Men who hunt for their women. Read the following passage about wild birds. Imagine the juxtaposition of your sterile plate of hot plastic goo with their timeless poetic arrangement of food.

To a large extent, proper care, immediately after shooting, determines the ultimate excellence of flavor in wild birds. While the bird is still warm, the neck is split and the carcass bled. Check the neck for any undigested food and remove.

To tenderize and improve flavor, it is necessary to hang many wild birds, specifically partridge, prairie fowl, ducks and plover, grouse and hazel hen—unless they are to be roasted. How long to hang depends first on age. Old birds can be held longer than young ones. A second consideration is the weather. In muggy periods ripening is accelerated. The third and most important is personal preference. Some hunters go to extremes, holding a bird until the legs stiffen, even until head and body part company...

We all have to eat. I am an apprentice chef. There are moments while washing the factory chicken when I feel a rage pulsating at my fingertips. I want something to strangle. I feel an urgent need to pluck, to tear, to use my incisors with their original raw intentions. I want a rainy fall morning with light just dawning and the barrel of a .12 gauge, cold in my hand. Rain turns to snow, I am not the feeble, whiny, Winnie-the-Pooh hunter who will shoot and miss three times before finally bagging a kill. He picks up death carefully while his friends watch and laugh—the hot breath from their lungs has scent traces of Listerine. These are not men. Inside I know they're crying over the senseless death of the bird. Their loveless wives are back at home with the children, pouring pasteurized milk over sugar cereal and dreaming of macaroni-and-cheese for lunch. The hunter's confusion is a constant, silent startle inside himself, like a thousand frightened partridge taking flight from the cover of pine and powder.

The neck is split and the carcass bled. That natural beauty is forgotten.

September 23

"She said, 'Somewhere, there's a far away place
where all is ordered and all is grace.
No one there is ever disgraced.
And everybody there is wise,
and everyone has taste.'" —Lou Reed

The obvious question: Where is heaven?

Here are some answers from a booklet some smartly dressed Witnesses dropped at my door. They left in a hurry when I told them that I already love God, and don't need a donation, thank you. I think their book is too confusing. If you want to convert the modern mind, don't use words. Words are no longer productive. Laxatives and trickery is smart marketing. Over the last hundred years, diarrhea is the most effective way to get God's name called out loud. Sex is somewhere in the middle. Joy is at the bottom, tied with finger slicing and toe-stubbing.

Anyway, here's an excerpt:

Page 1: Wally's (God's) Witnesses
Q: Where is heaven?

#1 Under your feet, asshole.

#2 What you see at the exact moment you wake up
#3 In the blue house across the street
#4 "Acklebantinklebicow!"
#5 Oh God! My toe, my toe, my toe!
#6 Wherever the dog sleeps.
#7 Forget it. Unless I can smash your face with this shovel.
#8 Behind that cloud.
#9 Sleeping.
#10 Definitely not in Bob's garage.

• Free laxative

Page 2: Wally's Witnesses

Take laxative before reading...

Do you love? Then you are in heaven. Hold on tight. Let no one harm your love. We are strangers at your door. We do not love you. The man next to me standing in his sharp suit has a dog he loves more than anything. Before he gets dressed he sits at the table with coffee and stares into his puppy's big brown eyes. He will outlive his dog, his father and mother, maybe his sister and brother, all of your family, the dog's family—Oh my God, not my babies! Oh my God! Excuse me, but I have to go to the bathroom...

Hold on tightly to your love. That is heaven. Let no one come and take her. Heaven is the child wrapped up in your arms. Heaven is her safe keeping. But it's all up to you. God is your enemy. He put the evil bastards on earth. He created these sorrowful storms. He killed the two skunks we drove over on our way to your neighborhood. He darkened the skies that drenched today's crusade. He threatens us with fire and brimstone. He murdered Job's family. He will murder your family! My wife and children are at home unprotected. Oh, what am I doing here? Oh my God, why am I dressed like this? Steve, give him the Lord's poem and take me home. Jesus, my stomach... Brother, can I use your bathroom?

We are all in this together. Where is heaven? Do not let anyone hurt her. Stay out of the car. Don't fly in an airplane. Wash your bodies. Cleanliness is a smart way to keep God and disease at bay. Eyes wide open. Constant openness. He's gonna get ya! No chance. No heaven. We need a new word for that dream. Earth. Laughter. Helplessness. Art. Beauty. Everything under the sun except car parts. Skin. Where is heaven? Leave us alone. Say, "I love you," roll over, and turn off the light. You can not get away.

I'm sorry about my friend. It must have been the tacos we had for lunch. Here's a piece of a poem about why you should push me outside and kick my ass immediately:

...O let the print
of her hurrying sandal
be unrecorded in the
meadow's thousand deaths
yet upon his heart
it has signed the angel's
name. For him the
distance of the world
is never less than when he is forced to think
how all he loves must soon be taken away

—Kenneth Patchen (from Heaven on Earth)

September 24

The rain is keeping me indoors. I love the face of forced laziness! Walk throughout the house today. Make an apple crisp, and waste an hour to smell its baking. These are the cool days when boys stop talking and just do. What do they do? Well, if they want to be men, they do nothing at all. Just throw on a flannel shirt and read a good book under the light. A good book damn you!

Here's what I want all of you to aspire to...

Sunday, September 23:
The Day the Artist Clipped His Toenails

Frank lived with his family in an old logger's camp at the base of Mt. Hope, two miles in from the highway. The road to his cabin could not be traveled by car. He had to walk to get food and mail. It was 1943, a year when all of America came this close to eating their human kill. Frank wanted nothing from the outside but food and mail. He was patriotic enough for the U.S. Postal Service, and fond of Sam, their mail man.

Frank's wife and child were content and peaceful. He often thanked his lucky stars for that stroke of good fortune. They kept their dreaming personal, that is, the daughter walked the dog around the lake while the wife calmly waited for the landing of the loons. The days were magic. "To be human," he often thought, "was too beautiful for words."

Frank painted a thousand watercolors of the mountain. That was his art. Portraits of the mountain in the seasons. Mostly of the rain and snow, when his model was barely visible through the fog. Nobody bought them. Sam, the mailman, would reassure him. "Really, these look a whole lot better than a smiling Jap." Most of the time, on his walk back through the forest with his bundle of mail and milk, Frank would come to his senses and push the sorrow out of the way.

Meanwhile, the whole world was at war. Sam told him about the murder of his sons and nephews in the Pacific. It made Frank sick to his stomach and once, he threw up at Sam's feet, over box elder and wood rot. "Isn't everyone sick Sam?" Frank foolishly wondered. Sam sighed. He tolerated Frank's questions because there were only two men left on his route. The other guy was an old WWI vet, who sometimes shot rock salt at Sam, imagining him to be Kaiser Wilhelm, the mailman.

Sam shrugged his shoulders, "It's war Frank. It's ugly, but it's war."

The summer of '43 passed just like the summer of '42. White flowers and the fresh green leaves of lazy July. The geese sounds in the gray overhead mingled with the hopeful smell of dinner in late September. This was the artist's simple routine. NOW, stand Frank's calm melancholy up against the wide-eyed fear of your only son ten thousand miles from home the second he spies a flash of light from the brush, and the next second when he sees his mommy kissing him good night. He's dead. Do you understand? Oh boy, here I go again. You gave him life and now it has been taken away. Who took it? The President? Yes. The mayor? Yes. You? Yes God, you. You horrible parent. You rotten human being. You devil's devil. You no longer possess the instinct to protect. What kind of mammal are you? Why aren't you tearing the flesh from your son's murderers? How can you justify this? Is your child a rabbit? Did you make love to his father who was a rabbit? Can you squeeze out a hundred more of these before you die? Mother sends her child off on a train whistling straight to his grave. What a cute face. Showered and shaved. What an ugly thing a bullet does to his precious face. But war is ugly, and that's a fact. And thank God almighty your son was murdered, Mrs. Smith. His sacrifice really slowed Tojo and Hitler's advance. Yes ma'am! That's what the letter says, so it must be true. "Morning mom. Wow pancakes, thanks!" No. He's dead. His happy face had bullets shot into it. The letter gives thanks for your son's life. They dragged his dead body over the bloody wasteland, tossed him into a used coffin, and dropped him at your door. And tomorrow if Mr. Pres. says we're going to the Middle East, then let's go. Hurry up! Yes, by God let's go! It's got to be more exciting than listening to those silly bird calls and waiting. Just waiting. Always the endless waiting. Acquiesce. Give in to the power of your elected leaders.

Frank? Where's Frank? Why bother with Frank? Oh I am so sick and tired of stories. I wish Frank was a glowing hot steel ball shoved up your colon.

So instead, I clipped my toenails.

September 25

Last night work was very slow, but I made the best of it. I am the highest paid cook, so I better contribute once in a while, even if they put me at the fryer where the most capable heart and hands in the dirty restaurant are at the mercy of a tub of hot oil. I pureed some fresh strawberries and heated them with cream and sugar. Some gelatin, milk, and banana liquor... A dash of salt. Strawberry-Banana Panna Cotta. Then a slow, deliberate chicken stock that I maneuvered between heat sources, so not to disturb the ornery cooks who become violently possessive over their assigned stations. "Don't boil," I told the stock. But the stock already knew. I tell it to teach the others. They boil all their soups and stocks. Especially Covey—he's the best at ruining the possibilities of food. The cooks are guilty. They come to work and expect money. "I'm here. Pay me." They gamble or read gun magazines. They think about beer and coffee. Television for a day. Not an egg-thickened sauce. I say, "one bubble to the top of the stock every four seconds..." You hope that is enough. It is a gentle thing, the stock. No. Even the sous chef hates living. He dips his tongs into the pot and stirs with a fury.

September 27

Grabbed the homemade astrolabe off the table as Rachelle was walking out the door with her mother. Quite an instrument! Within seconds I had our latitude. 43.5 degrees. Just above and exactly below the line where all the polite, unconditionally sad people wait. Oh Screw it! Just words. I feel. I awoke in the cold dark, got out of bed, stood on two feet, envied my sleeping wife, and began the routine. First I peed for quite some time. "A lot of water," I thought, "for a six hour sleep." Then I came downstairs to begin the day. The pig, the cats, the coffee, the dog, the writing, the oldness I feel on top of my eyelids. What is happening?
It's all bad.
What is?
Everything
except silence
tears
laughter
and a gentle voice.

I am not telling the truth. I have no idea why I am here. I like maps, my child, my wife, cooking, picking herbs, housework, cleaning horse stalls, driving with coffee, getting up before dawn, home schooling, reading (sometimes as little as a paragraph a day), listening to music, eating. I like football in season and the romance of the past. I would like to know what the hell is going on. I need to know beyond a doubt that to like these things is good and enough. That to try to like more might make me explode. I would like to believe in God so I could put an end to all these things. I would expect a universal, undeniable assurance, acceptance, and congratulations for cutting myself down all the time, and making about as much noise in life as an amoeba on a log in a forest out of sight.
I love imagination. Ah, but it can be so disappointing when we know where we are going. I need to get there with poetry, yet there might not be one person on this planet who has the same desire. Yes, that is depressing. Yes, that opens up every new and old door to anger. Yes, I feel like some dirty trick has been played on me. I never wanted these poems in my head. I did not expect to think wrong or right. I never

thought until I began to think, and now for the time being everything is ruined. Even the simplest chores like eating... Without God there cannot be hunger. Without God there is no satiation. If you expect the morning to be there, then you do not know God, and you will be suffering with me until the end. This includes everyone waiting.

Little ball in space
go the other way today
These thankless wretches!

Rachelle and I read about Sweden. We were both fascinated by the pictures. Marie took the day off from work and drifted off to sleep while staring at a Sami girl standing on the ice. Our baby is inside her. On a boat the little girl and wild animals sleep. They drift down a clean water river. The gray fox and the brown bear watch from the bank while waiting for their fish dinner. The trees are tall and old. The sky is blue and arctic cold. These Swedes are very beautiful.

September 28

When cats get asthma, they are very stoic about it.

You want magnanimity, eh? Here's a refresher course for the low low price of fifty dollars. However, we are not responsible for what the hordes of toothless overweight morons will do when they get a hold of these papers. We suggest practicing gifts of kindness and gentle manners on your cats and dogs at least five hundred times over before attempting a beginner's loving kindness routine on your first human infant.

With *Magnanimity Again* you will learn the lost ancient art of being human, (or was it just a spittle dream?) Chapters on trust, goodness, grace, tact and beauty are sure to make improvements even to the most psychotic and perverted intelligence. And there are over fifteen thousand colored pictures to keep the brain awake enough to read. "Can't kick the cat or spank the dog, hold the fish out of water, or even swing the guinea pig on a string. Not unless they're being really nasty and cumbersome."—from chapter two, *Don't Kill With Your Bare Hands*.

Order now, and for just $29.95 you'll receive the *Helen Keller, Look,*

Hear and Talk Like Me Ball. A small state-of-the-art electronic device that sets under the tongue or in the ear, and, with a charge lasting up to seven hours, will get you through most complicated societal encounters. You won't be able to hear your colleague when he leans over and whispers, "I'd really like to have sex with your wife, but her pubic hairs are too long." You wouldn't see him either, or talk back, even if you wanted to articulate, "How does this feel?" while carving "scum bag" into his chest with a boning knife.

I had a very bad night at work. I don't want them to read, write, make tasteful jokes, ask how my child is doing, toast my good fortune, say words like "splendid" and "happiness." No. All I am saying is that there are children with cancer, emaciated mothers feeding their babies lead-soured breast milk, and the incredible fleeting beauty of sunlight's shimmer dance on your wall. There is still hope. Because dying things aren't cracking "jokes" about pubic hair, I want these sick bastards to die, or to be dying. It is incredible how taken for granted breath is. Just a small head of kale forced into the mouth, a firm nose plug, five minutes watching his eyes pop out of his head, and then a roll-over into the cold river. I don't care if I am discovered. Magnanimity doesn't mind prison. Just $79.95 and I can have them all killed? Wonderful. With a *Look, Hear and Talk Like Me Ball* I can eliminate my enemies of the human race? Good show! Simply splendid! "I should get a promotion for this!"

September 29

Asthma. The first morning of the heat switched on in the house. Winter hates me.

I will begin this day with a letter to another hack writer, some other young failure, who might be just as confused. I will drop it in the mail on my walk to work this afternoon.

Dear writer,

I don't know you. I know very few outside of my beloved family. I have two friends, Kevin and Pat, but they are suffering from our disease too. They do not make attempts to contact me via the soft spot. My heart's feeling is very strong, and I am aware that the world is crushing

me. My art is wretched. Nothing I write is useful. I am a good cook,
but asthma wants me to copy a rabbit's diet. I am thirty-three years
old, married, rich enough, and a father of one, and one on the way.
Where are you?

My hope is that you are in need. Did you write from the heart today?
You probably didn't show it to anyone. Do your parents wonder what
went wrong? Did they send you to college to become a millionaire or
a man? Do you work in a factory next to TV monkeys who get their
art feelings while driving by car dealerships? Are you getting up at five
a.m. to hack out words because you see a richer, more abundant life?

I don't mean to bombard you with personal questions. But I do feel
the need to get personal. I must seek a colleague. Such a huge country
and I do not know even one poet. Yes, I am shy, but isn't everyone?
Why not? I don't want to be completely shut out. God, it's so wrong
to write for nobody. I laugh at myself so often, sometimes out of a
false humility, other times because laughing is better than thinking.
How crazy to be humble at the pursuit of your own desires. Humble
to the point of crying out, "Oh to hell with who you think you are,
Ron Throop! You think you are better than everyone else, eh? What
about your family? How are you going to feed them? Do they want
your anger, your contempt of strangers, your persistent god damn bitter questioning of everything?"

So I begin to distrust my own creative intuition. Why? A feeling of
being the only line cook left in the world, working alone inside his
hot kitchen, cooking creative dishes, and serving them to no one. He
must be crazy. "Pick it up on the point Marie!" he calls. But Marie
never comes. Food? What is that? We don't need your culinary art.
A waste of time! My contemporaries are overly satisfied, gluttonous
blobs depleted of nourishment. Now they must eat their own fat to
survive. My neighbors do not want me. I am not useful like the bad
cook who might feed them one night a month with a cut piece of cow,
powdered potato mix, and dirty salad. To the blobs that is fuel and fuel
is useful. Who wants long menus of scatter-brained confusion and anger, especially the disillusioned poet's very personal flights of distorted,
disturbed, sometimes demented confusion and anger?

You, I hope. Can you help my career? Give my confidence a boost?
How about a letter a day? Some morning exercise to get the juices
flowing? How pleasant to know that someone else strives to create lobster soufflé for beings who fleek saliva at the mention of Burger King.

It's a comforting feeling to know that another shares that insecurity. I can cook you a fat partridge I choked myself. How about some small, round potatoes stewed in the bird's own fat? We'll meet at the table and discuss our future plans. A novel? Ah, phooey! That's a Whopper with extra cheese. Why waste your energy for those saturated fat-in-the-brain pigs with shoes? Pass the snails. How about this for a cover..? A picture of the blue sky and forty or fifty gigantic blobs with canned raviolis pressed into their slime chasing me down a hill...

October 1

Fruits and vegetables on the tablecloth. On this cool hazy morning I shall execute the perfect dog walk. I know my themes are repeated over and over. If I do this enough times, I might end up with five or six perfectly picked and placed words to explain the entire horror show of modern life. Drive slowly by beauty walking through the leaves. Songbirds sing along with her and the wind in the trees. Coax beauty into your van with a false smile and caring. Then pull the door closed and slap your devil face back on. Proceed to carve her up while she cries out for love and compassion and gentleness.

Today I live for the shes in my life. When their eyes open wide, I will clean, bake, play. I will kick right into gear for love. Yesterday in bed with Marie I let her have it with the angst. I cannot be so selfish to forget about her. She never blames anyone. The child inside... Both imaginary and literal.

But get a load of this...

Further on I promise to write about my chef. I have been wanting to do so for over a year. There is so much meat on his bones. Spoiled meat for the starving to pull from the garbage. Writing about him will not change the world, nor improve a single moment in the life of some poor and neglected human being. But it will show my grandchild what I was up against, the blockheads I had to fight just to get my hour a day, maybe two, to do the things I was born to do.

It would also be fun to write about some of the other characters who work with me into the night. The shared pulse of no-life, therefore no poetry or love. The death of life standing upright, propped like an Irishman at his funeral, usually with whiskey and a sham of a good time. Human beings ruined from the top down. Exhausted. Pooped out. Circumstance has nothing to do with their miserable lot in life.

They are able to eat and pay rent for less than a forty hour work week. That's a job. The strike babies of the last century were fooling themselves. This cannot be the hopeful result of the brotherhood of man. These spineless animals? But yes it is! Their own grandchildren and great-grandchildren. A club on the head for an eight hour work day? If they didn't strike, they were mere slaves. Who really wanted to stop work at five p.m.? What did those lazy buggers give back for that luxury? More bars. More men-only games. More spousal neglect and abuse. More children ignored and made to wait to grow up miserable like Dad. Nothing has changed today. A thousand revisions of tried and true cover-ups and alibis. No better love. No better devotion. No better humility or caring. Death to compassion. Death to passion. A concave curvature of the spine. A hundred years later and we've developed the freedom dreams of captive horses. My sous chef puts on a heavy flannel coat—wait. Rachelle just woke up. She stands next to me asking if I'll clean up the dog's vomit. Time to keep my promises. I will catch up to my reading public later.

October 2

My sous chef puts on a heavy red flannel coat. It's a cool autumn day. A pumpkin patch in the neighbor's yard. Crows on the mowed lawn. Crows on the porch. One crow eating grease out of a can hanging from the portable grill. My sous chef bought a pellet gun at Walmart. He's twenty-two years old. Crows and squirrels eating. It might take three or four close shot pellets to penetrate a layer of crow skin. It stuns the bird. He flaps in the yard crying. Reload and point it a foot from his wide open eye. Fire!

What kind of father made him and kept him?

Sous is a French word.

Of course man is evil.

When I was eight or nine years old I aimed my BB-gun at a fat bumble bee resting on a peony. I pulled the plastic trigger and petals exploded into the air. Last night I picked up a pincher bug and put her in the garbage can. Over the years I have killed a battalion of mosquitoes. Because of malaria in the tropics I pretend that it is war with the mosquitoes. I won't harm a spider.

Last night I quoted Kenneth Patchen to him after he justified his backyard crow massacre. "They were noisy," he said, "while eating the grease off my barbecue."

"There are no proportions in death." I replied. I should have quoted myself, and followed that line up with, "That means your precious pale hide is covered with crow feathers. Your daddy and mommy are crows. You are pecking at the grease of the world and creating a nuisance unknowingly to a thousand living things a minute. How many pellets to penetrate your thick skull? Do you see why it's not a tragedy if a hundred crows ate your brother? What the hell is so god-damn human about us? If to be human is to be merciful, caring, or just a little bit careful at least? Romantic love and the slaughter of cows. How do we make love with such bloody hands?

Today is a school day. We have a hundred apples to bake and books to read. Rachelle my sweet baby child, reveal your true cruel heart. There are happy squirrels running to and fro. I intend to teach you how to rip off their hides with boots and your bare hands.

I love my innocent babies. I am a daddy crow.

October 4

Was it this day Marie was told to remember? Something would happen to change her life forever. Her mother bought her a psychic and the psychic said...

She told me that she loved me five years ago today. Yes of course I remember. A gray cool weekend in New York City. How cocky I was back when I smoked a pack a day. How strong and durable and hopeful. How ignorant and wonderful! An aspiring painter-poet wanted to court the girl of his dreams. I was dreaming about her for over a year. One day lived full and unforgettable is fuel enough to transcend a lifetime of disappointment. To be a failure in love, to stay in love, making backwards adjustments whenever necessary, to acquire and then release yourself of the burden of everything... To go back to nothing—that is my greatest hope for us. To be content with a poverty that moves with nature. Do we understand that first love is the only true love? And I mean love, not safety, not comfort, not money. No lovers are free if two cannot spend all their money today, right now, and finish their first cold autumn night together slurping soup on a bed. Where are we going if not backward? Forward to death? No! To smell the autumn evening with you by my side. Look, that's the moon. That is enough! For our lives to be everlasting, we must remain poor and glad and eager.

October 5

Am I rich enough to stop for longer periods of time, to sleep at least an hour into the sunrise?

I need a massage of the lungs. Asthma is stealing my breath away.

And the getting up before dawn to write. What good is that torture? Write it down in a big black book. Oh, but the first sentence never looks good on paper. Handwriting for Ron Throop is such a cumbersome task. Too bad! The big black journal moves with you. One is not forced to write at a table in the dark. Nor made to get up at dawn for lack of a better time. Write by the river, in the grass, from the teahouse. Most important of all... Write nothing if it's time to be a better human being.

Time to be a better human being.

I have beside me a wife, daughter, a living yet unborn child, a dog, two cats, and a guinea pig. This is immediate reward. This is a very personal public. I want their love and happiness. I want mine too. But theirs must come first.

Last night on our walk to get cat food and coffee we bought a scratch-off lottery ticket "just for the halibut," as any seafood line cook might say.

"This is a spit in God's face," she said.

"What do you mean?" I asked.

"We're already so lucky. Why do we push it?"

Last night's walk home. No span of five minutes was ever so beautiful. No walk more great, more poetic, more heroic. We came home with cold cheeks and sleepy eyes, and pushed our bodies together to keep warm on a cold night. I picked up Thoreau's journal and read a few entries. A great man. A great thinker. Writing so beautiful and flowing. Writing. Words.

Beautiful? No.

Just an Immortal? No. Dead.

Am I immortal? So far, yes. At least until I die. I will sing my lover's praises. I will sing my families' life, our days and nights. But most important of all, I am singing for us, the wife, daughter, unborn child, dog, two cats, and a guinea pig. As far as I'm concerned we are the song of the world.

October 12

I have asthma. I wish I had an easy breath, one that could be forgotten. We're convinced that I am allergic to our cats. The doctor told me to get rid of them. Human beings aren't really humane are they? A good movie to watch, if just for the courtroom scene, would be Dr. Dolittle. His defense for himself and the animals is a true rhyme. A good chapter to read to find out how weak in the spine man is would be "Higher Laws" in Thoreau's *Walden*. I think I'll read that today.

American Football's Popularity Rising In Equal Proportion With Mass Infant Circumcision

Why do it
After listening to those glad humming sounds?
Why slice
after the giggling,
The evening tummy rubs,
The bouncing rides..?
Surely these jolly moments might preclude
the beginnings
of ecstasy outside the womb
You know,
actually a happy, gentle, caring child.
That's all us boys dream of
even after they snip off our foreskin.
Happiness
Wisdom
Strength to stand up for the uncircumcised
For the whoosass in the lunch line
To fight for his honor
To let him know in no uncertain terms
that sure you're pissed off
that the first thing they thought of
after nine months of sweet dreams
was cutting up my dirty little pee-pee
and Frank and Sal's and Dave's
dirty dick

Now we're all nuts
having the potential to murder too
because after circumcision
they didn't stop and hug us and give us dolls
We played with trucks, footballs, and guns
And looked down into our shorts
always in the know
that something was wrong
Very very wrong
So incredibly wrong
that's it's no small wonder
each of us hasn't thought
more than once about
hanging from a tree.

How out of place do you feel?
The circumcised watch Monday Night Football.
Little boys push a backhoe
Little girls color horses on the floor
Girlfriends and wives
think about hair and skin products
and improving the smell of the house
I mean
how do you look on the couch?
Do you stare at them and wonder "how
can their movements be so pure and innocent
after they've done this to my prick?
How can they want me?
Where did hope go?
What is a man?
What is money?
What is a job?
Why am I so selfish?
How is it that all of us know what football is?
That angry player just said "Mother fucker"
These are pigs who have nothing in common
with me
and yet everything is sadly the same since
we've been cut back to expose the head.

Football. TV. The Presidency. Paying taxes and the garbage bill. The company. Health insurance. An entire row in the supermarket dedicated to dog food and cat shit. The Internet. The 40,000 dollar truck. The 10,000 dollar used truck with rust. A stereo. Video games. The radio. So many shirts and pants.
I want my foreskin back. I want to be different.
I want at least twenty feet of foreskin
to make up for the difference
of years of not-knowing what I am.
I want to be a man

November 27

I think I might begin writing again. Long month of many happenings. The tooth fairy flies happily through the faraway clouds and different sun of childhood. Ask me about it tomorrow. I need to teach.

December 3

Boy, am I filled to full! Birthing classes, a healthy baby, demi-glace in beans, and a tall stack of school subjects to organize, pancakes, recipe writing, reading *Huckleberry Finn* to pass a cold morning with my daughter... And an apartment to build in the back.
A frigid day. This business is my fire to tend to, my stock to feed. There is no neurosis. There is a selfishness reigning supreme over our emotions. It is an early 19th century Christian world. My fire, the cow, the children, cooking to survive, sewing to keep warm. I'm going to make you understand my position. Everything prior to this was a feeling out of the situation. I can show you crazy. I can easily point out the insanity of you and your friends. But I would rather raise sane and happy children. You don't know me. You never will. You can't find me. Yes I am famous, but I am also invisible and fleeting, thriving in a world of my creation. This is a France of the past in an absolutely cheerful and carefree future world. Honest, good, wondering, creative children make up my village of grown-ups and babies. I swear this poet's heart has the power to categorize you, to condescend, to label you and your friends as old chickens in the yard behind the barn. Is anyone hungry? If you hope and pray not to become dinner, step out of the lie, as a chicken, and we will feed you feed, and care for you as a pet,

and love you like our own. But as you are, you are nothing more than me, or the bark of some old, dead tree, fallen deep in a cold forest that you haven't torched—yet. There are no proportions in life, or in death. Our sameness with tropical sand creatures and the beaver damning a small stream running out of the Hudson Bay should be as obvious to you as your own skin. Why then is it not? Why so blind? Here is a nineteenth century primer for the eternal man inside you who should have as much of a concept of "century" as the hungry fox stalking the snowbird.

January 2

Beany the dog ruins all potentially happy mornings because his nose is attached to his ass. I stood outside in the cold for a half hour while he chose the perfect square foot of snow to soil. Yet because I let him look, I must be a good man. That should cheer me up.

Over the years my grandparents had dogs for love and company. Probably very delicate prima donna mutts like Beany, who were also careful about the placement of feces. But they had land. Beautiful land! Trees with tall piles of snow fallen on their branches. Intense quiet. Fluff. Pine green and cloud white. The blackness ahead, The unknowing. Yet a friend with a nose like healthy human eyes in broad daylight. A happy soul willing to take you along on his morning walk. Time to meditate. To be quiet. To dream. Who am I?

How can I help give my beautiful wife the happiness we all seek? What is a perfect day? What will my grandson grow up wondering? Someone wants to hold my hand. My dog loves me. How many more mornings like this one? I used to skate with her when we were young and didn't care. I don't want to burn garbage. Won't answer the door today. I will stay dressed in my pajamas. The most useful gift I ever received was a pair of slippers. No one knows who I am. My dog lives for these morning walks. What have I ever given worth a dime of happiness to another soul? Everything has a soul. My dog deserves more than this. I want to play for the rest of my life. I just don't know which game.

Oh your beauty is so upsetting. I am mad because I can't take that photograph and fold it into a shape sharp enough to poke into the chest and through my heart. I want you here, where I can never get. I have no control. I will always be less than fully alive.

January 12

My life is a flux of noisy Spanish colors. From the front porch I see the Northern Lights blazing fantastic colors. An invisible crowd of strolling men, women and children are speaking Spanish. "Azul, verde," whispers a faceless voice. Oh, Spanish! Those are deeper colors than blue and green. The only way an American can be persuasive with his voice is to say blue green lake, wait a few days, write several thousand pages trying to explain to another man the madness of "blue green lake," and then promptly go into despair, bash his own skull on a big slab of granite, and wait for the slow tide to cover his dead face. But if he could understand and speak the language of those many things which trouble him!

The beautiful changing colors.
Working in America
The Weenie Omnipotence of Doctors
My Mother's Friends
A Book on How to Make Better Tips
A Book on How To Quit Your Job

But first I'll begin with a love song to my daughter.
It's her eleventh birthday!

It is in your eyes
that thing keeping me alive
What's behind your eyes—
You are singing from your eyes
what you see in the leaf
what you stir into eggs and honey
what you touch on your barbies
when you lay them in bed
how you ask when you are happy
how you ask because you trust me
I don't know and I don't care—
The real meaning of a man
is what you say it is

Everything has to be what you say it is.

Once again, I've quit employment. I have no one to talk to. John stopped at the house yesterday and bullied us with his vile and confused gab-a-lot. I swear to God there are no men! Here's a Laundromat poem of the twenty-first century. I want everyone to go to hell.

Why Do I Quit?

Oh, very smart question
to be asking yourself in a Laundromat!
Isn't it obvious?
No?
"That's such a nice purse!"
That's such a good answer.
"That's such a nice purse I want to die,"
I could say,
and the zombies walking by,
my bulging eyes just miss them.
Oh the minutes here tick tick tick tick
by you the man
who swears he's the only man left
willing to shed these clothes and quarters,
this car, your car, more clothes and towels,
a pair of underwear for each day, socks, pants, houses,
the agonizing, tortured thought of sockspantshouses...
You can buy me a wardrobe
I might thank you
but I don't care
I've never been moved
I've never had anyone to thank
Nothing makes me happy to live
Nobody is smart or bright alone
and if a thousand people think you're good
I WANT YOU ALL TO GO TO HELL!

I need a man and woman to cuddle up across the room
two heavy wool shirts
washed last August not last night

He must be a fine goy
with Scoottish aukcent
He has to be a Scoot
It's much more manly to be a Scoot
NO, IT REALLY IS. I'M NOT WANTING TO BE FUNNY.
The sheep know him
They know his hands
A man will be judged by the look of his hands
We must look at a man's hands
We have to stop reading
Jesus Christ
I should just leave a bomb somewhere.
Cuddle up with my wife too
and Jack and his wife
Oh the smells of our women in the kitchen
the wind howling against the pane
the empty black freezing night
a thousand miles of sea and storm
Nobody anywhere but here
Not on Mars, not in the city
WE ARE SCOTTISH MEN ON A HUMBLE FARM
We are unlikable ornery pigs without money
So not here
So sad here
where everyone is alone with expensive stuff.
Go through your house counting every thing.
It will take a year I promise
You are not Jack Scot
You are no good
They made you this way
needing nothing times a million
and a Laundromat littered
with stubbly boys in hot fluffy coats
wide-assed from pizza and sitting
short-necked from pizza and sitting
Little soft boy lips
voices like zoo animals with human heads,
pizza and television
Good God

Christ
Popes and Kings
and pus-lipped
hunched back
peasant men,
Hard useless quiet monsters
THERE ARE NO MEN!
I'm running out of paper
Even the mass-murderer has plump titties
Say,
if we move this camera in for a close-up
maybe the god-damn sops will believe every word we speak.

It's a Mexican Christmas
by Rachelle Throop

When I was young and happy the world was a ball. Every morning I awoke with a troop of small helpless animals just like me, and we'd pray together, and whisper softly words like "joy," and "sweet," and "love". We would lay together in the sweet grass, the leopard, the muskrat, the bunny, the squirrel, the wolf, the myself... I was so happy to be alive. I wrote a story and it was very important. I read it to my family at Christmas. Five miles into the forest deer stood in the snow that fell from a sky that went on forever, black and cold and empty way up into itself. I love you. I don't know what it means to be sad. I have no heartache.

¡Hola! Welcome to Mexico. Now I know we're not really in Mexico, but let's pretend we are. Outside it's warm and sunny, flowers are blooming. I'm going to tell you about all of the Mexican holidays, that come at Christmas time.

Flowers are blooming. There is a child nestled safely in my wife's full belly. Yet I have no idea what that means. I am afraid for her. I don't even pretend to know that a child is with us always. We have been making love with our baby listening. Any day now a child will be born. I have the calm piece of mind to write my thoughts because I am a scared piece of shit. Everything in our lives should explode with wonder. Science, man, the universe... Children should fight the last crusade. Bite the hand that feeds them. Then maul the hand and eat the rest. They should be merciful and band together and kill us. Then have a tea party.

I am so much in love with the child in me who has been beaten, mocked, and left for dead. I am a scared little boy because I grew up and there is nobody out there older than me. Please help.

A Poem I Wrote For the Kale and Cantaloupe

The saddest part of knowing you're dying
is hearing *Squeezebox* on the work radio
I'm so in love with you...
Picturing her thinking that when she looks at you
Feeling that from her eyes when
life was a blazing sun
Knowing that you knew once
life was a blazing sun
maybe in another life,
but knowing nonetheless,
Hearing The Who's *Squeezebox*,
I'm so in love with you...,
and having no erupting thought
beyond that of making a pretzel.
Boil a pot of water
All creation rolled up into a pretzel
I'm so in love with you...
Oh I can stand here in a white shirt all night long
mocking life
cutting up, dishing out, scraping off life
It's the stream of bullets shooting into my mouth—
I can't hack away enough the thought of
you being so in love with me.

Oh yes to God my love of my life, my every second's
hope and prayer is for you to always be
so in love with me.
But more important than anything ever
is for all men to go on living
passing on to a higher plane
with a wise and cheerful blessing

that will not come from a true heart
until I've lived the rest of this life
so in love with you.

Last night Kevin called to talk to me about my latest quit at the restaurant. He's a good friend and a good man. In fact, we could become men if we tried a little bit harder. But that's neither here nor there...

We talked about my crazy boss who hasn't come out of his house since June. I compared him to Mr. Potter from *It's a Wonderful Life*. He really does push buttons and expect the best. I have always pitied him, until the inevitable moment when he has pushed me too far, and I am unable to make a measly paycheck because even I, the poor Chinaman, can see him laughing at my ancient pride. I up and quit, more to punish his audacity, than to defend my ancient pride.

But it comes. Ten times now. Because I am an artist, and an artist can live on bread alone. No, I mean live on bread alone! So any one can see how that confounds the businessman. Especially when the artist is working amidst a creative stream and the money rolls in and the boss is getting a real pretty steak put on an ugly plate. Even more so when that artist lives alone among men in a small community of fat-jowled, dental plan, "Geez I can stay this way and even get worse until I get my twenty years in" state workers and factory men who have no ancient pride or modern pride or any pride that would have them abandon that shiny new truck payment. I help empower the businessman who sells creativity by making beauty a cheap thing from a minimal food cost.

So I quit. I hate making people money. I would like everyone to quit so the boss could cry for his mommy. Kevin likes this idea deep down, although, ever since we became friends, he's played the Devil's advocate all too often. There is some embarrassed presence blushing within Kevin that makes him bow before the man with more means. Two winter's ago, during a snow storm, the boss called him out to the bar and told him to get a broom and brush off his car. He didn't ask me because he knew I would have slashed his tires. Not that Kevin doesn't have any pride. But it's precisely that Chinese acceptance that makes such a timid America. It never sits well with me. I was born. Isn't that enough right to rule the world?

Anyway, most of the cooks got laid off because the boss is losing money fast. Even the chef got tossed. That was a huge loss for me because he alone was making my work life livable. Come in at four. Leave at ten. Six hours to think about work. But take the chef away, and the cheap artist will do the same thing for next to nothing. That's what the businessman who's falling apart thinks. Now triple the effect of that destructive philosophy because he won't come out of his house for six months. Bad business. Now he hasn't anyone besides the flaccid-jowled, "I gotta keep gas in my car and coffee and cigarettes and a six-pack a day habit" restaurant workers without any sort of benefit plan, and the boss has a very nerve-racking summer ahead of him.

Of course we could benefit, all of us, the boys and me, by forming a guild to protect ourselves. Mr. Potter doesn't have to be the only devious planner in Bedford Falls. But I have never known a more pitiful people than American men. Look at them yourself and wonder why the persistent slave mentality. All for two hundred bucks! All for our little world not to fall apart! And we think that our measly two hundred dollars held it all together...

No, we could never organize because it is so much safer to be a poor coward than a poorer hero.

January 13

So Kevin called me the other night, half drunk, and gave me a subject for a book that would make money. He admitted that it would be no literary challenge, and that it might even be embarrassing to write, but any publisher would take it immediately because of the mass market opportunity. Will they ever learn? Just because I know bread, that flour, yeast, a little honey and water make a loaf worth eating, if all goes well in the process, it does not necessarily follow that I would have success at creating the perfect shit white bread that Americans love to squeeze between their dirty fingers. I have about as much chance of writing a book entitled "How to Make Bigger Tips" as Tim Johnson at the Wonder Bread Factory has of baking the perfect French Country loaf. If he works at Wonder Inc., he has never baked a single loaf of bread in his rotten, degraded, strip mall-minded existence.

Man, I want all of you to be this simple! Right now, mimic the life I imagine and together we shall skip through a kind, ancient forest and be friends to ourselves, each other, and all living creatures. Let us organize to destroy what is so unnecessary in our lives. History proves that humanity, when inspired toward a common cause for the greater good, is earth's most capable destroyer. No more empty words. No more happiness if it has to remain merely a word for the rest of our lives. If everyone, even poor old Helen next door, lit their drapes on fire, and scooted the family and the pets out the door; if every neighbor did this right now... And ripped wires out of their standing machines. If men pulled their shirts off and women flipped off the old homes that kept their lives full of radon and misery; if each neighborhood mass huddled together in one giant ball because the night was cold and the stars were out, and everyone came this close to a terrifying death, then that would be the best way I can think of for making bigger tips.

My unemployed chef came by for coffee yesterday. The first sunny day after a month of snow. He told me that he went over his finances at the kitchen table while thinking of suicide and the fear of tomorrow. He'd be all right with his unemployment insurance, that is, his house, utilities and truck would be covered. It was food and fuel he could not afford. Not without some other income.

We should all have our legs sawed off for being this stupid.

January 15

The most emotional day thus far in our married life. But I won't go into that!

Fanaticism can be a strong piece of artwork. These words you hold in your hand right now are the necessary product of heart strangulation. A steady, methodical choking inside the most sensitive layman to enter paradise in a long time. A good old-fashioned wrenching of the vitals is my reward for being born. The truth is I hurt more than any of you. It's the year 2001. Someday a hundred years from now some lazy boob like me will have romantic daydreams about my world—the kind of dreams I have about Walt Whitman or Henry Miller. A drafty corner to set up my writing station. Paintbrushes standing in a cup. Borrowed music playing on the Victrola. A wood table. A wooden cup. A pair of warn corduroys, shoes and a hat. Mr. Miller goes for a bike ride along the Seine. Thunder in the sky. Couples run off the path looking for shelter. A grin from ear to ear. He'll meet a friend in a cafe, tell him of his latest wonder, and take small sips from a Pernod, a drink I find absolutely awful tasting. He'll get back to his room at twilight, the smells of the city fresh in his mind, and write with an incredible burst of energy before bedtime. Seventy years later I'll look over what he wrote and feel my stomach full and content. I do almost the same imagining while reading Hunger or Pan. The fanatical authors write living books! It's impossible for me to be further away while reading *Tropic of Cancer.* Here's what I'm trying to express...

There's a kind of truck parked at the store. A pick-up truck, with a hood taller than me. A diesel engine cranks in the cold. Everyman wants one, the young and the old.

It's forty thousand bucks of big tires and music. You can put envelopes in or hang a scented tree from the mirror. I can't prove how sad Everyman is today. Logs from trees he cut down? Bales of sun-dried hay?

The sound it makes in idle. You must know the truth about man's demise. These trucks are twenty times bigger than men with cigars. Thirty times larger than most of their wives.

You can buy one blue, green, or black. Only three colors now because nobody cares. I can play you a song about a slow-mo death. Played for the young, dumb and the dumb, young acting old... Just walk past a diesel idling out in the cold.

January 16

I will slip into my journal another piece of writing that could have been some use to the world, but my sweet woman prefers to lay low, not making any big noises in this life. Lovers must compromise. She put up with enough crap from me over the years.

Thank God a man can still get dandruff. Good old-fashioned dry scalp to remind him that he's alive and has poor hygiene.

Look here,
We do not want the

Hepatitis B shot
into our baby
Thank you
You see we worried
wondering if any one would tell us about it
Nobody did
so we're telling you—

We are not in need of decision-making by others for our living child.
Please God give us the strength to endure their reckless abuse of life.
We determine the gentle movements of tiny heart, lungs and brain.

And Thank you for helping guide our baby out of Marie.

Ron had an experience with Rachelle. She was born, thank God,
alive, but quiet until the myconeum was sucked out of her lungs. The
labor was long and mild, until the doctor said "Let's break your waters,
honey." She whispered, "No, please," but he stayed firm and unmoved
and not interested in "No, please." So he stuck in the pin because he
wanted to and then
  Pitocin and then
  Epidural and then a
  Spinal and then probably a club against her head
  if she didn't scream the baby out of her
  But she did
  Thank God
  So now I'm religious
  Every "No" we are screaming at you with
  hot religious zeal
  All decisions are religious
  We are religiously concerned that we decide
  how to birth our child.
  We believe in our hearts
  that you wouldn't trust a bus driver
  if he broke through a mountain gate
  and drove the bus over a cliff—
  not unless he delivered your children safely home first.
  Please let us react to you without fight or flight
  the day our child is born.
   It is not by mistake that we have read so many books on the subject
of babies coming into the world. We love our child, and want the best.
That is why we have chosen your house to give birth. That is a high
compliment—
However, books are in my hand, on my lap, laying in the grass beside
me on a summer's day. They give answers. No nurse has stopped by to
relax my worry, to comfort my mind and remind me of the beautiful
days to come. Instead of building a trusting human bond with mother

and father, modern medicine has got up and gone to work performing duties that pay well enough to stay alive without worry. So have I, the cook. I perform my duty in a small restaurant along the banks of a dirty river. When someone comes over to my place for dinner, he can get onion rings on his Steak Au Poivre, although they're not on the menu, and I know in my heart that eating that garbage will kill him, eventually. He's paying for a service that I and my fellow colleagues provide.

We shall not buy something we do not want.

Here is a birthing menu. We are very poor renegade Amish farmers stopping by to give birth to our boy Samuel, or our girl Beth.

Big City Birth

Appetizers

Rupture of membranes
(Served with stubborn impatience
and baby not quite ready)..$7,069.00

Fetal Heart Monitor
(Dressed in discomfort and as accurate
as listening with old man's ear)....................................$8,678.00

Pitocin
(Usually served with rupture of membranes via
impatience, and just as comfortable
as getting a gorilla to wring out your uterus
with his hairy hands.)...$43,000.00

Entrees

Epidural
(Might relieve mother's pain, but Samuel
will grow up attracted to farm animals).................$69,000,000.00

Spinal
(In the year 903 A.D., sitting on a stool in
a stone hut with wet thatch on the roof,
and a mild outbreak of bubonic plague

devouring everyone of house and field, Miss Jackie
O'Leary had a safe and happy birth without
a needle put into her spine. The doctor, who
was her brother's milker, said she saved her
father's family six hundred hen's eggs)
....$Involuntary Cranial Shutdown

C-section

(Why don't we just tell the truth about
God? Let's write the most foul, Satan
infused blasphemy, and get it over with
quick! I am so ready to cross the line of
humanity. All it will take is for that rat
bastard to reform me into a wild dog, and
I'll take to the streets mauling every living thing
in sight. Why are we here? For obstetrics? No
you cowardly little mice! We're here to give
birth to our own Jesus Christ! How much
for your knife? You're getting the little
gigglys aren't you? Can't wait to stick the
blade into my sleeping virgin wife?
Oh boy this civilization has become
the shoddiest bunch of high-falutin'
screw-ups and crackers. If I can prevent
one helpless young man or woman from
entering med school.... If just one young fat
head after reading these words thinks twice
about pleasing his vile, rich mommy and
daddy, then all of my mornings will be justified.
You don't love me. You don't appreciate me or
anyone in the world who doesn't leave your
paneled, sterilized office before bending over
to wet your pallid white ass with his lips.
You don't believe. You don't love anything
but money and power. You are an empty, dead God-player.
So much for your Hippocratic oath.
Faker! Liar! Thief!... $Slavery!

Please no pipe or cigar smoking in the delivery room
And then this to my senator...

My child will be born in one month, hopefully happy and
> > healthy. It
> > is my right as a man and my wife's right as a woman to deny
anyone
> > the
> >chance to touch our child without permission. What kind of
> > frightened coward dare invoke bogus law to challenge our
God-given
> > right
> > to make and raise children? Who are you to write these laws? The
"terrified to think for yourself" medical profession is
> > not
> > my mommy. I cook for a living. I think most Americans could eat
> > cardboard and enjoy a better diet. But what right do I have to
> > choose
> > what a man eats? Filet Mignon with Sauce Choron? No, I'm sorry.
>That
> > gas
> > alone could choke your neighbor. You're going to eat bulgur wheat
> > and
> > rice cakes from now on. The day New York State walks into my
home,
> > rapes
> > my wife, kills me, and assists in the birth of her bastard child,
> > then
> > that is a day to stick any needle you want into our baby. My
> > religion,
> > my philosophy will dictate to my conscience. Not doctors. Not
> > lawyers.
> > Not judges. I swear to God, if legislators were told by any moron
> in
> > a
> > coat and badge that heroin was now a good thing for babies fresh
> out
> > of
> > the womb, they'd be getting the little jiggers in their hand just

> > dying
> > to sign new mandatory heroin injection laws. No one will touch my
> > baby
> > without permission. Thank you.
> > Ron Throop

Rachelle sleeps downstairs on the couch. Marie sleeps with our baby inside her. The sun must be over the ocean now casting its light on the waves. Seagulls are warning the world of its coming. Sunrise in Newfoundland. Good day to the world. Being alive in Oswego in winter is like living inside a cold rock at the bottom of a deep cavern. I'm not pretending the world is better anywhere but here. It most certainly is! I want my Walden! Give me my seagull eyes and the strength I lack to hunt for the lives of my children.

Does that sound silly?

Welcome to a manless world.

Letter to a Mother

You do not always give. You are potentially half the world, but you do not always give. You can be a traitor to your child. You do not necessarily understand love outside of you. You might think you are giving love when really just some days you're a damn good organizer. Much too much is written about you on your behalf. You feel sorry for yourself. You should. You might not even want your child's happiness. You might take her last dollars she saved for a dolly and spend it and hope that she never asks for it back. You could think that money is important. You might love money. You would take money happily. You want to be smart enough to make money. Maybe most of the world's evil began as a woman pretending to love a child, but really loving money.

Tonight she is cold but happy as long as she does not suffer your schizophrenia. Do you have a clock? Do you have somewhere to go? Are you always going? When she grows up and has children I hope she is her father. She will lay warm with her lover. She will always know happiness and want it. The furnace in the basement will believe in the work it does and proudly pump heat into a happy home. When I am angry I think I am telling the truth, when really I am just being an insensitive ass. And, I am a poor communicator.

"Then there are the middle classes—the bulwark of the nation, as we blithely say. Sober, steady, reliable, educated, conservative, self-respecting. You can count on them to steer a middle-of-the-road course. Could there be any emptier souls than these? All living like stuffed cadavers in a wax museum. Weighing themselves morning and night. Saying Yes today, No tomorrow. Weather vanes, shuttlecocks, noisy amplifiers. Have kept up a good front all their lives. Behind this front—nothing. Not even sandbags." —Miller

January 18

Winter should just ride by on a horse and slice off our heads with a sharp sword.

And yet I'm still relatively happy. Probably because yesterday I got my mane cut and body sprayed with soap and water.

You should see me laying in bed with Marie at two in the afternoon. I am a scared little boy. Do you see what they've done to us with money? I know I've been brainwashed simply because it hurts so much to think of the good without a steady income. One wonders if it's all hopeless. Then one wonders if one's own family and loved ones are trying to kill him, or drive him to kill himself because they know he's not employed, yet they go to Walmart and buy jeans. Or they send twenty dollars a month to Rico in Columbia because they want to be good Christians and feel useful by giving, and yet they don't see their own child or nephew or best friend tying and untying frayed pieces of rope in his teahouse. Yes of course he is lazy! Yes, he doesn't dare work for a living. He just wants to experiment with his own life to see if these jackals really love him. "Stand up on your own two feet. I picked beans when I was starving. I picked fights when I was bored and picked my ass whenever I found myself standing with nothing to do. Christ, I was always able to make money. What the hell is wrong with you, Hmm? And if you're going to write... Geez, c'mon! What the hell is this crap? Just a simple whodunit? would do you some good. A novel about a lawyer or a cop. Have the bad guys burp and fart and use foul language. Make the good guys say "important files," "witness," and "testimonial." Or, if you can't do that, Jesus Christ, drop the damn fries in the oil and count yourself lucky to be alive. I don't believe a word of it either. At least not since I was ten years old."

Then give to your alma mater. Some people send as much as a hundred dollars a year. Some give to God on Sunday, but then God gives their quiet daughter double pneumonia probably because three dollars didn't cut it. Just buying a cup of coffee is a spit in the writer's eye. Leave the seventy-five cents. You'll buy from a begging Girl Scout. See, we're teaching her to beg. "It's good to ask for money, honey. As long as we give cookies in return." When I was twelve I participated in a bike-a-thon. They expected me to go door to door asking strangers to become my sponsor. So much money per mile. A total of twenty-six miles. Mrs. Smith sponsored me a quarter. I rode my one speed bicycle up and down hills on a hot day stopping at designated rest stops for a McDonald's hamburger and sugar juice. I worked hard. The kids with MS got cable TV. The doctors who research MS got a free spinach salad at a lunch paid for by the hospital and money towards a down payment on, yep, you guessed it, a bright shiny new silver Jaguar.

So come over and visit, but please come with a quarter to sponsor me. I'll work upstairs in my little room for three hours. A quarter an hour. That's seventy-five cents. Almost a dozen eggs. If you want to stay and visit I'll fry you one. I can't cure MS, but I can cook an egg thirty ways. I can pick up my dog's poop with a quick swipe of a plastic bag. I can string together sentences with poor grammar faster than you. That's got to be worth some of your old pennies, yes?

Man, everyone is in business taking extra and giving back less. Then what's the problem? Supply and demand? Oh, c'mon...What do you really demand? A bird feeder? Molding? A pad of lined paper? A magazine? Gasoline? I'm a good man. Toss me a bone. Or pennies. I'll take your dirty pennies.

Friends, family, worthy strangers... Come to my door if you are in demand of anything which I can provide. A cup of coffee? Come over to my house. I'll charge you a quarter more than what it's worth. A hamburger and french fries. A quarter more than what its worth. Stop giving to the faceless man, the greedy corporation. Do you need a pedicure, a haircut, your oil changed? I'll do it for a quarter more than what it's worth. Please don't force me back into line cooking if I can write French fry books instead.

Years ago my cousin had a sponsor. I thought it was wonderful. So did my family. They fed and housed him week after week in the summertime while he played the New York string of the PGA Mini-tour. His sponsor bought him a used Cadillac and paid for a chunk of his travel expenses. I don't want a Cadillac. I want to eat. For twenty-five cents a day I promise to win the U.S. Open.

God Please Give Me a Mop Large Enough to Soak Up the Schlop of Xerox

Just look at the awesome size of it!
It takes some time to pass this pile of
squares beside squares next to
little squares, big squares
on top of so many squares
Call 'em walls
Steel, granite, gypsum
slabs of death-in-a-box
Hard, bitter waxed floors,
more squares, two or three rectangles,
a triangle and a tiny
octagonal shape from the shy zany architect
who committed suicide right after Xerox—
Two minutes to pass
at forty-five miles per hour
All these squares,
two thousand or more and
wires weaving through wire mazes of
small wires, fat wires, long, very long
thin wires and outlets to outlets to
boxes to more squares
Six hundred thousand outlets
with screws and twelve million nails
Six billion screws
Two trillion black top pebbles
crushed beneath
a constant stream of human headlights
going round and round in circles
around the biggest square of squares
O whippee shit
Big sky my ass!
Big clouds, big snow

O whippy shoot shit
Big sun my ass!
Big moon?
O whoppee whippy shotty shitty woppa wumpa shit my ass!

Xerox in the middle of a forest by a lake
Deer turn a fuzzy muzzle
"what the hump is that?" They ask
Weasels, wrabbits, wraccoons wonder
the tubby house fed squirrels duck under
logs and sticks they stop
they thunder
"What the crap is THAT!"
This is dawn of winter's day
Look Mrs. Doe, it's a Xerox!
If you need copies for no reason,
oh my dear deer, you have
bound and leapt to the wrong place.
Probably have to skin your own hide
and wrap the meat up in a butcher's bag,
drop in the back of a bearded factory
hairy-faced human's truck—
He'll bring you inside to his break table
Throw you on it and say something like
"Here Jack. It makes damn good jerky."

A Xerox
Jesus, bandit the coon,
the nicest old lady in the place
would stab your pups with silver knitting needles
before giving up her
data-entry job with benefits.
All of 'em, every one
would walk by your head on a post,
over ground
and forest dead and burnt
acid in a stream
clouds raining radium and
constant heavy low moan sounds

rolling across the putrid air.
Any price for squares
cable TV, used boats
fishing poles
shaving cream
bumper stickers that read
"Topless, it's the law!"and
"Greed is an act of fear"
huge tires
envelopes in the mail
dirty carpets to clean
over and over again,
purple knickknacks
and—
O I can't write worth an industrial complex today!
Simply put
the absolute truth is this:

Each man and woman to walk through the doors of Xerox would fornicate with a bunny rabbit, if no one knew, and it kept them their jobs.

January 19

Marie and I attended Rachelle's Passport Club in the basement of a little church on Main Street in Cato. Happy children sitting in folding chairs with hands folded. Thank you so much Mr. Happenstance, for letting me see the light! Humility. Honorable humility. The smiles. The worry. The happiness I have given. The open doors... How insignificant and wasteful is grown-up land. I want to go to *Beauty and the Beast on Ice* to see my beautiful child gaze at the wonder of nonsense with a thousand other contented, simple souls. The light shines through the church window. The grownup light is dull, usually blocked by a mail truck or moving van. The skaters are beautiful. Everyone wears woven mittens. Rachelle and her friends Constance and Laurie hold hands. There is light. They are breathing. I know that any father who loved his child, and gave to her, and thanked her, and then lost her, has gone crazy and died.

Her caring hands.

On Sunday Marie was crying. She came into our room and gave Marie a back rub with her small hands. Sad music. We are all so fragile. Tell me how daddies find their way. I sent my poems to a publisher. It appeared his company was friendly, so I also included three books that cost me almost forty dollars because at certain weak moments in the day I am a vain idiot. I never received a reply. No "thank you." Nothing. I went to his website (he's a poet, but more famous as a publisher of poems), to see if their was a "Thank you" posted to me. No, nothing like that. Plenty of past newspaper articles about the importance of poetry and news. The words "Zen" and "San Francisco." Blue phrases that are underlined. Hit them with the cursor and travel to another childless world. Oh man. There is no poetry. How important it looks. You can have some believing, but god dammit there is nothing there! A career of word arrangement. Bad words too. They all want to be rich, and rich can very well mean having a lot of people know who you are. I want nobody to know who I am! Your stupid words! Your bullshit inspiration! How clever! What a foggy special world of your own and your circle of soft-fingered men! You are no better off than a lawyer and friends sitting around a fire talking trash about their one slim chance to be alive on planet earth. It is all the same fake language you speak in the same circles. Leave the poems alone! Why aren't the children celebrated? I know. Because they are not powerfully clever enough. They weren't there at the right time—at the rally, in the cafe, on the court, on the march... And they don't toss in the word "fuck" in their poems about snakes and winding rivers and sunshine glimmering on the mountain lake. Oh the lasting, true beauty of children... How insignificant the basement of the small white church where the homeschooled kids gather to learn about Spain. How dirty and bleak the farming village of Cato, N.Y. in January's gray dull light. This is a statement to all men, and women who pretend to be men... The following curse I launch is aimed at your kind of spite and self importance that blows its foul stench of words into the prevailing winds, hoping to choke my child and her happy friends before they realize that choking you might be a better time on roller skates.

Ron's Curse on Mankind

May all your money turn to ducklings
Your possessions burn to stone
May your well full of water
dry up like dinosaur bone
May your dog and cat forsake you
All your food spoil and stink
May your wife run off with neighbor Joe
his rat pee in your sink
May all the hopes you had in life
fall like a Hippo on an egg
May you live a hundred lifetimes
but first you'll have to beg

You really have to leave the children alone. Stop for a few seconds and breathe in through your mouth and out of your fingers. That feeling running from the heart, through the chest, arms and hands, and finally leaping off the ends of your fingernails...That small, wonderful feeling is all that you need to cope with the wrongness you have practiced thus far. First get the feeling and then work off that. Repetition is what we're after. The sameness of that wonderful feeling. The children feel it in other ways. You have to feel it this way because it's the only way you have left. Take in a deep breath and let it out past your fingers. If successful, there is a sunny, tropical paradise waiting for you. Lavish mogul empires to ride through slowly on horseback, dressed in finery and in charge. There is a whole spinning earth to walk around on dizzy with glee, at least as cheerful as the eager children listening to a lecture on Spain, some tired spot on a map called Europe where old people grow up to die.

January 20

Baby Throop any day now. I am so excited, tense, scared, emotional... Jourdan or baby Jane...Which grace awaits?
Today, after writing, my main concern will be consommé. The doctor says Marie can't have any solid food because I think the doctor wants more than anything to cut Marie open and have a look at her inside out. Doctor's orders. I believe we should rethink our attitude towards

the medical profession. How can it be trusted? Why do we reward it with our trust? Marie is pregnant. She needs energy. The doctor and the doctor's friends would rather her not have enough energy to push the baby out. Twenty-four hours without food. They hope birth will end up in surgery. They love to hear their team called for over the hospital intercom. I think we trust the doctor because we think his life is not as boring as our own. We trust his encyclopedic knowledge although most of us shy away from encyclopedias most of our lives. Doctor has her eat nine months straight for the baby's sake. Don't drink. Don't smoke. Eat good. The doctor doesn't know what the last order means, so it's left up to the father to translate. Fine if the father is an artist, but the other ninety-nine million derelicts have their wives settle for Happy Meals and Stoeffer Macaroni and Cheese Dinners. All of this "good" advice from your doctor, yet the mom and baby are expected to fast on baby's last day in paradise. Then if mommy cannot push because she just hasn't the energy, the wise doctor will provide plenty of options for her to consider Quick! He will want to release a very painful synthetic hormone into her veins. It is called Pitocin and it pretends to be a contracting uterus. Then come the offers of drugs because mommy's pain must be relieved. The doctor pushes the drugs even though they are linked to childhood mental retardation (the kid grows up wanting to be a doctor). Then an episiotomy (to satisfy the doctor's disturbing urge to slice open perineums), and forceps or vacuum extraction for the stubborn, sedated child. All that before Junior can squeeze outside for a breath of fresh air. Oh my God! What if he can't get out? Maybe his mom is too stoned to feel. Don't worry. Doctor will put mommy to sleep with more drugs (definitely not nicotine or alcohol—those are relatively safe compared to the crack house he works out of). While mommy sleeps, the bloody baby fairy magically appears to cut open her stomach, whisks her only child off to be inspected past a gauntlet of unloving hands, like the convicted entering his prison. Mom can look at the thing, but *do not touch*! Doctor's orders! The good baby fairy left a smiley face scare, prolonged intense pain, and a devastating bill of sale. For thousands of dollars, they got you that thing alive and just slightly deranged and unprepared for the dangerous life ahead. For an extra fifty, if mommy happens to push out a boy, the good doctor will cut up his little penis with razor precision. There... Now that's a work of art! Doesn't that look nice? He's screaming and could possibly go into shock and die from the agony alone, but heck, I'd fuck it, wouldn't you? Here's some ointment for the eyes because we assume that you have gonorrhea. Well, maybe *you* don't have it, but those dirty street people sure do. Can't take any chances. Sleep now. Rest mother. You worked very hard for this joy. Sleep, sleep. Rest now. For in just a few weeks my colleague, the pediatrician, whom I trust with your child's life, although I don't know his face or name, will have his army of toxic inoculations ready to invade your baby's healthy immune system. Two weeks, then twomonths, fourmonths, sixmonths, 1st year, 2nd year, school age, DPT, Polio, Vertigo, MMR, Chicken Pox, fever, diaper rash, meningitis, pink eye, hepatitis, tonsillitis, boils, hemorrhoids, ear infection, stress, depression, the maddies, vomiting, high blood pressure, low blood pressure, societal pressure, asthma, allergies, toxemia, scabies, lice, ringworm, strongyles, tapeworm, rabies, poverty, poison oak, poison ivy, pigeon toes, nervousness, neurosis, convulsions, temper, fear of grown-ups, fear of doctors, the wanton abuse and torture of animals, inability to make friends, selfishness, greed, anger, hate, jealousy, despair, Tourette's Syndrome, bad manners, poor dresser, easy target.

Yes, it's just plain smart to simmer consommé today. Healthy humans do not need to go to the doctor. If I can convince two people today to avoid the doctor tomorrow, and these people can do the same, right down the human line ad infinitum, then we can oust these dangerous quacks from our previously unmedicated planet earth.

It won't happen I know because most people are oblivious. I've had a sinking gut feeling ever since I met our doctor. Of course she can't be trusted! Why should we trust her? Because she loves us? Do we trust anyone before love? Yes? Why? Because generally we are stupid. Is trust a noble trait? No. Why? Because people are good and bad to each other and my life is not a roulette wheel. You must earn my trust. I will not take chances with my own life, let alone my unborn child's. So what can I do about it? Well, unfortunately Marie refuses to have the baby in our bed, so we're going to the doctor's work house, who more than likely would not miss dinner out tonight if earlier in the day she delivered a stillbirth. I pity her if any seen or unseen injury damages little Jourdan or baby Jane. Isn't it a lovely world that coaches a father to begin his child's life with threats and unjustified accusations to invisible enemies? Yes, it's not my fault! As a newborn baby boy, I too was on the pediatrician's rigorous schedule. Modern life was brought to me, not me to it. Maybe I was sick, but damn everything! Now I am diseased.

Just a moment ago I let Beany run loose into the backyard. He and Frisky the cat love to chase the birds and squirrels. It gave me some free time to think. Yesterday, Marie and I went to a family doctor for a consultation. We wanted to get his opinion on immunizations. This "feeling out" of prospective physicians has become a common practice for us lately. We don't trust anyone! Well, to tell the truth, it is me who won't trust anybody. Marie is a Libra. Libras see every angle, but unfortunately for the Aquarius, they tend to side with the guilty party. Libras appreciate both doctors and the criminally insane. No, it is I who searches for the "right" person when pressured into looking for a doctor. I could spend the rest of my life without one, if repeating nuisances such as asthma attacks or my child's exploding eardrum could be avoided. These misfortunes happen because of my own negligence. Proper home care and prevention hinders development of both dumbness and disease.

As a young man I was willing to take the doctor's opinion as truth, if not law, which should be one in the same thing. I had no reason to doubt his learned expertise. Really, I could care less what was done to me as long as I got better. I had very few doctor visits in my life. The first one I can remember happened during my freshman year at college, after two long years of avoiding my swelled and monstrous left testicle. It had become too big not to notice. When my roommate brought back a pamphlet on testicular cancer from the health center, I knew that it was time to see a professional. I can't remember the doctor's name or face. He asked me to drop my pants, said "Oh my," and two weeks later I was out like a light, under the knife, and sent home with a monster scar to show my girlfriend.

Yesterday we went out in the cold late afternoon to visit with a prospective client who will oversee our babies' medical emergencies. We can trust the doctor to handle an emergency. All minor and major ailments, from the common cold to influenza, ear infection to rabies, diarrhea to pink eye, and any other childhood discomforts and diseases will be sent over to our offices, Marie's and mine. She's a mommy and I am a daddy. Who is better equipped to handle infection? The licensed cadaverous physician clutching a clipboard, shooting off his mouth and gesticulating his body as if he were playing air guitar, to prove a well-researched and documented point-of-view? Off his sickly, green tongue memorized medical terms and phrases jump past his white lips with frightful intentions. But he's wasting his time. Words make us angry. We are not poor, ignorant teenagers voicing a "yes, doctor, what-ever you say doctor" answer to every problem. We are intelligent adults there to find an emergency care provider. The stuff of broken bones and deep wounds. All other visits are just a waste of our time, money, pride and joy. He doesn't agree. Now he doesn't trust *us*. That is what this world of books and cars has come to be. The idiot thinking the other guy is stupid and always so depressingly vice-versa.

I bet there is an Erasmus society in existence on the web. At Oxford or Harvard paid academics discuss discussions over what discourses Erasmus discussed with his eager students. The poor doctor had books. Greek books. Roman books. "Get back to the classics fellow sufferers. For the next hundred years we should dive into the pool of ancient learning, and dog paddle there until we tire and drown."

Yes, an ancient scholarly twit like Erasmus is studied because he studied Roman law and wisdom, and was so amazed by their utter simplicity and cleanliness. Of course the poor dirty beggar Erasmus was impressed! He walked about the shitty streets of Europe just gid-dy in anticipation of the next eggs of knowledge to ingest, those to nurture his mind and the minds of his well fed followers. The cult of "oneupmanship". To know more than peasants and kings. It is no different today, except that knowledge finishes last in a one man race. To know is to pass tests is to graduate is to set up practice is to get rich. Any dwerb can know. It's the greatest failures of the heart who actually get rich off knowledge. And failures of the heart prefer long nights of study. It takes discipline, hard work, and a well-trained ignorance of reality to memorize the difference between fibula and tibia. Memorize well, stitch a few bleeding gashes, brush up on your failing memory every couple years, put an MD after your name, and live the life of money and prestige because you copied better than the uneducated, drippy nosed, disease spreaders watching prescription drug infomer-cials in your waiting room.

I tell you, the persistence of modern science has ruined humanism. Humanity, when it is thriving, considers people like Erasmus, the Popes, or Ted, the barber from Havenshire, as colorful individuals from a glorious past. A sweeter time before the invention of toilet pa-per, when it was okay to juggle colors and images in your imagination during a walk to market to buy milk. Books are fun for the purpose of pleasure only. I will let you in on a little secret. I know nothing about Erasmus! I saw a painting of him with his pointed nose, holding down a fat book with Latin letters printed along the spine. Isn't that wonderful enough? Everything I need to know can come from the colors of my own imagination. Colors. He is whatever I want him to be. I can argue my point-of-view, even if that point develops into a circular confusion of contradiction, and I end up thinking about Erasmus' incredibly funny looking red hat. It's my god damn brain! If I can't enjoy it, who will? Science wants it. It can't have it. It is so easy to see what science wants to do with my imagination. It does not pretend disinterestedness. It wants my brain. It needs my brain to survive. If peoples' minds are too busy with happiness, nobody can get sick! If no one gets sick, the American Medical Association can't show off the elegant swan ice carving and twelve foot long pâté en croûte at their annual Marriot Hotel convention. Membership will dwindle fast. Only the most dedicated and impoverished doctors will meet in a clearing of the ancient, dark forest. With big fat frowns they'll share the latest findings from *Medical Discoveries Magazine*. The peasants are too superstitiously happy to accept this grave band of learned men. When Ted junior, the barber's son gets sick, Ted makes a funny face and hops up and down like a bunny rabbit. When Ted's village gets struck with the plague because one of Erasmus' colleagues made a visit to Genoa last week, and while contemplating muscle structure during a lecture on Roman anatomy, stuck the end of his quill pen in a rat's ass and then put the quill in his mouth, then Ted, his family, the village, the surrounding countryside, including all the asses and sheep, perish.

The day I trust science I will enter medical school with a thousand colorful syringes dangling from my skin.

So if you want to know something more about Erasmus, find it in a book written by some scholar who researched the subject well. The libraries are filled with reference about his life and teachings. Why? Because us little illusion-stuffed gluttons of science imagine ourselves to be as important as Dr. and Dr. Jones, the medical, political, botanical, psychiatrical, archaeological, anatomical couple who have everything, a Mercedes-Benz, and even knowledge. We trust them to know the truth, and to keep us safe and warm. Why? I cannot answer for the mob. It takes only a matter of seconds for my imagination to picture the privacy of my doctor, a moment to himself when he is all alone, practicing some filthy habit or dirty routine of ignorance and prejudice, or just plain stupid acts of mental retardation. I need only picture him watching TV or eating a fat piece of chocolate cake to convince myself of the dire need to avoid his practice like the bubonic plague of old.

So far every doctor but one I have visited is an fool of institutional science. Books. Books. Damn the books! This baby and books have got me into a lot of trouble. It takes just one sentence to screw up the brain of a noble father. "The vitamin K shot given to newborns to prevent hemorrhaging has been linked to childhood cancer." Oh shit! Really? But the hospital frowns on those parents who won't accept it. What if your baby has cranial bleeding? What if the doctor drops the baby on the floor and bleeding happens in the brain?

January 22

Snow and wind last night. This is a great humility in Oswego, to live and be covered in snow and ice. It puts technology in a corner of your playroom, with the colorful balls and figurines. A man's life in winter hasn't changed significantly in sixty years. Oh sure, the phone rings and he can pick it up and walk anywhere with it, but that's not much. He can have a thousand channels of TV, but so what? The wind howls and his garbage can cover flies by the window. The snow turns in violent circles under the street light. The man will have to sit and wait despite what new "toy" he has to play with.

Chicken for din-din. The oven uses gas, as it did sixty years ago, but now it can clean itself. No it can't. That's a distortion. He has to clean it. But the oven has a timer, a fancy built-in instant read thermometer, digital clock, professional BTU's, and an endless inner light to illuminate the carcass... Yet it still does not possess the necessary robotics to take itself to the store and bring you back a chicken. Nor can it sliver the garlic, poke tiny holes in the breast of the bird, and insert the slivers for you. Oh but it's shiny and pretty and brand new! Technologically advanced. State of the art (Strange to label the most artless monstrosities and tiny black plastic boxes as "art"). A good technological advance would be an automated device invented to inject a serum into a man's brain immediately upon entering his vestibule on a cold winter's night. A drug to make him think that time improves a man's outlook, that advances in science and technology open old stubborn, painted, glued and screwed shut doors of happiness. That air cleaners, DVD, Surround Sound, the Internet, computer station, stainless steel dough mixers, microwave ovens, snowblowers, and riding mowers, to name just a few beautiful shiny new things, are not only really fun, but fill up the empty places to overflowing. A drug to wear off by morning, because I believe the sun still possesses some magical powers of rejuvenation. (Most men still dream in the early morning, without TV).

Unfortunately, no such drug-injector exists at the present time. They're still working on the light sensors. It won't matter how tipsy a man is when he stumbles past the door late on a winter's night. He'll be quite satisfied with the television, an invention of the 1940's, to sooth the growling yawns of his inner, sleeping animal.

Wait. Now here is an example of technological progress. I just got up from the table to use the toilet. I plugged the toilet. I searched every room for the plunger that has been hiding in this house since 1958. Without a remote control finding beep, I found the tool, brought it to the bathroom, and jabbed it into the toilet to upset the dam. The stool broke free. I sighed, and came back to work.

Now this isn't Tolstoy. I'm not genius. God does not write through me. The plunger is enough. Because of technologies' stubborn advance, the aspiring modern American writer types with the same genius and sense of purpose that Tolstoy's great, great grandchildren use to club-hop and cocaine snort their typical Friday night away in Moscow. There are no young geniuses. One would think that time-saving devices would help in the output of more works of fine art. True, there are plenty more artists today struggling with a car payment. Modernity can boast of great strides in art. Particularly in the field of abstraction. The age demands easy expression, some abstraction being a short-cut with paths that widen in equal proportion to the artist's knowledge of *The Brady Bunch.* Had Tolstoy the opportunity to view an episode, he might have come up with a creative way to carve out and cook his own spleen. The sculptor of today who possesses a clear vision of Bobby Brady's favorite t-shirt can produce a masterpiece out of the stale beer cans, twisted wire, crumpled nudies, broken glass, and empty quarts of oil strewn six feet high, found in his Uncle's mini-landfill of a back yard. He'll call it, "The Final Destruction of the Soul," parade it across the country, from one artless museum to the next, settling in at night with gobs of take-out, TV, and perhaps a point to make about Tolstoy's Russian madness, during the commercial breaks of course.

Every single artist my age who was born in America has heard of *The Brady Bunch.* The juxtaposition of that piece of embarrassing information with Tolstoy's worn, calloused, and bleeding feet is the best lobby

I can offer for the dire need we have of constant, repeating improvements in technology. The slim chance of survival that the artist has today remains to be seen in the complete destruction of creative spirit among his contemporaries. Because the artist is drugged silly by the supposed ease of modern life, rarely has he the strength to stand alone against technologies' invisible army. The ironic battle cry of "We just want to make you more comfortable," often proves to be their final, victorious charge against the American artist. The white flag is raised from the desk chair, bent over the dirty litter box, while out walking the dog , or upon arrival at the front door holding a bag of groceries a four course meal with the eight dollars the artist found in his coat pocket. Three of his favorite syndicated shows are on after dinner, and he'd really like to get this piece finished before *Laverne and Shirley*.

What options beside madness and suicide are there for the man who is true to his art?

This: He must do his absolute best to avoid as much gadgetry as possible. Unfortunately, avoidance will give him neither strength nor courage. It might bring him sanity, provided there is one like himself fighting inertia in the same town, and they have the lucky chance to meet. For art to endure at least another century, the artist must scrap everything holy in America. Presently, and probably indefinitely, toys are the most holy. He must start with the toys then, and toss out at least one a day. Oh yes, and he must always do the exact opposite of his neighbor. Not the easiest program to follow! What began as a quiet personal, monkish struggle, will end in a declaration of war against man and his technology.

Oh but woe to the simple artist, for the enemy has an endless supply of ammunition from an ever-expanding arsenal of weapons. It has an army, navy, air force, and marine corps of square-headed goons with very powerful G-12 processors. It has the popular backing of nearly every man and woman on the planet. All domesticated pets as well. The house dog is taught to turn on the master who changes his diet from an egg yolk on kibbles to "go out and kill a rabbit you lazy mutt!" No, there is no chance in open combat for the man whose life is dedicated to art. He must avoid his enemy guerrilla style. The sane artist will retreat into the jungle to practice his future strategies while living the life of a rainforest hermit. He's a lone warrior now, one who doesn't love a soul connected in any way to making his life easier. He likes the hot, steady rains of the jungle, and an occasional hurricane to humble his growing dependency on technology. He might take for booty a pair of sneakers to protect his feet from the sharp forest floor and raid an unlucky troop of tourists using his path to the waterfall. However, he will not hastily assume that his enemy is everyone. No, it's not wise to combat with any joker holding a wireless. These days, even a promising young painter will be carrying one of those! When the hermit steps out of his hut in the hot morning ready for confrontation, any human being he spies will be carrying some little gadget to play with. Along with American TV, technology has invaded all remote spots on the globe. When he leaves his hut looking for a fight, the artist must take along the same advice given to Marsha Brady by her father Mike when she needed the courage to give an oral presentation. He told her to imagine the audience in their underwear. The artist must go a step further. For his war to be won, he must rip off the underwear and make every body naked. Stark naked and stupid, just like the day they came into the world. First he strips off their clothes and sets his face eye to eye with each captive. He is looking for the same sign in everyone. There is only one difference which separates the artist from the technological man. No matter how fat, thin, pallid, pimpled or pussed the enemies' body, the artist soldier focuses his entire inspection on the eyes. Nothing can separate him from his enemy quite like the eyes.

For my outlook to improve at all, I must see hope's death hiding in their eyes!

January 25

We must abide then with the major advances in technology made during the last half of the last century that make men faster, stronger, more idealistic, optimistic, healthy-faced, and preening with glowing red cheeks from this constant game of internal tag between desire and satisfaction.

What, you mean to tell me that your new car doesn't do those nice things to you? So, you can't tell the difference between the crisp, clear melody of the CD surround-sound system and the crying, screaming agony of your own heart's lying to itself?

Let me tell you, this morning I know my writing to be a useless, very selfish form of torturing the ones I love. Any day now, my child will be born. How can a man be so blind and so cruel? I love you Marie. To touch your lovely skin where the insides ache is my duty. I scream and spit at the man who can cover up all of God's most joyous occasions. Let this also be a point made to anyone unfortunate enough to read this. Ronnie Throop hates himself as good as the next guy...

February 1

ON JANUARY 27, 2001, BABY JANE THROOP WAS BORN TO OUR SMALL, GLORIOUS HOUSEHOLD. EACH NEW DAY I FIND MYSELF TO BE MORE ALIVE THAN THE LAST.

Marie is a remarkable woman. Her labor was quick and relatively free from doctor intervention. Janie has a strong neck, healthy lungs, mostly a cheerful disposition, and roving, inquisitive eyes that follow me around the room.

Good God! I write about the luck and joy and fortunate bomb of birth like some university professor. I must be too stupid to live! I love baby Jane. I am a marked man!

February 2

The problem with writing, then, is that I have already quit my night job. I pretend that I need to write a million more words before I can put one true word to paper. Nonsense. When my brain is alive as it has been this past week, I should be quite able to turn on the faucet and let the images and feelings flow. More than anything I need to tell the truth.

On Monday while driving Rachelle to her horse riding lessons I had a very clear vision of a contemporary American home and neighborhood. Now I've forgotten most of it. The gravest error of writing is that I will try to recapture the images anyway, probably because I need something to do now that I have quit my night job.

We have no souls. The Protestants and Catholics of 16th century Europe had big fat Christmas ham souls. We eat a pile of dead, flea-bitten, Bubonic rats off our platter. We are not pleased, and never content. We have no belief, no moral code, no fear of something greater than ourselves. One should be able to walk into an American neighborhood any which way he pleases, and that might be called freedom but it ain't no soul that I can see. While driving down the county road, every home's inside was unfolded to me. So many rooms! So much space! So many things to fill up the space. And the sameness in the space was re-markable. Each house shared not only the same staples— TVs, sheets, clothes, shoes, and food bought from identical stores, but kept the same personal touches as well. The cookie jar, knitted sweater, shotgun, goose and flower drapes, the children's toys, the motor oil—these and much, much more were exactly the same stuff bought from a similar place. And although the outsides and insides of these pretty country estates were exactly the same thing, or kept so damn well close to it as not to matter, I could not detect even one tiny soul to share a sameness with. These unfortunate dopes hadn't a soul anywhere. In the garage? Nope. Just a bunch of same stuff and a sport utility to keep warm and bright. In the basement? Nope. Just a brand new laundry center washing the same socks, underwear, and Starter sportswear. On the roof? No. In fact if you turn over any shingle, it reads, "Ha-ha, we're the same thing too, dingle-butt!" On the tire swing in the yard? Nope, Goodyear and a Lowe's rope. The tree? Yes, but never affiliated with the dopes. Okay, okay, no soul. I get the picture. But do you really care? You're comfortable. You like your car, your dough mixer, your books, the computer that cost you an arm, a leg and a soul... What are you get-ting at hypocrite that you haven't got to already via the weak, bloated pulse of your own sick heart?

Jesus Christ, don't you get it? I am the same soulless prick as you!

Pray tell us why you feel different then.

Because not a day in my life goes by when I am not disgusted at a human or humanity. There, happy?

Sure, whatever. *Hey, how do you like the Audi Ron?*

In sixteenth century Amsterdam Lars and Mindy were devout Protes-tants inhabiting active souls in a household at 1313 West Faer Street. Their neighbors, Pope idolers, Charlie and Joan, had busy souls too, and kept a hundred candles lit in their abode to prove it. One morning Protestant Lars got out of bed, coughed blood, walked through the cold over to Charlie and Joan's house, smashed their stained glass statue of Jesus Christ's mother's friend's donkey, leapt into the couple's bed, and cut up his neighbors in a crazed fury. Then, after setting fire to their home, walked back through the cold to Mindy, who stood wait-ing for him in the doorway with a hot bowl of oats and sheep's milk.

Our daughter baby Jane was born this past Saturday. Yesterday my mother picked up a back issue of the local paper, so that we could cut out the headlines and paste them into little Jane's baby book. Oops, Janie was born on a day when the headlines were coughing blood.

January 27, 2001: *Man Pleads Guilty in Murder Trial*

(APP) Associated pissants and pilferers. Did you know that there are degrees of murder? One, two, and three? If you kill one, it might be dropped to two. But if you look like you're truly sorry for sticking that old lady in the gut with a sharp piece of glass, it might even drop another degree. How do we know if you're truly sorry? We don't. So wear a sharp suit in the court young man, and the judge might take pity on your non-existent soul, and issue a sentence for manslaughter although you pulled the eyes out the back of her head, and chewed on them. The lawyer representing the killer has no soul. The judge playing judge has not a smidgen of a soul. After work he picks up his little girl and squeezes her. He is lying. He loves something not his daughter. The father of the killer has no soul. So what if one balmy day nineteen years ago he had sex with a woman, and then fed the product of that affair sugar cereal every Saturday until it was old enough to kill. Does that give him the right to pretend he has a soul when a woman is dead with cut glass stuck in her forehead? The reporters, the courtroom audience, the secretary in the room next door... They have no souls. The people in the street, out in the cold walking by? No souls. The good folks in their cars passing people on the street? Nope. Why? Because an old woman opened her door last May thinking the boy was polite enough, and she might like another subscription to *Good Housekeeping*. Sure, but there wasn't a soul in the vestibule, so he invited himself in to have a look-see for himself. Nothing there, so he killed her. The coroner who found glass shards in the roof of her mouth—he doesn't have a soul. The cops that came to call, and saw her lying there in a pool of blood. They will never ever, even if they were bunnies with badges, have a soul. And without a soul, one cannot develop children with souls. Not first, not second, not even third degree murdering souls. Not one of you nips reading this soulless babble has a soul. You might hope that the priest at the funeral service has a soul, but you don't hope, because you know deep down, in your bottomless empty pit of a heart that there isn't even the tiny, starved bird of a soul trying to break free.

The boy was nineteen. The boy could not possibly become a human being. That is what it has got to be now. Every Homo sapien shall be born with a soul. However, soon after the soulless mother or father touch it with their trembling soulless hands, the soul disappears, and with it, its humanness. I know this to be true. The entire courtroom should have been set on fire that afternoon. All of their soulless bodies should have sent billows of smoke up into the winter sky. Because there isn't a pope or priest out there who believes in God, death is the only sword I can wield. How could that old lady's children not annihilate the house wherein sat their mother's murderer? Why did they rise from their pews in the house of law, see all that dirty money exchanging hands, the smiles, the lying tears, the grease on the chin of the lawyer who could actually stomach a burger during lunch break, and not run up to the man who cut up their mother with glass shards, hold him down, and ram a burning torch down his throat? How could her kids stand up and vacate the building without leaving a courtesy bomb in a basket with a bow tied around it? I don't dare say that I write for God. I am a scared little punk just like you trying to make a comparison between the sixteenth century murder for a belief, and the inability for Homo sapiens of the 21st century, who can't believe enough in God to play God when their own mommy is slain because she opened a door to buy a magazine.

"We are more humane in this age," says the President, says the working man, says the soulless father and mother who don't believe because they are so afraid. No, God damn us, we are spiritual cross-dressers, who can't muster enough humanity to construct even the tiniest moral code. There is no God. You know there is no God. The fear that you have because there is no fair God, makes you helpless. You fear the man next to you, who might send you to a prison where inmates swear a lot and have sex with the same sex, if you decided to meet that soulless nineteen year old who killed your mother face to face, with an eye to an eye; or Jesus at least some kind of similar avenging attitude, other than "It's out of our hands," or the even more pitiful, "How can he not show any remorse?"

Why doesn't he show any remorse? Because inside he is laughing an imaginary head off! Inside he has got a thousand sardonic smiles stuck all over his body. Inside he walks up to you laughing at your mother's death with a thousand smiles. He knows that in the end you will agree with the jury to feed and clothe and keep him warm for fifteen years to life. He knows it. You know it. You might go home and do your taxes tonight to prove it. But you won't do anything about it because God does not exist and you're so incredibly afraid my sorry little soulless orphans. Oh fellow spiritual degenerates, why not form a circle around his tied down body and jab it with tiny little cut pieces of glass? Secretly you want him to beg for mercy, to plead and scream his sorry ass off for mercy. We can let him beg, even make it look like he may get off the hook, wait a couple hours so he can think about his crime, then launch upon him like a pack of starved, wild wolves, tearing at his flesh with our own, very useful incisors. Afterwards we shall wash up, step outside into the bight sun, clap our hands together and sing Hallelujah! Then of course, by all means, go back to work or play, and mourn the wrongful death of another innocent soulless creature whom some of us happened to love enough to kill for.

It has got to be this way. We believe it. We just don't know where to begin. I'll tell you, the early years must be dedicated to acquiring humanship. And the few, the very few, who graduate, those receiving the understood blessing and carefulness of being alive, they alone are in the running for soul reacquisition. Those with a soul will teach by example. If the priest happens to possess a soul, he will direct the funeral service for the woman who was murdered by cut glass on a march to the jail, and bomb it. If that isn't enough, and the people still cannot see, he'll march them to Albany and bomb the houses that say it's okay to kill—just be prepared to eat and sleep for free, fifteen years to life. If that doesn't work and the soulless monkeys come to arrest the priest, don't fret a bit. There's a good chance that he will be captured in a state that kills their undesirables humanely—with gas, electric shock, skin peeling, esophagus stuffing, brain bleeding.... But your soul-stuffed priest probably won't care. He'll hang himself long before they can agree upon and organize the proper manner of his execution.

She would have bought the magazine, really, and piled the issues on the table of her soulless home. There are civil murder trials. Pretty neat, eh? I might be misunderstood, but I love that slain woman like my own mother. Cruel and unusual punishment? Please God yes! Enough to make up for the slow, but firm advancement of civil cowardice over the years. I beg of you, dear Lord Almighty, please bring back the braver souls of yesteryear.

February 3

No more thinking! I love my children, my wife, my family. I fear my own mind.

February 4

Quote for today:

"If one quarter of the American people are today living on a level of subsistence far below the norm, there remain nevertheless a hundred million who enjoy comforts and advantages unknown to men in any period of the past. What is to hinder them from revealing their talents? Or is it that our talents lie in other directions? Is it that the great goal of American manhood is to become the successful businessman? Or just a "Success", regardless of what form or shape, what purpose or significance, success manifests itself in and through? There's no doubt in my mind that art comes last in the things in life which preoccupy us. The young man who shows signs of becoming an artist is looked upon as a crackpot, or else is a lazy, worthless encumbrance."
—Miller

I am excited that it's Sunday. Rachelle comes today. School will start up again. We will bake sweet treats, and I can go back to normal thinking.

Yesterday lost in the dreamy haze of newborn glee, Marie, my mother and I talked about my idea to beg a simple living. First, let it be known, we are very happy people. The cold February, the unemployment, the very simple mornings and even simpler gray afternoons, have made baby Jane's first week of life a post-womb bliss. This is happiness. It's also very rare, and confounds my mother often to the point of distraction because she's never known a couple to be so cheerful while in the wake of financial ruin.

Anyway, I feel good enough this week to talk to her about begging. Why not? Sponsorship has always been the artist's plight. Why should I be ashamed to ask my fellow man for five cents a day? It's the 21st century and the economy has never been so fat. Just a nickel a day. Five pennies. A dime to secure me for two days. If I could acquire say, forty donors spread out across the United States, perhaps even the richer countries of the world... Forty people each sending me a nickel a day—then that would be enough incentive to quit the hate mail I send out to the non-existent addresses of disinterested Americans. For two dollars a day I might even concentrate on creating something beautiful. Practically fourteen dollars a week will be enough to silence my criticism of everything that cost more than fourteen dollars a week. I could concentrate on beautiful writing, like something straight from Jean Giono's mind, although not nearly as well-written (I know my limitations). Detailed descriptions of the countryside, brilliant colors of the sky, animals with strong limbs, a kind gesture from a human being. The money would help pay for two simple meals a day, arranged by my own two hands of course, and an hour or two to walk about the town meditating on my next book. This I would do for five cents a day. It used to be two hundred a week. Now it is five cents a day.

Of course I would gladly accept more. Generosity would not go un-appreciated. I would dedicate the rest of my books written before death to the forty original sponsors of my plight.

A nickel a day. Thirty-five cents a week. What, do you expect me to live on less than that? After our afternoon inspirational, my mother sent me to the store for steaks. "Nice big juicy sirloins for Marie and me," she said. Fine. And I didn't even consider the cost, at least not until this morning, after the buerre rouge, the sauteéd mushrooms and pearl onions. The spicy black beans simmered in garlic and olive oil. Then I wondered about money. Why should it bother me that each steak costs five dollars and I've been planning the last few meals out of a pot of black beans? It's her money. She earned it. Why does it matter that her son just spent an hour giving her a lecture on the virtues of begging, and that even the paltry sum of a nickel a day, thirty-five cents a week, $18.20 a year would keep the budding American artist not only humble to the very core, but deliriously happy because out there somewhere, is another contemporary as foolhardy as he. Why is it that she can give Price Chopper Supermarket a two dollar profit on the purchase of a steak, simply because they supplied the cut piece of cow, but that it breaks her heart to know her son seeks a five cent profit for his artistic endeavors? How can an artist's own mother not sense his reoccurring frustration and outrage?

Because Ron Throop, you sniffling idiot! She can eat the bloody steak!

February 5

In the morning I can have no worries. Is it this way for everyone? Most of my writing happens before dawn. That has got to account for the cocky child in me. It's quite a different story in the night, when my mind is a heavy, overloaded glutton suffering the ill-effects of a fat illusion diet ingested throughout the day. This morning I awoke on a warm, sandy beach. The tide was high, just tickling my toes. The East was light. I sat up, feeling clean and new to the approaching day. A pelican stood in the sand watching me. A blue heron caught on an air wave cruised silently by, and the thoughts in my head and myself were the same. I was a me not separated from my thoughts. However, when I proceeded to get up and act (I thought I'd wade up the shoreline for adventure), the clear-headed thoughts chose to stay behind and made their cozy secure homes rooted down into the sand. Every few waves I turned to look back, so as not to lose sight of my fading thoughts.

Further down the shore, my body yearned toward the sea. Since the sun was up and birds were singing, I felt brave enough for a morning swim. I fell into the warm waves, and pulled myself over one, then two. The water was changing shades of green and gray. I knew this was the best way to live, and looked back to my thoughts for agreement. But a crowd of feeding seabirds blocked my view of the shore. No matter. I had plenty of time to get back to this morning's light.

Suddenly a whirlpool grabbed hold of my toes and pulled me out to sea. Far, far away from my original thoughts. Then I panicked. Going down, coming up. Believed I spied the shore when it was just a head full of air and water. I guess then I must have died, and heaven was a glorious dawn on a warm, sandy beach with the light in the East, and a pelican wondering about me.

I simply woke up to think about another day.

What are these illusions that in the morning are virtually non-existent, but by early evening drown you in violent whirlpools of confusion?

Where do I begin? You see, this morning I feel happy and free. The world is an infinite exploration. I awake with a blast of anticipation, excitement, belief, wonder, hope, joy, real strength of character. I can even have positive thoughts about begging. And unlike the evening, the thought stays true, and keeps itself clear without the illusion of other people's feelings getting in the way. A current reality I am dreaming up is to attach a wooden box to the side of the house and cut a slit into the top. A collection box wanting for nickels. I imagine donors walking to the artist's home, not for the artist's sake necessarily, but to knock themselves out of agonizing routines. This morning I am certain that joy will come to the man delivering a nickel, whether it be to God, the hungry old woman, the Children's Aid Society, or to yours truly. In bad weather the nickel donor can take up a staff and obtain an old sock to stuff his nickels in. Already his life has improved significantly. A walk across town on a nickel delivery might turn enough envious heads from inside their cars to really make a difference. "Hey, isn't that Mr. Howard, the shop teacher? What is he doing walking through the snow? Why isn't he in his car? Where can he be going?"

Mr. Howard finally came to his senses, picked up his dinner plate, and threw it against the wall. "Freida, where's the coin jar?" he said, and then wondered why he didn't know where the coin jar was kept. From that realization he moved on to the next obvious one. He was near invisible to the people in his life. His loved ones saw right through him. Sure he kept his toothbrush in the holder beside the others, but the big question now was: Would they stop brushing their teeth if his toothbrush was gone? Sure, being a shop teacher earned him a mountain of nickels, but even that couldn't keep Freida from thinking about her gorgeous foot doctor—the blonde, blue-eyed Adonis with the incredible hands. Son and daughter were touched by Dad once long ago, when he played football with them and Buster in the yard. They pitied him for putting on a show. Suzy was five, Tommy was six and Buster was the puppy Mr. Howard bought with a bag full of dirty nickels.

Now he takes another look at the home which he hath provided. "Why aren't we begging for nickels?" he wonders. "Man, we all got it too easy. How is it possible to appreciate anything? And thoughts...! My God, what do they matter? Thoughts, dreams, they are nothing in a home overflowing with nickels. Why did I not see this before? I guess it's okay to teach other people's brats how to cut factory wood and tighten bolts, as long as my own brats say, 'Thank you father,' and 'I love you father'. But they never do. And Freida puts that god-damned plate of food on the table every night. I don't know, but she might have spread ten toxins on her body today to give it that shine.

I wouldn't stop to count because the days and nights are streaking by and I have nothing to show for life but a house stuffed chock full of nickels. When Suzy and Tommy open their mouths to speak, nickels pour out in a stream. Freida's a walking sheet of noisy nickels. I got nickels falling out of drawers. Buster won't take another treat for going outside. Now he hoards nickels in a pile by the garbage. This morning I was late for work. It took twenty minutes to clear the nickels off the driver's seat. Since I heard about the man in town with a begging box, every turn I make confronts me with a wall of nickels. I never knew I had so much until the other guy made a complete ass of himself. Now I cannot will the nickels out of my mind. I have to rid my thoughts of every last nickel!"

So Mr. Howard takes up a staff. Yesterday it was a broken branch fallen after a west wind. Today it is a staff. He stops at his car to pick nickels out of the ashtray, and drops them in a tube sock. He ties a knot in the top and walks out into the street swinging his sock.

"Where the hell do you think you're going?" yells Freida standing in the doorway.

"I am going to the artist's house to drop these nickels into his begging box."

"You are like hell!" Freida screams. She's in a rage. Her eyes are hot. She feels the heat behind her eyes getting hotter. She shakes her body and waves her fists at her husband. She curses. She stamps and screams. Mr. Howard returns her fit with a look of cheerful indifference. This gesture makes her livid, beside herself with a red hot hated for her husband. Her temples are flaming. The heat starts to melt her eyes and suddenly her head explodes. A blast of lava-hot nickels erupts out the top of her head. They land whoosh-whoosh onto the frozen blacktop, shooting bullets of steam into the cold sky.

Mr. Howard walks up to his wife lying in the doorway, steps one leg over her prone body, pokes his head through the door, and yells up to the kids to bring him down another sock full of nickels. "And clean up your mother," he says. "I'll be back in a few years."

You must have no idea about your status as a non entity. That is the greatest illusion, is it not? You're not that important. So stop fooling yourself. You need me. I need you to provide water, light, heat, razors, toilet paper, food, certain types of entertainment, practically everything out there necessary to sustain life. Jesus, I'm an artist, not a mountain man. Of course I need the newspaper editor. Once in a while I must pretend to look for a job. Sure I need the grocery clerk to arrange cabbages, the farmer to milk the cow, the nuclear engineer so that I may flip switches for electric light. You need them too. Then what use am I?

I am here (alive and breathing) to put the original thought back into your copy-cat brains that the artist is no more an anomaly than the shop teacher, Mr. Howard, the butcher hacking meat, the stone mason picking up rocks and putting one on top of the other, the assembly line worker at the cereal plant making sure each box is sealed with glue. Listen, we are all useless! The more so if we actually think that we contribute to the whole. "I perform a succession of meaningless labors until the end of my day, everyday, until retirement, or death, or death in retirement. I do this for the good of society. I am needed. It is needed. We are needed." No, that is an untruth. Nobody is needed. The world will keep turning without a single human being left living on it.

That is a depressing thought. So what? The whole will always smother the importance of a single man. The whole is the most silly illusion, yet because it has been allowed prominence for so long, it boasts as being the most dangerous illusion of all. Deadly. We believe in the whole because that is what the whole wants, but what we *need* in order to keep ourselves from empty space. It is a feeling of being a moon rotating around a center. The moon is dead. The center is a sphere possessing air, light, dark, life, hidden caves, and tall green forests. Giraffes and lions race across meadows of yellow and blue flowers, tiny creatures swim in a cool water stream catching the sun's ecstatic ray dance. The center is one man. One individual man. And yet it is also the whole. The illusion is the whole, but it is really just one man, one immense population of many "one mans." Every creature inhabits that center at birth. The grand illusion is an entire life, spent dedicating a better part of it to reaching a cold, personal moon which does not exist. The moons are out there. They are very real, and yet nonexistent. So much the better for them to be spared our luckless souls. As a whole we aspire to become a frozen clump of inert rock, nickel-hoarding non-entities. Each individual a whole, needing just a nickel a day to eat and dream up things like cold, personal moons.

Oh fellow non-entities, empty your coin drawers, boxes and jars! Become an artist. Explode a lonely moon!

Words are so wrong. I read what I write and it doesn't make sense to me.

February 8

Your House Is a Fat Whore Shitting in the Street

My fingers smell like urine
My baby coos in bed
My dog stands at the door
He's smarter in the head
What we say we know we know
You know it isn't known
That crap about the light of day
reap what we have sown

A plumber on my road
has four llamas and a spa
A house with twenty rooms
and soul for bacteria

He's sneaky and he's dumb
a dangerous, rowdy hood
He's smelled his ass too many times
Would lick it if he could

The truth is my dog
just waits to wag his tail
He's real to himself
unlike the human male

He sleeps and dreams and whines
when he's hungry or he's mad
and not like the lonely plumber
will cry when he is sad

The depressing truth o man o man
Is that you're not a dog
my buddy waits before the door
and I won't make anymore stupid rhymes to honor his most selfish
  beauty.

From this day forward I will be a child. I am beautiful and not-knowing. I have a mommy and a daddy and a step mommy. They take care of me. My homework is real. I'm doing a presentation on healthy alternatives to common sugary soft drinks. I have dreams. I don't want to kill. I have a picture book about my favorite singing group. On each page there are empty spaces for me to write information about myself. The saddest day of my life was when we had to bury my pet rat named Slick. We carved her name and the years of her life in cement poured in an upside-down metal can cover. I can lay in the grass for an hour. The taller the better. But Daddy can think of nothing else but when to mow it. Even when the day is sunny and hot and we can go to the lake. I don't want to be like my Dad. I am happy with my dreams and playing. Daddy is wrong.

Is it time now for a climax? Yep! You Betcha! Followed by twenty or thirty more pages of fanatical cynicism. Anyone who can read that far will either be a close relative or a better pessimist. It's not difficult to see that I am crazy. I actually want, more than anything, to be content. That should make me crazy, because I see it and have it in raising a small, very close family, in the midst of poverty. Selfish, selfish poverty! Because I am vain enough to want to publish small books, I feel that to be an end, when really it is only a means to get back to a beginning.

Clearly I am not singing man's praises. You can say that I am writing to save myself from disease. But that is not true. Before I said that one true word is enough. It isn't enough. I lied. Yes I lie, I cheat. I am a coward too. O God, all the beautiful men who were so careful. Those beauties who left us their perfect writings, those wonders who were so clean and misunderstood, but lay in bed night after night convinced of their immortality. They practiced their immortality. Man, they were more phony than I could ever allow myself to be.

You see, I am a living man. I pity mankind in the same way I might feel sorry for myself. Do you think that I would not want to write an entertaining book? My God, I'd give anything to be able to produce a thrilling novel or a book of poetry that sings so sweetly about life and living. But most importantly, how I pray that I could have the gift of knowing my own strength. To be like Walt Whitman, peddling my knowledge door-to-door. Or a Thoreau in the forest singing my praises "as lustily as chanticleer in the morning..." God no, I cannot write like that. I am no great man. I am such a mixed up confusion of this and that, that I wonder if I am a Throop, a Ron, or a crazy idiot.

These are not confessions. I know myself, and myself is not me. I am what all of mankind is right now, and isn't it a sorry state of hell man is? I mean we just have to kill morality. We are too dangerous now. I am not talking about the half-men; there are plenty out there so terrified enough already. They know who they are. You can bet they didn't read this far. They got to the shelf and picked out something from Diderot instead. He wrote well. He spoke French. He wore a wig, which is some big difference to seek on a Sunday stroll through the bookstore. Anything is better than what you are at the bookstore. No, I write for the man I am, which is what some of you may be. I do not know if it's a level below or beyond, but I am precisely not the ex-con talkin' jive about why I ain't allowed to vote. I am not him, nor am I the billionaire CEO, kicking the tile in one of my twenty-six marble bathrooms. I am nobody but I am everyone. I don't give a constipated hope about man. I hate my neighbor. I don't fear him. I hate him. The only thing I fear is the loss of freedom to shit in my own crooked pine wood bathroom, if I happen to strangle my neighbor because he never introduced himself to my family. Yes, I would kill him for buying a snowblower and wasting the morning cleaning the snow off a sidewalk that he will never walk on! Yes, I would kill him, if I was desirous of murder. But then the freedom to hide to pick my nose, and be as vile as every man hiding, is lost. And I am thrown into a prison to live beside things which I consider better dead than alive. Why? BECAUSE THEY WEREN'T SMART ENOUGH TO STAY FREE ENOUGH TO LEAVE EVERY SINGLE MAN THE HELL ALONE!

February 9

Dreaming is fun. I like dreaming. To be at a slumber party in some unknown room, and all your friends are there, some of them digging your music, is just a wonderful way to stretch through the five and six a.m. hours. To pee in a toilet and wipe some clear, caramel-like substance off the seat, and get a wink from the doctor in the room, who says, "It's all right, no one ever did that before..."

And then suddenly you're in Los Angeles joy-riding with Marie, looking for proof on a billboard that Roy Orbison wasn't as ambitious as Dick Clark. Then you're chastising Dick for being so fame-hungry, and Roy's life is now very beautiful and sad, but oops! Is this Sunset Boulevard? Hop in! We'll take a turn here in our '74 Plymoth. This might be the road that winds through the hills to the ocean. There's some kind of fancy private club—there to the left! Let's go round this bend to s— Oh my God, the ocean! There's no Shore! A massive wave approaching and we're floating. The old Plymoth Fury is falling into the ocean!

Not if I can help it! I turn the car around with my feet and steer back around the bend. We park at the country club and step out into the bright California sunshine, stark naked and dripping wet. We go inside. People dining, and any second we might get chased through the halls and rooms. Now we're clothed with Rachelle and baby Jane standing at the curb on some hot, garbage-stink street in the city. Marie wants to eat across the street, at some greasy spoon. "Are you kidding? We'll be killed! A band of hooded hoods gather around us, but appear to pay no attention while they talk about how the landlord's done them wrong. We walk from inside of their circle toward the ocean like a moving illustration from Monty Python's Flying Circus. The road we turned up before is straight ahead at the end of a line of magnolias and weeping willows. Suddenly we are in the country club talking with my arch enemy, Marty, his son, and a doctor. Marty is laying down a blanket so I don't get my ass wet on the chair. I walk over to the window looking out for the lights of Los Angeles. I know it takes seventy-two hours to get home driving straight through. I bet we can do it in two days.

I hear an announcement on the radio. Then I taste my breath and feel the weight of waking up in the dark as old as I am.

So, leave us your dreams, proud working men of the 21st century. They have got to be more fantastic than the life you've formulated to fit the exact same life as everyone else passing by in a car. Sit at the stoplight, idling in your safety seat, and stare out at them. Count them. Surely they are very different than you, no? No?

No.

Maybe in the manner which they leave their beds and end up in a car. There may be some slight difference. But everything else is the same. That is, the clock alarm might be set to a disc jockey saying "ass" rather than "Azerbaijan". News radio is modern rock radio is 90s pop radio as long as the entire population of the planet can differentiate between these three things. You in the Mercedes, and you in the '84 Ford with the muffler dragging, can and shall be satisfied with one of these stations, whether you tune in from Knoxville or Nagasaki. The barely literate scum bag holding up a convenient store will sing along to the same hip hop radio sound that the high school jock was singing five minutes ago, before he was shot to death for fifty dollars and a pack of Starburst. (You know what that is too, don't you?) Our barely literate dust-brained murderer sings the "Hey, mother fucker..." song while merging onto the freeway. He gets lost in the music. He doesn't hear the siren screaming up from behind. The cops were listening to Brittany Spears on Radio Disney when they got the call to chase a dangerous suspect. They like Brittany because she's got a hot ass. When that particular song is playing, they imagine their dirty beards pressed into her navel. Sometimes they get inspired enough to abduct a barely literate street girl and rape her in the back seat of their squad car.

Oh well, they got him. Five to ten years sentenced by the judge who drove into the courthouse parking lot, listening to a story on NPR about Israel's election. He didn't think about the Congo, until it's president got machine-gunned off his leather chair. It had to be a machine gun or it wasn't news for NPR. Actually, no news comes from Africa, India, Iraq, Bolivia, Iran, (name forty or fifty other countries of dark-skinned people), unless significant numbers are dead from famine, disease, disaster or fear. The news is for Caucasians about Caucasians, and Jews are light enough to pass for Caucasians tanning in Florida. So it's necessary to learn about the terrors in Tel Aviv, even if the Pepsi vending man still follows the same pick-up route through Jerusalem. Jesus Christ, good Pharisees and Allah, it's all about money. Don't you dare get in the way of that. Not even if they're bashing each other's skulls in. The judge likes to "get the news" before he dons the noble robe for a long day of playing God to goof-balls. Yes, the judge is brain-washed. And so is anyone who turns on a radio for pleasure. If Togo fights a civil war over the debate of forced female circumcision, then the judge will want to listen. He's wild over the wacky women of Togo and their anomalous labia. (He heard that story too on NPR). Yes of course the judge is a pervert! Did you expect anything beautiful to be born out of his status-seeking existence?

The barely literate scum bag is in prison now, eating Apple Jacks for breakfast. (You know what they are too, you damn robot). He listens to Christian radio because it will look good for the parole board. In the prison yard standing with a friend, our wiggling bag of scum laughs and laughs and laughs. "Yo mane, dare sendin' in a whitie today mane, to in'view me in ma cell. A pubic radio show, some seriesshit man 'bout prison life. Ize cansay whatever ize want to— muttafuckas shit dat's right. Dey call me Joe and Ize cansay stuff like 'Ize like to kill people,' and 'Ize don't feel no 'morse.' Stupid muttafuckas. Say mutterfucka, waz fo suppa? Deyz givn' us dat cheese shit man I don't like dat shit. Makes my shit stay up in my ass."

What is wise? Are wise men extinct? Emerson thought he was wise. He had a national following. And for good reason. His hundred and fifty year old wisdom still holds true. But it will never be enough until taped on the end of a stick, and sent running amok in a world gone wrong. Here, read it:

"Life is a succession of lessons which must be lived to be understood. All is riddle, and the key to a riddle is another riddle. There are as many pillows of illusion as flakes in a snow-storm. We wake from one dream into another dream. The toys, to be sure, are various, and are graduated in refinement to the quality of the dupe. The intellectual man requires a fine bait; the sots are easily amused. But everybody is drugged with his own frenzy, and the pageant marches at all hours, with music and banner and badge."

Sorry Ralph, but now our world has become night and day. That lazy bean-sowing friend of yours, Thoreau? He was right. But only part right, because he couldn't keep himself away from men. And worse yet, he wrote about why he stayed, or couldn't stay away from them. What business was it of theirs? Still, I wish that in your life you were half the man Thoreau was. Writing a whole lottocrap about self-reliance and letting them applaud you on and off their crude, manure-stink stages. Ah, go to the Devil Ralph Emerson! We need to be like Thoreau in his extreme. A man today must come to that end, or he's simply no longer a "man" beyond the biology. No difference of heart or mind can separate him from our meanest citizen alive, unless he flee to the woods and remain out of sight of everyone. Retire in obscurity to befriend the raccoon, or revolution in the streets. I tell you it's got to be one of these two things. Shake imaginary hands with the river rat or war with any population of men who cannot value the life of you or the river rat.

Lies, lies, lies! Emerson was right. I just changed Janie's diaper, and understood the world of men to be a crying helpless baby wet and shitty with saffron colored digested mother's milk. I tell Marie that the baby is lucky that this is a world without Doctor Spock. Otherwise, she'd be singin' freedom songs from her playpen cell. And then I start to dance around the room with Janie singing, "Rocka my soul in the bosom of Abraham..," I change the words a bit to make the situation more humorous. "O rocka my soul in the bosom of mommy..." And then, "Spit up my soul on the bosom of mommy..." Falling back into an even deeper, more plush pillow, I tell Marie about my fifth grade music class, when I imagined a slave baby being rocked by Abraham Lincoln, not the Abraham of Issac. I didn't know the Jewish story. I had Alpha Bits for breakfast and waited for the yellow bus to take me to school. Then I played jump up and down with my little friends while the bus driver listened to the latest reek of news to blow in from the Middle East.

The situation is much more precarious than that. What does this 'banner and badge' crap even mean? The sots are easily amused... In 1847 the sots went to Fourth of July picnics. They were amused by a parade and the noisy bangs of Chinese exploding paper.

Folks, you must juxtapose. I like that word because using it properly, might drive us insane enough to make a difference.

So let's juxtapose.

In the year 2002, how are the sots amused? You tell me. It must be understood that two to two billion people do not matter much if just one man or woman over fifteen years of age, has heard, and understood an utterance by a civilized human being.

Living in society means pajamas after thirty, slippers after forty, mother's milk in infinite varieties of processed foods, local taxes, far away taxes, shoveling the driveway, watering the lawn, "the right way," "the wrong way," anybody's way but your own way. Even the most expressive person cannot create without some major help from society. The painter must purchase the paint and flush the toilet. The writer writes at a desk and turns out the light. The dancer twirls on a stage, and rents a movie for later tonight. The musician bought a folding chair. He goes over the score while smoking a pipe and cleaning between his toes. It's a piece by Beethoven because people in the twenty-first century have no idea how to play their own music on a log. God forbid that there is a fool somewhere who would take up the violin solely for enjoyment! No, for that he must succumb to a life of Beethoven and sweeping floors in a dentist's office. Nobody gives a hoot about him or his violin, until he comes to the concert hall, dressed in his pajamas and slippers, reading a symphony that Beethoven wrote in his head while peeing on a wet log.

What good is a Beethoven? Any sot today can buy a CD at the world's biggest mall. That is not beautiful. How can that be beautiful? Whistling "Erotica" from beginning to end while searching for toothpaste above the tampons, next to your favorite hair shampoo, is a destruction wrecking more devastation on the inside than a nuclear bomb on the outside. The reason there are nuclear bombs is because of Beethoven. It's all his fault. Not the man's necessarily, but his music. How shall I prove this to you? Who do you think Beethoven wrote for? Us? Do you really believe he cleaned his stinky toes and washed behind his ears in anticipation of our appreciation for him? The notes go up and down to the rhythm of his boots avoiding piles on a street walk from piano to pie maker. He wrote for Claus and Heidi, his father and mother, Napoleon, any German lake, fish in the water and birds in the sky. Now the same man buying—(Listen, it's always buying from now on. Nobody makes beauty. Sometimes we might put it together, but we must buy it first, already assembled or in pieces.) Now across from the man buying a Beethoven box set, stands another man in his pajamas holding an Eminem CD. For those of you reading in the year 2030, Eminem was a shrewd criminal brain who gained fame at the age of twenty for sipping his mother's milk from a slipper, while rapping, "When the cops weren't looking, I raped a pickup truck. And when I got through with that bitch, I rammed it up a duck...." Beethoven and Eminem. Finally! We are beginning to juxtapose.

2002. 1803. Emerson had his high thoughts about illusion. He would be the first to say that Beethoven was drugged with his own pleasure of music. And he'd be right of course, in 1845. Ludwig would be the intellectual type who required a fine bait. Besides the fiddler at the dance, the sots knew themselves to be the gifted music-makers. Music was made by the sots themselves. If they felt the urge coming on to sing, they sang. They laughed and cried in song, thought in song, stirred cornbread batter in song. They sang their songs. They alone were the living creators. Which of them was strong and lucky enough to climb over the Alps and get permission to come inside out of the rain to hear Beethoven and his friends go "da-da-ta-da" with a score of washed musicians playing with their polished and finely tuned instruments? Maybe a thousand people in the world heard Beethoven while Beethoven was alive. And I promise you that the ears listening were the richest most uncreative morons of the early nineteenth century.

Don't you see? Beethoven, like Emerson, existed in a higher state of sotdom. He wrote for music students and professors of music who had an "in" with the right paying society, the princes and princesses.

Now juxtapose Emerson today calling on Eminem and his mommy at their city house on a street. "What!" he will wonder inside himself while walking through the ugly of a Detroit or Cleveland, "Society has come to allow this thing and its mother Beethoven's freedom?! Oh my God I am so sorry I did not see this coming. New York was bad. London was worse, but they all got theirs with a dish of the smallpox. I was so wrong to pursue my own illusion down such a straight and narrow path. What kind of philosopher was I?

Thoreau was right. I should have requested his tutelage—not the other way around. Did that boy just say, 'Yo fukamudder, washyouma-kin'bigshit'boutRalphie?' Did he just say that? My God, what is it?"

"Ma'am," Emerson asks, "Did you make it?"

"What?"

"Did you make this thing?"

"You mean my son, mister?"

"Yes if you are not so ashamed to call it that."

"Well, I gave birth to it, and it was such a sorry-lookin' thing when I done it. But it was tough raisin' him. His Daddy worked overtime most the time at the plant, and little Em here started calling me fudderfupper at a real young age. I dunno, two, three. We thought that was something' though, so we bought him a 'Sing along with Beethoven Mini-studio' at Montgomery Wards, and he just looked so smart singing 'slap da bitch,' and 'bust ya face,' that we thought genius like that should bypass maturity and concentrate solely on being stupid and ugly. This is a free country, ain't it Mr. Emerson? You see, I know where you're getting at, coming back from the dead and all just to interview our boy. You want to know how nuclear proliferation, and sick, twisted anomalies like my son here can happen in such a short time after hard tack and gathering fuel for the fire. What amazes you the most, and it's no small thing I'm sure mister, is that some simple-minded daddy of two, and husband of one, can know about little Em from so far away in the February of a cold winter, upstairs in an old house that was built during your lifetime and only two hundred years after man had to dress up in a deer suit to get dinner. I agree mister, that is amazing.

"Yes madam. But tell me, where does a quiet, unobtrusive philosopher catch wind of such foul stinks like your son here? No offense."

"Mister, the only offense I take is what little Em dishes out. He probably heard about him at his job—he has to have a job, mister, if he wants to live in society—And anybody who works today knows about Eminem. My boy has made quite a stir! Or, he might have heard them talkin' about Em on the radio. National Public Radio most likely. Especially if your quiet man wears an old-fashioned Irish cap and has day and night dreams about money."

"Dreams about money? We had a lot of that in my day too Madam."

"No mister, not quite like us. It's not the same thing."

"How so?"

"Because I think if you was poor back then, you darned socks and sweaters and starved a bunch. Sometimes you might have thought it'd be nice to have money to stay alive, but you also dreamed about Africa's wild elephants or sailing on a green sea in search of anything besides socks with holes in 'em. Now money ain't like that anymore. Even having a bunch of that can't help us."

"Why, is the cholera still a killer."

"No mister. But my son is. Would you like to buy his CD? He makes ten thousand dollars every time he says 'fuckdabitch,' on live television."

"No thank you madam. I think I'll go start a fire in heaven. Maybe ravage that little Alcott beauty, stick a vein, or piss on the world. I thank you dear woman for creating that useless piece of horse crap of a son of yours. Good bye."

"Bye mister. Watch your step on the stairs. Little Em leaves his Matchbox cars there all the time. I tell him not to, but he just laughs at me until I start to cry."

What is the truth about Beethoven? Was he civilized? As civilized as today's average monkey? He had to dress up in a heavy wool coat and walk to the concert hall if he was to hear one of his peers conduct a concert. That was his illusion. Snowflakes falling, an intricately carved cane donated by an admirer, and a musical walk down a busy street. The movement of many people. A pig in a box. A horse sneezing snot while trotting by. Firelight. Beethoven was every other man and woman, but different with the gift of concentrated illusion. He had a purpose and was praised for it. He had everything everyone had, plus one big thing: The desire to express thought, dream, history, happiness, madness, peace, beauty, and the galloping animal world of the black forest, through music. Beautiful music! Intoxicating music. Music to sooth the beast in us—not the beast to make the music—which is what happened not long after the death of men.

When did men die?

You tell me mubbafucka.

February 10

We are in the midst of a winter hurricane. The downstairs door flew open in the night. Winds are striking the walls and shaking the windows in their frames. All we are left to fear these days is the weather. There should be tanks riding up and down West Seventh Street. Bombs could be dropping from the sky. Freedom is gone, so let's make the most of it. Arrest me.

February 11

Went scouting the library for magazines to send my poems to. Each one that I picked up read like not one of these fat doves accepts the existence of a single McDonald's. What a pile of beautiful fairy shit! I hate the English language most of all because it is so full of ways to beat around the bush!

I remember the clown at Woolworth's like it was yesterday
and my mother held me in her arms
and pulled my blue hat down over my eyes...

A hundred bucks for that? Who the hell reads this crap on purpose? When *Friends* is on at seven and it's quarter to, and that god damn fucker in front of him is only going forty-five! Pintos and cheese, soft tacos and sour cream, I'd like to pull the poet's intestine straight out his asshole, dangle it in front of his eyes, hold it up against a wall, drive a fat nail through it, carve "liar!" up and down with a blunt butter knife, until it falls onto the floor in a mangled pile... Then he can tell me about his blue hat at Woolworth's, and his mommy's gentle hand playing pee-pee with him in the tub.

Oh Jesus Christ, what has become of us? Every Journal or Review that I picked off the shelf would only accept previously published poets on query. Each poem came with a list of credentials. Dr. Cornelius Imasad. Professor of American Literature at the University of Minnesota. Published in *The New Yorker* and *Georgia Review*. Dr. Imasad divides his time between the Greater St. Paul area and the warm plasmic lining of his mother's uterus.

"Who did you kill with your bare hands, and why?"—That would be the first question asked to our submitters. Our quarterly would be page after page thoroughly stained with the blood of the poet's own heart. No library would dare subscribe. Each issue comes with a neat little World War II explosive, because our editors believe that is when the human race should have cut itself off from existence. We do not recognize humanity after the year of our last happy child, 1...9...4...5, ready or not, I'm gonna blow the tiny heart out of your body!

This quarter our chief editor's talented daughter submitted some fine material. It's a play in one act about a court of justice trying the crime of misuse of a singular verb with a plural subject. She will play the part of the judge because her little friends voted for her instead of Mira, who tried so hard to say one clear word during her audition. Mira has a speech impediment, but that did not affect the children's final decision. They voted her out of that part because she couldn't make them understand a single word she said. Mira was not offended. She knows what she sounds like when she talks, and took a lessor part because she also is a gentle, soft and truthful creature. BECAUSE THIS TINY WORLD OF GRACIOUS CHILDREN ACCEPTS HER HEART AS TRUE AND BEAUTIFUL, NO MAN SHALL EVER HARM HER. Their poems, plays and stories are the truth that is spoken with every gesture. Our editors want them. We publish their true tales about the death of man. Only those grown-up poets, playwrights and writers who tell their tales through the eyes of living children are accepted into our quarterly.

Myself? I write to kill any man who would make a bomb to murder this beauty. And so should every poet. Anything else is just another firecracker contribution to the supply shed of my daughter's murderers. If poets were true, which they are not, they would write witness accounts of civilization's cruel and brutal slaughter of their babies. This would make these poet-warriors very dangerous, because after the word comes the deed. And the deed is a mad fury and rush to tear out the bowels of the lying, careful word picking professional child-haters lurking in moneygot universities.

We must write about our beauty. The real stuff. Not the professional toy box tears that give the fat poets more time and enough money to buy another cheeseburger. Juxtapose our real beauty with the sham that they are making of it. Then write anger beside our beauty. It has to be this way, or we shall all perish.

February 12

Last Night in India

Last night in India the power went out
The blackness just got blacker
if you can imagine that.
You can't
So I'll tell you
They froze to death.
Some soldiers marched into their hut
Kicked a body out of its bed
and assumed the whole village dead.
Everyone was wearing hats.
Thirty or forty people frozen
They stopped counting at lunch.
Lunch happened and they stopped counting.
The government got a wire.
The international press was having lunch
So the news never got outside
the frozen Indian village of dead people.

But Sita did.
She crawled out from beneath
her mother's embrace
whimpering and crying, upsetting the tiger
who was prowling the village for lunch.
He leapt toward her with a roar
and a hungry guttural growling
his coat rippling with hunger
Sita saw the starved tiger,
stopped her tears in their tracks down her cheek
and began to sing the lullaby
her mother sang while she froze.
Now this tiger was very moved
calmly waiting a long moment

even sitting his haunches back on a ground stone
while her lullaby sang careful and slow.
Then he leapt onto Sita
eating her very quickly
from her tiny head to toe

What?
You thought the tiger would
take Sita by the yellow scruff of her sati
carry her to his cave high up the mountain
nestle her in his warm softness
for many many cold nights to come
and teach her the tiger's strength and courage and beauty—
What?
Why should the tiger clean up your mess?
He's a wild animal
But so heavenly beautiful
in truth
that the least I expect from him
is still a whole lot more
than any human would do.

Prove to me otherwise
and I will sing man's praises.
Until then I sing for the tiger
the dumb hungry moose,
the puppy, the cat,
the Sitas in my life—
who know no lullaby but hunger
and warmth and play...
The earth is a wild ball
Let us walk upon its turning
devouring evil
which can only be a human thing
because they know how to spell.
I tell you
the only evil in the universe is human made

February 13

The Perfect Unsurpassed Beauty of The Ox Creek Calvary 4-H

It will take me a while to get to the point. Beauty is obvious, when it happens to the beholder. However, the world beholds nothing until I declare what will be beautiful. Is this not what poets and prophets are called to do? It must be the lure of democracy, television and union paying jobs which persuade Americans to decide for themselves what is beautiful. Most of the time they are wrong, simply because beauty cannot arrive at the door like the newspaper, everyday, at exactly the same time. Anyway, even if it did, it would just get used to perform some degrading afternoon chore, like wiping maggots out of the garbage can, or picking up a winter of what the dog left in the backyard.

Usually it takes me a while to shove beauty down a throat. I lack the necessary skills of a writer. I am not a writer. I am a beauty-copier. Last night I witnessed a show of human perfection. Since it was physically impossible for me to squeeze the 4-H farmhouse meeting into a ball small enough to fit inside a mouth, I promised myself to take in the perfection quietly, as a shy, unobtrusive bystander, and later use the weaker persuasion of words to shove beauty down the infidel's throats. When magic happens, nothing and no one can duplicate its meaning. I said that I was a beauty copier. Which means that I am an artist— translated, "the great fool" in the mystical tongue. Only perfection has the sense to leave magic well alone, and I am quite a distance farther from perfection than your greatest illusion of infinity. So as always, I digress. I tell you, it's a whole lot better than cooking French fries.

That being said, and most likely, misunderstood, please join my daughter and me on a cold winter night's drive through the country.

Getting the Best Results From Choking a Blind, Spineless Grown-up

Well, legally you can't break his back, even if in the long run it proved to be the more humane thing to do. So I would like to open our discussion about knitting squares with... Oh wait wait wait! First the *Pledge of Allegiance* and 4-H pledge. Laurie, could you hold the tiny flags please? "I Pledge allegiance to the flag
of the United States that would kill me..."
All the girls and the one boy pledge their allegiance, without the least

bit of thought about the meaning of the words. Why should they question this allegiance? Why think for themselves? The mommies and one daddy have their right hands on their hearts too. They pledge. And so shall the children.

This is the first sad revelation of the meeting. Nothing could be more defeating of hope than this display of tiny hearts giving allegiance to the United States Army. This is the beginning of societies' dementia. The children! How can the loving parents allow this horror to happen? How can we expect the following 4-H pledge to hold any weight, a pledge which is so much more true to their hearts than the first madness they are taught to recite? The 4-H pledge respects their rights, but more importantly, their dreams. The pledge to country is provided in part, by their parent's paranoia. It is they who give the state power to lure their child into pledging her heart to the devil's own symbolic flag. It is they who press their six-year-old to memorize war cries before her mind is ready to consider the actual horrible significance of those words.

Ironically, the 4-H pledge follows the *Pledge of Allegiance*. Why is it of second importance? It's a 4-H meeting, and not the Boston Tea Party. Does anyone know the definition of "allegiance?" Whose hell is this anyway? You brainwashed jingo Johns and Judys! They are learning about the horse's digestive system and helping each other prepare for their presentations on Saturday. Now the soldier parents march their babies' vulnerable hearts across the entire country, pledging allegiance, as if come a declaration of war, the little girls tore off their retail clothes for cooler camouflage, and tossed aside their nifty four-color pens to be replaced with automatic weapons. What else does the pledge of allegiance do besides will them to gaily run out the door holding hands through a mine field?

For the organizers of this wonderful institution to ever gain my respect, and it alone is worth more than a library of written law, the first pledge to the United States must be eliminated from the program. How cruel to mix up the children's horse dreams with nightmare enemies of state. Children giving their allegiance to a flag? Dementia. Why not a pledge to the Tennessee Walking Horse, the Palomino, the Lippizaner? Why are they here at 4-H anyway? If there must be a pledge to the U.S.A., make it be to their parent's mutual, acquired fear of their government. It might be a better truth to have their little minds start believing in.

To truly pledge their heads to clearer thinking, which is the first line of the 4-Her's motto, Mr. or Mrs. President of 4-H has got to scratch out the flag brainwashing which jump starts each meeting. If children were truly allowed the freedom to think clearly, they might grow up to be morally strong, individually wise women and men. Those kind of humans dissolve all dishonest institutions, a United States included.

February 14

I pledge my head to clearer thinking
my heart to greater loyalty
my hands to larger service, and
my health to better living
for my club
my community
my country
and my world

Where was I?

Oh yes, perfect, unsurpassed beauty.

February in farm country. If you are one to want both trees and stars to preserve their quiet, and moonlight to remain a practical benefit for roof building, please join my daughter and I, as we ride the frozen, dead corn hills of Cayuga County in our smart little German car. Rachelle reads by battery powered lantern light, while I steer, accelerate, and stop my brain's many distinct illusions. By this hour on Monday night I am usually frazzled silly. My day began before dawn and went non-stop before getting behind the wheel to relax.

It is quite a distance to the clubhouse. Twenty-five miles south of our smarter routine of staying at home, eating a scrumptious feast of a dinner, and slowly pulling our tired bodies up the stairs to bed. In winter the nest is enough—for me. But it's not just me, is it? In fact, it's more for them than me, shouldn't it be? God how scary if the opposite were true! Raising children has got to mean more than that unconditional-love-until-death piddlybunk two housewives discuss over coffee and toast. Their little devils play together on the floor, rudely hoarding toys and growing up in fear of everything.

Raising children is slavery. Call it any name you like, but I know its true name is slavery. And yet it is the highest form of love and bondage potentially attainable by man. That precisely is its virtue—a complete devotion to a god of his own spirit, depending on how awake and persistent the slave be. Tell me, what mythical, untouchable god enjoys a fraction of the sacrifices we bestow upon our children? What Buddha, what Yahweh, what angry volcano deity outwardly possesses more divine right than your own son or daughter? And which force would you prefer to keep the most healthy and alive if you were called on to care for both?

If the children only knew their real power! There are plenty of opportunities for our masters to abuse us. A good slave knows how to watch his tongue and behave, else his master turn against him. Or maybe I keep to myself this amazing good fortune. I know my master would never take advantage of me. Not on her life! I am an alert slave, ready to perform every duty before it can be noticed undone. I am on a constant watch-to-action. That is the difference between a good slave and bad one. The better the slave, the better the daddy, and the more happy and more lucky as well!

The clubhouse is an old, abandoned four room farmhouse set alone at the top of a hill. Fallow fields stretch a mile out to the tree line. It's been a long time since this old house has seen any cheer. What a joyful place! Without 4-H, it probably would have housed another round of poor, greedy dirt farmers.

We turn into the front yard right on time. We're always on time. It's one of my constants. Good slaves keep an eye on the clock. My master is a very poor judge of time. Back when I was a young master, I knew by heart every second's tick. The networks programmed their shows on the half hour, and I programmed my daily life to fit the network's schedule. Long ago, before 4-H, children watched television to learn about time. When Rachelle was born, I took control of the TV for fear that time could be such a waste of my master's energy. She would know when it was time to play, time to eat and time to sleep. I would tell her. I know that now she is better prepared to greet the many dangers of the day— but only since I have bared the burden of time in my brain.

In short, we always get to 4-H exactly on time. We gather our things and go inside. I bring my manuscript along so to keep my head buried in words and my eyes focused on anything besides people. I am afraid of people. Mostly grown-ups. No, I am afraid of every grown-up. It might take me two years to warm up to the most determined man or woman seeking my acquaintance. You can see that I am practically without friends. Like the child, I am so very shy when called upon in public. But unlike the child, it might take me a thousand times longer to approach a potential playmate. Personally, that is a great disappointment in my life.

But just look! All of Rachelle's friends are here! Laurie and Georgia, little Constance and Emily Smith. Their smiles are enchanting. Envisioned in the wrong light, they may appear drunk and uncaring. Not so. I believe "carefree" to be a more appropriate word. "Wild" might be a better one. In its meaning one shall spy the bleak desert chasm separating the bright sun of their true hearts, from the cold, black, acquired knowledge trap which the crafty grown-ups have set.

The wild ones remembered the rough drafts to their presentations. Next Saturday will be the real thing. And although that kind of time pressure would drive me to the limit of my neurosis, the children aren't nervous at all. They revel in the present moment. Again, you see, it is my duty to take on my master's worry. I twist my guts inside-out so that she may live her days peacefully—this is a tacit bond I share with the other slaves in the clubhouse. We are servants attending to our master's whims; mere porters, coachmen, drivers, cooks, launderers, groundskeepers, room cleaners, and tutors. Oh, but we better watch out what we teach them! A good slave is very careful. If he wishes to keep his master's trust and attention, he will constantly be on guard of his own dangerous mouth and deeds. So, "the mouth is the gate of woe." Yes, but any slave worth his indenture knows that the moat of action boils before the gate of woe. Say whatever you wish good slave, but the master knows the falsity of words spoken before deed. Some poor slaves find out too late, and are banished from their children's kingdom. Expecting deeds before dinner, the master got steadily poisoned with words all day long, and gradually, over time, had stone walls built to keep away the phonies Mom and Dad.

The mothers and fathers of 4-H have come this far, which means their children still love and respect them. That's reason enough for sincere congratulation. These kids are different. They are kind, compassionate, cheerful, gentle. They have so much *not* in common with the children outside of 4-H. There are physical and even some mental similarities to be sure. That is, Emily of 4-H can be forgetful as any child. But it is in her forgetting where might be concealed the kindest gesture. Last week Laurie had the flu. Emily made her a heart-shaped card at home, but forgot to bring it to Monday's meeting. Emily did not forget that the little bald girl who she saw in the store hasn't any hair because she is dying. Nor did she forget that pulling off the little girl's hat and laughing at her bare scalp, might make her cry real tears.

The other child forgot. There is a cruelty like that in some children. Not in the Ox Creek Cavalry 4-H.

Why?

Because in the beginning, long before 4-H, their slaves were truly that dutiful.

But this is not the time for parental back slappings. We know we're good. We paid our ticket to this show of beauty. We spent a lifetime tending our flock, raising our delicate flowers from seed, cultivating our pleasant gardens of Eden—You get the idea. No, actually, most of you have no idea what the hell I am talking about. But there will be another day to comment on the steady pointer rise on the doom meter. Few will seek my books, except maybe to burn them. Who wants to read a story about his own sick heart? But in the unlikely case that you read with some relish the exposé on the cruelty you pass on to your child, please understand my intentions first and foremost were to scold you. I can get right to the essence of the sour inside that makes you the greatest faker and liar. I know that the cruel child exists because of you. And to be ignorant of the awesome responsibility you and I have to this species, to not possess the instinct of gentle perpetuation, which, god damn it, evolution, or at least God, should, by all purposeful intent, have brought us to thus far—to care not about the developing perfection of your child, (and there is a human perfection to aspire to, I know), at least not until you can enjoy all the pleasant frillies that false living has to offer first—this my dear enemy, is the worst of all evils. It is the unnecessary black, infinity of the universe. Our children and ourselves possess all the universe we need to know. Because you ignore that truth, Mr. and Mrs. Slapdoodle, is precisely why humanity is wrong, and why so many parents can't find the time to participate in 4-H.

February 15

After the pledges, everyone sits down on the floor. Constance is the president. She picks tonight's theme for attendance. "Favorite color, okay? Molly first."

"Oh, I really don't have one specific favorite," says Molly, "I like all bright colors. Bright yellow or orange, light blue, bright green. Nothing dark and dreary."

Molly is eighteen years old. Her sister sitting beside her, is sixteen. They have another sister, Elizabeth, sitting across the room with girls her own age. She is eleven. Derrick, the only boy, is the next oldest at fifteen. Then there's fourteen year old Mallory, eleven year old Constance, Laurie, and Rachelle, ten year old Georgia and Emily, and finally little Shelby, who has spent six long years on planet earth.

What amazes me is that at eighteen, Molly can keep a lively interest in the 4-H. She has no qualms about hanging out with girls who haven't reached puberty yet. She participates without irony. She's grown up, ready for college, and the fast, sloppy world after college, and yet here she is sitting on an old floor in the cold of the middle of nowhere sharing stories and smiles with girls six to twelve years her junior. There's an American anomaly for you. Molly is happy! Why isn't she in the back seat of a car, drunk with some stupid boy squeezing his hands between her thighs? This is the heart of an eighteen year old girl? Here, at 4-H? She must have got wind of the sadness that awaits her outside the clubhouse. She must know some shitty truths about men—enough to scare her away for a little while longer anyway. Not that I am bitter. No, I also am kind and gentle and wanting realities' true intentions to shine. I believe in Molly. It's the monster I was at eighteen whom Molly has every reason to fear. And believe me, among my friends, I was the most sincere and well-behaved! All I wanted from a girl was a muse, even though at the time I didn't know the meaning of the word. Sex was on the brain, but not yet to my fingers. It's not the sexual desire that marks the eighteen year old American boy as a serious danger to avoid. No, its the entire cluster of mental disturbances shooting off in the brain of the boy that should scare the happy horseshit out of the 4-H girls. When I think back on the type of human being Ron Throop was at eighteen, a hundred pound mace is swung in my gut.

But isn't every boy a bit insane at that vulnerable age?

The majority, yes, of course. This is America, is it not? Our eighteen year old boys aren't truly healthy unless they're exhibiting some signs of extremely dangerous, irrational behavior. Selfishness and paranoia are stark normalities. Hate, prejudice, cowardice, and even sexual offenses are not discouraged at this age, because more likely than not, the father had gone and done the same thing when he was eighteen. The boy shall sow his demented oats before settling down to neglect a family, play golf, and never think on an uplifting thought again, if ever he had one at all.

I could write you a true story about the boys I knew in my high school. It would make very inspirational reading for skin heads. I hung out and drank beer with extremely violent examples of American insanity. To write down just a few of their exploits would make them suspect for possible prison time, provided that our government could hold onto a set of testicles just long enough to increase the statute of limitations for any crime to eternity. Listen, I am ashamed of that period in my life. How I came to be the man I am today would make an excellent subject for a sociologist's graduate thesis. Personally I think most of my friends should not have been granted life past eighteen. A better world would have cut their dangerous presence out of the way of real progress. But as is typical in America, the more dangerous or stupid one be, the better his chance for a high rise in paying society. Some of the kids I knew were clearing a wide open path to the electric chair. The other day I heard through the grapevine, and was not at all surprised, that the worst of them is doing rather well flying planes about the country. Here's an interesting thought to ponder while on your next pretty trip to St. Martin. The uniformed captain steering your plane toward paradise, covered the inside flap of my senior yearbook with a realistic sketch of a woman performing felacio on a fat penis. Folks, I knew him well, and that's the nicest thing he ever did. Is there anything wrong in that? Probably not to the couple vacationing in St. Martin. But there is some definite wrongness done to the eighteen year old dreams of Molly. And also to the innocent hopes of every girl alive at eleven, who desires a dream about horses after eighteen. I should mention this now, so as to get it in writing: I promise to kill with my bare hands the boy who forces his foul perversion upon my daughter. For his own sake, he might want to have an acute knowledge of 4-H and horses before strolling onto the dating scene. Or, to insure a safe continuation of his precious life, let him be drugged with the desire to win the wonderings of a gentle heart. I know the viciousness of an eighteen year old boy raised in the United States of Fatstomachs. I know the face he puts on is incredibly more dangerous than his father's false one. Daddy made it past eighteen, and I promise you he didn't do so as a gentleman. Dig deep enough into daddy's past and don't be surprised if you get caught up in a gang rape of a small girl in the snow, or the kidnapping of a black man walking down a deserted country road. It was your loving dad who tied him up, blind folded, and kicked his ass down the steps of the old root cellar out back. What did they do to him? Use your imagination, sicko!

I can hear the young man tonight, asking Dad his advice on how to love a woman. "Grab a beer son, and stick your fingers in like this..."

"No Dad, I mean, how do I make a girl happy? How do I get her to love me?"

"Marge, come quick! We raised a faggot boy. Jesus junior, take the truck tonight. Here are the keys. Now drink some beers. Go get in a fight. You're eighteen you silly little shit. Show me you're a man!"

So Molly says its bright colors she likes. Now it's my turn, and I say the same thing. Like I said before, I am afraid of people. Sure, bright colors, why not? "When I paint I use bright colors."

Next is Rachelle, who unlike me, always tells the truth. She thinks lavender is her favorite. The 4-H leader, Mrs. Beck, says lavender too. Can she have the same problem as me?

Oh God no! Absolutely not!

Around the room then. Red, blue, bright colors again, dark and dreary ones from the boy, Derrick. *Watch out for him at your door, Ron. Better stay in 4-H Derrick.* More bright colors, the many shades and tints of green, and then on to the next business of the evening...

Petty cash. Club savings. $18.54. $452.32. Both sounding so queer in a world of the fifty thousand dollar car. This is usually the time I fall back into a mystical mood. This little white farmhouse on top of a hill...

I watch my breathing. I can see my breath. It's this cold inside, and I'm the one closest to the kerosene heater! I wonder how anybody else in the room can stand it.

Constance Beck calls for the coloring contest. Each week the children color in a picture of a horse, drawn by either Rachelle or Georgia. They're the CCC's—The Coloring Contest Coordinators. This is not the Department of Defense. Wouldn't it be nice if our bottle fed generals could relieve some out-of-battle tension coloring in pictures? Say a piece on perspective of nuclear warheads lined up to the vanishing point of a smoky horizon? Or perhaps a desert tank caught in the act of crushing an Iraqi mother and infant? A sinking battleship with hungry sharks devouring sailors? Or say, how about this ambitious attempt for a Five Crayon General—Line art of a Chinese city with children's bodies just ripped apart everywhere? How satisfying to watch while these overpaid people killers color in a piece of human liver lying next to a manhole. Would they stay behind the lines? (Ha-ha, that's a joke.) Their salary is still paid by the taxpayers, yes? Well then, maybe for once we should give them something happy to work on. Rachelle draws excellent horses. All governmental paid killers please have yours in by the next meeting.

And why not? What the hell is stopping us from making the general color in the pictures that we hand out? Our children are in a coloring contest, and we the parents pay the general's salary. My child is eleven. According to the rules written by the murderous men we hire, (it's always men, and then when women get to be like men, they tow the line, so as not to screw up their chance to be like men), in seven more years Rachelle will be of age to kill people, if she so desires. She can join the armed forces. What's stopping Molly from leaving 4-H this moment on a search and destroy mission? What is preventing her from stabbing to death a charging Chinese girl-soldier her own age? Intelligence? Sure, why not? Compassion? Yes. Ambition? Of course. For each coloring she hands in, Molly receives five points toward free trailering and hay at the county fair. Not bad. My God, who really believes that six months of intense training at Camp Learnhowtokill can abolish Molly's desire to color in a picture of horse?

Gee I don't know. Maybe it can. And maybe it's time for me to grow up and lead the destruction of a species, that after two million years, still has not learned how to contentedly color in a picture of a horse and refrain from all savage urges to kill the neighbor.

Time for presentation practice. Here's a list of topics. Proof once again of the glorious beauty of children young and old:

Constance's Five Star Fruit Salad
Georgia's Saxy Music
Derrick's Misconceptions of Karate
Shelby's Secret Friend Zooey
Laurie's Rats Make Great Pets
Rachelle's Smart Dog Beany

Now let's have some fun:
Here's a little excerpt to shed light on the situation. For beauty to have

its rightful place in the spotlight, sometimes it is necessary to nudge ugly right up close. I am tired of allowing a billion arms to be thrown up into the air, "What the holy mother of God, would you have us do?" Here is an imagination game to play. Picture yourself sitting next to me by the kerosene heater. The children are taking turns practicing their presentations. You know their subjects. Now read this:

"The prestigious magazine, Science, has presented a number of articles over the years describing animal experimentations. An article entitled 'Chronic Uncontrolled Cross-Circulation in Unanesthetized Dogs'...is particularly noteworthy. During the animal experiments discussed,...two dogs were joined together at the neck with polyethylene tubing connecting one dog's neck artery to the other's jugular vein. The necks of the two dogs were then wrapped together and held in place with a plaster cast, forcing the animal's heads to tilt back—and stay back in place. The animals were forced to endure this treatment for seventy-two hours. This experiment demonstrated that blood could successfully cross-circulate from one animal to another for extended periods of time."

I quote that from a book entitled, *Clogging Your Child's Veins With Toxic Death—A Study of Immunizations and the Dog-fornicating Doctors Who Promote Them.*

Is it any wonder why I would want the parent who is not moved to tears by the two-headed dog story, to set this book down on the end table, and immediately explode in his chair?

Who, besides death can allow this to happen? What monster but death and desolation would make the lie even greater, and attend the child's presentation on Saturday? How many more dogs must be gutted and bled in the presence of crying children? Who besides death would wipe the child's tears without the promise of, "It's okay honey, Daddy will stop the insanity." I know that most of you are like me. You have your cute puppies too, and can't think of but maybe one instance in the story of mankind when the necks of two people were glued to a cast and stuck with two ends of a tube in order to share the same blood. I tell you this morning there's a man in prison picking over his breakfast on a tray, who murdered two baby girls after getting them to blow golden bee-bees up his colon. And you're gonna tell me he has a right to toast and coffee? Oh we give far too much credit to a non-existent soul. Prisons full of men, the type who are just itching to rape or kill anything on two legs. Why isolate this one evil and give it a name?

Think of the multitude of unknown monsters let loose in society... What do we call them? I am talking about the free men of this land. The corporal who was eleven years old when he joined the 4-H. The brain surgeon who quit when he was twelve because there was no god damn chance his father would pay his way through veterinary school. Or what about little Johnny, the scientist boy, who was born into the 4-H? His mother was an active leader for several years. Her pride and joy was a son who might one day win the Nobel prize. He proved to be the brightest, most ambitious member. When little Sally was through with her presentation on treats and rewards for the hurdling dog, he flopped a dead dog down onto the table, and dissected some chipped bone out of its lung. The other children cried during his presentation, much to their parent's dismay, who were all quietly amazed at Johnny's advanced expertise. That night while getting tucked into bed Sally begged her mommy to let her quit the 4-H. "Oh my God, nothing doing, you little brat!" Mommy scolded her child for not being as bright as the scientist boy. "You'll get your whiny little butt back there next week, Sally, and leave our stupid dog at home."

February 16

Break for a discussion about today's human drama...
I know that I am nil. Not right in the brain. Sometimes I feel unable to cope with reality. Sure, I am a frustrated artist trying my damnedest to stay sane in America. Sure, but I am also a man. And you can't put off that reality to suit your particular tastes for the day. That means when the family goes out with the baby for her first outing, and you stop at the bank to pick at your dwindling fortune, for the luxuries of bread and butter, and you are already wondering if you're fucking crazy because half the world is starving to death and you don't have the balls to say, I'll do whatever the hell I want in this pot-bellied country of filthy rich plumbers—I'll turn green if I must, and rot away, before I lower my head to these hermaphroditic cows. Work for a living! Ha! I'd like to see the man who works as much as I do. And my work ain't your idea of slapping on aftershave, day after day, until you retire and then you're dead. My work isn't saving up for Thursdays with the boys playing threes, fours, or twenty-one, or wondering why I was put on this earth, if not to frighten the shit out of any man who is not exactly like me. I work every waking moment of my life. I'm inside this brain.

I know. Great, so the true lord knows my worth, but I know that he's a wormy piece of shit too. Is he gonna pay me? Are you? Why not? I am a starving child of Africa you god damn fake-a-lot! I thought my illusions were too great to ever achieve happiness in this life. It's a fight every morning, not to get out of bed, not to love my wife, not to cook a fine meal, not to revel in merriment, not to joke, not to play, not to teach, not to learn, not wonder, not sing... *Never to sing*—Jesus Christ don't sing! If you sing, you're a goner. We'll just look the other way. If you sing without us; if you try to do practically anything without us, we will become your tormenting torturers. We fight like hell to get out of bed. No, we really don't. But we pretend to. We hate ourselves but we hate you more. Why don't you get it you poor baby sapling? We are not real! This is all here for you. It's your test. The car just went dead in the bank parking lot because we are watching you. We know Murphy's Law. We made that up on the spot so Marie would have something to say about the car dying. Marie isn't real. Not to you. We will decide when you are ready to love a woman. Afraid aren't you? Too bad! You're the only one. We're here for you, as instruments of torture. Look at us? Do you think we would actually look this pathetic in our real world? We walk like slabs of granite that received sentience five minutes ago. So get out of the god damned car! No one's gonna give you a red cent to write this drivel for a living. Can you turn a wrench? Join the plumber's union. Put your kid in school. Buy a car that works. Stop pretending that an artist in Paris is respected simply because some streets are named after dead ones. The artist is a worm anywhere. You don't write well. You have an eighth grade vocabulary. You stutter. Sometimes when we talk to you we wonder if you will actually start crying. Get out of the car! Scrap all the love letters. Feel around up your ass while you take a shower and guess right that we shoved something up there. We are testing you, and we are not merciful.

Get out of the car!

That's good. Now walk across the street to the mechanic and do what we do. Don't you dare set the car on fire. Why should Marie abandon a car for the rest of her life just because you say so? We tell her what to feel—not you gumbo! Get back in the car. Try again. Perfect, it started. Do you see? We knew it was going to start all along. Now get home you loser and keep up the sissy chores you call work until your wife and children despise you.

February 17

What happened last night? Hmm. That is why I am against the afternoon. I think the brain gets overloaded, like in dreams when the baby sleeps in the middle. One cannot fall deep enough into sleep to have normal dreams and forget about them. So he dreams about Michael putting his hand on your thigh. Never a beautiful dragon to befriend, who carried him on her wing and vowing protection from men.

At 3 p.m. my state of mind takes a turn for the worse. All downhill until darkness. In the night I am okay. I loathe to write in the afternoon, which seems to be the best time of day to scare the crap out of myself. I don't really have little voices telling me what to do. That is the dog barking while the rent-a-car girl bangs at the door. And all that garbage about Murphy's law? Marie could have stood at the door to tell me, "Time for cereal," and the bad day would die. Sure the car didn't start. Yes, of course I fear that no one wants me if I will not make a living with money. At six a.m. I can wake up feeling like a poor French farmer in February. There are chores that need to be done this morning but the afternoon is set up perfectly for idleness. By three I feel as though he never belonged on the farm. He spent the next hour dragging the anvil to the pond in the rain, and another half hour tying the rope to it and his legs. If he could stall just a few more minutes, the cold sun would set again, and the horse would need to be brought in and fed.

I can't help that my brain sits by a pond tied to a heavy weight everyday at three. It's been that way since I wanted to write, but knew I wouldn't be any good at it, and so not even the people most dear to me would care.

Now baby Jane cries. The French farmer in need!

Later that afternoon...

I believe in heaven and God.

There, now that is beautiful.

So is this:

After I am through with grown up lying, I want to spend the rest of my career writing about a tree. It would take ten lifetimes if I had any guts. Men cannot live for long with art. The art crazy man, the artist most true to his art, could never complete his piece, in any medium, whether it be music, painting, literature, if he were wise to the tree. One tree. It should be the beginning and the end. The painting cannot end. How can it? A true gaze cannot lie about its infinity. Only men stop and start anew. Not again, *anew.* The more trees the artist carries under his arm, the greater the artist. Nobody except the lunatic can be true to just one tree. And when I say "lunatic" I mean exactly that—the moon barking up the wrong tree type.

The presentations were today.
I will get to the story in a moment.
I held Janie in my arms while I wept to the music of the past.
Yes I weep. I am a man with a heart.
I believe in heaven and God
I believe in angels watching down
Our babies go to God
The animals go to God
You go to God if your food dish goes with you
I have never made anyone happy.
I am such a stuffed shirt of wrong knowledge
Everything is inside God
And he's gonna drag our noses through
the mud and stink of his own shit lies!
I love the beauty of heaven and God.
Whatever is so important about us not stopping
and going to see God?
This isn't even what I mean!
If I should ever lose my daughter to him
I believe in the beauty of a heaven and a god
I shall become the final wrath of him

I love her believing in angels

O the bitter hard eternity of
forever and not believing!

February 25

Now the only fiction to this journal, other than the name changes, are the dates remaining. I want to give the impression that I am losing my mind.

Yet no matter how bad the situation, it's impossible for me to lose it. I am aware of my sanity. I know that I am right because I am true to my belief. That is the second fiction. You watch—I will get desperate enough to lie to myself. What I promise not to do is give the truth anymore. Fools and fairy tales know the truth, and like to hear its bell's steady chime through the maddest kinds of chaos.

So tomorrow I will fake the date. The rest of this work is purely fictional.

March 3

Vive Los Cerdos Se Llaman Sammy y Rosita!

En la casa verde pequeña
Sentiamos en el piso
como "ba-na-na a-eating moan-key"
con ojos como grande
como tus ojos
dale a uno en la cara
mira fuera de ventana.
El noche de invierno
viene tranquilo
con un poco de copos de nieves gordos
y un mapache detiene
en las pisadas de la zarigüeya
mientras que un luz caliente echa
de aqui nuestro espacio pequeño
Los cerdos cantan las alabanzas
de el cielo y la tierra
y sus plato amarillo de
alimento humilde

Looks pretty damn good, don't it? Doesn't matter what kind of crap it is, I wrote it down in another language. Do you want the truth? It's written in the ancient Iberian tongue, "Ballazan". It was recited before the hunt to bring good luck and safe return of the men and their rabbit kill. I would attach a footnote like T.S. Eliot, to insure that enough college professors would know its meaning. Then everyone would be happy again. Ah poetic license! To rhyme *rain* with *again*, and jerk on and off to the sound of your own voice on tape.

But "Ballanzan" is Spanish and much too crude for dignified poetics. Now ancient Greek, there's a language that even Greek goats don't want to know.

"Mr. Pound, Are you interested in the price of partial immortality?"

"What do I have to do? Or rather, ᵒᵃ£¢∞ᵃ-tu-tu-agape?"

"Do you think goats would know it?"

"Not on your life Mon ser! Here's ten thousand pages of dribbling nonsense. Ten different languages and if I go a little crazy, some even shittier poets will climb up my pretty Venetian staircase to pay their respects. Shh! I'm pretending to be Metropolitan. I'm a high class chap with a cane. I know the American Negro should have cracked my legs broke, and given me some real reason to walk with a cane. I used to ride past Sunday morning church lynchings with my ont and ooncle ∞£¥¨å-˙µ≤."

You mean the great Ezra Pound actually lived in America?"

"Yes, I hate to admit it. But I am a small man. Though no less feeble than my goodfriend, T.S. (The initials stand for Takeanother Snackyoufake) His mummy and duddy had a sick psychic sense of humor."

"Who cares? We got you worldwide fame. Now write anything. Become obsessed with language. Say 'Viva Italiano!' Start singing 'Mussolini, Mussolini' before everybody finds out that what you fear more than anything is your arm being sawed off on a stump. We can guarantee a smart place for you in university books for at least a hundred and fifty years. You did much more for American letters than a tiny mouse taking a drink from a rain puddle, then scurrying across a sheet of looseleaf paper, dropping turds. If it weren't for your exhaustive efforts we might be living in a crazy world today, where children shoot children and poetry doesn't do a bit of fucking good!"

"So, where are you going with this my dear friend?"

"Oh, Mr. Pound, I'm so sorry. Some ancient Greek, a woman's scarf and a motor car. Twenty lines by next Friday and immortal fame. Fair enough?"

"£∂ßå-πø^¨¥-booka-book!"

"Exactly!"

Do you get it now? Drippy drippy snot boy is having a breakdown. I live in a warm house in winter with my beautiful family. A minute ago I let the dog out wondering if I could beg a dollar a week from a hundred people. Who in his right mind would donate to the enemy? Obviously no one wants to know the truth about the death of his eyes. In France I hear there's a man running amok across the land terrorizing

McDonald's. What words? There is deed. Words from the messenger maybe: "Bon jour fellow Frenchmen. You have five minutes to drop your burgers and vacate the premises. José Bové awaits his vindication! Au revoir!"

José Bové is a sheep farmer and a folk hero. It's not in his plan to kill people. But he has got to want people to kill themselves if he is ever to see in his lifetime all McDonald's erased from French soil. What does that even mean? Kill themselves? Are you speaking literally? Does José Bové understand? Probably not. He is winning the fight with action! The battles against timid quarter-men with money. Yet no matter how brave his disrespect for his own freedom, the man is still a silly phony. You have to do to the corporate men the same thing you do to the baby lamb when the children are having hunger pangs. How in such a short span of history have we become so afraid of death for a cause? I expect to be killed for my belief. There are many like me taking their life in their own hands. Why not fight first? What have we become in two hundred years? Where is the guillotine of old to get the bourgeois' legs up and running? If I was a shepherd raising my flock for food and raiment, and the majority of my fellows mocked and blocked my humble means of earning a living for the desire of a poulette de croquette, I could not stop at the polite burning down of their silly little eating houses. I would have three choices: Fight to the death anything that endangers my existence. Kill myself. Or run far away on this big fat planet to hide.

I would invite José Bové to come visit my street, never ever named after a dead artist, because America is a filthy degraded age old horror show of an old witch afraid of death and losing another tooth. Before my suicide I'd give the good Frenchmen a real taste of madness. A walk down the highway of a fifty thousand McDonald's. We would invite ourselves into the home of the squirming CEO of the multi-billion dollar franchise and ask him a few polite questions that have waited long enough on the tongues of true poets and warriors. Questions first asked at the beginning of time and repeated again and again up to the moment, not long into our future, when the last fat slob died screaming in his lounge chair, clutching a double cheeseburger.

José Bové will have his list, but I want mine to be the last words heard by the CEO before we force feed him to death, pound after pound of the shit he peddles to humanity. Just a few polite questions to get down to this business of the madness of more business.

Why were you born?

How did you get into this house?

How many people can you kill a year?

I want to know exactly how much an apple costs. How much dammit?

Where are your children?

What do you think of Jose's mustache?

Are you afraid?

Did you know that you're the last one we've come to?

How do you feel now?

Do you know who Rachelle is?

Have you heard of baby Jane?

Do you know Marie?

Is life glad?

Do you think highly of existence?

Why is there evil?

There is a woman on the planet who froze to death in the road last night. The baby wrapped up in her arms also froze. Two of your managers saw her lying in the road. Did you help kill her? Answer the truth or I will eat you alive!

Do you deserve to laugh?

If I leave right now would you send me a dollar a week in the mail? Even if I pay the postage?

Your turn José.

"Jesus Ron! That's why I don't like you wordy, poetic poops. You just take him by the hair like this. You put your eyes to his. You say, 'I spit on your ancestors and I make love to your wife and daughter.' And then you eat him. Here. Bon appetit."

March 17, May 1, and August 22

Now I am trying to create the illusion of time's wear on the potentially mad. I don't expect anyone to believe that insanity happens just like that, lickety-lickety. Really, I just want to end this crap because it's still winter and I'm sad on and off. And I need to write something beautiful, or get a job so I can end the selfish worry. Most of my day is a "what if?" about me. Yuck. That is not love. Nor is being a smart ass know-it-all and everyone else be dead wrong. Don't forget to tell them in writing so they hate you. They made you what you are by reading the paper and clipping coupons, when they damn well knew all along that there is enough fear and disgust of one man's idea of himself to detonate a massive self neurotic bomb in his garage full of gardening equipment brain.

Two real conclusions for the modern man who feels:

Conclusion #1 (rip out page to write last words here)

Conclusion #2

July 4

I got a job mowing lawns today. I think I'll start a landscaping business.

June 22, 2010.

It's Father's Day. Took Janie to camp. Rachelle called and told me to go to hell. I'm a shit father, she says.

Kevin and Jody are here to take Marie and I to the couple's tournament. I write only to show the futility of conclusion #2. America is no place for the artist. It's a shame when the only people he loves are American. Oh well, wish me a pleasant round.

From the gentle nuzzling of a pony searching your pockets for a carrot,

Ronald J. Throop

March Madness In Oswego

I am living in a house on West Seventh Street in Oswego. The morning is wide open. I am up early writing once again. I do this every day to save my sanity.

Yesterday I interviewed for a position as a bookseller. I am trained to be a cook. Over the years I trained myself to be an idiot. When I was twenty something, I actually dreamed up how beautiful life would be if I became the village idiot. Then I knew the real value of an autumn day. I used to pretend that I was one of Oswego's wild creatures. I collected horse chestnuts and dead leaves.

Anyway, the bookseller's job. It won't be available until May. It is March and ugly outside. Still, I was happy that the interview went well. That is, I didn't throw up on Mr. Biley. He did most of the talking, which was nice. Said he lived in Manhattan for twenty-five years and wanted to plant roots in Oswego of all places. But it was imperative that he and his wife find the perfect business first, otherwise, do like I do, and create a self-destructive philosophy, and then just see if he can feed his family with that! If I am fifty years old without roots, I will be a dead tree that is still standing. If I do not know where I am at fifty, I have prolonged life unnecessarily. You can see that I am very bitter. I want the wind to blow me over.

I think I got the job. He wouldn't tell me for sure. The clothes I need to buy would cost a week's pay. My old cook's clothes are too soiled to sell books in. It is difficult for me to digest the silliness of a minimum wage job demanding a dress code. I got paid twice that much for coming to work unshaven, unshowered, wearing holy shoes with last month's food stains stinking on the laces, dandruff, bad breath, long, foody fingernails, minimal or no grooming whatsoever... I can get paid ten times minimum wage sweeping floors at the power plant. For that position I need to gain fifty pounds in my boobies alone, and have no bumpy sores growing on the inside lining of my colon. I don't think there is any hope for people.

All week long I have had the nerve to dream about my next book. We have had some dangerous days this month. That I won't deny. I say

I had the nerve it's true. It is a sin around these parts to dream or be happy. No one believes me and is quick to say that I am being a baby. But I am telling the truth. It is practically against the law to be an artist in Oswego. When my wife was in school a dirty short Italian slum lord commissioned her to draw his rental properties. The pride in Oswego is twisted and demented. She got more money for drawing aluminum siding and hose faucets than I have made in my entire life through creative effort. In Oswego I can be a roofer and make a pile of dough on summer days. In Oswego some say there is an art to laying shingles. I disagree. All the men are envious of the shirtless roofers tanning in the midday sun. They are free to listen to classic radio, dream of draft beer, and ride their bikes home from work... It sounds like a damn good job to me too. But I promise you the roofer would be a bitter crying baby if he didn't make any money building roofs. Hence, no art to laying shingles.

I am through with politeness. It's over. I am no longer a gentleman. I am off that path, waiting by the road that forks into the forest. I am eating my lunch of bread and cheese on a log. I am thinking.

Hmmm. The one road leads to present day Oswego, N.Y., America. The other to revolution. The sign pointing to anarchy reads: "First with words, maybe with deed, but never with a god-damn care for human beings." The other sign, pointing to home and the electric bill, has a picture of a pot-bellied man with greasy hair, sipping coffee at a diner. It reads: "This way to the living death in Oswego." Gee, I wonder which path will be safer, which more fun? Revolution or the status quo? Always a very difficult decision to make. Either way I end up alone. The decision will be made after reading the signs, and comparing their levels on the heart's sadness meter. An inaccurate instrument for it can only make readings into a non-existent future.

It's been a long, cold winter. All I wanted were a few months of hibernation. To be left alone with my family and attend to our newborn baby with the necessary care squirrels give to their young in freezing weather. Food, raiment, running water, soap, flush toilet, entertainment, and warmth. And I was looking forward to some extra time to write. That was in January, when winter was young and I was impressionable. Now it's March and I swore last week that I will write a book expressing my disgust and bitterness. I swore that every Oswego man or woman blocking my path to freedom will suffer my rancor in words. Why? You'll probably laugh.

Because civilization wants me to shovel my walk.

Yes, believe it or not, that was the last straw. That harmless demand from a confused friend was the final push that sent me backwards over the edge. I just wanted to be happy and left alone, but he thought it his duty to tell me that if I am going to live in society, then I will have to shovel my walk when the snow piles up. He got upset after I laughed in his face. I feared that our friendship could come to a quick end, unless I humbled myself immediately with silence and a head nod. How is it that another man could not want the freedom I cherish? Last year our neighbors let their grass grow as tall as their oldest boy. "Wonderful," I thought, "now there are some neighbors to admire!" One day two police officers came to their door telling them to cut it down. If they refused, the city would hire a man to do it, at our neighbor's expense. That afternoon their boy came out with a reaper making long awkward swipes at the grass. Joe came over for coffee and I told him the story. He said the city should make them cut it. I said, "But what about the freedom we were born with?" Joe argued that rats and bugs get infested in the tall grass. "You're right!" I said, but privately thought of the human rats and bugs infesting the fat blades of houses on the squirrel's overgrown lawn.

That was it! Shoveling my walk. Jesus, if he just left me alone! They want me to be like them. A square and level walkway. Don't get it, do they? That is our damnation. We have always been and will always be exactly the same. True freedom in Oswego is a futile hope. A PVC pipe dream. They could never respect a man attempting the opposite of their inertia. Not while he is alive. I pray everyday to acquire the power from within to thwart the fears which menacingly confront me. I am bombarded! They do not understand that to block my movement in any way only strengthens my resolve to bury them out of my mind. It is energy that drives me. Energy and more energy. It is generated faster, more furiously, after each let down. I cannot stop it. It's going to flow, fast and hard. With just a spark, I can heat and light all of their homes for the winter. Why would anyone want to turn against me? I have power to give! I am a powerhouse. I am generating more wattage for their own good. They must understand that only a smidgen of my power need be harnessed. That if I am different and feel electrically charged now, over time's long drag, we shall balance each other out. I am going to get old and break down too one day. I'm just not ready to slow down and shut off. My best intentions have been blocked time and again with their massive wire nuts of defeatism. Now I will show them the damage they have done to a man with a heart and incredible energy. I have charged myself anew with a will to write out my vitriol because now I know, without a single doubt, that the negative is the last positive expression to a civilization that desires nothing more from its constituency than a mowed lawn in summer and snowless drive in winter.

The local artist true to his desire, his longing for the beautiful, must channel his excess energy toward creation. How can he not be wise to the embarrassment humankind has caused the earth? I write to eclipse the power of the status quo. I write like no other man. I am alone. I am the second moon stuck in orbit to observe our careless waste of life. It's cold and lonely out here. But I won't come back down until I believe in men. I have made myself sick searching for beauty behind their dry, wrinkled exteriors. I have been pushed and poked to the point of not believing. Yet I still possess the life force. I will not lie. I won't give man the satisfaction of my suicide. I am energy and energy cannot die. I believe in my energy. The ancestral blood flows fast through my veins, and I intend to fight with it until the bitter end. It is a fight I look forward too winning, for victory will have killed the bitterness. I will be a dancing, lunatic soldier. I will not fight to kill, but for the chance to spit in another man's eye, to kick him in the crotch, to laugh in his face while I kick him in the crotch. I don't want to put man out of his misery. I must put him in misery to set him free. I am an artist, not a general. I have no more interest in euthanasia than the gray fox who hops over broken beer bottles in the wet grass. I will do my best to tease and mock whatever it is men are claiming to be today. The reason? I didn't give man life for him to be such an aggressive intruder into mine.

I intend to write for my satisfaction alone. I am a good letter-writer. This then is my opening letter of complaint to the people of Oswego. I am driving one of your silly race cars at full throttle into your home. My words are the explosives taped to my chest. You would want that I make a detour going a 100 mph into a cement wall. No. You can't get to me that way. I am speeding off to California, Alaska, the most northern regions of Quebec, anywhere where I hope and pray man lives as I would want to live.

I have won. It was a photo finish. Lucky for me the judges were *life in every* form, and time. More than anything I want you to feel my nullity. I need you to realize that you're nobody too. I was an open door inviting you in to enrich my life. Together we could have been proud and cheerful citizens. You repaid my gentle manners by dragging your muddy boots across my floor. And then you stood in my home launching one display after the other of life-hate. No more. I write because there is nothing left to write in an unhappy world. I need to be happy. This is my exercise. I must write this letter from the perspective of the grass, the tree, the lake water—anything not human. I no longer share any similarities with that species of fools. I am a species-ist.

This is my microcosm. This is my America. I don't expect other non-entities of my neighborhood to suffer all the blame, but they should. I mean this is where we are living, and here stand piles of degradation taller than the stores of salt for the winter. It would be easier to condemn a Paris or New York. There the little masochistic poodles enjoy a sound whipping once in a while, after goose liver, or whatever it is the million monkeys are told to covet that day. No, I release my ill will into the air that I breathe. This is my home, for now. I should probably get a job.

Hopeless characters. Just got back from a drive out to Minetto. I am a cook by trade, and I heard through Oswego's half drunk grapevine that the old Dubois Inn is looking to hire a sous chef. That is always unfortunate because I am an artist, and the best man for the job. Usually a better chef than the chef too. Which does not sit well with the chefs. For some unknown reason I feel more alive today than usual, singing almost with a fury while I drive out to Minetto. Now I'm flipping off the houses I pass by, gladly giving them back all they have given to me. I know beforehand that I am overqualified for this job. That's a shame, because we could really use the money.

The Dubois Inn. You have to understand what's going through my mind. It was built in 1806. I have a meeting with an Indian at an Inn along the Oswego River. Word got out that the new chef of The Dubois is in need of a sous chef. "Dubois" and "sous" are French words and I am a sucker for what is French and not American. It's 1828 and the new proprietors, Gerard and Katherine Dubois, are rolling around in bed. The sheets are wet from sweat. It's a hot morning. A bell rings at the door. A traveler wants breakfast and his horse needs pasturing. Gerard takes the horse and Katherine leads the traveler into the hot kitchen. She takes two eggs off a plate and cracks them into a bowl. The traveler smiles at Katherine while he taps a silver coin against a tin cup. Katherine takes a quick, nervous look out the window, walks up to the traveler and hikes her skirt up past her hips. The horse whinnies and gnashes his teeth...

What am I going to do? Yesterday the bookseller said I might be called to work in two months, right about the time we'll have to start begging for our food. So I'm up against a wall. I have to go see the Indian. Otherwise I fear—

No, I'm not going that route. I am heading to Minetto on the grayest, ugliest road I have ever known. I am thinking of the Dubois road. I used to walk on it when my first daughter was an infant. I would sit on a log and draw a map of it and the surrounding forest. Still, nobody came out of their homes to invite me in. Not even an Indian. Maps! What the hell was I thinking?

It's an ugly road. Every road is ugly in the American North Country. But only because of human beings. Without their input, this wild world would be paradise. I am going to see an Indian about a job. I imagine some tall, wide monster of a man who'll break my back if I don't start work immediately. Earlier in the day I drove to the Dubois making the same piss offs signs to the empty houses.

Nobody was home. Not at 10:00 a.m. It's a work day, and I know well the loneliness of the statement: "Nobody's home at 10:00 a.m. on a workday." The Indian isn't home. He's not at work either. And the front door says they open for business at eleven. Oh man, I know where this is heading...

So I walk around back with my resume, cover letter, a brunch menu, and three page report on some interesting fish ideas for lent. More French words for my gracious hosts, the Dubois'. Sauce Choron, Codfish Cassoulet, Roasted Monkfish with Zinfandel Buerre Blanc. And some Portuguese dishes too—for Katherine, whose mother grew up in a fishing village south of Lisbon. Ttorro. Caldrada. Seasonal produce to use at the tail end of a miserable winter. Sauces to make the fish stink disappear. No wait, the fish are fresh. There's an unpolluted river flowing on the other side of the road. Men and boys are leaning against the trees, fishing. Wonderful! Who do I think I am? Ron Bocuse? Holy God, I am a fool who will be offered the job and take it. I peek in through the dining room window. The glasses come from sets once sold at the end of supermarket aisles, with the bath towels and animal crackers—flower decals pressed when Jimmy Carter was president. I walk around the building and knock at the side door, No answer. Boxes of dairy products piled up against the wall. This guy is no chef. I know that much already. But damn am I a fool! I wedge my papers between the whipped margarine boxes. I'm late for another interview that must be declined before I get the opportunity to let anyone know who I am.

Yesterday I applied for a line cook's job at a southern barbecue and bar. I'm so easy to hire. Just confide in me that you are an ass, and I'll work like a dog for you. No way. People are too proud of their spit pit, food stains, cardboard beer signs, dirty floors, even their snotty waitress who, "don't tell no bad news to the boss" for anyone. But she'll kiss the greasy ass of a customer for a dollar ninety tip. Jesus, I can't work here. Not even if I were starving. A place like Poorboy's restaurant in Oswego is a spit in my eye. Of course I am delicate. It's obvious to me that God prefers despair. What sensitive, puppy loving, leper-caregiver would not run amok immediately after stepping into such a hole for dinner? I cannot imagine the food any better than what a sweaty tenant farmer would rub under his armpit with cornbread.

But here I am talking with the owner in my pre-interview. I am dressed as good as it gets in Oswego. My hair is cut, my neck and face shaved. I am tall, clean, and pleasant looking enough not to scare children away. I have a resume and cover letter that would get me hired at any big city American restaurant, and eyes that might land me a carrot-peeling prep position in some obscure, country restaurant in France, (but only if I begged). Truthfully, I believe I must be well-shaven and give the overall appearance of clean. A glance at the resume. Then one should say, "Cut that potato and cook it with salt." I get hired if he likes the dish. Very easy. It's a line cook's position in Oswego at a filthy pit of a place to eat, and I am being pre-interviewed in my best clothes. Here's a piece of the conversation, exactly as it transpired:

"Well, it says here in your cover letter that you're looking for a well-managed place to work. I'll tell you right now, we are not where we want to be. We are far from well-managed."

"Oh, that's fine. I'm looking to make my life more miserable."

"What would you do if you had a confrontation with a waitress?"

"I'd pee in her salad."

"Okay. You should know that I have two jobs beside this one. I work full time as a Human Resource Manager at the power plant, and I am also an adjunct professor in the Business Department at the college. This makes it impossible for me to run my business properly."

"Oh well, that's okay. I am just another human being. Is there anything else you'd like to put into my ass?"

"Yes, one more thing. I don't believe in cooks not doing their own dishes. Not to mention I can't afford dishwashers and busboys and stuff like that. Friends would come over for dinner and tell me that my food was great, and that I should open up a restaurant. I have no experience. Tell me, how would you put away 200 pounds of hot pulled pork?"

"I'd cut open my gut and hide it in there."

"Wonderful. Let me just call up my associate to set up another interview."

And that is where I am heading now, on my way back to Oswego, to decline the opportunity to be a cook at Poorboy's Barbecue. I would never go back to that humiliation even if I were starving again in this new world. But Marie just had our baby, and we can count in our heads all the money we'll have over the next three months. It's not enough. So I go back to Poorboy's for her and the children. But I just go back to tell them to piss off with a smile. That has always been Ron in Oswego. Piss off with a smile!

I get home and there's been a call from the crazy Indian. He wants me to come back for an interview. Back at the Dubois Inn again, sitting in a metal chair, waiting to meet the chef whom I already disrespect...

Why "crazy Indian"?

Jesus, he's a man isn't he? He has allowed this to happen to himself and therefore lower the expectations for all men, has he not? He of all people has a desire to serve cut pieces of cow to old Caucasian widows, all of whom can trace their roots back to the wanton slaughter of his grandfather's race? There is a genocide outside of America, where the fanatics of the world murder their own kind. And then there is American genocide, tremendously more advanced because it culls from hiding, like in a sinister future world. Does he know that? There should be a voice screaming from inside his soul. But it's as quiet as death in there as it is out here. It's his restaurant. His game. I cannot blame him yet. I sit here and play by its awful rules too. I want money. Indians want money. This Indian will be no exception. How queer though, to make his money cooking chicken cacciatore for great great grandchildren of the men most responsible for his ancestor's premature dissolution.

Here I am, sitting on a folding chair, property of The Dubois Inn, looking out at the gray afternoon through a smudged window. The river flows another shade of gray. I could be more happy at the bottom

of the river. I want it to be 1806 or 18065. We need sixteen thousand
and sixty plus years to reestablish our kingly ties. We can't go back. We
won't go forward. I am waiting for my Indian to approach the table
with a wild stare, and fling me like a stone into his kitchen. "You get
to work you son of a bitch. I'm gonna make your life a living hell!" Oh
how I wish he had the guts to try me!

But Geez, just look at this place! A thick brown carpet saturated with
twenty-five winters of wet mud on the boots. Never been cleaned. The
floors themselves were warped by river floods and snow melt. They
creak louder than any dinner music ever could. Speaking of which, this
crazy Indian has an old department store turn-table stereo with paneled speakers set up against the window. If I was two inches taller, my
head would scrape the false veneer beams on the ceiling. The table and
chairs are all set crooked over the warped floor. And the smell! God,
I can't believe this guy is open for business! It's like he unlocked the
front door for the first time in ten years, taped the hours onto the glass,
reached around the wall to turn on the lights, walked into the kitchen
and started to cook. After ten years or more of rat infestation and other
wild animals spraying their piss in an abandoned Dubois, this crazy
Indian wouldn't dream of wiping down walls, mopping a floor, fixing
the ten slow leaks staining the ceiling tiles brown. Damn! This place
is worse than the joint George Orwell wrote about in his dishwasher
book about Paris kitchens.

Suddenly, I get the old reliable urge to run away. I stand up to leave.
But oh no, here he comes! A big goofy looking Indian for sure. Long
black hair, big grin, big hands... Okay, the place is a hole. I'll work for
you. Just say something French, or Indian at least. *Wild turkey throat
wrapped in corn husk, stewed in English fat...* Perfect! I'd stay with you
until the end of time cooking a hundred of those a night. Just speak
some French! Anything. *Merde en croûte with Pee-pee Allemande.* Tell
me with your first words that your hobby is food. That after a night of
sweat and madness, after the long, drawn out illusion of tricking them
to believe thirty dollars a head was a very fine way to spend a Friday
night in Oswego, you pedal your bike over two steep hills, out to a
small farm behind dirty and damned Minetto, lean the bike against a
fat maple, walk into the barn, feel under a chicken's ass for the morning's egg, skim cream off the top of this afternoon's milking, and fall
down into a pile of hay using *Gastronomique* for your pillow. Say, "Ra-
gout" you wild fool and I'll be your slave all the way, over many, many

moons time.

"Hey-hey Ron. Howayoú?"

Oh no. An Indian from Utica. Worse. An Italian accented Indian from Utica. Please, oh Cold River Spirit... Please set me free.

"Look, I'll be up fron-wid jew. Jew gotta a great lookin' resume. Yer cover letta really catches da eye, juno whatta mean. But jew gotta prove to me how good jew is. I hired dis guy last week, said he bin cookin' in dis bizniss 22 years. Jesusmuddermary, he didn't know hodda make a club saindwich! Juno, dis paper is nice and stuff, but it doan mean crap to me. Look, we do hundred-fifty a night on da weekends. Whattya think?"

"That's great."

"No, Jesus, it ain't great! I gotta do it all by myself. My son's in da Boces culinary arts program. He comes up on Fridays to help. But dat ain't enough. Jewed be my right hand man. Jew cook, just stay on da line, so I could move-bout freely, juno?

"Have you been cooking long?"

"I bin in dis bizniss fur yearz."

"Are you an Indian?"

"Yea. Oneida."

And then to myself, already in the process of getting my lips to form their polite "piss off!" smile... "I bet your kitchen is a stinking mess! I bet you can't hold a piece of meat in your hands and love it for the life of your son. I bet you never gave him a god-damn bit of wisdom, either, Indian. Wipe your face clean you dirty fake. I'm an Indian. I am the new Indian. I am more Indian than your mother was Indian. I was born here. I will die here. And in the between time I am going to bury this waste ball of human misery in a hole, fertilize it with fillets of trout, and wait for it to grow tall so I can eat it with salt."

Yea, I'm all messed up. I am thinking French when I should be sorting out the best way to murder him and keep his body put at the bottom of the river. Oneida Indian. Phooey! He's from Bleeker Street in Utica. French cooking? Oneida cooking? Listen here, I am the new Indian. At five a.m. on a hot August morning, this fool's naked ghostly ancestor could dive screaming through my window, knock me out with an iron spoon, and drag my wobbly ass to the center of some huge cornfield. And Dammit, I don't care if I ever come out. I'll walk around and eat bugs and corn all day and night. I would live out the rest of my life in the sun and tan. I am the new Indian. This is the menu he planned?

Prime rib, Porterhouse steak, Chicken Cacciatore?

At first I felt sorry for him—an Italian Indian out of Utica, into Oswego, better off floating in the clouds, or burnt to ash to live eternity with the fire ants and worms. But when he shot off bragging about the huge bakery in the works, the beer and wine bar, the party he booked for 250 sober Easter Christians next month, and he being the only employee... No dishwasher, no prep person for lunch or dinner, the broken equipment, those pathetic tiny tongs, the toaster grill, and finally the funny talk about the modest wage I should accept until we got the ball rolling... Wow, that was all I needed to offer up my blessing to his body and soul. The same blessing I give to all eager entrepreneurs. I prayed that he will grow rich and fat in Oswego living out the rest of his life in this dilapidated food factory, lying and cheating people out of their money, infecting their hopes, and dreams.

Please Mr. Oneida Indian, please take their dirty money, your money, take all the money there is in the universe, sell ten slaughtered cows a day, cut three different ways, to be cut down even further by their false teeth, rotten intestines, and clogged arteries. You are my partner in crime. Your efforts combined with those of the other restaurateurs in Oswego, are pushing me further towards France. And France is release, restitution, freedom and paradise. I am not working for you. I will continue to cook alone these grand meals and memorable feasts for the one horse traveler, the thirsty Indian, the merchant's daughters stepping off the canal boat into the brilliant July sun. Their eyes are sparkling gray like the river water. You poor sorry Indian! I know that after a busy summer's night, Katherine Dubois won't appear in your kitchen bearing her soft loins and wet mouth. I know you're more of the living dead than Gerard's great great grandson placing an order for sole meunière in Oswego NY. Some psychotic Irish culinary grad will decorate the dish with basmati rice and raw pieces of triangular-cut zucchinis, even on the coldest night in February! No, I feel the greatest pity for you and any living Indian ghost haunting today's America. Sure I pity you, but I also hate passionately your standing before me. I was hoping for a real Indian to teach me how to cook. I wanted to see and hear the ghosts in your stories, to watch them hover above us, dangling their strings of lake fish and hearing some wise laughter to mock and befriend me. After five hundred years of suffering casual oppression from the white man, I would hope that any Indian wanting to open up a French restaurant, would at least know a thing or two about porcupine butter, raccoon con fit, venison a la birch wood fire, Bitter tart of bear gut and crabapple...

No. Nada. Nothing but Prime rib and Chicken Cacciatore. An Italian Indian from Utica, although he says Oneida. Probably employed a few years at the Casino. Now we should fear the Indian mafia. English deck of cards, German beer, and French chef. It is well-known that money bad medicine. Me want Porche and slutty white woman for wife or two. First drink white man's fire water. Get mad and fight children. Then gamble white man's money. Get rich like white man. Eat rich food. Drink fire water. Next, sell drugs and sex to Oneida farm boys. Buy Utica. Buy Rome. Buy mayor's daughters. Watch movies. Go to sleep.

Oh go skin a buck on a truck! I think it's about time the American 86's all lands held by the Indian. Take them away. He is no longer worthy. Is anyone? Tuck that wasted, spent culture safely into a museum box where it has belonged ever since Ozzie the Onondaga pedaled a bicycle for a good time. A big box crate for each tribe. Not much to toss in, I'm afraid. Three arrowheads. A sweat stained deer hide. Some smooth, brightly colored stone a little brave hid in his ass two hundred years ago out of fear that his grandfather would find it and chastise him for coveting things like the white man. The Mohawk box. Oneida box. What, five, six, ninety-six boxes in a room? Stacked one on top of the other beside more pieces of ca-ca humans leave around for a thousand years, for wanting to keep some semblance of rational continuation to steer the races toward an exploding finish line. Bunk and bull! The Indian culture is gone. Dead. Long ago vanished. Spirit remains but not to be possessed by any human who respects it with Proctor and Gamble toothpaste. Babylonians, Semites, Cretians, Vikings, Romans, Iroquois, Sioux, Navajo, and nincompooop! Holy, holy turtle earth, sister sun... Stop the preservation of death! The Indian goes to Walmart. Get the picture? The Oneida uses American money to pay for milk and cream from American cows. Anything useful an American gets in return is born from a dream of the eighteenth century. The clash of cultures, when men had real choices and living opportunities. Before New York could develop into the butt hole that crapped out Philadelphia. And what of it, if Mr. Oneida Indian chef can privately possess a trace of beauty? Well, dammit, so can I! I have English and Italian blood. But where is my Stonehenge to lean up against and wonder about the stars? What Vatican shelters me from these frequent internal storms?

What forest surrounds my home that I may get lost in it freely? What wild creatures are left for me to respect, to follow, to hunt? I was born. The Indian sitting across from me... He was born. Why is he rewarded land rights and the opportunity to believe in anything without cement sidewalks? Why are deer left alone to romp and run in his forest, until one of his brothers is hungry enough to kill it with his bare hands? I have to watch pot-bellied middle management kiss-asses waddle into the woods carrying the firepower equivalent of some African nations to bag their two or three girl deer, whichever the government tags happen to allow. The Indian is granted eternal rights to a lush green paradise in summer and a quiet empty, meditative winter stillness. He can also order strip steaks and ranch dressing from Sysco Inc. Yes, and perishable dairy products to lie in the sun rotting as I write this. Mr. Oneida is stopped at a convenient mart pumping gas into his '94 Toyota pick-up truck. No chef worth his hat would leave sour cream in the sun. No Indian in my dreams would open a French restaurant for money.

The Dubois Inn. What a joyless creature a man is.

Reading Ralph Emerson at sunrise. His words call from a remoteness of a million or more years into the past or future. Still, his books are sold regularly, even if nobody reads them. Some young poet might find a sentence that inspires him while lying down beside a running river reading a mass market Emerson paperback. But all will be forgotten the moment he gets up from the grass and walks across the parking lot to his car. Where is the old man who reads Emerson how Emerson himself would want to be read? Presently it's just me. I am alone. I am the Oswego County representative to the New York State Emerson Society. Our state's other thirty-one representatives are out shoveling their driveways.

Soon I will type in a few quotes from this morning's reading to get you on the right track. For the next one hundred pages or so, I will attempt to make clear some very similar themes. Therefore no human fake-artist will pick up my book a hundred years from now and lie to himself. No quotes lifted from my book with pride. I refuse to help prove theories, win arguments, change a mind. No high school papers about me. In fact, I will stop that horror from happening right now...

Vaginalips.

Artists must nip in the bud any future time for their name and belief getting butchered by the living cockroaches. One more time...

Snacklefuck anus. There, that should keep me off the shelf beside Tennyson and Thoreau. I would be happy to bury my books with me. I don't write timeless literature. That is for fops and fake-artists.

Oh, anyway... Quotes from Emerson:

"Society everywhere is in conspiracy against the manhood of everyone of its members."

"Whoso (whoso?) would be a man must be a nonconformist."

"The poet is least a poet when he sits crowned. The transcendental and divine has the dominion of the world on the sole condition of not having it."

That is enough. I get sick in the brain reading Emerson. Too cerebral. Why didn't he write, "The poor poet is God?" Why words so carefully strung on a line? If men truly spoke like Emerson wrote a hundred and fifty years ago, and over time their brains adhered to a natural progression of development, then certainly by today, we would have developed into limbless balls housing enormous brains. Our end would come soon no doubt, with just our big heads rolling around in an open sewer of thought. Thank God that along the way language got butchered! I trust my arms and legs. I need their attachment. The evolution of language is for the university and the university is for a regular paycheck, medical benefits, 401K, coffin insurance, and sixty-four days of vacation a year. Mr. Professor would say I am just lazy, that usage of the English language can be very beautiful. It is intellectual cowardice to judge language by one's own inadequacies. No, Mr. Professor, you are a dumb-dumb. Language is not beautiful. It is confusing. It's bad architecture. It is built like a skyscraper for field mice. Those who know its most precise perfections are grossly maladjusted human beings. You know what you know, and if you happen to learn something new, use it again when the situation demands it. I write for joy and expression. I do not give a dirty dump about language. I want to communicate.

The English language began on a cold ancient continent one morning when Fan the Visigoth met Texapple the Viking. Fan had a hen's egg and Texapple a ladle. English was born out of the grunts and yowls made while fighting to death for the prize of what the other one had. Texapple stuck Fan with a stick through the heart, and the word we know today as "egg" was born from the sound Tex made while puking up a puddle of the egg he ate.

Can you prove to me otherwise? Can you do it without using any tool besides your own body?

The age demands letters to and from wandering souls. All men must feel the same jiggers in his belly that I do. Of heart and soul each man is a wanderer. It is the universal calling, the true vocation. Language acts to cover this truth. Then it holds truth down with a pillow on the face, and truth suffocates.

We must butcher the language to save our sanity. Don't be afraid. Language has value. You are fifty and like your boat? Write about it. Sing about it. Make like the cricket and play us your summer song. You are sixty and like to read mystery novels? Fine and good. It's the same as playing tennis, but it is not literature. Not life. Today's literature must bleed from you, if only to transfuse wisdom back into your children. Return unto them the literature of what has been real to you.

Your regret. Your success. Time will warp their memory. Two painfully written pages to represent you to the following generations is enough. It will be from you. Your blood. Sons and daughters do not need your money. They need you to write a small volume and bury it in the earth. A treasure map instead of a will. I know not one man of seventy years who would suffer a boil to save the literature of his blood. At eighty, see if you can find him in the shade of a tall oak writing poems to a bird or a mole. You should look to save yourself. Yet you want to be fifty years old holding on to a job and things. Walk into the forest with your little book and a shovel. Dig two holes. One for the book containing the literature of your blood and one for your dead body that will rot to bone. Beautiful writing is a luxury of the past. The age demands that you write like me, letters to invisible men. Love songs to frigid women in a future angry world.

I think that I would write about Oswego because it houses my home, and I am lucky to have one. I am also fortunate to still have life with just minor physical deformity. The rest of this book shall become a joyful hop, skip, and a jump onto the dead body of why I don't believe even a scrap of the lie I just wrote.

I am a sensitive human being. One would think I could appreciate this life and its living to the fullest. I should be properly drugged on an all-life bender of my own cheer. I could share joy with a friend or two, or a thousand. But I haven't any friends, and joy farts of constipation. I have a wife and two children, but rarely do they believe a single word I write. I am goofy and I make them laugh and feel like I do. That is the positive on a sunny day. Unfortunately I am wise to Oswego, its all-consuming ugly, and the pretty dessert I can make of it after building up several convincing layers of solid salt cake lies.

Presently I am studying local history books to obtain a clearer understanding of our past. I want to get it right. So, I have spent the last two afternoons reviewing some scholarly works about the initial growth and inevitable decline of our fair city. One thing keeps popping up in my mind while reading over their careful words—probably more so because the birds are chirping and spring is caressing more body parts than my mind can control. What I wonder is this: Have any of these scholars ever aroused a member of the opposite sex? These authors have published dry, authoritative books. I know how difficult it is for me to write clear, grammatically correct sentences passionately, especially when I feel the need to get some angst off my chest immediately. I loathe the words that cloud my meaning and put rules and limits to my desire.

I am a bad writer. I too often wonder why I have chosen word arrangement to help make my art manifest. Perhaps genetic connection to the yankee masochist lifestyles of my forebears. I seek constipation. I need to feel the acute pain of squeezing words out onto paper, otherwise I would not be able to justify my work. Still, I know that the more serious my writing, the less joyful my manhood, my sex, and my rise and fall of personal happiness. History, local history to be sure, should excite in the mind creative ways to improve one's sex life. Most other explanations, I believe, are a type of depraved mental masturbation. One can place himself into the imaginations of dead people, what a man ate, how he ate, and the enjoyment he got out of eating. It is fun to put a life into ghosts. More fun to give them an imaginative sex drive. But man, if you just read the garbage I checked out from the library... It's as if the living, breathing men and women of yesterday were walking, talking wooden beams, thinking only about money and never moving a muscle to brush away the layers of dust collecting in their skulls. This cannot be true. And why I never respect the work of scholars. Unimaginative bores. History is only a game, folks. It should not be as sacred as the hallow dirt wherein skeletons lie. We are 21st century men. It's bad enough that we are so lonesome, frustrated and undersexed... But to bring the dead into our thoughts and forego spontaneous erections... Depraved.

For two days I've bombarded myself with the insanity of what scholars think is human history. They research only what is written, and what is written on the pages of Oswego's history is enough to make a young buck desire sleep instead of food. The philly to turn against the colt, the colt to leave the fat, dripping nipple alone... Yes, it is well known throughout the kingdom that the story of mankind depresses animals to death eventually. You may wonder why it is your dog will not read. But I know professor, that if he read a single word of your book, he'd lose the stretch in his back and the warm pops on his tongue that give him freedom of movement and the delicious desire to lick himself clean.

Even the animals are wise to the need of why history must be avoided. Man is specie-centric to the point of imbecility. The animals have been laughing at us for quite some time. We know it too, which makes this business of history an even more ironic and embarrassing affair. The university professor, eager with an idea to write about nineteenth century architecture in Oswego, wakes in the morning with a dead man's house opening its doors to her brain. The brain is a fungus smothered with an incestuous family of fat parasitic worms. It hops up the lake stone stairs marking the caller's path to the non-existent mansion. A squirrel with a nut sits on a stone where the wrought iron fence was once attached. He takes a curious look at the brain while it waits for the invisible butler to answer the knock. Too beautiful an autumn day for a brain to call. But it does anyway. It makes every attempt to ruin these beautiful days. The most obtrusively rude organ of the body, the brain. "Yes, madam?" The butler asks the brain.

"I'm here to see the master of the house."

"He's counting his matches madam. He's up to a 149,546,760 at last count."

"Matches. How odd!" Replies the brain.

"Each match is worth .01% of one penny, madam. We have an elevator and I am a dumb waiter because of the matches. The mansion is built on matches and dead Irishmen making matches for money madam. So will you please go away and take that filthy body with you?"

"Well, I've never!"

The squirrel drops his nut and runs off in terror as the brain leaps up into the body of the professor. The brain in the body gets into her car and rides off dreaming about Turkish pillows and camel leather toilet seats in a bedroom of a house that does not exist. Neither the body nor the brain see the squirrel leaping into the road in chase of a round nut rolling in the wind. "Kalump-thump." Squirrels on tree branches and sidewalks turn to witness the hit and run. They are wise to the stupid evil your lazy history causes. The brain in the woman rides off into the sunny morning. "How amazing," she wonders… "Matches made all of that." And the squirrel's last breath is wheezed in the road. There might remain a remnant of his carcass left when her book comes off the press.

For the life of a squirrel, the passing of a day, and the teeny titillation from another rude brain, the following is the professor's creative account of a once in a lifetime visit to the ghostly match kingdom:

"By 1906, the Diamond match factory hired 500 workers and manufactured 150 million matches per day (two matches for every person in the United States)."

Facts about nothing. I am stopped in the head right now. I can't think straight. I am a poor historian. Also, I am incredibly horny these past few weeks. My wife's hormones are focused on baby care. It's not her fault that I exhibit the stallion's flehmen posture anytime she gets too close to me in the same room. My lips shoot up past the gums. I show my teeth, and I might even be grunting. But she's a mare with foal, and I best be careful, else a hoof in the mouth is the only piece of her that she'll give willingly. So to divert the loins to the subject of creative history, I'll write the story of this old house.

Out of the folder of records obtained from the real estate agent, was a map of our neighborhood in 1875. All the houses on this street were blank squares. Except for ours, which had "SAL" written on it. Saloon perhaps? Yes, why not? It's 1875, Tall ships at port, and sailors on the prowl. There are working men getting rubbed the wrong way for the six thousandth time, and slutty Oswego girls, just like today, giving sex for drinks, but plenty of drinks first. I'm sitting in the kitchen/dining room of what was once, 127 years ago, behind the bar on a Friday night. Good business this Friday in summer. The sun just set itself down for the trillionth time and there's a city full of thirsty men. Ah, it's a blessed bygone era when wives are kept and abused coolies, and husbands are free to do as they please. If the worker gets caught cheating on his wife, she keeps her mouth shut through dinner, and asks for a new hat at bedtime. If the woman cheats on the man, she gets beaten to death and arrested soon afterwards. The role playing world of 1875. The men work for money and drink. The women slap the kids and bake. Oh yes, and a good chunk of the world dies off early because no one is taught how to properly wash faces and hands.

Here we are at Throop's saloon, me an da boys. Aye, it's a roody noyt dis soommer. All day long we set at they docks unludin' loomber in ure wool pantaloons. Me an Jack, we bean to Flangee's bar oulready. Aye, un ware tahnked full abrew. Dis life is a pacer, ware tinkin'. Aye, an eats a good ting to da polite bubs o society dat weave refraned froom blowin up da whole show, yaknow. Ha, lookee dare. Aze tat Mayster Condee? Aye dey reech fat baysterd. Hey Jack, lookee dare. He's taken to yer seester. He best be a watchin' out, cause Ize got me ize owner. Ah goad damnit! Sheeza laufin' with em. Ah damnit, now sheez blooshin'. Holy mudder a Mary Jack, Abbey's walkin' out da door wid dat fat ass. I'll kill em I tellya, if he even tinks a-touchin are wid his fat grasy fangers. Ah shoot up jack, ya parevert! For da lard's sake, man, sheeze yer seester."

West Fifth Street in the summer of 1875. The lawns are freshly trimmed and the street dust has finally settled. The crickets in the brush play a happy tune nobody can hear. The buzz of a million wet manure and piss drunk flies drowns out any chance for a peaceful moon rise. The night is hot. The servants leave their master's houses, wide-eyed and ready for whatever the night has in store. Some walk up to Throop's saloon. Some go home waiting for their husbands to come back from Throop's. The children from the big houses play games in the road. If a dirty Irish or Italian boy skips by, the rich kids call for the nearest butler to chase him away with a stick. The sun's gone down and the moon is up.

Compared to the shacks set up around the rest of town, these mansions are enormous palaces. The gaslights are lit. The mosquitoes are out happily spreading disease. Master Condee and Abbey, hand-in-hand, have turned the corner and are heading toward his four story palace at the end of the street. He made his fortune in textiles. He's the richest man in Oswego, but thinks himself no stuffed shirt like his millionaire neighbors. He's got a rise in his slacks for Abbey, and is starting to pant slightly while they push through the thick night air.

"Aye, mayster Condee, yashare know ow ta make a goil laugh!"

"Thank you Abbey. It's one of my secrets. Let's not tell anyone." He brushes his hand across her ass.

"Mayster Condee, please, no," protests Abbey.

"Look, you Irish whore, I'll fire your pretty ass right now if you don't let me look under that dress." He takes hold of Abbey by the shoulders, shakes her up a bit, and throws her down on the grass in front of the Lewis House.

"Please Mayster Condee, no!" He falls on top of Abbey, muffling her cries for help with one hand while climbing up her dress with the other. A voice calls out from the Lewis House.

"Hey Condee, quiet down. Jesus Casanova, give the girl a break!"

"That you Bill?"

"Yup. C'mon Condee, leave the little vixen be."

"She's Irish Bill, come have a feel."

Bill Lewis puts his finger to his lips, gets up from his porch chair and walks across the lawn to where Master Condee and Abbey are struggling.

"Well, okay Condee. She sure looks pretty good. I'll bang her if you promise to keep the screams down. I don't want Alice to hear."

The two millionaire Oswegonians begin the rape of the Irish girl Abbey. Suddenly the millionaire's heads are cracked open with wooden bats swung by two figures standing over them in the darkness.

"Well lookee dare Jack. Deez tings have anoother use now dontay?

"O Patreek ya play da game o baseball bater dan any man I seen." Jack bends over to help his crying sister get to her feet.

"Did da peegs getcha Abbey?"

"No brudder. Dat fella dare, he come close dough. I taught he was un nice man. He said he would take me out of da factree, an give me a jewb washin' his cloothes. Aye da peeg!" She kicks Master Condee's bleeding head.

"Yo jack. Let's take deez bastards away.

"Ware to Patreek?"

"Aye, down to da docks. We'll send em out ta sea nailed to da hull of da next tug. I tooed ja ya shadn't let em taker outta Throop's."

That is the most concise history of the nineteenth century in Oswego that a living man need remember. There were tall people, short people, Polish people, Irish people, stupid people, smart people, violent people, gentle people, horny people, dirty people, weak people, strong people, rich people, poor people. There were parasitic people who spent their lives enslaving people with lesser means. And there were people who let them. Nothing has changed. Besides culture. In that arena, today, rich or poor, everyone is exactly the same. Especially here in Oswego, where there is mutual respect for bad history.

Man they're all just too white for me. This city is so old. White old. Every face is so god damn pale and old. The women who stay here, the younger women with children, artificially tan to hide their white oldness. These brown-faced women with light hair, they're all so old already. And their voices! You have to be an outsider to hear the Oswego dialect. A phenomenal tongue. You would leave thinking of the depressed white planet, Oswego, and everyone almost dead with just a few more stingy breaths to breathe. Even the children are sad and their depression takes on new and interesting forms of mental derangement. They're white too. So white and dirty. Sometimes it's almost too much for me to bear—Wait. I'm jumping ahead of where I want to be right now. I'm already at the Walmart check out when I should have limited the first twenty or thirty pages to Oswego's rich and colorful history. But no, it's not going to be that easy. This old whiteness. It is all encompassing to a sensitive man. What the hell am I doing here? Cold March winds, and I'm out walking an empty downtown night with my face buried into the collar of a thick red plastic coat, made in Paraguay. Oh God, please bury me head first in the hot marshes of Paraguay! Let only my feet stick out for the sun to tan. It's a different sun in Paraguay, I know. A happy sun. A sun of the four seasons. A dangerous, exciting sun. The natural born children crawling through the tall grass are thankful for civil things like laughter and cooked suppers unexpected. They play around the white man's feet stuck out of the ground. God must have put him there. Imagine their thirty cents a day went into sewing the coat laying beside his feet. Each Paraguayan is truly happy that a day worked is another yam purchased. How proud a thing the human being should be.

This afternoon I became infected with the 24-hour bug of Oswego. It can turn a proud man against himself in a day. Make him want to butcher the art of French cuisine and open a corn dog stand and deep fry in fat for kids. Oswego children look a worser white in white. The bug in the brain. It's built every business downtown. It took over operation of *The Palladium Times* and shows itself in the photo of a hockey player on the front page of section two in every winter issue. The thirty-six hair care studios have the bug. Artificially browned women with dyed blonde hair gossip about whose husband is screwing the baby-sitter. All are either reformed or presently smoking coffins and alcoholics. Oswego's bug is inevitable and true. It's disease is widely accepted and recklessly encouraged.

I tell you that, once infected, no matter how free in thought and step he once thought he was, the proud man of this city must re-decide each new morning whether or not to step in line with the rest of the white brigade. At all times in Oswego, there is an internal battle being fought, one with effects more damaging than any petty skirmish played out by cowardly soldiers of the past. The men who played shoot me for pay at the fort across the river—they alone knew the joy of a bullet in the eye. Man the whole town in the nineteenth century stunk like dirty animal ass everywhere. If I was a young farmer spending my Saturday evenings watching my mother wipe the brown grease off her belly rolls, I too would jump at the chance to fight the British. I would wonder out loud what the taste of lead was like, fight hard, and die glad without any prior knowledge of the statue to be erected in my honor a hundred and seventy-five years after my death.

Honor me? For being a farm boy full of holes? Jesus, if the stupid fools only knew what I was really made of. Looky here... Girls my age were scarce in 1814. Dad looked the other way the day I pressed up against our cow. It felt good, and I did the same for Dad. "Ma's belly stinks, son," he would tell me, while dropping his trousers. Then crazy Willie came by the barn that night to tell us the British were cannoning the fort. "Aw Dad, lemme go an fight! Please?" And Dad kinda felt sorry for me cause when he was young he had Indians to kill and squaws to play cow with. So he said, "Sure son, you go play with crazy Willie. But cha can't take my musket." So I went to the fort and the fellas there made me Colonel cause I didn't bring a gun. They said "You'll be our fifth Colonel. Don't expect to live long. There's a cannonball with your name on it, farm boy." But I didn't care. I didn't mind dying. And so that night a cannonball knocked my head off.

But then jest the other day I was bobbing my head down from the clouds, as I do now and then, and there was some old hag who looked just like my grandmother with spectacles on making a speech by a statue. She was talking about me! Said I was an unsung hero of the War of 1812. Wow, that shore made me angry. She said it was people like me who made life sacrifices so that people like her could waste their lives away dedicating statues to illiterate cowfuckers. I got mad right then and there cause my ma always told me that to lie was sin and sin was death. So I undid my trousers and started to pee on my own parade. Shoot, I didn't die for her or anyone else. Liars and thieves I tell ya. So I pissed on her until she finally stopped talking to pose for her portrait beside my statue. And then when everybody went away I let the sun back out.

Now I smile from my home in the clouds whenever I see a drunk taking a leak on my statue. Once a guy stopped to read the inscription beneath the stone carving of my dying self. He laughed so loud that the fish stopped swimming to listen. I knew that he knew me better than any old hag without life in her blood. I knew that he alone would tell the real history of Oswego.

More white stuff. Every man and woman in this town is white, and white is bad. To be one thing always and not the other is a recipe for bad, for wrong, and for worse. I know the old lady the dead farm boy peed on. She's the self-proclaimed city historian. As white as they come. Even more white after her daughter went to bed with a black man. More than anything the daughter wished to shade her mother in between the lines of her most blatant white parts. The white of this city would blind the eyes if the tears weren't welled up to dilute the glare. Those who aren't crying are walking with back bent and head down. Actually, they seldom walk. They're driving. Always driving. Bridge Street is a constant stream of traffic on Friday at five. Nobody walks unless the weather's perfect. And then it's just a "look at me with my brown skin and blonde hair" march about town on a warm July night. No, even the city historian, always spry and quick-witted, leaves her gingerbread house driveway seated in her green station wagon at exactly 4:50 pm every single day of her life. She drives over the same bridge to the same restaurant, arriving at exactly 4:55 pm for the same drink and food, as if every day in Oswego was a purgatory of the same thing, over and over, with just enough statues and public readings to create the illusion of a personal heaven or hell.

I know this bird. She has been in my life for as long as I cooked in town. I say she has cheated the people out of their rightful heritage. Oswego is just one town of ten thousand in America rich with the history of despair. There was never any culture here to speak of. Our claim to fame is Oswego tea and the Safe Haven. Safe because there was a fence around it. Wouldn't dare give the refugees dignity. Not for free. Jew Boys fondling Catholic girls? Scandal and outrage.

Each man here is a lone activated fear bomb. To say what you want to say is suicide. To think the truth is a finger quivering over a well-oiled button. To be truthful, well—there's a press down, and a two or three second delay before—BOOM! Death and taxes here, as usual, as always, and an obituary column in the local paper to remind the living fear bombs that they better just watch it! No one is allowed an obituary longer than one or two hastily written paragraphs. Unless he or she has some local celebrity status that will sell more newspapers. Perhaps he was the mayor twenty years ago. Or maybe a famous race car driver. Or she was the self-proclaimed city historian! Yet if he worked as a fork lift operator for thirty years and kept quiet as a member of Holy Trinity Church, his obituary will mention just that, and only that. The right people weren't aware of his existence. He didn't create a stir and it's probably better this way, because nobody remembers him well enough to laugh at him.   His wife mourns in front of the grandchildren. She broke down for the neighbor too, by the sweet peas, but the neighbor already knew that her husband was an asshole. So did she. He was dead now, thank God almighty, but there were mourning formalities to follow. After two weeks of hiding indoors and finally sneaking out to get her hair washed and dyed, she met the city historian for lunch at The Ritz Diner. She ordered macaroni and cheese with toast and margarine, and said it was the best meal she ever had.

Ho! Ho! Mr. fork lift operator! You have passed on with the same notice given to a dead seagull floating in the river sludge with the wet garbage and stinky fish. You are gone. You did your part. You picked up that crate and put it over there. You sang a hymn on Sunday. But the newspaper says you accomplished nothing besides some grandchildren in Texas and Maine. Do you believe it? I don't. I know your life was an infinite universe. Even if lived miserably wrong, it was still life, and life is long. They don't care about you. You could have asked that your flesh be melted and mopped over your favorite street, and still no one would care. Not unless you were melted alive. Then indeed it's front page news!

However, this is not the case when the city historian croaks. Now that's a top story! Last night she choked to death at her favorite restaurant. She was startled when a little boy walked through the dining room wearing a baseball cap. She kept pointing and grunting, which the other diners thought quite normal, and so ignored her falling to the floor. They watched her reenactment of the Colonel's death a hundred times. "There goes Mrs. Rarebit, the ham. Up to her old tricks we see." Only the waitress knew she was choking. Hot damn was she glad to see the old bitch finally go down!

The ambulance came but the paramedics were too hungover to perform a proper Heimlich maneuver. Due to her age, and looks, mouth-to-mouth was out of the question. So the city historian took her last breath on the floor of her favorite restaurant, which used to be a strip joint, and before that, a place where soldiers had holes shot through their bodies. The reporter rushed to the scene, loaded to the gills, and could barely scribble down "choke" onto his pad of paper. He passed out on top of the city historian never getting his big break at a front page story. That's when I step in. I was the cook who charred her steak, so I feel partly responsible. I will write her obituary. I doubt my imaginative descriptions will ever get published in the Pall Times. Here's the piece anyway. Written for the *Heaven and Hell Daily News*:

"Last evening at 5:52 p.m. exactly, Mrs. Martha Rarebit choked on a piece of red meat and died. She was seventy-nine years old, but looked twice that. Mrs. Rarebit was as white as they get in Oswego. In fact, she had an obituary already written for the press. My editor looked it over, and decided that, because she was dead, we could safely say that everything she wrote down was a lie. So this reporter has written a more accurate obituary for Mrs. Rarebit. He hopes that his more entertaining story will persuade her to not squat down in the clouds one day to piss on him.

"Martha Rarebit was born under a tree next to a barn in 1922. Earlier that week her father brought home their first working toilet and told Martha's mother to birth the child outside, so to keep the new toilet accessible to her husband.

Mrs. Rarebit grew up tall and strong compared to other girls her age. When she was eleven, Martha exhibited the strength of ten men and didn't cry one tear during the winter of '33, when every animal on the farm died from the dreaded hoof and mouth disease. In fact, knowing the seriousness of the epidemic, she put down her favorite pony alone, with an ax, and later made a plaque out of its skull.

Martha was an excellent student, and in 1940 graduated top of her class from the Oswego High School. She decided to skip college and use the money her father left in his will to stage an enormous production of an original play she wrote entitled *General Montcalm's Fight with Dysentery at the Battle of Oswego*. Martha paid for the construction of the tall ship and played the leading role. The old folks still make talk about her extended diarrhea soliloquy.

The day after Pearl Harbor Martha was wed to her wealthy first cousin Reginald Rarebit. During the war, the two set up housekeeping in Oswego, where Reginald made a fortune selling headstones to the wailing mothers and widows of dead soldiers arriving in the harbor daily. Reginald patented the world renown Oswego Memorial and invested in a quarry along the shoreline on the east side. Within ten years he was fabulously rich, and built Martha a Gingerbread house made out of wood.

Reginald passed away in 1955. A year later their little girl Cookie was born.

Not much is known about Martha's private life after Reginald's death. She remained indoors for thirty years until that fateful morning in 1986, when neighbors watched Martha drag Cookie by her pony tail down the porch steps screaming, "My daughter married a negro!" That afternoon she chopped off Cookie's ring finger with a putty knife. The mayor pardoned Martha to the loud protests of Cookie and her new husband, stating that Mr. Rarebit once saved Oswego from financial ruin, and a finger was a small price to pay for the fat chance of culture coming to Oswego's working class citizens. Then he warmly thanked Martha for the museum she promised to build free of charge, and arrested Cookie's husband for being black.

That day marked an end to Martha Rarebit's isolation. She soon became the most active member of the community, proclaiming herself to be historian of the whitest city in America. Due to her many efforts over the last two decades, Oswego can now boast of its own made up stories of the past.

Since then she has been mentioned in the local newspaper exactly 2,036 times. Her photograph has appeared on the front page 406 times, twice with her hair down scaring the shit out of the children on Halloween. Along with her impressive list of appearances, she has been cursed privately 342 million times, desired hanging from a tree twice, (both times by the author), scalped, stuffed, and tacked to a wall twenty-three times, and her mouth sewed shut 623.5 times, (twelve and a half instances which this author can claim).

I know the truth of Mrs. Rarebit because I have had the actual experience of her. Once she helped me quit my job. She wanted the whipped yams as a side dish for her steak. I told the waitress no, that there was a limited amount reserved for the catfish special. The waitress called the boss and the boss called to tell me that Martha pays my salary, so I had better give her the sweet potatoes.

God dammit they were yams! So I quit and came home to tell the wife and child. Damn! I wish she could have choked on her steak and yams that night.

Once I might have joined her roly-poly band of restoration helpers, after I had made my fortune in Oswego selling pizza or beer or submarine sandwiches. I certainly would have left Mrs. Rarebit the hell alone to tell more enormous falsehoods for future historians to screw up further.

She will be sorely missed. Calling hours are at—ah hell, any stranger's house that takes money for burning her body. The funeral will be held all day next Thursday on the outskirts of Biloxi, Mississippi. On a hot day. In the church of her son-in-law's parents."

Lately at night I sleep lightly like a vagrant dozing off in an upper class suburbia. I hop up out of bed the same second the baby cries, which is several times after midnight, and jog to the bathroom for a wet cloth and diaper. I stop at the door to look out the window at the eerie scene the street light creates in the frosty air. "Oh man, you better think of something quick! What are you going to do?"

Night after night I repeat the same scene and question to myself. During the daylight hours too. In fact, not a moment passes without a glance out the dirty window of my brain to think of my current situation. I feel corked, dry and useless for at least the next twenty years. And if forgotten, to turn bitter at thirty, vinegar at forty, found at fifty, then uncorked and poured down the drain. Worse than that, I feel like a New York wine. An average grape with a false fermentation, addicted to refined sugar. Artificially sweet without any personality. Too sweet after so many years of bitter solitude. Then to go bad as a fake sweet thing? Oh my God, the claustrophobic false joy of existence!

This is my America. It's something gone bad that was never any good to begin with. Its bad is the horrifying realization of it not being real. This morning while bouncing our baby girl on my knee, I got to thinking about a trip my oldest daughter and I took to *The Enchanted Forest* when she was five years old. When I was five, my sister and I traveled there with our father and new stepmother. Even as a child I was an over-elaborater. To me *The Enchanted Forest* truly was enchanted. Even without the miniature train and plane rides, small red and orange boats going round in a pool, a wild west town complete with a saloon to buy a snow cone or your favorite ice cream, a merry-go-round, a model T car riding a winding track past the facade of a tiny village... Wow! And dotted throughout the park were fairy tale rest stops with huge figurines come to life. Cinderella, Robin Hood, Peter Pumpkin Eater. One stop had a giant Indian tiger calling a cobra out of its clay pot. Another, a six-foot long dachshund named K.C. There was even a petting zoo equipped with live sheep and goats, pigs and a horse. Yet the greatest time of all, the most awe-inspiring wonder of The Enchanted Forest to the five-year old boy Ron, holding on tight to his pink cloud of cotton candy, was the half hour sky ride over the entire park and back again. It was more than I could ever dream up on my own. To while away a chunk of the summer afternoon cruising above creation. To have all these wonderful things and then flight too at the end of the day... I was overjoyed to be at *The Enchanted Forest.* I would come back every summer if I could. Such a joyful, lasting impression it had on me.

So of course I would want my daughter to experience the same. Although at the time I was blessed with never knowing the need to provide her with happy times. She made her own dreams come true by the hour, alone, without my help. Born seconds from death, into the danger world of the volatile Balkan Peninsula, she learned very fast how to appreciate and love her time in America. Never in her life had she experienced a bored moment up to that glorious, tender age of five. Quite an achievement without the child-drugs of TV and video!

Well I saved up my precious dollars to take her to The Enchanted Forest. On that bright, windless July morning I packed her bathing suit, play sword, and books into a small bag, and drove away from Oswego intending to give her what I got almost twenty-five years before. In my rusty, white Chrysler we rode into the summer heat, past wickedly vexed Rome, NY, and the many damned farming villages saddening the view from the freshly paved road heading north. Eventually the mountain air brought a cheerful coolness as the pines became more prevalent. The mountain air reeks of enchantment, when, even if driving past the depressed and hopeless homes of America, everything can be right and wonderful in a world gone wrong. Here is where my happy youth would be revisited. I too wanted a full day devoted to creating joyful memories. And I was not disappointed, thanks to my daughter's angelic innocence and beauty.

Did that last sentence sink in? Read it again. They're not just words, folks. Moms, it's the truth your babes cried about right after sliding out of you. Yes, of course divorce is inevitable. Look at Dad! That's your husband? That American ding-dong? You know, he will make every effort to impede your child's progress towards the truth. He will cut the invisible wings truth brings with each delivery. It is true, our babes deserve all the credit for whatever flowers they can bloom after this daily malnourishment of defilement and degradation. I know her tiny hand alone has guided me through the insane, store-bought jungles of your America. And on that beautiful summer's day, she led me through it once again, with her angelic innocence and beauty.

The NEW AND IMPROVED Enchanted Forest.

Listen here, do not give the American man any significant length of time alone with beauty. Does he ever look quite comfortable with it? Don't you understand that when you look away, he is pressing beauty's face down into the dirt? Jesus, it looked like the place was bombed and cleared out to finally put an end to childhood fantasy and play. Immediately I thought of strangling to death the millionaire who thought up this monstrosity. A water park! Those enchanted, childhood memories left fallow in my mind and much improved, only to be strip-mined and cemented over so some American finger sniffing jackass of a millionaire could plant a twelve story water slide. Oh the evil greedy men! Oh the insane insanity of money! He thought that if he built it in the mountains, and made a jingle to endorse its sham of a good time across radio waves, then they would come to it to slide down it, and make his filthy money make more money. I could tear his guts out for the joy he cheats us out of!

How fortunate for Mr. Millionaire that on that glorious summer day we sought out and discovered Cinderella's magic pumpkin. The bright orange color had faded and the paint was chipping, even an ear was missing from the mouse changed back from a horse after midnight. But he is lucky we found it. So she sat in it. I sat beside her with a sword in my hand, and we posed for a picture that I will keep forever to remind me of this eternal war I have declared against greed. On the outskirts of our magical dreamland, the new water fun park bustled with whistles and screams from the violent panicked offspring of the millionaire's America. I came to his forest and found our paradise neglected. I noticed. Mr. Millionaire will thank his lucky stars today, tomorrow, and for all the moments he has left to live that she did not. On the contrary, she played happily in his wasteland, oblivious to the weeds shooting up through the cracks in the concrete. I was aware though. I felt the sting of the madness which drives the millionaire to ignore the children enough to profit by them. Maybe once upon a crime he wanted to be like Walt Disney and create an imaginative playground for the kids, and consequently, a living for himself. That insanity could be forgiven, provided it was honest and sincere. He was a child once, who believed as a man that a giant painted pumpkin could make a little girl fantasize. The six dollar admission fee would help pay his rent, and in the end be just enough to make a family and living of his dreams affordable in a glorious, enchanted forest. Right? Wrong. Very wrong. Too wrong in a world we've created with room and time to invent gasoline engines and television. Now I know his true intentions were to sell enough six dollar tickets to purchase an estate with a maid and swimming pool. As a boy, I came to the forest when it was the pride of the tiny mountain village. I came with the desire a child has for ice cream. I returned as a man and brought my daughter along with me. The horror show I witnessed is an America I shall never forgive. I will always remember. I will write of the concrete path time cracked and Mr. Millionaire left cracked to stub the delicate toes of the princess. I will write my hate letters to millionaires because she opened her eyes wide to the floating boats and the track driven model-T car. She was tall then for her age, which made her look somewhat retarded, and therefore even more beautiful seated inside of it. She straddled the six-foot long dachshund, drank from the fountain of youth, walked through the concrete petting zoo of twenty emaciated farm animals, laid out nearly dead from heat exhaustion. She did not wonder why Mr. Millionaire wouldn't pay a shepherd to tend to them. But I did. Oh I curse this economy over and over for giving the millionaires life. It is all American. I hate America's dreams of living the life of the millionaire. I hate an America that neglects its children. It is the fakers and liar's paradise. It wants and respects the millionaire's desire. It wants Walt Disney's monied empire, not a true magical kingdom for the children to get lost in.

So Dad, how can you avoid becoming a good faker and respectful liar? Simply step up into that fat and faded pumpkin to wrap a towel around your daughter's long, flowing hair. Tell her that she is a maiden. Then ask her to close her eyes and keep them closed until you return. March off with the eyes of a man who has just witnessed his family slain. Break into a run with a wild, frantic look to find their murderer counting dollar bills upstairs in an office that overlooks your paradise. Force him out the door with the threat of her plastic sword driven straight through his heart. Poke him along, over to the million dollar water slide he built with more money. Grab hold of his head stuffed fat with dreams about making money, and bash it against the steel rail. "You dirty pig. Go clean up that petting zoo. Feed the animals the best cabbages you can buy. Provide for them shady lush pastures to run on and joyful music to their ears. You have the money. You do that for me right now or I'll drown you in this sliding piss pool you call a good time. I'll do this without any fear for my own freedom. I will do this to save an eternal life of happiness for my dear princess beloved."

Then not waiting for a reply, you fetch the wet rag and diaper for your precious infant child. For the moment you forget about the men and their millionaire dreams. Close your sleepy eyes my babies. Your slumbers will be blessed. I cannot promise a safe and joyful tomorrow. If I have not yet broke ground for a paradise in my father's land, then how could I ever expect you to build one after me?

O my innocent and deserving children... All I can do is give you time to play and dream. Father is a weakling. The millionaire lives to exploit you. I am afraid your Daddy is doomed to a lifetime of many calm, methodical, and imaginative murders of the millionaire.

What am I going to do? And this isn't enough I suppose? You want me to fall back in line this morning, find a good job, and do to Saturday what every man does with a Saturday after he gets a good job. I could make a thousand Saturdays to come my own private, special world, and grow up just like that miserable neighbor of mine, Tim the snow-blower. Of course if it's snowing on Saturday, the day after I get the great job to beat all jobs; if it's snowing and I could be leaning back on the couch in celebration, I'll make sure to shovel the driveway first, just to relax and not get too excited about my excellent job. Of course it must not matter to you that I would actually jump through the roof if I sold a piece of my writing for five dollars to an interested reader. No, the great job has come into my life with benefits and all those sick and personal days accrued. That there is a difference between being sick and personal I never knew. The employer must anticipate the employee being a fat liar. The personal day was invented for the employee to call in sick and not worry about being seen at the McDonald's drive-thru.

401K, dental plan, health insurance, excellent pay with room for more? I could shovel my driveway and hope to get a great job. I could spend all day Saturday dreaming that I am as good as the next guy. But I don't want to be as good as him. Probably because I don't think he's any good. It's too careful and safe a thing to be employed with benefits. Because somewhere at the top of that ladder there's a millionaire kicking over his filth onto you. The price paid for security is high, too high to spend any night on a couch waiting patiently to view a movie made for television. Was it just a dream last Saturday, of some time long ago when I ran shirtless along the rock face and leaped off into the shimmering light dancing on the water? I don't want the past. I'd rather the holy spirit slap me on the back and my teeth fall out. 401K? Man, I repel the future as much as the past. God, how can any man think that far past tomorrow? Why would he want to? What spell has come over the men of this country for them to wonder if at seventy there will be any hair left to comb? A powerful spell it must have been to have such foolish worries when knowing that hair or no hair, there's still those flabby titties to consider? Is everyone with a good job a frightened, quivering bunny with a car payment? If I ever got a good job I'd be too embarrassed to walk out my door with my head held high. How humiliating to be given a title that the world of men can understand.

"What does he do?"

"He's a mailman."

"Wow, I hear they got great benefits at the post office."

"Yes, but he had to pee into a tiny plastic cup. He got some drips on his fingers, and walked over to the nurse with his head down. She got pee on her fingers too, when he handed it over. She blushed and giggled with embarrassment, not because of the piss (she gets that all day), but because she knew that getting a good job is a very humiliating thing to happen to an honest man.

And then there is the rectal exam to consider. Your employer needs to know about your colon. In fact, a good interviewer will decide immediately if you're the right man for the job. Any man is the right man who would allow a stranger's finger in his ass. It can only go up so far, but once that's checked out, it's three percent of yours to five percent of theirs until you hit sixty-five, and are considered by your employer to be dead and gone, no matter how many strong Saturdays you think you have left. Don't bother getting your shovel out to prove a thing! You could have cleared the whole block of snow, but if you pick up a fifty pound box of staples and a disc pops out of your backside, then it's an early retirement for you. We're sorry, but the truth is you are a highly expendable piece of furniture. Which means we don't give a bird about you, Mr. Folding Chair! Your great personality cannot pick up that box of staples, can it? So sayonara! What good are you to us without a strong back? Heck, you can always fall back on the benefits, which is a safer thing than finding a gruesome abnormality up your ass, which might have eliminated any hope for you to get hired in the first place. A bump in your colon or a broken back? Neither are very beneficial, but one is much safer in the long run, don't you think?

I like to think of my brother in law, who shovels his walkway like a pro because he has a good job and would never eat crow no matter how many times they got him to drop his drawers for pay. I like to think of him bending over the exam table talking about drill bits or the Tuesday Night Movie to a frustrated doctor, who is having the damnedest of times trying to find his anus. (My brother-in-law has a very big ass.)

Well his colon and urine got a clean bill of health. Now he is as free as he'll ever be, with a good job to boot. It is always his own special Saturday to be exactly the same as the next guy.

Here is something men these days will not talk about. I think they buy new trucks to cover for the humiliation of dropping their pants for a job. Any job that pays well with benefits.

You might think that it is a personal quirk of mine, but no amount of money or security is worth a stranger's finger in my rectum. Thank you. Now I'd like to welcome prostate cancer and poverty to my retirement dinner. And leave all empty pillboxes at the door. I don't have a penny to fill them.

Thinking on my retirement... How wonderful it will be to work for minimum wage again. I am practicing that feeling now, by considering a bookseller's job. Who am I kidding? I want it. I'll take it and keep it for as long as it remains in business. Provided the boss doesn't ask any more of me than greetings to the customers, general shelf arrangement, dusting, vacuuming, and register check out. If I decide to retire come old age, rotten teeth, and an all-night wrenching abdominal pain, I will bow to my employer, expecting nothing in return besides the good memories we shared selling books. First I'll make sure my wife and I have a little something put away. Enough for first month's rent and deposit, plus two bus tickets to the Florida beaches. Leave it all up to providence I say. I'll get a job cleaning pools or selling bait and tackle from a stool. Because I want no one collecting my stool, I have thought out my retirement through and through. I will not pay that high a price for shoveling my walk on a snowy Saturday. I don't need to dream about the golden days, which was any time before succumbing to the acquisition of a good job. I am living them right now, for as long as I can hold out against the piss-in-the-cup and finger probing mob.

Wouldn't it be lovely if everyone you knew took on a minimum wage job? Your brother and sister? Your best friend? Joy is poverty shared. I know this to be true because I have experienced it and so have you, dear reader. But you have forgotten. We were young yesterday. I write to tell you that tomorrow we can become young again. Why wait fifty years not knowing where or what will become of you. The age of beauty is just around the corner. Prepare for it now. It is easy to see the end of money. I am a living example of that future world. And I am not a lone anomaly. There are millions alive like me who desire life shed of all its warm and cozy money blankets. I cannot find many of them. I should not have to look much further. I already know enough people who are fit to play some of the many games which the creator has graciously set up for us. Life is play. Your wife, brother-in-law, best friend, your father, mother, and anyone else that you know and they know, must burn their stinking piles of pretend money. It's time to play. We have our homes, the knowledge and ability to make food and collect it with our hands. But there is a long time lasting between the first seed planted and the harvesting of crops. I get so damn sad watching the old people die off without ever coming to this realization. Well.., never expressing it anyway. I suggest a playtime for the rest of our lives. Can you show me a better way? Can you honestly say the path you're on now is the right one? Or is it just the safest way to afford your coffin and save you the embarrassment of being dead and in debt?

But I tell you the truth and the truth says the reality of tomorrow is Ron's poetry today. I like you all well enough for surface conversation. Don't you think now is the time to dig deeper and pull ourselves out of this pit money's buried us in? Moments of clarity sing of this one, all encompassing truth. That we have suffered enough already, no one would deny. The age of beauty is flowering before our very own eyes. Why do we remain blind and crouched low inside our deep holes? We don't want to know about the easiness of sharing. We think that is a sin because the President tells us communism is a sin. Stop. Put the book down and dream about the sweet and happy passing of your childhood. I like to think about the football games I starred in after school. There's my room in the evening, and those mysterious jaunts to the dangerous lands within the boundary of my parent's yard. Even then they had us practicing to be alone. To take things as they come, alone. To live alone to die alone. It was a rare occasion when I was forced to share with my little friends. But when pressed, I didn't complain. A toy truck, a train, the igloo block maker... The grown-ups paid lip service to the virtue of sharing, but never practiced it. No example. Never. Never ever. Oh, Mom might offer her friend coffee, but not the house, at least not for too long. She would share her dinner, four, maybe five times a year, but not one square inch of her land. She would share the money with the borrower's promise to pay back fast and on time. But share it all as if it wasn't hers to give? And for a lifetime? Holy mother of God no, no, NO!

Now I will show all of you how to share. Let's have just enough money to buy us some time with friends who are smart enough to want to play games. This is what everyone needs after the roof, the food, the clothing and the heat. What is all this stuff we got if not a constant reminder of what little we have? Imagine now without my help the massive, smothering amount of waste laying about you. Layer upon layer. This is not an earth of you all alone with wild animals and no place to sleep. We have many places to sleep. We have the heaps of crap we've accumulated thus far. Some of it is worth keeping for survival in the age of beauty. In our homes, among our things, each will find what he needs to live out his natural life alone. Yet who is strong enough to brave the poverty and loneliness? In the age of beauty, it's time to use each other, to exchange only those ideas which bring us closer together, to share our energy and love before we die. This is not a good will paragraph. This is the truth. Once we remained together for the purpose of survival. That was noble and necessary. A warm wisdom in a cold world. Fences went up. The work was hard. For some, getting food was the most demanding chore. Now in the world of 246,964 boxes of Fruity Pebbles waiting at this moment on grocery shelves all across America, can we stop for a day and reevaluate the meaning of our existence? Do you think it will all go to pot without the Fruity Pebble factory? I don't. In fact I think our lives much improved without it, and the million or so other useless commodities. Uh-oh, without them some of you will lose your jobs. When a grown man loses his job he might as well slash his throat, since he has been conditioned to believe all his life that the job is the man, and vice-versa. Don't laugh! You're just happy that it's not you. Oh what a pleasantly cruel and pitiless intelligence we are! Human beings capable of wisdom again? What a long shot! In fact, all other creatures in existence are the wiser. The human being is a million years old? And this is what he has to show for it? God mocks us. But I don't have to tell you that. Go to your home old man, and I'll drive over to mine. And someday we'll visit our daughters and go out on Friday night with the Miller's and the Moody's. Everyone condemned to their separate house, separate home, separate family, separate friendships, separate possessions, separate ideas, separate hopes, separate plans for a future that most certainly will come exactly how we imagined it, because we bent over willingly and allowed a stranger's finger up our butts. It is the cruelest of jokes we play upon ourselves, to be so separately the same until death sets us free.

What is any wisdom worth if it cannot provide the outline for a deliriously happy existence? What old man wants to die unfulfilled? How can we respect the old man who died without ever giving us permission to play for the rest of our lives? These are questions to ask yourself before you are an old man, young man. I don't think I am crazy to desire my street to open up its doors this Saturday morning to show the people running out into the sunlight looking to catch the start of the next game. But it is so quiet today. All I can hear is the lone, cold snow shoveling from the nice old lady next door.

I'm finally at a time in my life when I can forget what day it is. Yesterday was St. Patrick's day, but I celebrated it the day before. Corned beef and boiled potatoes. There's an imagination in that which could keep a sensitive man cheerful enough through April. But a wise man would go deeper to tell you they chose the worst piece of beef and set it to boil for hours until it fell to pieces. Throw in the pig's vegetables and cook another hour. This was the faultless cooking of the Irish. The drunk's dinner. And we know it was the frigid night air that called him to drinking. I say they saw snakes because of the DT's. Saint Patrick picked his head out of the mud, puked green, and saw the snakes coiling all around his soiled clothes. I know it. You know it. So let's stop asallabratin' this instant Mr. O'Grady and march straight home to apologize to the wife and kids.

Also yesterday, during a heavy snowfall, I saw a cardinal fly over my yard and land on a fence. These are good signs. Northern inhabitants should change their new year to begin on the first of May. Of course for such luck to happen, drastic changes must occur in the business world. Did I say drastic? I meant murder. All the business people would have to be slain. Might as well scrap the calendar altogether and let nature tell us what time to get up, and which holidays to celebrate. St. Patrick's Day? No, *Cardinal's Day*. A green shag sale at the carpet outlet? No, *our eyes pecked out of our heads*. You didn't think the cardinal was fluffing his feathers out to impress us, did you?

My oldest daughter Rachelle is waking up in Frenchland. She's in Quebec with her mother and her mother's new acquisition to the family. This is the third man mommy has taken to bed in five years. There might be more, plenty more, but only three Rachelle thought worth mentioning.

He's brought them to the Frontenac Hotel. Quite an expensive weekend for my daughter to be on. He's booked a double suite. Why I wonder? Would their making love damage her mind? Yes, if they made love in America with Long Dong Willie and Moanin' Marilyn Mascara.

But they're in French-speaking Canada, and if he loves her Mom, she should already know how much he loves her mom. The French don't screw each other like drunken cowboys mounting a mare in heat. They live in small houses with locked doors, and are very careful how they make love in front of the children.

So many strange, disturbing thoughts come to mind whenever I think about the new acquisition. I still have not met him. I know why too. He's an American flapdoodle and I haven't the legal nor strong arm power to kick him out of Rachelle's life. I don't trust him a bit, and why should I? Last month he took her to a cabin up in the Adirondack woods outside of Lake Placid. He brought his own daughter along. Rachelle said she was bratty, but I already knew that because she attends an American public school. Anyway, he drove up to our house on their return trip from the mountains, yet stayed in the mini-van while Rachelle and her mother walked up the snowy path. "What chunk of brain has melted out of his ears," I wondered to Marie, "for him to think I don't expect to be introduced?"

That night while our little family kept busy with the newborn beauty, I got a phone call from Rachelle's mother. She said the new acquisition has a crazy x-wife who got their little girl to confess that she and Rachelle watched them have sex on the floor of the cabin in the woods. The x-wife called social services to react to the situation, and make arrests if necessary. Again, so many mixed feelings I've been having. Supposedly all this happened a month ago, and since then, Rachelle has been interviewed by a county worker who came into her mother's home to ask questions that should never be asked of children. County law decrees that I was to receive a letter in the mail explaining the delicacy of the situation. But it happened that the social worker was a friend of Rachelle's mother, and held back all pertinent information. She made a visit to their house anyway, to ask Rachelle about her weekend in Lake Placid. Did she see something to disturb her? Enough to admit to a complete stranger that she watched mommy humping up and down in the sheets with the new acquisition?

Yet again, a mixed jumble of feelings. Very soon I might go off in a thousand directions. Hopefully I will stop before I end up scaring myself. Unfortunately logic always circles back to a life or death situation for me. I see everything as night or day. Probably because logically, that is all existence can be. Logic is never the law unless the latter adheres to the statutes passed by life and death, night and day. Who do we believe in, the county government or the sun's light? Or both? No, logically that is impossible. You believe in the county government but expect the sun to shine down on it, and a moon to look pretty lit up over the roof of it. Logic is life and life is the sun. Logic is death and death is the moon. We are animals born into the world of life and death. We are a tiny fraction of a living world which does not need us. Man's law goes unheeded in a dark forest until the day he inhabits it. If a tree falls on a man's head in the woods, and no other man hears his painful moan, does he make a sound? We should burn our books collecting dust on the shelves. We should finish our ill-spent lives with a bookless moon to base the new law upon.

Grown up people screw. It's just something they do when boy meets girl and girl presses his privates. The woman who came over to talk to Rachelle about her mommy's promiscuity should hang from the ceiling by her wrists and licked all over by your most obese and sweaty county worker. She should suffer sexual humiliation. Why? Because she accepts an annual salary, paid in weekly installments for the perversion of stepping into a stranger's home uninvited, to ask guilty questions of innocent children. "Did you have a good time?" "Was there a lot of snow?" "How long is the new acquisition's penis?" What a perversion! How can she drive home at the end of the day unscarred? Any attempt to cross my threshold and I swear to God she'd be whipped in front of the kids. Or I could let my dog fuck her first, then whip her. That would give the county secretary a hot little book of perversion to file!

These sick, twisted minds hiding behind the desks of governments... Are they to look after my child? Are they the society caring for her? Who are they? Listen, I am in charge. I will decide if the new acquisition has harmed her. And if he has, I will be the one to stuff his colon full of rusty car parts. They will be delicate with the children. Judge? Secretary? Representative? Do any of these porn dogs know what dangers await behind the doors the caseworkers are paid to walk up to? Are only those hired who write on their application for employment "absolutely not!" after the "Do you have any self-respect left" fill-in-the-blank question? If it was my home, only bullets would get strangers personal time with my daughter. Remember that! I might be one to waste words, but they're shot from the Gatling gun of a dangerously truthful heart.

Where was I? Oh yes, disturbing thoughts. So I still haven't met the mysterious man in the mini-van. He must want me to create these illusions I am having. Or maybe they're not illusions because he can't hold his head high knowing that I know he ejaculated near my daughter. If he knew me, he would know that I don't care, as long as he loves like I do—with dignity and devotion. At least I didn't care, until he avoided meeting me again last week. He refused to come into the kitchen while I patiently waited for Rachelle to tie her boot laces. Her mother asked him if he was afraid. He told her no, yet he sat still with his back turned to my outstretched hand. All that I needed was his hand to make my acquaintance. No. He wouldn't even turn around to look at me! Then I knew he was guilty—for something, for anything, for everything!

I cannot get angry today. I hate waking up like this, boxing ghosts. So far, and probably forever, I think the new acquisition might be a lying fake snake. He even had the nerve to send my little girl a letter. Said she's a good example for his daughter, and he's glad he got to know her, and blah, blah, blah, kiss some more ass, American flapdoodle. Mister new acquisition, you foolish fop, she is my daughter's mother, and you can wine her, dine her and goose her thirty ways to Saturday for all I care. But don't think I will sit by with hands folded and eyes closed while you earn Rachelle's affection without first receiving her father's heartfelt blessing.

And finally a word to all county workers inquiring about my sex life—You do not want to come over to my house. Trust me. The same goes for any new acquisitions henceforth and including the latest cowering fakealot.

He is probably very nice. A fun guy to stand around the fire and drink beer with in a manless world. But I guess I'll never know because we are a no-community of broken-backed men and cowardly security-grubbing women, weighing new acquisitions for what they are worth to ourselves and never for what joy or harm they may cause the children.

Oh well, so goes my life in Oswego. Never a dull moment, until one happens, and then someone else is always to blame.

Night is falling on this side of the earth. It's impossible for me to become cosmopolite. I am an Oswego man and I am not to make a stir when a drunk college kid pisses on my lawn. I can certainly see myself cracking his skull open for pissing on my lawn, but it's just not wise to be so rash. We're even told to allow them pissing rights on our lawns and their yelling, "motherfucker" while our daughters sleep six feet above their steamy, stream of eighty proof white water. I may never live in Paris or even Montreal. Oswego will probably be my big city for always, I am afraid. But it's better this way since the men here are incurably stupid, and it's easy for me to aspire to an illusion greater than theirs. I pretend that this is a beautiful place to live. That I never knew a lake to be so blue one August morning was a good start. I saw a stillness there during my last summer at college, and thought, "Well, hmm, this could be a happy place to live." And the college library being so close to the lake... I could make a most charming paradise of this! What else does a poet need but room for thought, some good books, and a shallow shoreline to wade in? But the lake gets cold in the wintertime, the men get mean, the women produce a deep, prolonged sadness with weight gain, and if it wasn't for the old brick buildings to save my sanity on countless imaginative walks downtown, I am sure that by now I would have committed murder.

That's not entirely true. I had a daughter to care for in the early years. And I moved out to Red Creek twice on a whim. But in Oswego, alone in my youth, especially in thought, I had the strength then to imagine my city to be the greatest place on earth for an artist to take up house-keeping. A small city of artists just like me. It didn't matter how cold the gray sky, I would walk beneath it dreaming of some fantastic world. I had imagination. I had hope! I had time! I had beauty waiting around every corner. I walked with my head held high. And I had a best friend to keep me company.

His name?

Mr. Glorious Life of Poverty!

Great friend, but such a poor contributor.

I think that anyone pursuing a dream should move to Oswego. Here is a fine testing ground for a dream's fat chances. Only the strongest immunity to old men and their mind disease can keep steady to a dream after the onslaught of an Oswego winter. The cold is bitter and almost forever to a dream, but it's never the cold which finally kills it.

What then? There are colder places to pursue a dream. Regions left on earth that get frigid below zero in February, yet still welcome men bringing hope and idea and action. I believe, but I don't know where in the world, do you? Alaska? The North Pole? Houston, Texas?

Houston comes to mind because I have been dreaming about it all day long. My daughter says it is the fourth largest city in America. I imagine it flat with oil drills downtown. A city without nature in the way. The new city. The American city. Houston has the envy of every township in Texas hoping to become a Houston some day. And being such a huge hungry city, eating and belching millions of wayward souls, all of them thinking alike, dreaming alike, and not a single one of them arriving on foot or by mule, the chances are slim that at the tail end of one of its many brightly lit fast food strips, there awaits even a trailer's kitchen full of artists for Houston to devour. Maybe on the outskirts, on a treeless plain with pools of dust and rolling tumbleweed, where tornadoes still rip by after the storm, maybe there might live and breathe a teensy-tiny community of dreamy artsy folk. But I doubt it. Why? Because a true community of artists must create without means supplied via the millionaire's pocket. That means no government jobs. No part-time secretaries to the oil mogul. No art-inclined landscapers to discover new, decorative ways to make the rich man's lawn look even richer. Artists who earn a paycheck by other means besides art? "We have to eat!" they exclaim. Fine I say, fine and good. But eat and eat alone. Eat for fuel. Eat for fecundating. Eat for creation's sake. No chewing while you eat. Swallow fast and hard. No matter how belittling work was today, it had better be rice or corn in some form at sunset. Then a walk to chase the sun down and start the blood flowing again in Houston. The rich are rich because the poor want to be rich too. What is the middle class but a sour clump of feeble-minded wanna-be rich people? What are the poor and degenerate classes but the temporary disguise of filthy rich people with extremely bad tastes? Would any of these fakers pass up the chance to be a millionaire? Absolutely not. Everyone is eating. Sleep is inevitable. Creation remains on schedule. What pray tell is the problem with Houston?

It lives! Stop! Man stop! Don't let it get any bigger. Don't let Houston grow another hand to slap you in the face with nigger! You're down on your luck because of Houston. Houston is the cruel, faceless, unanimous vote against you. It passed a thousand new laws today. One would put you in jail for stealing food. Houston is not a sheep farm in the country. Laws. What laws? Laws to help build a huge house for him and a plastic poor box for you. This is not Hammurabi. If Mesopotamia had Houston, archaeologists would uncover petrified shoe boxes stuffed with porn, plastic wrap and mummified cheeseburgers smelling like Houston. Houston is not the artist's hope. It is his Antichrist, his judgment day, his netherworld, his hell on wheels. Every man for himself? Okay. I'm ready. Are you? I want that loaf of bread and I will set your house on fire for it. Houston is the monster of death. Houston is death brought back to life in order to create more death.

Houston eats her degenerate poor, then shits out streams of laughing coins. Reflected from the monster's eye is a picture of your loving mother. Mommy would never hurt you. She smiles asking you to come closer so she can see. You move closer. Then she kicks the sap out of your brain with steel-toed boots. Houston laughs the collected roar of a thousand whistling twisters mopping up your blood. It is not a war I call between the haves and have-nots. There are no have-nots. Everybody has and gots too much already. I hate the rich, but I despise the poor, and I could strangle all the fakers in the middle. The poor aren't great. The poor are not noble. The poor have not been noble in over six thousand years. The noble poor in Houston? Grandma buying her own coffin and plot, rotting peacefully underground until Mr. Bush drives an oil drill through her skull. There's a noble pride for you, Houston. An example of a sturdy citizenry. The poor are not beautiful. There is no poor beyond the naked and the hungry. Artists want to create something beautiful, while naked and hungry. Copy the artist's life. Especially if you are poor.

It is the people of Houston who make the ugly of Houston real for me. They have allowed Houston to happen. And Houston rewards their reticent acceptance of brain smashing-ins with splendid arrangements of trees and flowers in magnificent, irrigated parks, quiet air-conditioned buses with friendly bus drivers, new museums stocking the latest dead crap uncovered in France, a thousand "howdy, friends!" heard a day from the shoddiest looking bunch of human beings ever gathered together in one fat, greasy, malignant macrocosm—the best frame, plastic siding and asphalt roof offered in twenty-first century quick-build architecture, and extremely favorable conditions for the ordinary citizen to become a millionaire, provided he keeps wanting and hoping, always thinking new cars, and playing the lottery. The pretty landscaped drives are slick and friendly. It's a lovely warm day in Houston. Soon dark clouds will billow on the horizon, when the oil gush will paint a lighter shade onto a blacker sky. Do not fret, good citizens of Houston! Turn the radio dial to "Weather-talk" and listen for instructions. Click on the TV and wait. Don't bother to watch hail balls the size of human heads bouncing off the freshly paved blacktop. Just close your eyes rich or poor man, cause here comes Houston, gonna bust open your skull and rain on the sap of what's left of your brains.

Just warming up folks. A silly introduction to Houston. What I set out to do this morning was to relate another depressing, American love story. Houston could be a perfect backdrop in the following short take on woe. But since I've never been there, I better keep to what I know. Jane and Dick moved out to Houston last year. Oswego got to them too, but in a different way entirely. This story begins with a rare and beautiful love song sung by two little lambs of Oswego. It ends on a note of bitter dissonance, to the sound of sheep being slaughtered with chain saws. Their carcasses hung in the sardonic cold room of Jane and Dick's manipulative mind-thoughts.

Everything human is interrelated. The wheel is human. Whatever I write or think is only true in the sense that it is human. Animals don't give a fucktadoo about us. All trees want us dead. I don't like people as much as I do crows and dogs. So when I write a book about Oswego, but go off on a tangent dreaming about Houston, I do so because I can't free myself from the human wheel, the interconnectedness of all things human. I would want the people of Houston to know that I am on to them too. Oswego is my home. Houston is a hundred Oswegos without snow. How do I know this? Well, Jane and Dick of Oswego relocated to Houston because the money was good. The money is always good outside of Oswego. People should be happy enough to want to make money. So who could blame Jane and Dick for moving closer to money? For watching money like a hawk? For stalking sexy money? For sneaking up and pouncing on gorgeous, sexy money? Life is too short to not want a lot of money. I think Jane and Dick deserve a slap on the back for finally breaking out. Some applause for them please. Then straight to a drunken party of booze in a plastic cup. I don't think these folks ever received a proper send-off out of Oswego.

Me? Oh, I would be delighted. To begin then…

Jane and Dick are Amy's parents. Jane is her mother and Dick is her stepfather. Amy has a father. He married a bird, and is living on a hill where there is always money and a good job.

Amy was my third love. I was her twenty-third. I had a kid (Oswego terminology). I lived in a cellar. I settled down in it after two long months of living in the open air. I got retarded. I got happy. I saw some things the animals see in late September and October. You wouldn't know until you're homeless in the wild North. The trees are very careful about who they show themselves too. One must be either blindly ecstatic or an ignoramous. Either way, it takes a lot of trial and error to get yourself mentally prepared for the tree's respect.

I got a basement apartment and a dishwasher's job all in the same week. Lucky me. I had to call a friend to borrow money to use as a deposit for the apartment. I was so perfectly poor, wide open, impressionable... Practically overnight I fell in love with the bus girl, Amy, leaving her dirty plates, forks and knives for me to clear and clean. She was pretty and parrot-mouthed, with teeth awfully stained and crooked. But she was twenty and I loved her young, ugly beauty. I was the first poet to ever fall in love with her.

Jane and Dick liked Amy enough. She lived with them while attending college. She never went to class. She got dressed to go, waved goodbye, and at times even waited for the city bus outside Jane and Dick's bedroom window, to create the illusion of her going. She would get on and then get off over the top of the next hill. She never went to school. She came to my door instead. She failed on purpose.

There she is now, standing in the doorway of the November dawn. The wet air blows. Wet leaves stuck to the soles of her penny loafers. She's dressed up like a catholic school girl. Plaid vest with black skirt and tights. Ah, but she's beautiful this morning, and I've had my coffee. I touch every part of her body from door to golden bed, where we will make love and talk and sleep all day. There's not a window in the basement. I prefer it dark with the smells of coffee, mildew and sex. At three o'clock I get up to brush my teeth. I leave her there while I walk to the restaurant under gray, still, November skies. I am singing songs.

Jane and Dick take a cheerful liking to me straight off. How could they not? My eyes are wide open. I have a beautiful daughter. I love Amy. What more could they want for their loopy kid? Of course I don't think she's crazy. I think her heart is overflowing. I have seen her eyes well up with tears. I walked her home in the dark just before dawn, and she remarked about the black boughs and spider web branches of the young trees shining so wet in the lamplight. Sometimes the light is on in her little sister's room. She's up early getting ready for school. I let go of Amy at her door and walk back the way we came, wearing a wool overcoat and fishing hat. Now I am a man who knows ecstasy.

A short introduction to Jane and Dick: Jane worked for the power company. Dick worked as a button pusher at an automated garbage burning plant. Jane worked in Syracuse and drove a new car. Dick worked the swing shift in Fulton and had a sweet black pick up truck to ride. Jane left her husband to fuck Dick. Dick looked like Tom Selleck and Jane was going out at night with her girlfriends looking for Dick. She wanted more than anything his mustache tickling her lips so she could say she lived once before she died. She wanted Dick bad because all that her husband gave her were children and a garage littered with tools and PVC. He bowled with the fellas every Saturday night and drank himself a belly full of beer. Back then Jane was a hot teller and Dick liked music and dancing. He was single, over ten years younger than Jane. Dick had a sports car and respectable savings to begin their new life together.

So Jane left her husband to marry Dick. Dick always thought how lucky—now there was Jane and three little blonde girls to raise. Dick liked to think touchy feely, and over the years, got smart on how to make it look like an accident. Oops, up the stairs he lost his balance. Or when he couldn't reach those cobwebs in the high corners, and it was hot some summers so the girls dressed light... Oh Dick was a man and wanting enough to marry Jane, even if it was true that her tubes were tied. So he took on the responsibility for teenage girls not of his own blood. Dick was young but he wasn't dumb. He loved the children very carefully, from a safe distance, especially while Amy's Dad still had input.

Amy was the middle sister, and probably the most upset by divorce. She never found her cozy spot within the bosom of either family. Once she even dyed her hair blue and green. She was unknown in high school. Her older sister Lisa was the popular one. She was much prettier with straight teeth and an empty head, so typically forgiven of an American high school girl. The youngest was Melinda who would have Lisa's beauty if she didn't have Jimmy Durante's nose. She was young and impressionable and did not want to grow up to be like Amy. All three sisters liked Dick, but it was Amy who liked Dick a little bit too much. At the time, (simply because that time was so desperate to me), I never allowed such a disturbing thought to enter my mind.

One would think Amy might get closer to her Dad. This was not to be. Daddy forgot about his girls after he married a woman who looked just like a bird. In fact he called Amy a "freak for a daughter" when she showed him her new hair color, blushing and smiling her crooked teeth smile. "I have a freak for a daughter!" I don't think that the Oswego man is ever quite sure what his dick is really for. He creates a human life, and thank God it's a girl! But then he consumes the limited space in his brain with fattening dreams of advancement at the power plant. Why should he remain a lowly meter reader when he could change jobs in the company, aspiring to one with a better pension plan and a roof above him on rainy days? He bowled on Saturday nights and the boys slapped his fat belly and joked out loud, "You better watch it Johnny, you're getting fatter and Jane's looking elsewhere."

So Johnny reserved any real feeling he had for his girls to crying after the shrimp plate was passed on Christmas Eve. He broke down in front of me and the shrimp. We're standing in his living room, talking about football, and then suddenly he begins to bawl, gathering the girls up in his arms. "It's okay Dad." "Oh Daddy don't cry." "Why are you crying Daddy?"

Oh I know why your dad cries real tears girls. I know because I am a Dad. I just won't ever call my daughter a freak, that's all. I won't ever be guilty for building a big house expressly on demand from my birdlike wife. I won't buy a big truck while my daughter's living with a dishwasher in an apartment they can barely afford. I will never bowl if I can be with her. I won't allow a raise in my pay to buy another tropical vacation without her. I will keep my wife enthusiastic and happy and never choosing booze or a Dick over my strong arms and gentle heart.

Here I am girls, half your father's age, with the smarts to know what a dick is for. I'm a dishwasher with a daughter and a desire to watch football tonight before Santa Claus comes. I would be home with her now if her mom wasn't just like Jane, and in the beginning knew the real value of the egg she had fertilized.

I never got to know Johnny well beyond an occasional beep from his shiny green truck. Once he stopped by to visit while Amy was baking popovers. He wanted to give her the name of a man he thought to be a good catch. Another time he came over with the bird lady while Amy was painting and I was cleaning up my poems with a typewriter and new paper. Amy loved me then. A small temporary paradise discovered by his daughter, but poor butter-gut Johnny didn't know where the hell he was!

It's true, Amy had shitty parents. I loved her anyway. We moved to New York after she failed out of school. How embarrassing to Jane and Dick! At the time, they thanked me for taking Amy off their hands. Dick even drove us to the bus station and shook my hand as we boarded. But I was a fast failure in New York, and we returned to Oswego before a month went by, abandoning apartment and deposit because I couldn't stand life away from Rachelle. Simply put: Never again would I attempt to build a new home without her.

Amy went to Jane and Dick. I went back on the lam in Oswego.

Unemployed. Penniless. Homeless. March. Still cold. Still too cold to wake up under a tree, but I did. Jane and Dick thought I was living at a friend's house. I was not. I was freezing close to death. At dinnertime I'd sneak around the back of their house, and Amy would hand me a bag of food out the door. I'd steal a kiss and be off. That was good. In fact after failure and reduced to my begging for food, we still had hope for each other. By April I was back to work at the restaurant scrubbing dishes and trying to save up enough money for a deposit. Another basement perhaps? Why not when you're miserable cold and in love in Oswego?

Then one rainy night after another rainy and miserable day, I called up Amy from a pay phone in the park. Melinda answered.

"Is Amy there?"

"Yea, hold on. Amy!" she yelled, "The welfare case is on the phone!"

When Amy picked up, I heard them laughing. Dick and Jane and fourteen-year-old Melinda. They were laughing at the welfare case. I loved Amy and they were laughing at the man who loved her. Ah, "the bitter dance of loneliness"—I didn't realize it at the time, but the moment I hung up the phone, my life took a turn for the better. I discovered hate. Real hatred. And I rather liked the feelings hate stirred up inside. Hate was exhilarating. Hate was sublime. What was this fine line nonsense I heard so much about? Standing in the rain, wallowing in misery, poverty, love, I realized then that hate was something I had never experienced. Once I liked Jane and Dick. But I never loved them. And if love and hate were opposite sides of a fine line, once I must have loved them for as much as I hated them at that moment. No. Impossible. I realized that hate was a separate universe to love. It was not love's opposite as most believe. Oh no. There was hate and I had it. I was free to hate. Love and hate could no longer be expressed together in the same mood, in differing degrees of hot and cold. There was never any fine line at all. Now I knew beyond a doubt there was love and there was the absence of love. I felt hate and it had no intercourse with love whatsoever. If love was the supreme virtue, hate was never its vice. Hate would have its own place. It's own virtue. It's own life.

On that miserable cold and bitter night, I discovered the healing powers of hate. Because of the humiliation I felt, wrought by Jane and Dick and big schnoz Melinda, all snug in their cozy pajamas, laughing at my predicament... Because of the rainy night realization that love didn't matter a lick to these monsters, after the hanging up of the phone, the standing in the rain, the shock of tears pouring from my eyes, the idiot crying out, "Why would they want to hurt me?", I vowed to return their cruel carelessness with a hate so great it might kill them. I was going to love their daughter to make them sick enough to die. I would show how easy it was to hate and love at the same time. Oh there's your fine line Jane and Dick! The welfare case is going to love her all over. Are you ready? I may love every orifice of her, Jane and Dick, night after night, and you'll have no control. One day I will marry her and have children and raise them to love and hate exactly like their Dad. I'll pull each kid out personally, with fiendish glee, impatient to teach the newborns how to despise the smiling faces of their grandparents, Jane and Dick.

And for a while it worked. I most certainly drove them to distraction. They shook at the sound of my name. I admit that I helped fuel their hatred whenever possible. If Amy and I were out walking, and I spied Dick's truck coming our way, I'd pull Amy up close, take hold of her arms and kiss her. Then I'd turn my eyes upon Dick's hateful glare as he passed by. Oh that must have made Dick's prick shrink up inside. There was a time of desperation when Jane made an attempt at reconciliation. She wrote a note at Christmas, "Dear Ron, please let bygones be bygones. Love Jane" I wrote back a note telling her that was impossible, my hate is non-forgiving. Once, and this was when I knew for sure that I was hating them good and proper, she was so nonplussed that she actually called up my mother in Florida, and threatened to send Dick over to kick my ass if I refused to quit Amy. That is how crazy Jane was. I was a full grown man, long gone from the nest, with a child of my own, and this frazzled woman was calling up my mommy in sunny Florida. She never even met her. She was trying to persuade her woman's finer sensibilities. "Your son is angering my husband who is a six-foot-two, 210 pound Irishman with a bad temper." My mother called immediately, "Oh my God, honey, that woman is crazy. Watch out for her dear."

All in all in the end, Jane and Dick got the best of me. Or maybe I received hate's blessing, and was spared an eternity of loving Amy. Hate didn't want it's "A" student playing the fool again and again. Amy made a pass at my best friend while I was visiting Tony in New York. I said I would stay with her anyway. We could work it out. I think that I even blamed myself because I truly did love her. That's not what she wanted to hear. All night she packed her things. The next morning I awoke to Dick standing in our kitchen with a face on that warned me not to voice a single word of protest. I remember Amy trying to squeeze by me with my black teapot and cups. I grabbed the box out of her arms and ran downstairs out to the backyard. That was our last day in the love nest together.

Afterwards I kept to my daily routine as if nothing had happened. I cooked the meals, cleaned the house, played with my daughter, and on breaks, took my favorite book with me into the tub. Amy? She went on a fucking spree soon afterwards. Her spring time of life became a beer drunk and a sex binge. Never in my wildest dreams did I think she would go that road. Never a pretty sight in Oswego, no matter how popular. Still, I had to see Amy almost every night at the restaurant. I was promoted to a cook's position, and she to a waitress. It was the absence of love that kept me at such a safe distance. Once, soon after our break-up I did feel a sting of hate for her. It was in a bar, where she sat on a stool, snuggled up close to her man for the night. Fully inebriated, I bounced over to their stools to tell them that after sex, she would poop and pee with the door open. I looked into her eyes and saw such a rage flare up, I knew right then she didn't know what I knew—that love and hate could never stand together along the same line. Over the years we worked together, me in a state of the absence of love. She in a fire of hate she once thought was love. Cooks, managers, dishwashers came and went, and she scrumped enough of them under my nose, to be sure. Outside of my hours of cooking I lived quiet and slow like the snail. Poor Amy banged a big gong every night of her life, thereafter.

A particular agonizing memory stands out from the years we were together. One spring morning her father came over to visit with Amy. He'd stop by whenever the guilt got too loud inside. I wasn't there at the time, but Amy confided to me the gist of their conversation later that evening when I got home from work.

Amy wanted a Dad, but Dad wanted his daughter to be more like her Mom. What a masochistic spank-me-hard that Johnny! Over coffee he made his intentions quite clear. He told Amy she was too young to be living the married life. That she should go out and experience more. She wasn't ready for one man. Dating was a wiser choice than being shacked up with a line cook. Take on more pricks, dear. The more the merrier. Make a name for yourself in this small town Oswego. Be a slut or be nothing much of a woman. Life is too short, but the pricks are many. Don't forget that! Keep a ruler by your bedside to measure their lengths. Compare one man to another by the size of his pee-pee. Your mother did. I still love her. You look just like Jane when she told me about Dick's prick. Said it wasn't much bigger than my own, but he looked more like Tom Selleck, and I was growing a bowling ball and boobies, and that made all the difference in the world to her. I'm telling you this, believe it or not, because I think Ron's too good of a guy for you. When I see the two of you together, I sense the spirit of your mother smirking from your eyes. Ron should go bowling and have someone who is happy enough to live the quiet life with love and children.

Long after our break-up I had the naive belief that she was always true to me while we lived together, (except of course for the one attempted digression with my best friend). Over several year's time while going to the bar for my beer after work, I saw no less than twenty different men seated beside her. All looking the same, possessed of a like composure in assurance of the lay at the end of the drunk. What did it matter? I had absence of love for her. She took her father's advice. I understood. It was something she had to do. Then just last year a dishwasher got hired. He told us after the first night that he almost quit when he saw Amy walking by.

"Why?" asked the sous chef.

"Man I was dating her little sister when we were in junior high. I stayed over one night when her parents were out of town and she fucked me in her own sister's bed."

"Jesus, where was her sister?"

"In the shower, man."

"How long ago exactly?" I asked.

"Easter night. I know 'cause that's the day when my Old Man kicked me out for good."

"Easter night when?" I asked.

"I don't know," he said, "92, '93?"

"Please remember. It's important to me. A fish sandwich for you if you can remember."

"All right man. 1992. I know for sure. I was fifteen. That's the year, I'm sure. Boy was that girl nuts!"

That was the spring she fed me out the back door of her mother's house.

Amy never loved me. We met, made love, had good times, began to have bad times, accompanied by the absence of love, and then she learned to hate my face for getting in the way of her every fuck. Jesus, but I loved that crazy nut! After all it didn't matter. I was so much like her Dad. Just another masochistic spank-me-hard.

She's moved out of Oswego. Went to Houston to live near Dick and Jane. She's going to be a teacher. Oh I say, there are some mighty lucky teen-age boys in Houston! A mother and daughter team, a line up of tenth-graders looking just like Brad Pitt, and a 260 pound aging Irishman to bite his lip and watch. Oh I will hate Jane and Dick for as long as there is a Houston. But they're getting older to someday die unhappy like Johnny and the Bird, the drunken band of twenty-plus Oswego men, and dear parrot-mouthed Amy, who dared to fuck them all in the presence of my absence of love. Everything here is just a run away to find more money and flabby sad sex.

So now when I think of Houston, I know it's the right place for any-one who has never hated very well. It's for the masses of people who close their eyes to love and art and the paradise these wiser roads lead them to.

Impatient to get off and get rich are ya? To Houston then. To Houston everyone! It's the fourth largest city in America. Whosoever is searching for a new life should come to Houston. A new wife, a new job, a new cheat, a newness beginning and already complete. A ready-made life awaits you in Houston along with a friendly government to help you get rich. Everyone is screwing someone else's sweetheart in the sun. Houston is clean. Houston is a smart, new shiny thing. Houston is the fourth largest city of proof that the human heart is burned out. Every-one to Houston then for the finished life of more money and security, more Burger Kings, and an endless array of choice in hair care prod-ucts. Houston has everything in store for the stupid and getting more stupid. The most stupid never get to Houston. They live in Oswego restlessly searching for their Jane or their Dick. Some find an Amy to help piss and screw away another drunken Friday night. Some already had their Amys and are happy with a bird. All the people in Oswego, though, are interconnected with the lives of Jane, Dick, Johnny and Amy. All desire the help of Houston to protect the lies that keep them here growing old with money.

Crazy life I'm expected to participate in, here in Oswego, America. I can walk from my house on West Seventh Street, two and a half blocks to Byrne dairy to pick up heavy cream for our dessert, and a thousand mad images will pass through my mind to stifle any hopes of my ever becoming a valued citizen. The price to pay for being human in America today is too great, in the sense that Rockefeller was great, Carnegie was great, anyone was great who worked his fingers to the bone or got lucky in America. I tell you that everything here is money.

Everything! You know it too. Love is money. Once upon a time it was a trip to town by horse and cart for the overworked couple of the prairie. Those poor folks had no energy to love after three years of back breaking labor. Then Jake bought her tickets to a traveling Shakespeare play. She told him that she needed more than anything to imagine what love was like for the rich young daughters and sons of old Genoa and Venice. Her longing was for the romantic age of kings and queens.

Actually anything not of the prairie was desirable to her. Foreign love helped her forget the cruel prairie and the rough, dirty hands of stone-cold-sober Jake. Oh forget about Jake! From Jake onward, past a couple World Wars, all the boys ever dream about is money after getting laid. She needed the love of another's poetry to dream about while starving to death through another harsh prairie winter. Never a love of their own to cherish and protect, Jake and she. Never a prairie love. It was practical to work towards love.

Towards what?

What did I say?

You said love.

Oh. I meant money. More money of course.

Now love has everything under the sun. Opportunity for the glory of love has been widely available now for over a hundred years. It is a free fertile half acre plot on a wide open prairie with a thousand slaves, lush tall grasses and beautiful grazing beasts for your burden and your innocence to make more beautiful. Love is as obvious as toilet paper, but even that last privacy has become money. Tonight, along with the cream, I bought two rolls for the price of one. If I'm going to go broke with the desire for rich desserts, then I had better look for bargains to wipe out my ass with.

Face it America, we are rich and dirty. It's the truth, and most of the sorry hard bastards here love a good old-fashioned harsh reality. As far as I am concerned, which can never be too far for a lazy lovestruck man, everyone here is incurably insane. There is no wisdom. Not even a minor mental health. Love it or leave it? I would you stupid worm, but I like to hope I am wise enough to change things. Not for you. I am well aware of your psychotic mentality, and would not waste a minute more trying to change you. I have lived maybe half my life walking to the store the way I was expected to walk. Over the years I've made just enough money to rub shoulders with my neighbor, without pushing him too far to turn against me. But that is a fearful way to love, and I am so tired of being afraid of money. Now is the time to clean up this mess. I need to clear out the brain. I don't even know whose brain it is I occupy, but damn if I believe it to be my very own! I have got to break out to save my life. Where? And with what means?

Love has been expected from me since the beginning. Evolution is over and love must reign supreme. One must squeeze a thing almost dead to rid it of all impurities. One must walk outside his door, take in several deep cleansing breaths, and always be prepared to run amok.

Join me boys, on a short walk to get my things. Just a few necessaries and cream. We don't need much. But I do need cream if I plan to spend the rest of my breaths on earth breathing in the sweet air I was born to breathe.

My storm door is your door. Three factories make all the storm doors sold today. Open our same storm doors then, and step out into the sun. I am going to make it a summer sun to keep this ranting as cheerful as possible. We need cream for our desserts. What are you going to do with your cream?

I am making a custard. Wait, lemme run back inside to check for eggs.

I need eggs.

So my friends, what do you think of this day? Pretty nice, eh? Yea, there'll be plenty more, but I want to enjoy them now, while I'm straoght and tall.

What do you need Jimmy? What about you Burt? Frank? Teddy? Eggs too huh? And all of your wives have the mayonnaise out waiting to make egg salad? Hmm. Interesting. My wife doesn't do much of the cooking. Once it was my trade, now I keep to it regularly for joy.

What's that you say Ted? Oh, Joy? Yes it does rhyme with toy. And no, I don't cook on a jet ski. No Teddy, joy is something out of the Bible when you run out of toilet paper and wipe your ass with the story of Job.

Job? No Frank, no job yet. Geez, I don't know if I'll ever get one. Mr. Biley at the bookstore hasn't been all too clear with me, and it's already June. But I was talking about God's Job.

You don't say Burt? Your cousin's the priest? And he makes how much? Three hundred grand a year? Oh well, at least he gives back to the poor, provided the poor aren't Jewish and the check clears at the dry cleaners. That's okay, I heard the President wants congress to allocate more money to America's houses of worship. Do you know why he does that Frank? No?

He has a personal mechanic, cleared by the FBI, to check the transmission fluid in his SUV limo. Can't have the President stalling on parade. He has a general too, and after a Sunday morning pretending to love God, he tells the general to send a plane over to Baghdad to shoot the limbs off little Muslim girls. Jesus, it's his job, isn't it? So it cannot be helped.

Yes Frank, Job had a hell of a time of it. Lost everything. His wife and children, his sheep, goats, ox, pet rabbit, most of his slaves (some were dumb enough to wait around for the wrath of God).

What Jimmy? Her? Yea she's got a nice bod, I guess. That's what a winter of tanning and a spring time of bulimia will do to a girl's figure. I'll get the door gentlemen. Jimmy, Burt, Frank, Teddy, each man to his eggs then...

Hey Burt, check out the deal on toilet paper. 2 for 1. Is five dollars enough? Just enough, right? Good.

Eggs, cream and toilet paper. A wise man could live on these staples and some wild herbs of summer. Dandelion greens, burdock, wild horseradish. Strawberries. Apples and pears in the fall. That's the truth boys, and I agree it's a scary thing to think about. Let's go home and tell the wives about it, huh? We'll pool our monies together and buy some land out in Sterling. Wow, just imagine! A morning hunt once a month because we miss the taste of meat. We'll join together with bows and arrows and skill. Our wives will learn how to make their own mayonnaise with eggs from our chickens and grease from the bear we slain. We'll build sound structures to last throughout our lives and our children's lives as well. We will live together boys, with our families. We'll stay simple and vote on any complexities that arise. I don't suggest living off the land completely. We should take jobs for money to buy plumbing and music. My wife would like some fabric to sew a hat for your wife, Teddy. What do you think of that? We'll vote on all expenses. We can even have television if it will make most of us happy.

Every man can fend for himself and his loved ones. I don't want a communist commune. I want a small, real America in Sterling, NY. I'll buy your eggs Jimmy. You can charge me an extra quarter. But no more! I know your children don't want to read the same books mine read, so we will need a little bit of money in circulation. But we won't pay taxes. We will plow the snow ourselves. We will police our own yard. Eye for an eye painted to a sign stuck in the ground, every fifty feet. That should do it. You do mind paying taxes, don't you Frank? You don't really think it's okay to help pay the general's salary, do you Burt? So he can drop bombs on people and eat a roast rabbit in the same night? The fire department? Wouldn't need them, would we boys, if we schooled the children ourselves and cooked our meals in an outdoor pit? Street cleaners? The mayor? The mayor's helper? The mayor's secretary? Twig collectors? Computer technicians? Whose computers? Look at me boys, I am plum worn down from being afraid. You know it's fear Jimmy, and nothing but fear, that gets you up to mow the lawn, trim the hedge, wash the car, clean the cellar, remodel the kitchen, the bathroom, the hallway, shop for new porch furniture, file the tools, arrange the tools, separate screws by length and head into individual labeled boxes.

The fear of not conforming. Well fellas, I am here to tell you we can change all of that. We are little and weak. We are so tiny and small and helpless. Weren't ready for that one eh?

Thought you were a big, tall boy, didn't you Teddy? We are cowering in fear of our own illusions of Job's prosperity. Fear of God? Yea, right! What God? Where? In our hearts? Which chamber? The right or left hypocrite? Look at your god's representative Burt! A timid chubby girl man, bent over in his skirt, begging your money and paying you back with the Lord's wrath? I am sorry Burt, but there ain't no god up there God up there. The new god is our government. And not one of us has the balls to cross the new god. Life has not become more complicated.

Fear has. Fear is our ever-present satan, and his little devils are you and me, boys, not living the freedom we were born to live.

Look there Burt! That's a funeral parlor. You know it's against the law to bury your dead wife in sacred ground. She's gonna die someday. So are you. So if she goes first, why can't you cover her with the dirt of your own back yard? It was your favorite grass. You mowed it once a week for fifty summers. You rough-housed with the boys and helped your little girl train the dog to jump the ladder. You grilled on the deck, cultivated an herb garden, and buried a time capsule under the pine tree. They allowed you that one, because there was nothing bigger than a dead dog in it. And now every moment you go out and stand in the yard to see your dead wife come to life, hanging the laundry, weeding the garden, scraping the paint off an old door. Who are the dirty buggers gonna get paid off for the death of your beloved? Who are they Burt? Did you love your wife? No, you couldn't have. Not if you gave up her dead body to these greedy coffin pushers. Who wants to take care of strange dead people in America? Everyone! Why? Because it pays so God damn well! Who will give up their dead to the big house at the end of the street?

Everyone! Why? Because we are a country of fearful, crawling midgets afraid more of our own laws than death's inevitability. If you went to bed with her Burt, every night for over fifty years, if you loved and made children with her, if you miss her laughter and are beside yourself with grief and loss and the hope for her spirit, then drag her sleeping death, as old and feeble as you are, out the back door and across the lawn. Drop her in a hole you dug with the same spade she used to plant azaleas back in the spring of '96.

You run along home now and give her your promise to treat her in death how you tried to in life. You do this now, over egg salad sandwiches, and I will take back every word I said. Look at that place Burt. It's almost a mansion. You see the fat chimney? Down at the bottom of that hole is where the rich mortician gets his hands dirty shoving your wife into the furnace. Where are you? You're signing papers in the office? You're giving the woman behind the desk three thousand dollars in cash? It took her twenty years to practice that frown to perfection. She knows when exactly to break the ice too. And how long to refrain from beeping "Hello" to your dumb look in the yard while she drives past you and the memory of your dear beloved, whose death happened to be the final payment on the Cadillac she beeps from.

Listen boys, I am truly sorry for the morbid thoughts on such a beautiful summer's day. I know you think I'm crazy. Anyone for checkers? Great, bring the eggs home to your wives, and meet me back here as soon as you can. I got lots more to say and all day to say it. I'll talk right up until dinner if you'll let me. I'll talk until the thunder booms in the west. I am clean, well-dressed, and thin. I feel so good today with you boys. My mind is so clear. I am looking forward to the evening and the summer stillness. Checkers then okay? All night if we have to. Until the lightning flashes green, the thunder cracks golden, and torrents of rain soak our gentlemen's clothes. Then it will be time to tell our wives about our new plans. Then we can listen to the storm all night from the safety of our beds, and dream about tomorrow's game of checkers.

We could have our own chickens, you and me boys. The hens shall peck around our feet while we play checkers and smoke. That's how the day goes by in paradise. Did you know that there is a law against keeping chickens? You can't have your own eggs made. You can't abuse your pets either, but the dog catcher can set your cat on fire. Can't block the sidewalk, can't swear too loud, can't be loud, can't get too drunk, but you can get drunk, plenty drunk just can't drive drunk, or you can't get caught driving drunk. Must abide by their electric code, their plumbing code, their living code which even the bravest boob will not dare decipher. The code of living has been set by god our government, and no man is free enough in thought to attempt to break it.

Hey Burt, you're the first one back. I'll be red, you be black.

Burt, did you know that the code has been set by our god the government? That means you should give money to the poor kids in Baltimore. It's humanitarian even if in Baltimore the idiots pay their quarterback a million dollars. It's all according to code. We pay for him too. So Burt, when your cousin, the monsignor, gets caught red-handed screwing a twelve-year-old altar boy, the quarterback in Baltimore sends his pennies to Oswego to have it checked out. It must be humanitarian when us humans opt to take care of our own religious pedophiles. Your poor cousin has two deities to fear. He pays his dues twice, once to god the government and then to god the bishop of the arch Diocese of Syracuse. Today the bishop is in Albany to tell the Roman senators it's not okay for insurance companies to cover the cost of abortion. The Pope doesn't consider it medical necessity to ram a vacuum cleaner hose up a woman's vagina. He believes women are man's property, and that every homosexual must be brought to Italy to be tried and burned at the stake. The heat from their pyres will keep the Pope's robes warm around the clock. Burt, your cousin's dues paid for the bishop's Mercedes. He drove it to the Romans this morning. Later he will have lunch with Senator Wright, who agrees with the Pope one hundred percent, but won't give his vote until the holy father calls for a final crusade against the faggots.

Taxes are necessary Burt? Why? Will they pay for the promise of never being annihilated? Do they provide your wife with the necessary peace and safety to mash her hard boiled eggs, olives and mayonnaise? I don't like olives in my egg salad Burt. King me.

Oh hello boys! Welcome back. Please gather round. Sit under the tree in the shade with me and Burt. Everything is screwy. We're playing checkers. I want us to be like old negroes in the old south. Negro means black in Spanish. It's braver to be negro in 1934 than blanco in 2001.

It's god the government taking our birth rite, first black and then white, and sicking the dogs on us whenever we get the guts to say no. I'm afraid. You're afraid. I just got enough sense to play checkers this afternoon while I sing to you my swan song of summer. King me Burt.

It is not a conspiracy. I am guilty Burt. So are you. And you just lost. Who's next? Okay Teddy, set up the board. Where do you think you are going Frank? The egg salad can wait.

Besides, it's better if you let it chill. It's obvious you're not waiting for a dough to rise, or the cakes to cool before frosting them. You're guilty Frank. You too, Teddy. Jimmy's not coming back because he is too afraid to show his face. Each one of us is guilty for letting god the government inside. It's not a whole big thing. It's not a monster. God the government manifests itself in one man's fear. It is god the government being its own Job and Job's creator/destroyer in every man. Please Teddy, be honest, why aren't there more checker games being played in Oswego? I mean the kind of man's game to gather round and not look conspicuous. There exist all kinds of games to take the fearful out to play. There is golf, but limited to four suburbanites with haircuts, and four wussies cannot overthrow their fears of god the government. King me.

Okay Burt, good point. The bar room. Yea, but do you actually listen to their conversations, Burt? They want to believe they're free to talk about politics. Damn the President! Damn that woman senator, what's her name? I think the mayor wants to smell the police chief's underwear. Everyone laughs because they think that last remark safe and local. But it's just beer politics for fear of god the government. Did anyone climb up on the bar waving freedom's flag?

Who said Saddam is right, America is Satan? No one did Burt because they know in their hearts that they are fearfully free enough already. Don't push it. Have a few beers, watch the nightly news. Oh, we bombed Iraq today? Good Teddy, but not in the genocide way you're thinking of. King me. Just look at these old men in bars. Some of them are still young enough to fight. But Jesus, just look! Tip toe, shhh, softly, shhh... If I'm really, really quiet no one will notice me dying in front of my warm beer. Hunched over at the bar, pickled and forgotten, when they have the real freedom to join our checker game in the shade. How embarrassing! What tables would turn on our god the government if we gathered together under this tree every summer day to play checkers and exclaim, No more!

It's just not worth it. They can have all the goodies. We are no longer bored. We're dangerous. We know the cops can't get rid of criminals. We don't think the President is tough on crime. He'd have a noose around his own neck if he was. King you Teddy?

Why? What fear are you crushing today? One would think that constant fear would eventually cancel itself out. If everyone is afraid, there would exist no measurement for fear. Or that after a couple generations of depreciating manhood, we could trade each other in for a replacement nullity just as useless, but less careful and not expecting to rust away so quickly. I won't king you Teddy until you go home and burn your Bible, your W-2, your pension plan, your neighbor's mail, put on your coat of mail and come back to my tree for a final game of checkers.

Bring ten egg salad sandwiches. It's going to be a long afternoon. It could go on all night. Do you hear the thunder in the west? It's not coming from the clouds. Our President nuked Iraq this morning, seconds after a sorority of republican co-eds visiting the White House blew him to get their way. The thunder rumble you hear is Buffalo moaning. Rochester is next. And then a big fat one to fall on our checker game. Yes it's a staggering reality when earth's annihilation can begin without our permission.

All right boys, forget it. I have said too much already. And I can see that I don't have your confidence. Do you understand we have no real control of destiny? We can form a clan tonight, after checkers. Not a guild or union. America does not need another special interest group to make and break its own laws. It needs more clans to stop god our government from dishing out Job's fate to its families.

Teddy, time out for a minute.

Boys, gather round. I have never been more earnest about anything. Come closer while I whisper this revelation to you. What the hell are we going to do when other nations come to bomb us? Will we act like everyone else and sign up for the big fight? Will we get angry like Pearl Harbor? You know Roosevelt knew the Japs were coming. He wanted into the war. He thought it would be fun. And he could forget, at least temporarily, about his paralysis and that annoying, dandruff-forming head itch. But that was an easy and slow time way back then, to end up with a piddly-diddly atomic bomb. Do any of you know what's in store for the next war?

No. I doubt any of us understand at all. In fact Frank, I could swing a steel pipe against your skull, and I think you'd get up after a few minutes to finish checkers. We are drugged robots. We are at the mercy of our own technological, totalitarian government. We are a nuclear democracy, a hydrogen bomb republic. No man is a man. No woman can be a complete woman.

Who has control of the buttons? Would any of us trust even our own, dear, fearful fathers with such unlimited power?

God our government is picking a fight. It's their Persian Gulf, not ours. Get out. I want to make friends with the women of Baghdad because they must be some of the best cooks in the world. But I can't get to their food, and neither can they because of the sanctions. A half million happy children are dead now. Rules of war. Rules of pre-war. Starve their kids. It's not good form to storm into a country and slice off the head of their psychotic leader. It's proper pussy protocol to rain bombs on families sitting down for supper instead. Hi Honey I'm home!

Boom!

Sorry Teddy. Just set the checker board down against that smoking stump. I'll wrap things up, and then we can all go home. It was easier for Hitler to kill eleven million than for the Allies to find Hitler and cut off his head. It's a funny rule, don't you think boys? To leave the insane mass murderer alone and starve and bomb his people instead?

La-te-da-te-da. I'm a little boy in Baghdad hopping down the street. I got a loaf of bread and a jar of goat's milk for mommy—

Ba-Ba-Boom!

Are you getting the picture boys? God our government is a killer. It says that it's all for protection. It is not. It helps put fear into you. It's also damn good money for the rich and less manhood for the poor. Supposedly we have elected Mr. President into office. Supposedly it is against the law to kill babies, women, and men without guns, even if they eat couscous and fried grasshoppers. That law is meant for you and me. It's murder if I kill my old man neighbor. It's protection if Mr. President kills Assan Hassan's old man neighbor. The senator sits passive in his seat. The air force bombed Iraq today. The senator had diarrhea all morning long, and is not a bit interested in what the President is telling him. He looks to his right and then to his left.

Everyone else seems okay with it, so he is too. He won't object. Anyway, he can't stop thinking about the fish sandwich he ordered last night in Georgetown. Suddenly he shits his pants. The news camera focuses in. Senator Poopalot of Nebraska is considering the gravity of the situation. I can't tell if he's happy with the President's request, or if he just shit his pants.

One hundred people to represent 300 million? They must think our brains have melted.

That's no good. In the last election we were given only two to choose from, and both were greedy fat lawyers. The House of Representatives? Really? Be honest Frank. Whose interests are represented? There has got to be one man in the bunch to stand tall, with back straight, and denounce the slaughter of children, to agree with Saddam that America is Satan, to get on TV and tell us never to vote again, and to stockpile weapons because Waco was wacko, but only because God Jehovah was getting too tough for god the government, and the stronger god had to prevail. Oh yes, and it also killed their babies.

Enough! Politics is always an easy target. The truth is obvious boys. God our government is our own damn fault. We are struck blind and deaf by paranoia. I wonder sometimes if our brains are goo. We were born and for the first ten years most of us liked egg salad and a hot day for a game of checkers in the shade. The problem is puberty, TV, and both parents joining the work force. We can stop two out of three from happening again. Then it's only a matter of time for clans to be reinstated. Ask me about it during tomorrow's walk to the store for tuna and milk.

But I won't unveil the final terrifying truth until I have won twenty or thirty years of your confidence playing checkers under a tree. Boys, I need to be absolutely certain where your loyalties lie.

Good morning spring! I know you're under there! Come up from beneath the ground you froze last night with winter's wind.

So many more turns of the earth needed before the soils warms up enough to bust open the buds on the trees. So many days before the winter coats get hung back up in the closet. Time is too long and drawn out, this waiting day after day to open our windows and doors. Winter begins fast and furious in early November. It won't leave for good until mid May. Such a stubborn thing to kill, winter. A short one lasts five months. A long winter will stretch itself past the half year mark. It is difficult for men to remain happy in gray cold for any length of time beyond a weekend. Oswego's cold is not unique. It's just cold. That's all there is to it. Cold.

After Halloween even small static shocks of joy are rare at best. Winter is such an uphill climb. Thanksgiving is happy because nothing is expected of anyone but to eat a grand meal and be lazy after the dishes. The snow is always pretty in November. The smell of no smell is new and anticipated by everyone. Then the cold is a tonic, an interesting change to warm the blood. The leaves aren't dead. They have fallen. Gourmets feel the most open to experimentation. Now is time for cakes, pies, stews, roasts, crinkle-cut root vegetables... Slow cooking warms the heart and the home. There's a drunkenness come over the man who can walk out into the new fallen snow and pick fresh thyme as green as it was after an evening rain in May. Wine is not necessary, but if there's an extra ten dollars a week, it's a whole lot more cheerful than sautéing with tap water.

These fresh new winter mornings are the reason why the majority are tricked into staying here. But there are seemingly endless days and nights to come after Christmas when all is dead quiet or appearing like it's actually quite dead. Oswego's face looks sinister to the gourmet after the second or third coq au vin. It sneers at him mockingly, like a delinquent searching for the right button to push, the one to finally send him over the edge. It actually calls him a liar for making a French stew in Burgertown. And then "fool" for spending that kind of money on chicken and egg noodles. Free range chicken, $4.79 a pound? Wild mushrooms? Bottle of burgundy? Unbleached flour? Twelve dollar beef stock? To keep his sanity he learns to speak the language of the car and truck. They won't tolerate a chicken prepared like that unless he's got fries and an oil filter to go with it. After Thanksgiving Oswego turns into the land of the automobile. Every man to his machine, the steel block engine calling from the driveway, as it warms up the plastic seat for his pallid ass. Salute to the wipers that be! Look proud to the green anti-freeze. Praise for the carpet that exists in the brain to get dirty then cleaned and dirty again. Suck in that air bag belly. Stand as tall as you can sit at thirty-five miles per hour. Signal right to turn right. Or signal left always and drive in circles until you run out of gas. That's okay. As long as you own a car. Live once. Look silly.

On Friday after Thanksgiving everyone drives a car. You in the car want a new car. And what better time to buy a new car than on the busiest shopping day of the year? Always a sale. Marked down for the Holidays. Why pay $24,000.00? It's yours for $23,800.00 (pronounced twenty-three-eight to new car buyers). If you get in it now and turn the key, you can be to the mall by 4:30. Turn the two hundred bucks you saved today into Christmas gifts for the kids. They should get a little something too. Two hundred dollars is enough to buy the latest video craze, and temporarily remove any traces of guilt you have for birthing the children into automobile land.

26-6. We know it's a fix. A new drug every five years. Demanding copper as an alloy might make us men and not boys. But it's an advisable, encouraged addiction, to be ripped off and not care. Even if the car costs as much as a warm shelter for life, us big boys like our toys. Girls get their thrills. Here is a perfect example why romantic love is dead.

"You look like a big boy Mr. Throop. You must think that you need this new car, or you wouldn't be here today, would you? These Oswego winters are harsh on the heart. I understand. For 36-6, this one will getcha through snow up to three feet. For 46-9 this one won't do much more, but with sunglasses on, you'll look like a movie star! That is our guarantee. We promise. If you're not entirely happy with this purchase, we will reimburse you up to 3/5 the total cost an hour after you drive it off the lot. And if you try to hound us for mocking your pride, we will call the police and have you arrested. Because it's legal and encouraged by the corporate charter for us to strip you of dignity, Mr. Throop. It really is."

"So trust us. This is what we drive. Mine was 29-7. Hers was 28-5. Together we pack the suicidal energy of several thousand shivering elk racing to leap off an ice cliff. Ford or Chevy? Volkswagen or Audi? Buy now before Christmas and we'll throw in a barbie doll to take home with you and your purchase. It will be easier to tell your daughter that you traded her education for a car. "Don't cry, honey. Here. It has a retail value of 7-98," (pronounced $7.98 to the last man in Oswego who used the last money he had to feed his children).

"You'll throw in the barbie too?"

"Yup, for 35-5 you can make your daughter feel happy and occupied in the back seat while you day-dream freely about your next purchase, and drive the new car-truck into a tree.

"Yes, but is it safe?"

"Safe? Why Jesus yes. I should hope so. If you're hit head on, twenty-three airbags inflate immediately."

"Wow! That's great, isn't it honey? And airbags save lives, right?"

"Yes, but only if they're installed on a tricycle and the tricycle rides into a gigantic pillow at 3 mph. In fact at any speed over 42 mph, upon impact, there's a 95% chance that all passengers will die painfully... and without their heads attached."

"Oh. Well heck, but it looks great! And I need something big and warm, like a womb, for me to climb into. It snows a lot in Oswego."

"Actually, no it doesn't. Global warming has had its affect on the county, especially in the city of Oswego. Scientists claim the warm-up is due to morons like you spending thousands of dollars to look big and clog the atmosphere. But if there was any significant accumulation... No. It would be wiser to buy a used Chevette for a hundred dollars. But, if I'm going to sell you a car today, I have to lie outright. Company policy. They already know that if you are here, then you're dumb enough to buy one. It wouldn't matter if I told you that while you were checking sticker prices, me and the mechanics were sticking your wife on the lift. I could say you have the balls of a cricket and at the same time hand you a pen to sign the contract. It's a tiny piece of yellow paper with the three words written on it— "I hate myself", and a place at the bottom for you to sign."

"Well okay, it's a deal. Does the barbie come gift wrapped?"

"No. And I think you're making a terrible mistake."

"No no. 35-5. That's the price we agreed upon. You won't get me to pay a penny more. Just roll her up in one of those paper floor mats will you?"

"The barbie or your wife?"

"The barbie. I'll take my wife up front with me."

Just before Christmas I get a renewed contempt for the new car buyer. Last December that's all my chef talked about. His Ford Expedition. And every one wonders why I quit my job over and over again. I am one of those few curious Romans who thought Jesus of Nazareth was a smart cookie. I was no Jew about town. I was pagan out of habit and laziness mostly. And I loved being one of several personal cooks for Senator Ipicus. Mornings I got to inspect the fish the minute it was brought up to dock. He also allowed me every expense, which meant I could use however much garum and sea salt I needed to create a supper fit for the gods. So the days of my life were always pleasant and easy. I had a bath once a week and spent my coin wisely. Then one day I met Jesus. What a fanatic! He didn't like us pagans one bit. "What's wrong with money," I asked him on the morning he marched down to the docks with his band of rowdies, cursing and flogging the Hebrew fishermen for selling their catch to me.

"Oh, go get a Ford Expedition. It's shiny crabapple red with four-wheel drive!" was his answer.

What a queer Jew that Jesus! Ford Expedition? Four-wheel drive? What is a crabapple? It didn't sound right. Like something out of the frigid northern corners of the Empire. Some curse of the Britons maybe. Nor would he tell me what it meant, either. He just looked up to the sky shaking his head, and then he took out that weird-looking penis and peed all over the Hebrew's full nets of fine Turbot and Hake.

What a strange bird, that Jesus. They finally arrested him. I knew he would get the cross if he didn't shut his trap. Each morning during crucifixion week, I'd hike up the hill to where the crosses were planted. "Jesus," I pleaded, "This is driving me crazy. What the sheep's dung does 'Ford Expedition' mean?"

He'd smile and say, "It's got four-wheel drive and is crabapple red."

Every day I made the same determined hike up to Crucifixion Hill to repeat the question. But Jesus wouldn't budge.

Finally, on the morning of Slave Slaughter Friday I made a last ditch attempt to get my riddle answered. "Look Jesus," I said, "Tell me now and I'll get you off this thing. You'll be back down at the docks in an hour. I am the cook for a powerful senator who's back from Rome on holiday. A dinner of little lamb a lá verjuice and a bucket of wine to take along to the beheadings tonight, and it'll be a cinch to persuade him. Just tell me what this Ford Expedition means, and why I should get one. It's your freedom for a riddle. What'll it be, Jesus? What will it cost? Please Jesus, I beg of you, how much for a Ford Expedition that's shiny crab apple red with four-wheel drive?"

"35-5."

"What? Are you out of your mind? That much? Man, I might be a pagan Roman dog, but nobody, not even the glorious inbred Emperor himself, is that stupid! All this time I wasted and now I don't even want to know what a Ford Expedition is. If it's that much, you can go straight down there to Sheol. 35-5! Jesus, you can hang there all day, but I ain't bringing you a single coin. 35-5. You know Jesus, I got a senator to cook for, and two kids to feed after that. I can walk to the docks... And Jesus Jesus, it doesn't even snow here. Four-wheel drive for 35-5? Now you're just pissing me off! Marcus has an ox. Tiberius a trained boar. What the Christ do I need a Ford Expedition for?"

Christmas is car time in Oswego. Everyone is driving at this most wonderful time of the year. I drive. But ever since I began to drive, the holiday has lost its appeal. Even I would walk for Jesus, and I am the worst Christian among men. There exists an immense ball of self-loathing expanding beside the heart of the good Christian as soon as he steps out of his new car on Christmas Eve. The big ball triples in size during the time it takes to stand by the snow bank and lock its doors using the plastic remote control key. He must feel the pressure on his heart about to pop while walking up the church steps to Midnight Mass dressed in a long, black coat. When their Jesus comes back... Boy! Is he gonna have one helluva time with the hypocrites! Wait, not their Jesus. Rather, *my* Jesus. They just assume that their Jesus will pull up in a new Cadillac with shrimp cocktail and a hat full of thousand dollar diamond rings, one for each good Christian woman. Jesus, I hope he comes in my lifetime. Otherwise it's still ten dollars going to Christ in the collection plate and a $419.35 signed check to Chrysler. I imagine him picking out the grandest churches on Christmas Eve, and being everywhere at once like Santa, standing by the holy water with a dirty face and ragged clothes, looking like the worst beggar in Christendom. Any person giving him a cross look will immediately be stripped of possessions and set on fire, or put out to sea alone in a row boat. Time to think long and hard about his transgression while the cold fish and weary gull petition Christ to get his shit off their lake.

Not one man or woman I know believes in Jesus Christ. And yet everyone is a Christian. No one really believes he even existed to ever come back anyway. It's a sham Christians have played out since smallpox stopped eating their children alive. Not even the most devout priest could possibly be Christ's friend. How would I know such a thing? How can I call out such blasphemies in the name of Jesus Christ? Because my poor little lost lambs, I am him! Here I am, Christ almighty. What do you think about that? The second coming. It's me. Do you believe it? No, of course not. It's impossible. "You're just like us," you'll say. St. Elizabeth's Hospital? That's not a manger in Bethlehem. Forceps didn't pull out our beloved savior. If you're Christ, prove it. And then here we go all over again!

Jesus is not love. Jesus is a thing to hide behind, a symbol to allow illusion's powerful reign to endure. All the little old Oswego ladies setting up their mangers on Christmas Eve believe that Jesus wants to take care of their souls when death wakes them up in the night. Jesus is the grown-up's Santa Claus. The toys he brings are life ever-lasting, and safety for all of God's children who believe. He would come if they believed. But they don't believe. It takes each old lady an hour to get ready for mass. And then a very short drive to it, seated in a shiny new automobile, the most decadent display of pagan wealth ever spit into the face of a people's savior. Some poor Christian ladies even pray to have one of those too. They know who they are. They got their gobs of spit warm and ready. I'd be careful if I were you Christ. These people will eat your face off if you threaten to change even a minor routine in their existence.

You can see how my winter in Oswego gets off to such a bad start. What a heavy climb it is. Yesterday a March storm dropped a clean white blanket upon us. I woke up happy again, a feeling I hadn't felt in three months. I called it holiday cheer. If the spring wouldn't come, at least I was able to rewind winter's tragedy to its innocent beginnings. While making crepes for breakfast I started to sing "It's Lovely Weather For a Sleigh Ride Together With You". In March, singing Christmas carols. Did January and February ever happen? "Where is this coming from?" I wondered. "Have I been asleep all winter?"

More proof to my theory that if man chooses to keep the northland his habitat, he needs to hibernate like the animals. Have I not been practically asleep since January? A rough slumber for sure. My head itched. I got dry scalp and dandruff. My skin paled. I ate twice as much. I started to think low thoughts. I couldn't fit into my jeans. Rarely did I step outside. From time to time I glanced out my window to see all life still asleep. I was pushing back despair. I was fighting to stay awake. Why bother? What was there to keep awake for?

So much autumn life now playing dead. Why must man be so cocky about everything? Even life? Why force himself past these terrible winters, when, year after year, he should just curl up and sleep through them instead?

I believe the Oswego man in collaboration with the Santa Barbara man should offer their skulls up to science after death. It would be an interesting and revealing comparison to prove my following hypothesis: Homo Habilis is alive and degraded in Oswego, N.Y. Homo Sapien, the thinking man, cheerfully resides in warmer climes, like Santa Barbara. I predict a noticeable difference in shape and structure between the skulls of the two beasts.

The skull of the Oswego man will show a squarer jaw and flatter top, the latter enabling him to properly balance enough weight up there to impede even the most stubborn dream to get up and leave. The Santa Barbara man will show a more rounded skull and less pronounced jowl, most likely shrunken from the advantage of a winter of fresh vegetables to eat and thick green summer grass to cushion his walk.

The jaw of the Oswego man has sixty-two very sharp teeth. Used to tear meat and appear mean even while whimpering like a sad puppy over his supermarket kill. Over a lifetime many of these teeth wore away and needed to be replaced, due to the beast's high intake of New York Strip Steak in winter. The Santa Barbara man has six teeth, one for each small cup of food he took in daily.

The orbital cavities of the skulls bear a marked difference as well. The Oswego man's are larger, reamed out after many years of winter's rot on the eyes. This peculiarity happens when a Northern man closes the lids over the eyes too often. Without a pleasant world to look upon, the eyes are purposely kept without sun or exercise. They begin to rot behind the lids, and the rot spreads into the skullbone, evidenced by two significant cracks splitting down past either side of the nose. One good jolt in life would have resulted in Oswego man's face falling off. Fortunately he was rarely moved, either by earthquake or inspiration.

The eye holes of the Santa Barbara man are smaller, showing no evidence of life rot. Most likely the result of a lifetime of keeping his eyes wide open to the sun. A strong squint strengthened the muscle and bone around the eye, to give Santa Barbara man a more secure possession of his face.

In conclusion, this scientist casts measurable doubt upon his own sanity. Being an Oswego man half his life, and a northern man forever, he believes the life rot has already begun to eat into his skull. Therefore, suffering this condition makes it impossible for him to carry out a decent hypothesis, scientifically. So he's left both skulls in the middle of the street for the snowplows to crush.

To hibernate then. Oh the future springs we'd celebrate! I know that I would make my urges heard. On the first warm morning of sunshine the music would play ear-splitting loud. I'd throw open the windows, unscrew the door from its jamb, break the door over my knee, and leap out in the road to shake off the dust and entropy.

After a full, revitalizing exercise, I'd breathe a deep sigh of relief, walk back to my house and burn it. Time to start all over. Let's destroy our dusty wooden boxes in spring and look forward to a hot summer of renewal. A sympathetic mayor would allocate some tax money to the cause of local joy, and fully endorse the meaning behind the slogan of "one man, one hand grenade". Time to raze these wooden boxes that have kept us caged up all winter. Set up tents this April and build beside them your house of lake stone and mud. Or like Thoreau, build a wood box with a window and be ready to settle down this autumn with nothing to do. House cleaning should involve dragging your furniture out into the yard and mopping up the mess you left of winter. No one will want to accumulate furniture because it's too much heavy waste to maneuver on such a beautiful May day.

Just look at our boxes. Is it me? Am I the only one who is ashamed? Is this simple and wise living? If sheetrock is an inevitability, can we limit each person to four sheets and a pamphlet to persuade him to do without? What is the meaning of common sense? Where do its new boundaries lie if in the eighteenth century it meant building a wood box before the first flake of snow and making friends with the Indians? I go on my walks about town looking for even the memory of sense that was once shared in common. One could search a lifetime yet never find a shred of common sense in his community. Unless common sense is common stupidity. That would make more contemporary common sense.

I have over sixty sheets of sheetrock screwed throughout my house. It took me four years to cut, shape, screw, tape, and cement their various shapes into barely decent looking walls. For what? Just more flat painted places to lean up against and wonder if life can really be such a drastic waste of time. Four years of breathing gypsum and joint compound dust into my already damaged and tender lungs for the right to be just as troubled as my neighbor. A common absurdity. Common to look common. Every house on my block is the same. Every block in every city. Today any structure built for sleep has it's walls made of sheetrock—plaster and lathe, if the inhabitants are still poor and lazy. Never a noble poor or lazy wisdom to have them avoid renovation altogether. It is common not to know what our time is for. It's common to envy. It is common to buy cheap and look rich. It's very common now to want to be rich, and to have no idea what rich is, so long as you can count as many rich things as your neighbor. I have always measured my richness on what little I have. The less, the more. I like to sit out in my yard in May and watch while the fools run orange extension cords across their lawns. Oh I have made the same mistake before. Like I said, it took me four years to put up sheetrock, always making the promise to myself that once finished, I will ease myself backwards, like I used to, and listen to birds, watch my daughters play, play with my daughters, or in my mind's perfectly relaxed state, plan the best menu for the evening's feast shared with my family.

No. Finally, after four years of old house renewal, I have been inducted into the *Oswego Common Sense Society*. That means they believe me now when I say that I am in it for the long haul. Even so, because I am a rookie, I have not yet gained my elder's respect. That will come over time, after I have detailed every facet of my existence down to an exact science of common sense.

I want to build a bathroom for you. On paper. Members can stop in the society to pick out a how-to for any known home project that he would like to take on. Say a new bookshelf he wants to look just like a nineteenth century law library. There will be a copy waiting with the plans laid out in detail. Of course if he is a member, he knows that it's common sense never to while away the day reading. It is more common to build something unnecessary, like a book shelf, as long as it looks rich and the wife can get a mess of used hardcover books for cheap during the summer garage sale season. There are handouts on any common how-to imaginable. Plumbing for instance. Pamphlets for underground, over ground, in a room, through the roof, metal fixtures, copper, galvanized, couplings, tees, streets, 90 degrees, 45 degrees, putty, teflon, male, female, screw-on, glue-on, ABS, CVC, black, white, cream-colored plastic, 1/8 inch up to three feet wide, (if it happens you have a whole lot of ca-ca to hide). There's even a sheet describing how to arrange several thousand different types of screws in your shop, using a computer data base, twenty old shoe boxes, a thousand pill boxes, and a pail of glue...

Anyway, here is my current contribution to the Common Sense Society of Oswego, NY. Just a simple square bathroom design—It's no longer common sense to leave our waste outdoors, nor build our homes beside the bathtub of a lake. Now that it's an easy world we live in, time to prove why I have often thought it no less than a miracle we have common sense enough to inhale and expel air from our lungs.

I am going to build my bathroom in a crooked old house. The floor is not level. Common people would choose not to walk downhill to take a pee. It will take me an afternoon to figure out the best way to level it. I am not bright in these matters and will need the assistance of an elder member. He says I should buy a longer level, but for now, a thin strip of sheetrock and a tape measure will do. The floor is off level in so many places—one inch, then two, then level, then two inches... The elder says that tomorrow we'll have to jack. I suggest building a subfloor to save time, but he gives me such a sour look that says, "Watch what you say rookie!"

On this day, I peed twice behind a tree and held my bowel full until I got to a house with a bathroom installed.

The next morning I met my elder and we went down into the basement to jack the floor. There wasn't enough room to stand up straight. With hunched backs we jacked the beams, agitating the asbestos wrapped around the hot water pipes beside our heads. After a day of abusing our backs, my elder came to the conclusion that we failed to level the floor. "Tomorrow," he said, "I'll show you how to build a subfloor. These are the materials you will need. Have them delivered tonight. I'll see you in the morning."

That day I peed once in the corner of the basement, and once in my pants. In the latter instance I was needed to steady the jack while my elder finished his cigarette. I began to smell my own smell. I finished my toilet in the evening at a house with a bathroom installed.

The next day I was up at dawn to arrange the delivered materials. Four sheets of plywood, forty-six feet of ¾ inch furring strips, two 10 ft. lengths of 1½ inch ABS plastic pipe, (with its large array of black tee's and elbows to fit), one length ½ inch, and two lengths ¾ inch supply plastic pipe with their necessary accompaniments of elbows, tees and couplings. Two 10 ft. 4-inch pipes used for dumping our waste down to meet the sewer river underground. Acid and glue, six-hundred 2-inch screws, joint cement, floor leveler, a seven inch circular saw blade, ten-inch hacksaw blade, and finally a file... I was all ready to go when my elder arrived. We spent four days setting the floor over the plumbing.

On the fifth day my elder called for the help of another elder in the society who specialized in leveling floors. He showed up after lunch with a three foot trowel and smoothed joint compound (known to cause cancer in California) and proceeded to level with the grace of a dancer dressed up in the old, torn jeans and stained t-shirt of a plumber's crack ballet.

During those five days I peed beneathe the pine boughs, and constipated myself for fear of not finding an installed bathroom on time. Nevertheless, at midnight I was forced to go in the creeping myrtle with the neighbor's cat watching. Now I smelled really bad, and on the morning of the sixth day, took a bath in the lake.

Finally I installed the floor and it was fun. I felt excited being so close to a working bathroom. Screw down not ten, not twenty, but exactly 756 screws into the plywood, making sure the screws sink so they won't crack the tile when the latter is laid. That took a day. The spring was in full song and beautiful. I peed three times behind the grapevine. It would have been twice, but my elder and I shared a beer to finish my day's work. So close we were to finished that I could taste the toothpaste on my tongue.

Then to the tiles stacked in a box. Each box weighing 50 pounds. Six boxes set up against a wall. "You'll want to stagger the tile," my elder said. "I'm going to play golf. See you in the morning."

One should start from the center, but I always take the quicker path, which is to guess. It is tile. It will be stood upon. That's rookie talk, I know. Impatient to use the thing before it is complete. Sacrificing craftsmanship and detail, for the cause of hurry cramps and diarrhea. Tile is cheap. A tenth of what the bathroom cost. Oh hell! Let's get this done. Then I can go read instead of pee under a tree.

Geez, a little off center. I wonder why? Even after three days of glue and dry. This time I evacuated in the yard in broad daylight like my dog. On the last night of construction I took my wife to the lake, for I needed a bath now, real bad—the spring had turned hot, even the nights were muggy, and my smell preceded me by several feet. No love snuggling on the rocks, like we used to before I joined the Common Sense Society. She said the lake water smelled of dead fish and that wouldn't do to wash away my sewer stink.

On the final day of construction the elder came by to inspect my work. "The tile's not centered. The glue didn't dry. You go too fast, and you haven't learned a thing." Then he helped me carry the tub, toilet and sink up the back steps into the new room. We hooked up the cvpc, with shut offs at the floor, and two where the clothes washer would go. That took all day and into the night. So for the last time I swear, I took my bath in the lake of the dead fish.

The next morning I rose early, eager to use the first room built by a rookie of the Common Sense Society. I don't want to scare anyone. But I haven't included all that there is to know. It is the golden rule of common sense never to spell things out for another. Common sense is a secret the elders are very careful not to tell. I think because the elders know they are wrong and are too scared to admit it. Anyway, that would be cheating. They tell me that once I know, I will under-stand its fairness. Still, at present I think The Common Sense Society has every single screw they ever set, loose, and presently cracking the tile in their brains. Why the indoor bathroom? It would be better to have an outhouse built in a day. It is our own stupid, reliable common sense that taught us how to survive in this climate. But to be fair, even the common senser in Florida doesn't possess the wisdom to set up an open shower in the backyard. Thoreau wrote, "Our lives are frittered away by detail". Plumbing this way is wrong. Period. I don't feel the need to give my digestive system so much privilege. Maybe without bathrooms, we would poop less. Who wants to run outside to get rid of his stool in sub zero temperatures? I do. Because it's cheap and re-vealing, and queerly, even a bit alluring. Maybe without the ease of indoor showers and cozy steamy bathtubs, we'd finally kick ourselves below these miserable latitudes. That story I wrote about Santa Barbara man? It's true but definitely not the whole truth. He has his screws loose too. How many shampoos can he count? He got the toilet in, the sink and bathtub too. Now where will he put the shelves to house his battalion of toiletries? He might live in a better opportunity, but he's grown steadily cuckoo like the rest of us. We should keep our soap dish by the back door. Take the soap and go. It should be hot with nothing to do today. Why not a public bath? The Romans did it. They lived most of their lives outdoors. Why can't we? Not enough common sense? No, too much common nonsense!

We have a common council and a mayor of Oswego to oversee the operations of the city. Each member of the council is elected by the Common Sense Society to represent his ward, or district. Non-Common Sensers are allowed to vote, but their vote is never counted. Oswego is a small, crooked city of small crooks, and their many tiny crimes and misdemeanors. Usually what happens is this: Common Council representatives are elected who also happen to be leading elders in the Common Sense Society. They make important decisions affecting the manner in which human beings must live, if they choose to live in common.

Their grandfathers passed the initial bill for the indoor bathroom. That same day they voted to clear out all remaining horses and chickens, and ever since, code-making day has become the most popular event for our elected common-sensers. The day after the bathroom was written into law, over four hundred codes of construction and conduct were passed in council. Not only was the resident forced indoors to flush a toilet, but now he had to worry about making his toilet clean and quiet. Today there are codes for flower growing, driveway maintenance, furniture placement, lawn height, snow removal, plumbing, electrical, and building codes, and enough permits, certifications, and licenses to stunt the growth of any man who believes that he isn't finished growing. There are even codes passed on how to design and print the how-to handouts. This week for instance, the Common Council voted to rescind an old ordinance prohibiting girls the right to dance naked in clubs downtown. Now just yesterday I saw a sign on Bridge Street which broke the code that limits sign size. It read: "Nude Girls Coming Soon".

I was stopped at the light thinking about *The Winter of Our Discontent*, and how the title didn't fit the prose at all. My eleven year old daughter was doing her schoolwork in the back seat. The distinguished members of the Common Council are very lucky that she kept her head down and her mind absorbed with a book. If she saw that sign, and asked me "Why Daddy?", I would not be able to hold back my most precious, correct sense. I might have very carefully constructed a personal code for murder, and vowed a midnight visit to each member and his dirty dick of a brain.

Oh you sneaking little cowards... I know what you're trying to prove. That modern, functional bathrooms means more clean girls. You Common Sensers find it perfectly sensible to meet up with each other after Monday's meeting for a beer and circle jerk. As long as the girls wash themselves in code approved facilities. I know you. I know your wives. I know how slow it is on a Friday night for a couple over forty. You need to speed things up a bit, to pretend it's some exciting place you live in. Cocaine in Oswego? Yes, why not? Mr. Common Senser gets his from Crazy Marty. And when his wife sniffs it, he strips her naked with the baby-sitter and then does it to himself while they lick each other goofy. Life is wonderful. At least on Friday, when he's a big shit in Oswego. At full length, on his tip toes, he's five foot two. He can make his penis grow a whopping five inches erect—but damn it feels like a ten foot length of ABS plastic pipe when he's fully railed and lucky to have a wife who goes down on young girls. Yes, little Oswego needs the capital gains from a nudey bar. Money will pour into the economy, like cold beer into a frosted glass. The revenue from lap dances alone will pay the mayor's salary. And now the lucky grown men of Oswego have exclusive right to legally come in their beer.

We of the Common Council, made up of the most distinguished Common Sensers, run the show now. Next year it's a whorehouse across the street from the elementary school and a choice of XXX movies at the theater. What's new from Disney and the underground world of Los Angeles porn? Just crawl up our butts to find out. Friday nights in Oswego will be like they used to be, when the power plant was pumping millions of dollars up our noses. Only now we have the advantage of getting wired *and* naked. We don't look silly. We are important. Let's see... Who do we get for opening night? We got a whole college of juicy girls to choose from. The ones we get will be ugly, of course, but that's okay— our wives are ugly. At least the coeds are young. Yes, young and juicy. I'm starting to get a rise just thinking about it. But we need a prop. A headliner. A top dancer to showcase. Some babe with big jugs. She won't need to flash her box. She'll be that special. That's it! Great suggestion Mr. Alderman. All right boys, Jack says he's got a daughter nursing her newborn. She'll dance for a hundred bucks a night. She's pretty enough and lucky for us she's got huge tits aching full of milk. She can make 'em spray too, right out into the audience. We'll call her "Milky, Hot Mama of the Third Ward". We'll get her to tickle her nipples. For five extra bucks the fellas can line up and take a drink. Those Kanucks will break down the border just dying to get a taste of her!

Listen, I am not trying to be moralistic in a moral-less existence. Why bother venting our plumbing? The fumes of town shit have been choking us blind since birth. We should wipe our asses with the codes the Common Sensers pass in council. They are meaningless as long as we demand that our digestive systems remain personal property. It took over ten days to build a bathroom, the cost of which was more than a shack set up in paradise. No kidding. Yet it's not a financial consideration I'd have you make. There are better reasons than money to abstain from indoor plumbing.

The power of law enslaves mankind. Law has turned us into domesticated pets and beasts. One can be a dog, a cow, or even a fish in a bowl. But choose one, please, because he cannot be a man anymore. It's over. He might think he is free, but free like a horse in pasture. He could try to eat the man, but knows damn well he would starve to death without master's hand to feed him. He's so very free to leap the fence and run wild forevermore. But he built the fence, and knows exactly why he built it. He has that fear, no matter how deeply concealed. "No one is above the law." That is man's motto. Law's power is the law. After breaking in the cow, the horse and sheep, man turned on himself, and made a domesticated dog's life of his own freedom.

That is why I cannot believe in man or man made things. I do not trust man. I do not respect him. I don't even like him. I live in a town of men, but to me they are just fearful, upright mammals conditioned to obey. This town is the quintessence of fear, and fear passes laws. Hundreds and thousands of laws! When the invention of plumbing came to Oswego, it should have brought joy, but codified more law. Electricities' advance meant new paths to waste and destroy, and another book of laws. Interesting how much money and energy is devoted to harnessing electricity, compared to that of processing plumbing fixtures. We have a massive billion dollar power plant corporation groaning up the road, yet no plumbing factories to choke smoke into our skies. There's a lake and a couple small unobtrusive buildings to filter our water and empty the sewers. Simply put: shit doesn't pay. Water is cheap. So are wax candles. We need light for our night reading. We need a little heat for the luxury of cooking. Don't eat meat and we wouldn't need heat. We would freeze to death, or get the hell out of Oswego. That choice should have been made the moment a law was passed detailing a man's evacuation of feces. No. It's much easier, and potentially safer to suffer the consequences of his own made-up laws.

We talk so lovingly of democracy. We buy a flag at the store to thank our forefathers. The owner of the store is a fat pervert. I saw him the other night trying to have sex with a wall outside the strip joint downtown. We say America is the experiment of the world. No. The Iroquois were the experiment for the world, and America drained them of their blood. At its best America was once a land of farmers needing food to survive. If a thief had time to steal an ear of corn from the farmer's field, the elders voted in council to cut off his fingers and cook them to replace the farmer's corn.

In a real America, men represented men. The Iroquois were men, not from long ago, not in a past world. Their world is right here and now with new eyes and ears. For instance, reading this book will open your mind to the Iroquois, or close it forever to a new book of laws. I can write what I want. In real time I will be dead soon. I shall not feel wrong anymore in a world I did not create. I am doing what I can in continuation of the great American experiment. I am trying to overthrow my mind. A bloody revolution for all is not applicable. It would be like invading a pasture of sleeping cows with a fully equipped modern army. It's true, that a handful of desperate men could easily decimate the entire country. I don't want that. I want to live peacefully among men—but on my condition. Because I know that it is a freer, more glorious America I dream of. Maybe I hate men so much because I love what they could be. It only takes one gesture of the hand to change direction. One final "No" to break the chains. Is there another man in America who prefers to shit in his own backyard? Is that so bad? Is that all I have to bitch about at a time when I should be jumping for joy? Men of Oswego, listen to me, there are clean and easy ways to defecate now that we have domesticated ourselves. We have time and safety, which are luxuries we haven't had since the pact of the Six Nations. How can we feel in common the freedom our forefathers felt while walking down the public road on an orange autumn day? Freedom the Mohawk felt in summer while running his string of fish back to the village? Freedom that the former slave breathed in as he stepped off the train in Chicago? I'd like to meet the bug in you that wants to build what it does not need. Bacterium or virus? I should like to squash it, and have your own blood wash up the mess it left. For that to happen, you will need to come to me to learn a thing or two. Ha! But such a proud stupid animal man!

A yellow tint shows through the morning rain. The drops are heavy. In a day they can make an earth green. I should like to get on a train and travel for a month. I need a dose of reality, a ride through the deep south where animals and men still work and play like animals and men.

America has its wild preserves. I suggest a man preserve. In Montana perhaps? Or does everyone there still think cattle and wheat? What is the difference anywhere? Iowa grain or New York textile? Both think they are wiser than the other. Both will get rich the way they want to and write their invisible epic legacies about shallow beginnings, dry gulch aloneness, smokestack prejudice, high rise nervousness, deep canyon hatreds, wide open illusions...

Finally, the first signs of spring. I don't think the rain has any intention of becoming snow. Still, one can think worms and robins during a white-out if he so desires. There are two early springs. The yellow rain falling now. This is the cleansing wet side of March. Earth cleansing, part of the eternal wheel, a drenching reminder that life is worth living. I walk a dog and there's the outdoors everywhere. Rain pouring down on meadow and forest and man is just a small thing not in the way.

Then arrives the sun of March—pre-Easter and downright sad and hopeless. People step out of their homes to pick up garbage and dog poop accumulated in the yard over winter. Gray-black smudges of winter stain every crevice. The roads are brown cake of winter's salt and car exhaust. The sun shines. The car is filthy. Windows smeared. October's newspapers collected upon layers of snow, suddenly revealed to expose their old, sad tidings. Every home's front yard is drab. The trees rigid like cold stone statues. The air is carbon. Even the sun is choked by man's careless waste of what is truly life and real. This spring America, north of the 35th parallel, has the look of an apocalyptic wasteland.

But at least we have indoor plumbing.

Here in Oswego it's even worse. That wonderful cleansing rain has turned back to snow. And I know it's a lie to believe a man fortunate to be alone in the wide open spaces this morning. Here is a small city of men without access to a path in the woods. That's okay—there's a beautiful lake to view. Stand at the water's edge. There. Now forward is the breakwall. After that a sea of fish, a great lake of good and plenty—an endless supply of carcinogens to catch and eat. To the left, the tallest man-made structure in the city. Twin smokestacks stuck out of the oil burning plant rising into the gray sky. You can see their poisonous presence from twenty miles away. The lighthouse of the damned. Burning oil to make electricity? *Shh... That's not the woods. Keep on the path.* To the right, close enough to dominate the shore, but four or five miles from the city, stands the final reason why men despair. The Nuclear Power Plant. And it's not the potential danger, nor its incredible size that contributes to the gnaw busily eating away our internal organs. No, our pain owes its beginnings—*Shh... Quiet down. That's not the path.*

There is no freedom of land. You want to walk but you must walk on a paved road. You want to walk to the country without taking a road. No, it's illegal. Get on the road so they can sneer at you from their cars. You look suspicious. You might be dangerous. If it's night, the worse for you. They have dogs to bark and snap at any shady looking character passing by. Their children speed by in cars. Sometimes they throw a can of soda at you, or a stone, or a brick. Some young ones are so ambitious that they want to club you with a bat. You were walking a deserted road in the dark. What town justice would be sympathetic to that? Of course you were up to no good. Who were you going to rob? What were you hiding from? The boys are sentenced to a heavy fine and a year of weekends in the county jail. This for dragging your bleeding body off to the side of the road, kicking your head, pissing in your mouth, laughing and spitting, and getting back into the car.

Now is the time to arm ourselves. I won't stand for pain and humiliation. I want to walk on these roads with a gun. And no one can know I have it. I will do what you cannot. I will kill for my body's trespass. *Whack! What did I tell you? One more digression and I'll chew off your toes! Now get on the path!*

I feel wild. Spring for me is something larger than loin arousal. I want to sing out, but I leave the house just moving my lips to song. Lip-syncing joy. "He's talking to himself again," they say, "That guy's crazy."

I must quiet down. The Christians want to keep all joy quiet. "Please keep your joyful noises down. Withhold your applause please, until after the performance." Man, they're all looking at me. I better take my song to the woods, like Pan, and wait there happily until I shout out all this Easter from my system. I'll walk west down Route 104, and take a left at the first welcoming forest I spy. *I'm warning you...*

Oh fiddlesticks, what's this? Signposts read "No trespassing. Get out! This land is mine, not yours. I have the deed. I own the land. It's my property. Get out. Get out. Get out!"

Surely this good man will not mind my walking into the woods. That sign is meant for the people of the smokestack whom I left behind. He is wise enough to love the land. I know because it's still here. Those trees are standing tall, and I can hear the roar of the flooded creek calling me. I'll just take a short walk. I am searching for freshet and wood fairies to take my mind away from human cares. *Yes, but be careful. And you know what I mean...*

Unfortunately, no matter how many of us would heave a huge sigh of relief denying such, these are the days of Christ. Although our land has always been more suited for Buddha, Dionysus or Rama of the highlands, Christ owns the property and he alone decides who may trespass. This is the northern forest of conifer and fresh water lake. Deities to run and dance wild around the life of man. America—once a ripe playground for adventurous gods—is now under Christ's domain, and every other god condemned to the sandbox. Mountains to the east, valleys to the south, fertile land out west with more forest for salvation. I was born here. Christ was not. Christ lived in a walled city. Born in a desert. He wore a robe. He ate falafel. The desert dreams which haunted him were the seeds of future chemical imbalances grown thick and hemorrhaging in our modern brains. Christ walked below homes of desert brick stained white to reflect the rays of the sun. He dreamed his dreams, and now those same dreams make us hot and sick inside. He never saw the leaves of a maple tree turn scarlet in October. What would he think of the raccoon, the woodchuck, the turkey or the deer? Had he ever seen a chipmunk? No. His dreams were about Romans, Jews, money, the funny monkey at the temple, no money, food and his father who was in heaven. After two thousand years of incredible luck and successful war-mongering, every man-made structure in America is a demented Christ devotional littering the once wild and majestic landscape.

Christ, Muhammad, and Zoroaster. Such mean-spirited Middle Eastern prophets-turned gods. Out of spite alone, Christ would beat Buddha silly with a sand rake. Even out west in the soggy forests of Washington State, where Buddha owned some influence once, during a wave of Japanese immigration, Christ moved quickly and dealt a low blow to conquer his weaker foe. He's not the Christ we learned about in Bible school. The timid turn-the-other-cheek Son of God. Not even the Pope's demented, circus Christ. The true Christ is the warrior Christ. The American Christ. That was the old Christ's promise to the New World. "Folks, you just plain soiled Europe. Now I plan to show you how real crazy your Christ can be!"

Anyway, after the death of St. Francis the world was made ready for Manhattan, plastics, and the Vietnam War. Christ got aboard all ships heading west, introducing himself to each immigrant personally. He let them know that America was cruel and tough and extremely dangerous. Every man for himself and for Christ, King of America. "I am no longer the Christ your father and mother loved," he explained. "I am the new Christ you must fear. I will see to it that you get what you deserve in America. And you will owe me."

He devoted all ship voyages to tossing overboard a thousand years of their baby Christ hopes and dreams.

The immigrants arrived to settle with Christ and the smallpox. Then Christ had them open up their prayer books to the Lord's fever rush of hell fire and damnation scare tactic chapter: "Hymns to Sing While in the Throes of Destruction." And by Jesus did those settlers sing loud and strong! "Level the Trees O Lord, O Lord!" "Build Us Sturdy Christian Folk A Powerful Empire", "Please God, Let Us Find Killing in Our Hearts." "Save our Corn, Eat an Indian," "Convert or Die." "The Governor is Christ's Best Friend." And then later when some American men became more like their own image of Christ... "Conform or be cast out."

Wait, I was sleeping. Repeat what you just said.

Easter is coming and the forest is getting ready for the death and resurrection. Birds are singing the coming of Christ. All is—*Fine. Look, I must step out for a few minutes. Keep it clean. Remember your toes!*

All life is stirring. The earth has awakened from its winter slumber. The snow has melted. Wild leeks are the first green born into the forest. I am gathering some now to make soup for my supper. Ho! Here comes a man with a gun and a dog.

"What the hell do you think you're doing?"

"Looking for Pan good sir, and wood fairies, and a spring freshet to lift my hopes and bring joy to my heart."

"You're trespassing on my property Jack. Didn't you read the signs?"

"Yes, kind sir. But surely all this beautiful land can stand the walk of a lonely man with a heavy heart?"

"No. Go back to from where you came, Mr. Freakshow. Or I'll make it so you never leave my forest."

"But you, kind sir, you're not cruel and hard like other men. You bought the land to save it from the dirty horror growth of factories and smokestacks. You saved the deer run and gave us back the cool blackness of the night."

"I did like hell."

"You mean sir—"

"Yea, I work at the oil plant, and my wife is the lingerie manager at JC Penny. We saved every penny we ever made to afford this land and a new truck, and a new house, and a fat savings account, and securities, and a garage full of tools and a snowblower, and a riding mower, and a trip to the Bahamas, and, oh hell— Anyway, it was my idea. I saved the deer run so I could shoot the deer. Great hide. Good meat too. After the butcher's through hacking it up."

"Oh, I see."

"Say, I'll let you off this time, seeing it's almost Easter and all. But if I ever catch you on my land again, I'll sick my dog on ya."

"Ok. Say sir?"

"Yea, what is it?"

—Don't you dare.

Ah damn! You're back already?

Yes. I told you I was only stepping out. I know what you were going to say.

You do?

"Hey, who the hell are you talking to?"

You were going to say, 'Now I'm going to eat you and your dog'.

I was, wasn't I?

Yup.

"Hey, I said, who the hell are you talking to? Yo Freakshow, I'm asking you!"

You can.

Can what?

Eat that filthy slob.

Thank you Pan.

You're welcome son of god.

Now it's time to write about Marty. No picture of Oswego could be accurate if I failed to mention Marty Lieberman. He's a local character, owns a bar along the river. Also known as "Crazy Marty," he and I go back eleven years, to about the time my first daughter was born. That's the Marty I know personally. But he was already well known about town before I met him. The rest of his story I've gathered from other people's accounts of him. Some reliable. Some criminally suspect. All of them funny. For Marty is funny. Nuts actually. Cuckoo, bonk-bonk, flipty-doo! About as nuts as they come without papers to commit him. Some say it was the booze which triggered his crazy. Others swear it was acid. An old cook once told me how she spent the entire summer of '76 with Marty on the roof of his bar, licking sheet after sheet of LSD. That would explain it. For Marty's not crazy like the mental health ghosts dragging their feet across the bridge and back again. No, he's not nuts like that. He didn't knock of a children's hospital in 'Nam, nor is he one of the unfortunate products of the brother-sleep-with-sister pastime made very popular in this part of the state. Old money in town has been very good to Crazy Marty. It's provided him freedom to roam the streets without a government card. But Marty refused to walk a block on his own two feet. So old money bought Marty a shiny red SUV. That satisfied him. Now he can turn off road to make a quick getaway whenever the CIA is chasing him.

Marty is nuts. But he wasn't born nuts. He's one of the classic few nuttys who became whacko on purpose. Marty's mind is a lot like that of the rock star: money, fame, and of course, drugs, have unveiled the big top tarp to his crazy. This is the sole advantage which keeps his one man circus from getting locked up. Old money and Oswego rock star fame. So what? It's worked for him. Marty's crazy, but he's got an SUV and his own bar. In Oswego that is the highest position of respect a man will reach. In Oswego, Crazy Marty is as good as gold.

Marty's origins are from downstate. Hometown son of a wealthy furniture salesman. No one knows for sure how he ended up in Oswego. Of course there is gossip and speculation. Anyone who has lived here long enough to drink six beers alone in one night knows who Marty Lieberman is. And each has his or her own opinion of Marty. Myself? Well I know that he didn't come for the college. That's for certain. He wrote me a letter once, a response to an angry note I slipped under his door. He told Mary I was mealymouthed. I was. I am. But he also said that the only literature worth reading was the *New York Times*. For some queer reason that remark infuriated me. I sat down and penned a scathing letter and addressed it to "Marty, my enemy." I sealed it in a blank envelope, walked it down to his bar, and handed it over to him in person. The next day I opened my door to go out, and there was the envelope with his scribbling on it. He wrote back.

Ho! The man was barely literate! Suddenly I became overwhelmed with pity. Marty pity. Self pity. I nearly cried. This was my adversary? This poor bastard? He could barely scratch out a sentence. I had to get a hold of myself. Where was I going? I was making an enemy out of an idiot. No. Mary still had the scars to prove that Crazy Marty hadn't the slightest problem expressing himself. So what if the bartender read the *New York Times* to him? He was still Crazy Marty, local bastard son of money from downstate New York. What if he couldn't read? He still had the power to pick up a woman by the hair and dig his fingernails into her flesh—

But I am getting too far ahead.

Two rumors circulate Oswego about Marty's true beginnings. Some say he's involved in Oswego's biggest drug cartel, the Mitchum family. Richard Mitchum is a ninety year old puritan lawyer with a blue-haired wife and an effeminate toupeed son following in his father's footsteps right down to the polished toenail. That would make up the entire cartel with Marty employed as drug runner and pusher. No, impossible. That family is rich from white money, not drugs. They're crooks, through and through, but not the automatic weapon toting type. Small time crooked lawyers who have used the best of time and trickery to amass a pretty fortune at their neighbor's expense. Scum yes. But not murdering scum. I have never seen Richard senior, but every Friday night while I was employed as a cook, I cut up Mrs. Mitchum's fried zucchinis into tiny bite-sized pieces. This was an extra effort I made on her behalf. And each time I offered up my mucus as a condiment.

A generous gob of spit from a not so generous, mealy-mouthed deep fryer cook with a smoky lung. Her and I go back too, both guilty by association, although she wouldn't know my face from one of her soiled diapers.

The other gossip, more believable, is that Marty is the illegitimate son of Senior Mitchum, Attorney at Law. Some folks say that long ago the Mitchum's were invited by mutual friends downstate to the Lieberman's grandiose home. It was a weekend party to celebrate the new governor's election. Mr. Mitchum asked Mrs. Lieberman to dance, and after supper, snuck upstairs and laid her on some of Mr. Lieberman's very fine, expensive furniture.

So Mr. Mitchum gave the Lieberman's Marty, and since sex scandal was very bad publicity for a Jewish furniture salesman and Puritan lawyer in the mid 1950's, Senior Lieberman made a secret deal with Senior Mitchum. "I'll take care of Marty his first eighteen years, and then he's yours after that, Mitchum."

The deal was made. Mr. Lieberman did everything he could to pretend that he loved his wife's son. He even enrolled Marty into military school, and every summer, sent him as far away from home as Mrs. Lieberman could stand. Like any successful business family in America, the Lieberman's grew very wealthy on a diet of suppressed anger, depression, and guilt. Mrs. Lieberman drank. Mr. Lieberman taught Marty how to use dangerous carpentry tools in the basement of their furniture store. In fact, he took Marty out of school early and gave him a full time job in charge of all repair. He knew that his son could barely read or write, and smiled a broad smile whenever he thought about it.

There was a cake for Marty on his eighteenth birthday. His mother was sloshed and tried to eat the pearls around her neck. For presents, Marty got some money and furniture coupons to use for his new home in Oswego. Then Senior Lieberman drove his son to the town airport and left him there without a single gentle word.

Senior Mitchum was busy in court all day, and so was unable to greet Marty at the airport. He sent his gardener instead. The gardener brought Marty to Mrs. Mitchum, who had been waiting eighteen years for Marty. She slapped his face while he set his suitcase down in the parlor. Then ordered the gardener to go collect zucchinis in the garden. "You son of a bitch. You ruined my life. I hate you with all my soul. You wipe that smirk off your face you little bastard. You think you're living in this house, well you're wrong."

So before Mr. Mitchum got home, Mrs. Mitchum set up Marty at his new quarters in the old grain elevator along the river. It was decided upon that night by Mrs. Mitchum that Marty would receive an allowance and a piece of the grain elevator to live in. Mr. Mitchum was never to call Marty, "son," and if Marty made trouble, then he would be denied half his weekly allowance.

None of this drama affected Marty. He got accustomed to his new place rather quickly. Oswego had its fair share of drugs, booze, and girls. Plenty of girls. College girls. Marty loved girls. He wanted girls. He was always on the look-out for girls and more girls.

Marty tried his best at the local bars, and had some luck. Once he got two girls to go home with him, and they slept with his roommate. Marty thought himself a bore. He just didn't know how to behave around women. He was popular enough when stoned or drunk. That is, he made the girls laugh, but he would not admit what it was about him that made them laugh. And he couldn't laugh them into bed. That made Marty very unsure of himself. His looks didn't help either. His nose was fat. His eyes were small. He had a forty year old look at twenty. It always took him a little something extra to get a pretty girl to sleep with him. Well, truthfully, none were very pretty, but Marty vowed to change all that.

He needed a gimmick, a scam, and found one eventually. Even as a young boy, Marty possessed the old school insight to make big in the present in order to secure a more wealthy future. He didn't want more money. His allowance was quite heavy already. Marty wanted girls! Young girls. He wanted his choice of young girls when he was old and more grotesque. He had a plan. A great plan. He would trash both of his father's old money, old school business practices. Sober rich people didn't get pretty girls. They got old. And their wives got old. Money wouldn't get its hands up a skirt quicker than no money. Marty recalled the advice from his third grade drill sergeant. "Ya gotta be mean and loud boys, to get what you want in life. Mean and loud. Remember that, if you remember anything!" Marty realized a man could not be his meanest and loudest selling furniture at a ridiculous mark-up. He called on Senior Mitchum.

"I want to make the grain elevator a bar."

"Marty, now we talked about this. You're going to open up a furniture store to compete with Goldberg's. Why do you think I had a shop installed for you upstairs?

"I want a bar!" Marty screamed.

"Now Marty, a deal's a deal. Oswego has enough bars already."

"Give me a bar you dried-up white prick, or I'll monkey dance all over your wife... *Dad*."

And that was that. Marty Lieberman, born into money downstate, gave up a career in money to open a bar to get laid for life. He got straight down to business, working as fast as other people could to carry out his plan. Senior Mitchum gave Marty a huge advance on his allowance. During the summer of '76 Marty dropped acid every single day with anyone who would climb up onto the roof with him. He took the advice of his half brother, Junior Mitchum, and used drunks and druggies for the construction crew. "Pay them next to nothing, Marty. Give them free draft beer on Fridays, and they'll be as loyal to you as dagos to their Godfather." After one real hot day, a couple guys called up to Marty demanding to be paid. That didn't phase Marty. He had a plan. He just rolled up hits of acid into tiny hot tar balls, and tossed them off the roof yelling down, "Take two of these and we'll see what you say in the morning."

So the necessary work got finished, eventually. Marty opened up The Old Grain Elevator in the winter of '77. He taught himself how to play guitar because he knew that drunk girls loved music. It was part of his plan. Still, past experience dictated that no pretty girl was about to fall for him just because he could play "Stairway to Heaven" cold. At least not without a gimmick. The bar was phase one of the plan. The acid binge was phase two. Already there were traces of paranoia swimming in his blood. Once a customer walked in, sat down at the bar, and asked for a beer that Marty didn't stock. Very slowly, as inconspicuously as possible, Marty got up from the barstool, and backed away, step-by-step on his tip toes, turned, and ran out the side door. Later he told the bartender that the request the man made was in a secret code the government used to hunt down communists in American bars.

"He asked for Utica Club, Marty."

"Nah. That means, 'Bartender, are there any communists in the room?'"

"No Marty. My Dad is the brewmaster at Utica Club."

"No he's not! Get the hell out of my bar spy! I don't want no communists here!"

"But Marty, my girlfriend's pregnant. I need this job."

"You guys married?"

"No, but we plan to be after next month."

"Get the hell out of my bar commi-pig. I know you're an agent!"

So the acid made Marty crazy. It was his plan. Yet he wasn't getting any younger, and the paranoia did not attract prettier girls to screw. He was drunk so often that a permanent white slime grew on the corners of his lips. Never washed away until the benders were over, when Marty looked in the mirror to brush his teeth. He needed an improvement to his existing plan. He needed to consolidate. Not all women were for him. Some girls never set a foot into his bar. Some girls didn't get drunk enough to puke. Most girls were repulsed by the white slime and the physique that was looking more and more like a bumpy albino squash. These girls were out of Marty's league. One afternoon while feeling sad and depressed, he took a drive down to Fulton to watch the naked girls dance. All of them were so friendly for a dollar. Some were pretty. Most of them were young. He asked the bartender for the manager's name.

"I'm him. Name's Freddy."

"Are you married to any of these dancers?"

"All of them."

"Oh... Okay Snippers, so would you like to tell me how you get them to take off their clothes?"

"They get to keep all the money that they find in their holes."

"Yea, but that's not enough."

"Fifty bucks, and I'll tell you my secret."

"Fine... Here. Now tell me."

"I've scored with some of the prettiest women in the county. I've been around. I was a lot like you—overweight and old with a yen for little girls—"

"Hey, hold on there! I don't want them if they're too young."

"What, are you in business?"

"Yea. I own The Old Grain Elevator."

"That's right. I heard about you. Crazy Marty! Man, you should know better. Any fifteen year old can dress up to be eighteen. You just have to get the right fifteen year old and a fake I.D. She's more girls than you would ever believe. I know. I'm up to two thousand minors, and six hundred broads between eighteen and twenty. And I'm as old and ugly as you, Marty. The only difference? I go for the babes with no self esteem. Remember that and your fifty dollars is the best money ever spent."

"Yet again Snippers, how do I get them to take off their clothes?"

"Usually with the prettiest girls there must be a preliminary investigation. Say you hire a bartender at your place, and she's gorgeous and just old enough to serve drinks. Chances are she hates herself already. Or she's confused. Very confused. Or she thinks that if she must live in Oswego, then the highest life she'll ever find will be at your bar. Great. Now is the time to make your move. She's come into your house expecting to get paid. Start prying into her personal life whenever possible. It would help if you acted a bit crazy about town. Then she'd expect you to be rude."

"I am crazy."

"That's right! Excellent. So you're all set. Look, I'll stop by your place in a couple hours. Wait, I like you. And anyway us scumbags got to stick together. Miranda!"

"Yea Freddy?"

"Come here, I want you to meet somebody."

"It better be good Freddy. That guy was reachin' for his wallet."

"Miranda, Marty Lieberman. Marty Lieberman, Miranda."

"What's your scam Marty?"

"Ah, I just stopped in to lose the choppers."

"The choppers?"

"Yea. FBI. You wired?"

"Yes. Can you guess where they put the bug?"

"Did your father ever make love to you?"

"No. But my Mom's boyfriend did. He took me truckin' all over the south."

"Do you know what real French Champagne is? How old are you?"

"Can I tell him the truth Freddie?"

"Yea Miranda. Go ahead."

"No. And 15."

"You want to come back to my bar? You can live in my bed. And you won't have to take your clothes off for money—except for me."

"OK."

Marty was in love.

His relationship with Miranda was rocky, to say the least. She bartended for a while until the temptation to take her shirt off every time she saw quarters lined up on the pool table became too great. Then puberty arrived and Miranda fell for a lead guitarist. She wrote Marty a "Dear John" and sealed the letter with wax and her favorite pink tassel.

The bartender read it to him. Marty was devastated, but glad to have the tassel and a loved-lost experience to mark upon his crazy resume.

That's about the time I come in, give or take a few years. It is a time in my life when I have everything a man should ever need, but I think I am missing something. A time when foolish, carefree youth becomes stupid youth, and steps onto the path of the wrong-way adult. Everyday I fought the truth. I hated the truth. I was young. Youth is forgiven repeatedly when it might as well be shot in the stomach to put it out of its misery. I will always regret participating in those younger days when I acted like a complete idiot for my own, miserable sake. I don't believe in a man having no regrets. I believe in man's desperation, which is an active, breathing regret. It inhales the self and exhales despair, and coughs the life force out of every one of us. I feel it. I wish it wasn't there.

Well, at age twenty-four I was young and dumb. I have no good feeling for that early Ron. Not one. The twenties. What a wasteful good-for-nothing rock, the young American man. So cocksure! So empty. So volatile, yet erupting nothing! And I thought I was the center of the universe! Youth is not wasted on the young. Youth never comes to the young. Youth is the old man's regret. I don't ever want the energy I had when I was a so-called "young" man. What a disease! What a lie! What a painful memory it becomes for those lucky few who desire to age with dignity. When I am forty-four, I will most certainly regret thirty-four, but I will never hate it. Not like I hate twenty-four. Now I am where I want to be. If you asked me what I wanted when I was twenty-four? Easy. I wanted whatever it was I wanted. Perfect selfish lonely moon!

There's a youth worth preserving. The one regret we all share: Our lost childhood. Our greatest possessions are those little memories of innocence and real joy we keep to ourselves and seldom reveal. They end the moment we know and can juggle in our minds the cost of three or more things at a time. That is, we want ice cream, but think about dinner too, and gasoline, and fixing something. Youth worth preserving would have stopped at the ice cream. Fifty-five cents for a double cone. And then the next hurdle for the day. For most men, twenty-four is sixty-four. Only sixty-four is physically and, in our country, mentally unappealing. That would explain why most sixty-four year old men long for twenty-four again. What a grand, happy, healthy, energetic youth, twenty-four! Thirty-four was older. Forty-four—this is the straight and narrow path the physically weak and mentally deranged old men of America wake up and go to sleep on everyday of their lives. These are the people who know the exact number of brain cells which die every second. They love and adore twenty-four. They are yearning for the wrong youth of twenty-four. How could they ever understand that eternal youth is the only wisdom of old age? We live in a time when old men identify their lost years by that era's make and color of automobile. That is not at all a part of the joy of aging which I imagine. America can have it's twenty-four. I've buried mine.

Still, I will need to uncover bits and pieces if I want to continue with Marty's story. I'll try to focus my thoughts more on him, and less on Ronnie, the mealymouthed masochistic, narcissistic moon at twenty-four.

It's ten year's ago last Thursday. I am living with my newborn and her mother in a very cramped, furnished upstairs apartment. It's a time in a young couple's life when everything should be handed over to them with the words, "Don't worry, life is beautiful". Instead you find yourself never more alone with a room full of cheap, plastic stuff. All except for the oak podium, a request I made to my father for a college graduation present. I stand behind it and attempt to write down my lofty inspirations. The baby cries. Re-runs at seven, but first the CBS nightly news with Dan Rather. Twenty-four had the absurd idea that current events exercised the intellect. Events? Of what? Whose events? I probably crossed my legs too while watching, and made witty political remarks to Mary which marked the beginning of death and the tucking in at bedtime any tiny flecks of passion left to fall asleep. This was twenty-four! The stage was set. The tragedy would come. The only light to shine shown out of my daughter's eyes, and yet, I was simply too selfish to notice. All eyes were focused on the array of goodies behind her. I read books like *Black Power* and *The Tibetan Book of the Dead*. Holy crap, my poor baby girl! I was too selfish to know, and much too weak as a man to care that I would be better off blind, and preferably deaf and dumb, or just dead and gone too. Blindness is a beginning to the humility men are in dire need of. A wise rite of passage would be surgical eye removal for every boy on his eighteenth birthday. And then a ten year stretch of a life without eyes. The perfect cure for a nation sick with fear and bad taste. Blind men cannot form opinions with discrimination. They are forced to doubt their power, which is like hugging on to dear life a live ticking humility bomb.

I was not blind. I was twenty-four. So if Dan Rather said, "Bombing in the Persian Gulf," I'd jump from my chair and yell at the television. "How could they? What monsters! Why can't anybody see?" Oh, but how ignorant I was of their perfect eyesight! At twenty-four I could have had the wisdom to cover my beautiful baby within the bomb shelter of my arms. But I wasn't blind. I could see the child of Baghdad held up against her mother's breast. Myself and the twenty-four year old fighter pilot saw the same scene. Both awake in the morning, putting on our pants, pouring cow's milk over cereal, and leaving the nest to explode the flesh off human beings. A blind man would immediately smell and feel the heat from the glowing fires of fear behind their lies. And if he could write legibly, would pen letter bombs from his podium addressed to the sixty-four year old men killing babies in Iraq.

Nope. Twenty-four was frightened without power. Oh, and the helplessness of being enrolled in my last semester of college... There was no hope for me. I was without any reason to claw the eyeballs out of the men in my way. So vulnerable, so ready to leap into a pool of boiling acid with my ideas. Another man's ideas that I cherished like my own. That autumn I baby-sat for the socialists. I won't name them for you because now I have the wisdom to know that all of them were twenty-four. Useless, incurably selfish creatures, neglecting and/or abandoning their own precious children for an idea. They had no intentions of paying me for my time spent looking after them. Oh, and such a rowdy bunch of crying babies they were! My baby girl waited patiently for the sound of my steps climbing up the stairs. A man's steps. A man with big hands to wrap around her tiny body. A man to be proud of his hands. No. He's not coming. That man will never come home. He got a job in Marty's bar selling slices of pizza to wobbly beer drunks.

Under the table work. Minimum wage. In at four. Out at two in the morning. Pizza to drunks. On any Monday Oswego is teeming with drunks. However, with more than a hundred bars, they seem to spread themselves out quite evenly over the city. So each bar might give the impression of having only five to ten hardcore drinkers in Oswego, when in fact, simple multiplication divided by half the college population being drunk at the same time, says that three out of ten Oswego men is stone drunk every single day of his life.

Marty's bar was popular on band nights, when the co-eds came down from the college to get looked at and laid. Then the regular drunks made their customary stop to drink from a plastic cup at Marty's. On

Friday nights his place would fill up fast. Monday's crowd was small. Thin-faced, red-eyed, draft beer sipping pool players all working jobs that they hated enough to come to The Old Grain Elevator afterwards for artificial gladness. This was Marty's awake time. When he walked back and forth from one end of the bar to the other. A lackey kept to his heels, always the most hopeless drunk with just enough personality to keep himself from being committed to Oswego's own, rarely vacant funny house. Earl was Monday's lackey. Earl with the afro. A piss drunk loser of the first rank was Earl. "Earl here, reporting for duty!" Marty paid him in beer, never shunning the great advice his hair-piece half brother gave him years ago. Earl worked with me on weekends in the pizza room. Slobbering drunk was Earl with the afro. Loved Marty's pizza like it was his own child.

"Marty got this secret recipe from an Italian in New York. We're making the best pizza in Oswego, man. Maybe the world."

"What about the Italian in New York?"

"What does he know? Fuck him!"

We'd be lucky to sell one whole pizza on the slow nights. Weekends were a little busy. I didn't have time to read about my precious socialists. I got to watch the girls though—all silently working like mad to make eye contact with the best looking guy they'd allow inside. Such a pathetic, alone thing, a pretty woman in a bar. More sad than the loneliest man who will end up there after a thousand insults from a world that wants him to hang. On Mondays there were no girls besides the attractive bartender Marty hired after many long hours spent searching for the prettiest and most self-loathing girl beer drunk in Oswego. Chances are that he already laid her, or at least received the proper signals for a future laying. I'd come in at four in the afternoon to make the dough. The first and only pizza had to be out by five thirty, so the paying drunk would not go home to his wife's cooking. Marty was a brilliant businessman. Pay lackeys in beer. Pay everyone else under the table. Write up bogus w-2 forms for the one or two self-loathing bartenders who were loyal to Marty for the shallowest of reasons. Calculating Marty. Not so nearly acid nuts Marty after all. Draft beer in plastic cups made ready for whatever comes out in decent weather to hope for the manness or womanness to express itself openly. In a public bar. Put the quarter in the jukebox. "Listen, everyone. This is my song, my personality. This is me singing." Enough beer to wake up to think, "I am a man! Everyone look at me." Marty to collect the dollar bills of their hope and to pretend along with the best of them. To sit at the end of the bar using whatever means necessary to get laid and paid at the same time. And who cares? Not me. I got a job. At the end of the night I walk over to Marty for my money. He wants to be smart and funny.

"I didn't see you work tonight."

"No, I guess we didn't sell any pizza."

"Why should I pay you?"

This exchange will go on for a few more minutes at two in the morning. I stand exhausted, waiting for my forty dollars because I am twenty-four kissing the idiot ass for loathsome money. He'll pay me, finally, in front of his drunk lackey army. They already know about Crazy Marty's "Why pay you?" routine. He knows I'll come back tomorrow, even after humiliation, because I am twenty-four. Why bother holding my baby when I get home? Already, at what should be such a hopeful, promising age, I am ashamed of my man's hands making the best Italian pizza in the world for an illiterate Jewish acid freak. Why should she anticipate my steps up the stairs? They only startle her to wake up and cry.

Calculating Crazy Marty. Not so crazy after all. Crazy men don't chase a skirt strollering a newborn baby. Scumbags do. Especially old scumbags with some money and a furry paunch. A crazy man wouldn't scheme tomorrow and the next day to win what's under a skirt a year or two from now. Sad old men do that all the time. If Marty was full crazy, he would have goosed her right there in the street. No, his sensors were lit up. Mary was young and pretty. That was obvious. She came up to the window of the pizza room so I could give our daughter a kiss good night. But her skirt sent out signals in a secret code known only to men like Marty who live their scam like a religion. She must have had a masochistic aura about her, a scent which Marty picked up easily after so many years of practice. It informed him to bag this girl immediately, at any cost. Experience knew what a loyal pet she would make. Marty could realize this after just one meeting in the street! A pro. A real pro Marty Lieberman. He knew I wasn't satisfying her. Not in the ways she wanted to be satisfied. Mary wanted to be taken care of. Whatever she was going to be, would become manifest through a man. A man was what she wanted. She never wanted herself. She wanted a man. I was just a pizza boy who read books and kept a journal. I knew I was on the outs when I asked for authors for Christmas presents and got a box full of tools instead.

She walked away, and Marty peeked his head around the corner.

"You married?" he asked.

"No. I—"

He was already out the door, practically running to catch up to her.

A couple weeks later I quit Marty. He came into the pizza room for the first time, and looked down at my book lying on the chair.

"What's this?"

"A book about Lenin."

"Oh! So I got commie-pinkos making my pizza!" He picked up the book and threw it against the wall.

Phase two of Marty Lieberman's plan.

Phase one was hiring Mary to bartend after her twenty-four-year old boyfriend quit the pizza business. (Marty never schemed in order. It was part of his crazy.)

Phase three happened right on schedule, according to plan, the moment she received her first penny from Marty.

It's not my intention to write the story of my lost loves. I was twenty-four. Marty was forty. I liked staring off into the changing colors of the sky. Marty liked to poof up an ass with cocaine dust and lick it. I went for walks pretending to be a wild animal in the forest. Marty went searching for antique furniture at garage sales. I could not trust any man who made business his business. Marty was afraid that the FBI would get him. We were different people, Marty and I. Secretly Mary chose Marty. I should have known. Then one day Marty called me up on the phone to ask why I wouldn't let him send a plumber over to fix the hot water heater. I was overcome with rage. Mary thought Marty's actions were perfectly normal. I left Mary that night.

It was July. I carried a paperback *Leaves of Grass* and collected cans to buy peaches and bananas. I slept on the lake rocks. I woke up and bathed in the lake. To be fair to Mary she needed Marty. At the time I needed Walt Whitman and a warm, very deep, blue lake to clean out my mind. My mother was sick. Her intestines got gangrene. She wasn't supposed to live through the night. I walked down to the bar to tell Mary the devastating news. She said she would drive me to the airport in the morning. Just call her for a ride. I went back to my rock bed on the shore to lay awake all night listening to the creeping waves roll my memory over and over.

Up bright and early, trembling. I brought my soap bar into the lake, and after bath, got dressed and found a pay phone to call Mary. What?

Nobody home? At six in the morning? Where is our infant daughter? I didn't know if my mother or my child was dead or alive. Holy God, the bar! Oh, that pig! That slut! Now I'm really mad! A hazy, hot morning jog downtown. By far my longest walk in twenty-four years. "Oh my baby girl. Oh my dear mother! My world is coming to an end!" I got to the bar and Mr. Mule, Marty's full time lackey, was spraying down the previous night's beer and vomit in the street. Marty always took good care of his drunks. I'll give him that. He let Mr. Mule live in one of the unheated rooms upstairs. For drinks Mr. Mule was Marty's morning clean-up man. The alcohol drove him mad. One could barely understand a word he said. Vicious public Tourettes and violent conversations with himself hid quite comfortably behind Marty hiding behind his old money. But I hadn't any reason not to like Mr. Mule. I asked him where might my recently departed girlfriend be. He grumbled and swore something incoherent, then pointed his finger up to the third floor. I took that to be an invitation inside.

Up the dusty stairs I walked in the early morning of my first fear. I knew exactly what waited for me behind the door at the end of the hall. It was left open a crack.

I walked in whispering "Mary?... Mary?"

Oh! There was pretty Mary and Crazy Marty, both stark naked on the floor, sleeping. Marty was snoring. I walked over to Mary and got up close. I smelled the morning booze breath which I had grown accustomed to during those break-up months. Jesus, as much as I saw it coming, I never got myself to believe she'd actually sleep with the sickly bastard. But there he was, naked and heavy, lying beside my daughter's mother, with his white slime lips, dreaming his happy-crazy dreams.

I walked over to Marty and squatted down beside his penis. I scanned the room. In the corner an oozi leaned up against the wall. "Just a prop for the scam," I said to myself. "Otherwise the door wouldn't be open and the gun would be within his reach." How clear and open was my mind. I saw into my future. Marty's penis told my fortune. I felt a peace and calmness that surprised me. I was not upset in the least. Not about Marty anyway. I took more time to study my surroundings.

Hundreds of dollar bills were scattered about the room. I imagined he set that crazy up in his mind a few hours earlier, while Mary downed the plastic cup shots he lined up for her. The windows were filthy. Every other one had a neon beer sign. The floor was sticky and stunk from old booze. The furniture consisted of an old couch and a small bar in the corner, with a few stools from downstairs set before it. A bag of cocaine lay next to Marty's head. I picked up a dollar bill and covered his penis with it. Then I stood up and walked over to Mary's side of the floor. I brought my face right up close and stared into her eyes to wake her up. She woke up. She jumped up, calling out, "Oh my God! Oh my God! Oh my God!" while fumbling around for her glasses. And I laughed a loud laugh almost hoping Marty could wake up to see how well I was taking his scam. My first question was a presage of many future last words I would have with Mary. "Where the hell is my daughter?" I picked her up by the shoulders and carried her to the toilet. "Where is my daughter?" I was loud with tears and rage. I knew that Marty was opening and closing his eyes to the scene. No man could have slept naked through my spasm. He was calculating, that Marty. Damn did he know when to keep his gingivitis closed to the world! Play possum. Very important rule to follow while floating naked in the pool of another man's agony!

But it's good to keep the past in the past. Start believing in these tricky mornings before Easter and one is likely to let too much out at once. That would be devastating. My wife and I just returned from the best walk of our lives. April has finally arrived with its bright blue sky of original energy. We are funny people, my wife and I. Happy. We laughed out loud on our walk along the river. Laughed about Marty after he drove by in his SUV staring at us. The brightest day of the year, this fifth of April. She's twenty-seven now with an easy laugh and eyes that wander like those of a sleepy cat. Who knows who she is at midnight when her eyes meet mine and we travel to the land of sleep with the baby in the middle? She's a beautiful girl who makes me laugh. That's what I know, and that is enough for me. How lucky I am to have her love! We revel in our shared joy. We congratulate ourselves often for being so smart. How many husbands and wives are out walking with their babies this fine April day? It's not a weekend. So it is true that most good folks have abandoned their families to amass a fortune. A few young families show themselves. Mostly Oswego's welfare dressed up in their finest Starter jackets and sixty dollar pair of sneakers. They could even look respectable, if not hunched over so. They are of a lower order. In Oswego's human junkyard we stroll down from the mountain-top like royalty.

During the course of our walk we spy Marty three more times. Is it him or his SUV that's so curious about us? My wife laughs while telling her own Marty story. She's laughing but she also sees right through him, and I can tell that it makes her a little angry. "Marty is thoroughly manipulative," she says. "He works girls over with shameless attention until they finally give in. He tried it once with me, remember? I told you about the Japanese lamp he wanted me to copy. That was going to be my summer job. I was psyched! Then he showed up at my mother's house and asked if I was ready to go to New York. Whacko! I told him before that I wouldn't go. He took me to Syracuse once before that, picked out music I liked and bought a hundred dollar bottle of wine. Said we'd have to finish it that night. I told him no, but he was fast with a back-up plan. He said the least I could do was have dinner with him at his restaurant. We could talk about the lamp. What a laugh! But the lamp. I really wanted to start work on it. On the way back to Oswego he began to complain about the helicopters following us... Whoa. At first I thought he was kidding. That he was just trying to make me laugh. He kept it up though until I realized he was serious. Okay whacko, let me out of the truck."

"He wasn't serious." I said. Then I offered her my theory about Marty Lieberman. How remarkably similar was hers and Mary's story. Right down to the hundred dollar bottle of wine.

"Young girls are vulnerable," she agreed. "He has a perfect seat at the bar to seek out his prey."

"Exactly," I said. "But how did you meet him?"

"My car broke down on Route 481. He and that pervert... Ah you know the one I'm talking about. The guy who tried to sell his sex movies around town. The hairy pig. Mac Davis' cousin. I forgot his name.. Anyway, the two of them stopped when they got a look at me standing against my car. I must have been as crazy as Marty for letting those drooling old men drive me home. That was one of the few bad decisions I ever made in my life. But that's how I met Marty Lieberman. Soon after that I swear he started to follow me around town. He was everywhere I was. He'd come to the restaurant to watch me work. He'd stop in alone and sit at the bar looking at me. He knew exactly when to change the subject. He noticed that I was getting uncomfortable. So he began to talk about the lamp. Just the lamp. As if he thought I would just ignore the fact that he was watching my ass for the past three hours!"

"But you didn't sleep with him, did you dear one?"

She laughed. "Yea in his dreams. He is so repulsive!"

Yes, it is a new and glorious April morning when I can see Marty's SUV drive by with his big head turned to look at me, and not feel a rage unsettling my stomach. I am lucky to have a wife who also knows that Marty is a manipulative fake. It must drive Marty even more nutty to see us together out walking. Poetic justice in my favor.

Great walk. Early spring's big tease. I say though, Marty stayed in my life much too long after I caught him and Mary in bed with the dollar bills and cocaine. Not long after my absence of love with Amy, I decided to go back to Mary. She was changed. She gave Marty a baby boy—something he wanted and was determined to have. I swear the boy was just phase four of Marty's plan to get girls. *Get a small child.* As far as I know, he still hasn't learned how to care for him. He would have thrown him away, like garbage if it wasn't for me. I asked Mary to move in. That got his attention. Then I asked her to marry me. That made Marty simply furious. He took Mary to court. He beat her up a couple times. He would pull the SUV up to our apartment building, beep the horn incessantly, and yell out the window, "Hey slut bag! Hey witch-bitch, give me my son!" Mary would turn to me while getting the boy ready, saying, "Now don't do anything Ron. Don't you see? He's trying to get you to flip. If you raise a hand to him and he calls the police, it's your word against his, and he's got Mr. Mitchum's crooked fingers into everything."

Going to court made Mary crazy. It made me crazy. Marty, who was already very crazy, became a regular reality in my life. Several times I would watch helplessly from the window of our apartment while Marty argued with Mary in his SUV. Actually, I think she began to like it. Once when I got home from work, she was standing at the top of the stairs holding some neatly ironed Oxford shirts. "What are those?" I asked. "I'm doing Marty's laundry for him. He's coming over to pick it up."

For a while she stubbornly kept her job at his bar. He told Mary he needed her. She would draw out fancy advertisements for him after our dinner of eggplant parmesan with the kids. We would be sitting on the couch casually discussing lawyers and court, while she concentrated on her pen and ink pattern that needed to go to press by morning. Marty drilled his manipulative screw deep into poor Mary. She was locked into his crazy power, becoming obsessed with Marty's negativity, as if she actually yearned for his abuse. Many times I suggested that we leave the country, or the state at least, to make Marty weaker in a court without the Mitchum's power to assuage a judge. Nothing doing. She was determined to lose her boy in the Oswego County Court, well known for its illegal promises and payoffs. Oh well. The masochist found her sadist. To this day she still accepts his abuse regularly. He gives it to her via the boy's innocent mouth. Marty tells his boy that Mommy is a whore. "Daddy says you're a whore Mommy." And she still allows the kid to visit him. Marty sure knows how to pick his women.

Poetic justice. An incredible learning experience in humility. I went back with Mary, no matter how wrong I was in doing so, to make things right for our daughter. Mary came to visit me at work one day during the summer of our reacquaintance. I leaned over to give her a kiss, and she turned away to look at Marty's bar across the river. "Are you serious?" I asked. "He's well over six hundred yards away. And we're sitting under a tree with thick August leaves. Anyway, why the hell do you care if he's looking at us?"

"I know he can see. He's probably filming us right now."

I put up with Marty and Mary's nutty behavior for about a year. I have always been the wiser for persisting in my folly. People should not learn from their mistakes. At least not the first time. I say if you think you've done something wrong, do it again just to make sure. Marty isn't the only crazy duck in Oswego. He just happens to be the loudest.

A final thought from the mealy-mouth to the illiterate, bastard sitting all alone in a bar along the river...

You're getting old you dumb fuck. You better make some more money fast. Senior Mitchum will soon be dead. I believe Senior Lieberman is already dead, and Mrs. Lieberman too, who was your last hope—I think she's dead. Junior Mitchum is bound to hang himself someday. So you can't depend on him. Where is this going to leave poor Marty Lieberman? You're getting older Marty. Even the most retarded little girls won't touch it unless you got a fortune to share. Invest your money. Start a trust. Or else, start sweeping up like Mr. Mule at your own bar. You better watch out—I might secretly persuade the new judge to sign your commitment papers. You crazy aging idiot! The acid buddies of the seventies all got their SUV's too. Only difference is they got little girls coming of age and old wives who are disgusted by your presence. They'll sign the papers. The coke sniffing girl-men that you partied with all through the eighties? Embarrassed! Caught red-handed pretending to be rock stars like you Marty. Anyway, most of them are into politics now, and have their own little girls to worry about. Many of their constituents are the old mothers who hate you with a passion. The effeminate men and their wives will sign. What about your favorite drunks? Your devoted lackeys? Where are they if you don't have any money? You had better start saving Marty. No amount of crazy can keep you from Mental Health on the hill, or the more modern facilities in Syracuse where they possess an official okay from the government to use electronic machines on your brain. Or perhaps one day the FBI, the CIA, or the IRS will actually be following you. Maybe they'll be looking for some back taxes or a fifteen year old girl buried in your basement. "Vay have vays of getting view to talk." As soon as Mr. Mitchum kicks, his wife's gonna take you out for zucchini. She's got a few papers you need to sign. Look left, look right. Call Earl, Matt, Monty, call every red-eyed loser in Oswego. Without a bar, without drugs, without money, you got nothing. You might have a little boy to wash your face and wipe your ass when you lose control of your faculties, if you weren't such a manipulative, selfish, nutfuck now. It would also help if you knew how to love.

Hardy ha-ha-ha.

Love. Marty, you and I go way back. Do you remember this piece of loving advice you gave the boy when he was three years old playing with trucks?

"Hey boy, remember this if you remember anything. Women are good for only one thing."

"What Daddy?"

"Blow-jobs. Remember that. Blow-jobs. Just blow-jobs."

And your loyal circle of liver-waste lackeys laughed. You laughed. Even I laughed, but not in the manner you would expect me to laugh. Did the boy laugh? No, I don't think so. He rolled his eyes. He didn't know what you meant. He shrugged his shoulders and rolled his eyes, and pushed his backhoe through the used pile of plastic cups. He didn't laugh. He got another memory of his Dad named Marty who was crazy and could not love him.

Sign Mrs. Mitchum's papers Marty. They're for your own good. Then follow her up the stairs to the roof. There's a helicopter waiting. Lick this sheet of acid here. Step into the chopper. It's going to take you away. "Are we going to Halifax?" you ask the pilot. "Because I want to go to Halifax. Gimme, gimme, gimme! I want to go now!"

The pilot turns around, takes off his head gear and grins his crooked teeth grin. "Guess who Marty? Didn't think I'd get my turn, did you, you dirty old man?" And I laugh the wild, exaggerated laugh I always wanted to laugh while I fly crazy Marty over my calm ocean.

I want to write about Oswego's physical beauty. The lake, the river, the trees—there's even a teahouse in someone's backyard. Oswego is a beautiful place to live, *in summer*. Just around the bend are some cheerful thoughts about the flora and fauna of my fair city. However, presently I am unable to write about the grackle snapping at the raindrops without including wet sheets of plastic wrap, a beer can, and a torn piece of stinky milk carton... I would like to wait until the ugly wears away completely before I attempt to write about the real beauty Oswego hasn't destroyed yet. By July most of man's winter litter is sufficiently hidden by things that actually thrive being seen alive. Why waste words writing about a lake if the lake smells like dead worms? Why sit through an afternoon of fog to watch a river flow gray and muddy when you know at its end swirl a hundred small pools of floating garbage?

There's a book in print entitled *Paddle-to-the-Sea*. Once I took it out of the children's library to read to my daughter. Recently I bought it for myself to call back some forgotten or non-existent wonder of my childhood. Paddle is a carved wooden indian sitting in a birch-bark canoe. A Canadian boy made him and set him atop a mountain of snow. The snow melted into a stream, the stream into a river, and the river into Lake Superior. That spring, Paddle set out to have many adventures, caught up in the zig-zag currents of the Great Lakes. This book expresses the true, innocent goodness of man coexisting with the hardy rough beauty of nature. With cheerful determination they work together for as long as it takes Paddle to get to France.

Paddle-to-the-Sea was published in the 1940s, before science got devilishly curious enough to ruin our lives with its half-life testings. The author is proud of men and their machines. The moose and bear congratulate the tanner and commercial fisherman—Here is a book about the state of the Great Lakes as seen through the eyes of a healthy mind seventy years ago. It's like reading an alien's description of his planet of plenty.

A very clean book. I suggest that all Great Lake locals read it and wonder why a man can no longer make his living on the lake's bounty beneath. Set the book down. Take a walk to the lake. Stand on the edge of the bluff. Sit on a large flat stone. Look out to the sea. Since 1950 man has managed to give all the fish cancer.

Seventy years have passed. Duluth, Detroit, Chicago, Oswego. Death to the largest fresh water lake chain in the world. Deep delicious water teeming with billions and billions of creatures. Every single living thing breathing the water that rolls over your toes, was poisoned for the next twenty thousand years so mankind could have its choice of laundry detergent.

Now it remains a surface visual beauty that I promise to write about once the weather improves. "Fish at your own risk," the government tells the man. "Salmon not good for nursing mothers. Neurological disorders to the newborn. Child grows up wanting to eat carcinogenic fish." Yet how regularly every season the fools line up along the river-bank for their catch to bring home. Bad time of year for me to take my walks down there. Men from New Jersey drive up to Oswego by the truck-load to catch horny salmon. One could dangle a rubber girl salmon five feet above the water and catch leaping fish all day long. No. These misogynistic sportsmen would rather stand together in the river with the best equipment fishing magazines can offer. I could live for a year on what one of these guys paid for his gear. He could buy twenty years' supply of unmirexed, farm-raised salmon if he'd sell that goofy truck he loves more than his own wife, wearing nothing besides rubber thigh-high boots in his fishy dreams.

A walk along the river in November rekindles my cyclic winter bitterness. For now let us be overjoyed in the knowledge that our parents and grandparents poisoned an entire lake and river in two generations. Rejoice in the present acid elimination of all Adirondack fish! Neighbors and friends, let's put our hands together and pray to God for the strength we need to kill every swimming underwater thing in existence. First the sissy Canadian fish. Then those oily Mexican fish. I got enough boxes of All Tempacheer to devastate Lake Chapala in a day! Stand together my friends. We need to buy all the plastic we can stuff into our homes at once. More stuff we cannot eat. More factories. More oil. Drill in sensitive areas. Down two miles, three miles, down a thousand miles, why not? Suck out a trillion gallons into the sea! More hazardous materials. More radiation poured into steal mesh balls and rolled into a coral reef. More nuclear testing. A lot more. Blow the fish sky high! Indiscriminately launch our entire arsenal on the oceans of the planet. I want proof that every swimming thing is floating dead by next week. Hurry up. There's so little time. Someone quick, get down there to Florida. Poison that pompous pricey pompano. You, to the sharks! You to the flounders. I don't care how you do it; I just want every fish dead by this time next week. Stock your chlorinated pool with a thousand guppies and goldfish. Everyone piss in the backyard stream. Pump anthrax off the shores of Newfoundland, ignite an oil rig—more mercury, aluminum, liquid copper to melt all the fish brains in the South Pacific...

Who would have guessed that the wrath of God was going to begin the moment man morphed from monkey? It is so clear to me that we are now in control of our own demise. Eager to be created to begin destroying. How easy to forget what we have been born to do. We are sent reminders of the encircling doom. Yesterday God sent a memo through the mail. Just another one of his pocket blueprints of destruction. Open up to page 3 in your *Oswego County Emergency Planning and You* booklet. Look at that face. Ring a bell? Isn't he one of the antichrist's smiling helpers? Mr. Almustead, Chairman of the Board. The most comfortable man in Oswego. He owns a couple classic cars, a pretty wife, and a pretty little camp set up along the Salmon River. He looks happy and content being a helper to the mass murder of you and the fish. He fries the salmon fresh out of the river. You can see for yourself the tumors pushing out from his neck skin. He sure knows how to groom himself for a snapshot before the blood-dripping human organs hit the fan.

Turn the page, and another happy helper, holding a pointer against a blackboard, looks like he's counting out loud the number of fish he can kill in a day. There is even a list of radio stations that one can tune in to to find out the exact time the earth will begin screaming. On page six some jolly firemen helpers get ready to release more radiation into the atmosphere. More black and white photos showing exactly where the wrath will be unleashed in this region. "In the event of a natural or man-made disaster, some residents may need special attention because of their physical impairments or transportation problems. Please fill out and mail the following card so we can make it look now like we won't be laughing later, as you struggle in your lameness to get to the designated evacuation site. Wait all day if you like, crippled Sally. That bus ain't gonna come. You can wait until the sky turns puke green and you cough your body up into a cloud of dust. Trust us. No bus is coming."

Oswegonians must think "Chernobyl" means "go out and play darts 'til a quarter to three". Ask the first five pot-bellied men slurping bacon fat at the Ritz Diner where they earn the kind of money that can afford an omelet a day for the rest of their lives. Three out of five will say, "I work out at the plant." The plant. The plant. It pays well. If they didn't have the plant to pay well, every man with his cup of coffee would be a dishwasher or a janitor mopping floors. If the plant wasn't there for eighty grand a year, Oswego might improve itself into a proud American hometown. Unfortunately today townie pride remains whatever Ford or Chevy built tough this year. Security guards making eighty thousand dollars on fire watch? What is fire watch? You sit in a room and if it catches on fire, you run screaming out of the room. What if a van load of determined jihadists break through security (which they could do with balloons if they wanted to), and jog straight into the reactor core? They will confront the janitor, my chef from the restaurant. He's down on his hands and knees waxing tile while talking on his cell phone to Ron Throop, the ex-cook/writer of ill repute. The chef was not qualified to wipe down walls in a reactor core. He applied anyway, after being fired at the restaurant for keeping a loaded gun in the file cabinet. "What?" asked the boss. "I got Wyatt Earp to braise my chickens?" He called up my chef and told him to 86 the gun and himself from the premises. My chef had a temper tantrum but thank God he didn't shoot anyone. Within two weeks the plant hired him to wash the walls of the reactor core. Presently he's on a six week stint for eight grand.

That's a lot of money for an itchin' trigger finger to pick an ass with all day long. It's hush money. So many of us got our dirty fingers on it, that it's bound to be respected. The chef mops walls and wipes floors. What do you think the smiling CEO antichrist with the fat neck makes? A million maybe? I don't know for sure, but it's enough to sedate the obese electrician who just got hired at the power plant. He'll make twenty thousand during the next six weeks. That is cash for darts and beer on Wednesday nights and a custom built snowmobile to breeze through the powder this winter, even if his autistic kid drinks a gallon of lake water a day and miraculously grows a third hand.

Oswego County has the second highest cancer rate in the state. The number one county was once the world's leading producer of asbestos. Why should that matter to anyone as long as they're getting their fair share? Always death by long illness to end a poorly-lived life. A hot dog and beer benefit to help pay the exorbitant sums the doctors demand to care for another human being. And not a soul is getting angry (besides the cancer patient, maybe). We know what carcinogens are. It's like knowing the murderer personally. Yet who's got the big salt potato balls to deliver the antichrist's ears to the benefit? Impossible. The antichrist is a standing army of every one of us, eating the "best grilled chicken we ever had!"

What is cancer? Are we too afraid to demand the truth? "Ah, Dick's got cancer." Then the funeral. Then everyone back to work. The eulogy was short and sweet because Dick's best friend was working the shutdown at the power plant. If he missed just one more day, he'd have to go on unemployment and make only four hundred a week. Dick is dead and the crow caws. No one thinks Dick's best friend is septic-sludge, because they know that Dick would have done the same. What a fool Dick's friend would be to take such a drastic cut in pay just for mourning. A waste of time. That won't bring Dick back. Anyway, the best friend has two other mouths to feed and raise insanely. Go back to work, Dick's best friend. You have already replaced Dick. We understand. We are exactly the same. Anyway, in a lifetime, what did Dick give? Dick gave to Dick and Dick got cancer. Those who loved him had a benefit. Everyone gobbled up hot dogs. No one besides me felt sorry for the pig. I know there are three stations set up for the proper processing of a dead pig. You need ten clean sheets for the blood alone. What do you do with a pig's freshly slaughtered heart? Let it bleed.

And then?

Eat the hot dog. Eat the bun. Eat the ketchup, the mustard, the gun. Eat the car, eat the wallet, eat the kid's new clothes, eat the meat, all the meat, eat anything that grows. Eat the earth, the sky, eat the other guy. Eat motor oil, and gunk if it's good, or potatoes, eat more potatoes. Eat four things on a plate, no, five—eat your mate, eat the stars, eat a book about cars. Eat cancer. Eat your friend who's got cancer. Eat the cancer before the cancer. Eat cancer's cancer. Eat all morals for dessert. Eat more, never less, and never ever gobble up the middle best.

Cancer is you and me. Childhood cancer? Unexplainable? Cruel? Yes! It scares the bleeding stools out of me, too. I love. I am no different from you. But admitting dying children into a Ronald McDonald House is insane. Do you know what Ronald does to cows? Have you any idea? And you're sending children into his giggling grease trap? Don't make your child crazy and sick because you allow that clown's CEO to bulldoze dead cows into a gigantic cow chipper. We are so desensitized that I feel silly and beyond naive just writing this down. "They're just cows," I am thinking. It's not vegetarianism I am asking for. It is wisdom-ism. Wasn't it Eisenhower who warned us about the malignant growth of the Industrial Guilt Complex? How can a man close his eyes to the way in which his food is prepared, and open them, just briefly, while his baby girl dies of cancer? His eyes will close in a silent agony after she is gone. Opened to drive to and from work, or to eat the saltiest carcinogens off the aluminum tray a lá Stoeffer or Swanson. He'll want to hate himself for her untimely death. Why? When we all know that Ronald McDonald is the most guilty one. If Dad could see, and was not afraid of seeing, he would publicly accuse the clown of child murder. Tobacco companies are liable? Then so are clowns who sell us poison to eat. Ronald stripped her land to raise cows for slaughter. How does that give a little girl cancer? Look for yourself. They keep adding another billion sold onto that sign. I know the creator takes five hundred of ours for every million of theirs. Flesh-eaters buying their meat from a clown. Top of the food chain? Absolutely not. Cancer rots our flesh. It chews our meat. It purrs with satisfaction, then settles down to savor the delicacy of our organs for dessert. Cancer is king and we are its servants.

Now, how to avoid this hungry predator...

Don't buy a Big Mac. Do as the Buddhists, who have known all along that cancer is a stupid, impressionable beast. Lay off the meat! There is a balance, whether we like it or not. One cannot eat up all the non-human death, and not get it back eventually. All she needed was to be born into excellent loving care. What is the best that you can give? Right now. Without waiting for the invisible scientist to tell you. The new wildness is human indifference. Clown apathy. The persistent hum of mellow heartbeats from delusional humanity. Its motto? To kill and not suffer.

"Eat your burger honey. A pothead in Oklahoma works very hard pushing dead cows into a grinder."

"Daddy, I don't want to eat the happy cow."

"You eat it right now, missy, or no Hot Apple Pie for you! What, did you expect me to do everything I do, and prepare your dinner too?" Fast food should be emergency food only. The rancher leaves an ax against a fence post along the highway. The children are weak from hunger on the drive back from Fort Lauderdale. It's okay. Dad can get out of the car, take the ax, chop off a piece of the cow, and leave a twenty dollar bill under the rancher's bleeding ax. Otherwise it's more cancer at McDonald's. And some more at Burger King, since their CEO was not crafty enough to set up a charity house in the name of their ridiculously dangerous, cancer-wielding mascot.

I will set the record straight. The death mess is everywhere, and unavoidable until we avoid it. Ronald McDonald is just one evil clown. There are more. The Burger King and Wendy, the Pippy-Longstocking look-alike. Any fast food cancer hole that markets its death-in-a-wrapper to children under ninety. In fact, don't eat any place where profit is the first concern. These clowns play Russian roulette with our children because we invite them to. Can you slaughter six thousand cattle a day? If you're a multi-millionaire you can. Or if you are a pothead in Oklahoma, you'll bulldoze the dead heap for the promise of more pot and one kickass wage. The clown will do almost anything to get them to digest his cancer. Shall we continue until the moon crashes into us out of disgust? Are we feeling alive? Sometimes I feel like I am writing invisible letters to stones. Ronald lives in McDonaldland with the Hamburglar, the Grimace, the goblins, and a horror-house stuffed with a million other fast food monsters. They're on the take. Their hush money infects humanity. Corporate executives in private jets have cocktails while discussing the clown's next funny television commercial.

"Hey, how about this: Ronald can take the Grimace by his purple flabby head skin and bury his nose into the dirt of a child's grave. All of the sudden like, the Hamburglar pops out of the ground, juggling a cow's vial organs."

"That's not funny Ray."

"No, but it's true, ain't it boys?"

"Yea, you got us there. Here's to you Ray!"

And the happy executives toast each other's greed while flying off on their mission to destroy faster than the creator creates.

Never has life been this ready to poop out. Is this not the age of doom? There isn't an exact hour and minute to certify my prediction of the end. I'm not sure how exactly we will get there. I know Jesus won't come. If he was the least bit interested, the human race would become extinct the moment he saw three rubber tires left in a swamp. But we are finished, of that I am certain. The age of doom can last until the next millennium. Or it can begin the same moment the last poet gets killed by a hit and run grapefruit truck out in the middle of nowhere. Nowhere is where I like to go witness man's life falling apart. Even in the boonies it is apparent that Americans are not interested in the beauty and freedom of life. The police will want to make a report: "Looks like a drunk got hit by a grapefruit truck, Sam. Oh my Lord in heaven Sam, look at the sky! Run!"

But it's not Jesus and a biblical Armageddon. It's a nuclear bomb from China finishing off the day's doom. Early this morning they got the big cities. At lunch all the suburbs and outlying school districts. By twilight every farmer and his cow. Tonight when the moon is high and those lucky few left are having a very hard time falling asleep, great China will blow the final death wind over our land to erase all flora and fauna, and the few humans still breathing. And why not? A walk in the country should never ever stumble upon a blue heron standing on a tire behind a Winnie-the-Pooh mailbox. But it does. And uglies like that must be a harbinger of doom. A rusty trailer with a fierce dog on a chain. A line of broken down cars, taken apart for parts to make one loud, big ugly car. Litter par excellence. A refuse ranch. You know the scene. Our noble country dwellers. Living away from the madness of civilization to watch television programming caught from a satellite dish big enough to swim in, make country crafts with glue guns, and never to play serotonin-swelling games with their neighbors. The husbands work in Fulton or Oswego. The wives believe in God and Winnie-the-Pooh. China will clean up the mess if we're not going to.

There is no freedom in America. There is posted property and cantankerous farmers. I could not build a Buddhist temple in Meridian, N.Y. The farmer boys with their manure bombs would terrorize me night after night. Call the police? You know you're kidding. The cops are even more crooked in the country, where nobody would see even if they were looking. Freedom in America is a freedom to fear, never complain, and be extremely careful about what we say to our neighbors. It's their word against yours. And if you happen to be one who yearns for freedom, you will be found guilty always, since it is the opposite of freedom which represents the law. So I got the temple finished last Tuesday. That night a group of farmers stopped by the well looking for my cows.

"You milkin', plowin', or selling meat?" asked the head farmer.

"No, nothing like that. Just a small garden for my family and an hour before bedtime to meditate."

"Where's your dog?"

"Don't have one."

"Tractor?"

"Nope. Got a bicycle though."

"You plan on collecting broken down cars to take apart, part by part?"

"No, actually, I am planning a Japanese garden, and a teahouse by the stream. I'll have my hands full cleaning up the mess the last tenants left. What are all these rubber tires I see everywhere?"

"We put 'em there."

"You're going to terrorize my life aren't you?"

"Yes."

And that is why Buddhism will never flourish in Upstate New York. Christianity rules the roost here. In fact, all the farmers are getting ready for the big Easter celebration this Sunday. Time for farmer Jim to wet down the head and join the folks dressed in his finest church clothes. There can be twenty in a room before dinner, each with his own robin to peck out the eyes, and not a meaningful peep out of any of them. The dead have risen. That should scare the crap out of Farmer Jim. Make him leap from his chair, run screaming out the door, and hop up and down like a monkey on the new grass. But no. Just strained conversation had over a salty pig butt with all the trimmings. Jim is the first to talk—a new tractor, the weather, or maybe a television show he saw last Thursdee on NBC about five new lawyers fresh out of law school. He sat down with his cow shit smell to view it with the wife and kids. The kids didn't want to watch the lawyer show. The Grammys were on and Junior's favorite downtown, cop shootin', coke sniffing rap murderer was nominated for best new video for his song entitled, "Watch Charlie Cut Up Copper." Welcome to America, Christ. Easter time. Glad you have risen. No one cares. It doesn't matter what form you take, they ain't looking for you. Anyway, if this is the mess you're watching over, then by Christ, you're one of them and will never convince me of my salvation. What a careless little American boy God you are, driving the speeding white car full of drunk farmer boys all over the county. Out hunting for poets taking twilight walks through the American wasteland. You find one, stop the car, and get out. You walk over to him hiding a bat behind your back. You mock him. The other boys push him around. Then you start to get mad at your own made-up images of him. You dance around his frightened body, poking him with your finger, and spitting with anger. Suddenly you fly into a rage and crack open his skull with your bat. "Drag him over to the bog, boys. Bury him in the sludge!"

What is our future? What would you call an age of doom if this is not? I will offer a random current event to help the reader understand the hypocrisy of Easter and the lie it means to be a United States Citizen. This is not separation of church and state. This is the total inclusion of church in state. Not all churches though. Just the American Christian church. Something disguised. No registered denomination. No deacon. No bishop. No rabbi. No priest. Not Catholic. Not Protestant. Not Orthodox. Not European. Not the African church of white rolly-polly missionaries sent from Arkansas and Tennessee to teach jolly Africans how to despair. This is the American Church of Nuclear Holocaust with Jimmy Swaggart as President. All citizens must participate like members of the KKK. Only the falsely accused, white lady rapin' negro is everyone of us. We're the ignorant self-righteous terrorists too, hiding our heads with hoods, and stalking the countryside to bash in any face that doesn't look like ours. The President supports the wrath of God, wholeheartedly. He is His messenger, and will announce it with glee over the radio, through the TV, into our cars and our homes. The situation is hopeless. We are helpless. You don't believe me. Write a letter to the President to tell him you are not happy and that you would like to punch him in the nose. Wait a few weeks, and see who stops by. Oh look, men with sunglasses and guns. Now tell me you're not helpless!

One man is nothing. All men must accept their small helplessness.

Those who do not are marginalized for life. Freedom in America? I think this will be the last generation to perpetuate that fat lie. The following is a true story about a current event in man's embarrassing and very dangerous existence:

An American Navy spy plane was nicked by a Chinese patrol plane in mid-air. The Navy spy plane was forced to make an emergency landing on Chinese territory. There are over one billion human beings breathing in China. There were twenty-eight American spies in the spy plane spying on China. They got caught spying with American tax money, and not one American knew about the American spy plane spying on China.

Spying on China. Spying on China. Spying on China. Is that enough? Are you sure? Okay. Concentrate really hard. Try to remember that an American spy plane was spying on China.

President Swaggart was notified over the intercom while wiping up after his toilet. He's a sucker for Texmex cooking. Chimichangas and lard cakes for breakfast. Consequently, the first duty for all Secret Service jobs is to scout out any unknown perimeters for the nearest bathroom. It must be secured in the event of an emergency.

President Swaggart has never been to China. He remembers when his Daddy used to call them the "little Chinese". They are not little. With over a billion strong, even if they were two feet tall, they'd still be bigger than America. Who are they? Nobody knows. President Swaggart doesn't know. Not even his specialist on Chinese culture knows. And he's third generation Japanese! No one will know China until China blows her black cloud over America. Then everybody will know China.

Publicly the President is mad at China today because Chinese officials boarded the broken spy plane and won't turn over the spies to the American embassy. Personally, Mr. President was in the throes of diarrhea at the time and could care less about the little Chinese, even if their police were torturing the twenty-eight paid killers. However, his aides, all of whom are without mommies and daddies who love them, told the President to make a public announcement denouncing China for their mishandling of "the situation". Bad China. Very bad China. A serious matter. Something better be done about it soon, or the President might gobble up another oily Enchilada.

Who is this idiot we hire? Are we going to let him threaten the Chinese nation of a billion and more because they want to deal with the paid killers in their own way? Was it last year when America had the most difficult time giving back to Cuba the boy who was stolen from his father? Little Cuba had no say, because their bombs weren't big enough. Now Mr. President and his aides are going to threaten my existence because twenty-eight paid killers got caught peeping their perverted equipment into other people's business. If anyone poked their dirty face in front of my window, I'd punch my hand through the glass, pull him into my home by his hair, and beat to a pulp the bloody face lying on my floor.

Who are these consultants and aids American voters do not hire? Why do we trust these faceless pushers who instruct our idiot President? Whose money supports them? During an election, neither candidate will talk about the huge fortune to be spent on the President's helpers—the veritable army of lobbyists hired to act as his brain. We allow it. We elect one man to have five hundred faceless people make life and death decisions in his name. We don't know China. We don't know America. A man can be alone with his wife and baby, telling the baby in baby talk that "bunny day" is coming. That a happy bunny will bring Easter presents and hopefully a sunny day for the American President to flush his toilet, walk out into the West Wing and begin the chain reaction leading to all out nuclear annihilation. That means a man picked up his laughing baby and both were melted in the time it took the President's brain to realize that he just shit his pants. A spy plane got caught spying and twenty-eight paid killers got the whole world destroyed because, after the final analysis, they just wanted to snuggle up next to their mommies. I say to the Chinese government— No, I won't say that. It is not my intention to be political. I want the truth so I can be free to pick up my baby and tell her that it's "bunny day". And then I want the morning to come and Peter Cottontail to hop out of the new spring forest like he used to before nuclear weapons. Like long ago, when Easter dinner came, and the excitement at the table was never Jesus, but talk about the spy plane that went down in the South China Sea. War with China could be heroic without nuclear weapons. One of ours to every five of theirs. Bodies to fall apart, piece by piece; they'll get charred and eaten by worms—but that's okay if those who die volunteered their lives for a paycheck. Death is always a fair and proper end for the man who volunteers to kill another man. This Easter after the ham, the farmer will talk about a new TV show. Lawyers fresh out of law school. If he didn't talk about TV, he would have to think on how he gave up the earth and his children for some hush money and a new tractor. He knows Jesus ain't coming. There is no Jesus, no Easter bunny, no nothing but a radio to tell him he better kiss his ass goodbye if the President has a bad shit that day. If his father could not stop nuclear proliferation, how was he going to? Would he have to be a hero to his own sons? No. He will help kill his sons. Grandsons too. Great grandsons. "Thanks for the chocolate bunny Dad. Now let the skies light up and melt me and my baby sister."

Doesn't it feel sunny sublime this spring morning, knowing that we're all just a big bunch of dumb slaves to the American lie? And it's only a matter of time before we get to watch our babies burn up to ash instantaneously. Will we do anything to stop that horror in the gut of the death wielders? Not a lick, I'm afraid. Pass the ambrosia.

And have a Hoppy Easter!

Woke up to the first thunder and lightning of spring! The flash in the windows. The roll of the thunder. All is perfect. The cycle never screws up!

Is it Franklin Roosevelt's birthday, or deathday? How do I know of either? Why should I know? "Because the brain is the bane of mainkaind." Oh well, not to worry my pretty face about it. After the sun falls up, we'll get the green grass. Men are silly. It might take the small fear I have for my own life during a thunder and lightning storm, to appreciate the good I got. I am in love, and there is evil. But it is not my evil, and I don't need to expose the evil in order for me to love.

So how come these little fear jolts?

Our cats leap up onto the pillow and purr their fear up close to my ear. They need to be reassured that the master is still the master. Beany the dog fell down the stairs last month. Now I must carefully coax him down from the very top stair. He stands looking straight ahead while I turn in circles. After each turn I expect him to follow me down. He might fake it with a flinch, but no, it will take a while. Sometimes as many as twenty turns—first thing in the morning, in the dark. I am a very patient man.

There is much to love in Oswego if a man is not afraid. Emotions are very disguised here. Tears are difficult. Wailing is a no-no, even if your best friend dies of cancer. It's like this everywhere. The seasons pass with little or no notice. I cannot easily hide the joy of my pantheism, especially during this drastic change of season. Winter to spring? It's like being alone an entire lifetime and then having a baby to love. I over elaborate in the fall, when life is at its most vulnerable and wild.

Pantheism. Life in all things. But humans will put a negative sign at the end, expressed as an "ism", to finalize their disregard of life, and never to show their tears. All things have spirit. Buddhists call it sentience, but limit themselves to what they believe are living things. All things are alive. Yes, even rock—no matter what the human scientist says. I am the fool to block the scientist. I am what keeps him honest and working overtime. The tree, the rock, the blade of grass, a grain of sand. I say that everything is alive and thinking. Why not? And what's the difference if I am wrong? Will it stop us from polluting and killing? Absolutely not. Believe in the rock with a spirit. Why? Because I told you to, Mr. Rock!

The wonderful thing about being a fool is the freedom to express the most profound truths and embarrassing wrong information in the same sentence without damaging his integrity. A fool is a fool. There's no going up or down. The fool can say, "The tree is a squirrel," and be absolutely correct, provided he expresses himself not to other men, but to the 74 trillion other living beings occupying the big planet we know so little about.

Nobody knows. Each man could very well be alone, and every one and every thing else a dream. Our chemistry is completely wrong. Why not? It is to the fish. Don't they get a say? There are seventeen zillion sentient beings breathing water in Lake Ontario alone. This does not include the uncountable anaerobics. Will man take notice? Not if he's busy. He is always busy. He'll be busy being about nothing. Nobody I know in Oswego would weep for the dead seagull floating beak down in the sludge. If a man can skillfully suppress emotion, then where do you think truth lies? Bingo! Truth lies. And anyway, what truths actually waste their revelations to the man who must use isms to describe peculiarities? Why won't he admit the futility of speech? He will have to one day, when the world is too weak to speak. The nearly dead might think twice about using an ism to label themselves. What was the ism after all, but a smart place to stop thought? A period to end his sentence? A "God bless you" after the sneeze? Yet some men spend their entire lives fighting to get their names typed down with an ism. Why?

A man should stop for fifteen minutes to observe his own thoughts. Then jot them down as quick as they come. He could tape his voice struggling to keep up with his busy brain talk. After a few seconds one realizes the impossibility of translating thought's language into speech or the written word. Thought's language is an unsolved mystery, even to our true selves. The selves existing inside us without language. Our sentient selves. The vision in the brain has no ism to speak of, absolutely no conformity to speech. Put a color in your head. Name it NOW! And describe in complete detail everything surrounding it. Ooops! You've changed your mind. Anyway, you probably said "red" when it wasn't really red at all. Is that a giraffe? No, but it looks li—Damn, it's changed again! Don't bother attempting to get your immediate thoughts down into your mouth and out of it. Impossible.

If a man can't say what he sees, but says it anyway, all is fine and wonderful with the world. When a man believes in the things he says but does not see—that is the time for everything else around him to run like hell. A lucky man will understand his awesome helplessness in the unknown. He must be able to say the thought he feels while noticing a lone goose on a hill, or feel enough to remark on the vole's black terror felt beneath the grass while the point of his shovel stabs through its passageways.

Men are so close to the permanent elimination of outgoing sensitivity. They will feel pain, always so well aware to the pricking of their own nerve endings. But never a breath of compassion for living things not man or man-made. Man has become oversensitive to himself on the inside, picturing all life in motion from inside his brain, as if he had the first power to put life into action, and to therefore cease its action if he chose to. A murderous robotic monster of his own creation, man. A Mr. Hyde without the Jekyll to feel guilt for each innocent creature his monster murders. *Speciescentric*. Now there's a new word for scientists to talk over and write on sticky labels for their Ball jars. Mankind has numbed his senses to pain and pleasure of all things not man. He acts as if all life was his to waste. Sounds juicy. It just means that man is the earth's asshole.

Back to reality. Dawn in the warm middle of spring. No leaves but the skies have the look of a subtropical paradise. The tops of trees set before the sky. Could very well be Jamaican trees. Am I in Singapore?

I think writing is dead. This small book must have some worth though. Desperation? Of course! And hope too. I hope one man, preferably a young one, who is still capable of feeling, lays down in the grass today with hope and bitterness, holding tightly to my book of mixed-up confusion. I want one good reader! One reader would be friend enough to help me understand my own garbled and confused word-speak. I want my world to provide fifty more winters to read over what I wrote and laugh at the words laughing back at me. I want to invest in the company that makes hollow cardboard tubes for toilet paper. I want to help the world turn. I want to be proud of the work I do. I need to feel useful. Sewer clean-up? Hell yea! And a cold beer after work!

This is not good. Nobody is interested in what I am doing. Why won't one man look at me the way I need to be looked at? Here is the intermission when I build up an even stronger more devastating disgust for my human surroundings. Now is the time to let loose! I am crazy. I need to be alive. I cannot hide out. Are you telling me that my work of art won't inspire you to give me a little shove away from the deep fryer? Do I have to go back to line cooking to save my sanity? A hundred years from now I want the people to know the truth. Art in America received its final death blow this morning in Oswego, NY.

But the last artist did not go down without a fight.

The money is gone. It's either dog food or a job. I don't like you. You are wrong. I don't write for you. I am writing for the man a hundred years from now who has a sick feeling in his gut every morning while the fortune dwindles. Hey future fella, what are you hoping for? Freedom? You found this book in the wall where I hid it. I published a hundred. They bought seven. Six of them went to my family. The one stranger thought there might be a rape to read about. My family put them in a box, said they were proud, and told me to get a job. I burned ninety-two and stuck this one behind the sheet rock that I put up to disguise my desire for all things not sheet rock. I tell you it is not constipation. It's gangrene. They have gangrene of the vital organs. All their fluids are stopped. Nothing flows. There is no more beauty. Beauty has become gnostic, and the gnostics treat it like a wall-hanging to uncover during break time and then, "back to work!"

I want to be free! I want men to come to my door and talk about revolution. After that I want to play catch with them in the yard. I need to talk and play with them while our wives and daughters cook dinner. Okay, okay, I'll cook the god damn dinner! I just need to be among thinking people. It's all crap, future fellow. The grown men are tuning in on Radio Disney in their cars, *for the children.* The children are killing each other. Hollywood is trying to get the children to want to fuck and then kill each other. Dear future man, I cannot even imagine the horror movie you walk into after getting up from the grass stuffing my book in your back pocket.

I am alone giving you this true account, so you can smirk at the historical lies they tell you. If you are so unlucky to have my book, you probably don't believe a word they're saying, anyway, and you are frightened. Go to the river. The cool flowing water. Find a favorite spot, and get to it as often as possible. Watch the seasons change, the

leaves turn color, fall, rot, and come back to life again. Watch the animals look at you. That is wisdom. Don't step into the mantrap. Keep
your eyes wide open. They are watching. Be careful what you say. You
have got to be so alone a hundred years from now. There can't be anyone left. I think that even you might be a traitor to me.

Future fellow, I am finishing this book for you. It must be for you.
When they read this, they won't understand. I'll be properly placed
back into society by the time I save up enough money to publish. I will
publish it for my friends who don't even care if I die trying. I want to
beat my best friend to death to get him to wake up for the next life. He
should already be beside me, helping to plan our next move. He comes
over to plan about how he's going to make more money. I don't have a
best friend. Everyone is in hiding. Do you believe that illusion is death?
It is. First comes illusion, or a soldier with a machine gun, or a get up
to shave and shower and drive to a meaningless occupation every day,
but making enough not to think about how cleverly illusion's world
enslaves the life of every single man, woos him with money promises
and payoffs until near complete coma, and then slices his entropically
depressed balls off.

There are so many mad images passing through my mind right now.
All of them an example of man's hypocrisy. It's okay to be a hypocrite,
the word has no meaning anymore since everyone became one. Two
hundred years ago "gentlemen" would duel to the death over that in-
sult. And then the victor would go home to ask his overseer which
nigger picked the most cotton that day. Man is a dirty hypocrite too in
2001. How is he on your side of the river? What's it like in Oswego in
2101? Are you born with a bag of Sakrete for a pillow? Or do they just
break it over your soft newborn head and mock you if you cry?

I tell you it ain't getting prettier. I'm shot. They're winning. I got to
move to the woods because men make me sick to my stomach. I want
men! But they don't want the man within themselves that needs to be
seen. I want the Oswego man to love his children enough not to put
them in school. They must stop faking love. It's making me sick. Who
is teaching? The children are neglected, unwanted. They know evil already, before puberty. The men here, out of laziness alone, do nothing
but push them to impossible goals—always a cruel, confusing lie about
happiness and money. Do you know that I know that by the time
of your reading this, something had to give. By now man's brain has
undergone a permanent particle change. Or a plenitude of hydrogen

bombs detonated in your mom and dad's time, and you're down by the river, stark naked reading my book, while choking up pieces of radiated lung. Evolution kept good to its promise to take man to his desired end—the violent, red-hot hatred of life. Beauty is dead. Words—gone. You can read. But what did they have you read? *Treasure Island?* It? Poems by Anne Bradstreet? Of course words will have to be dead. I cannot be a friend to you, future fellow. You scare the shit out of me. I am looking out my window now, in the know that no matter how many words I put to paper, they won't be enough without the power to inflict mortal fear, to scare men into self-constructing a loving, happy home. I know the failure stuffed inside every American house. Absolutely no signs of it changing for the better, either. Man is not happier than he was a hundred years ago. Quite the contrary! He is more afraid and more dangerous. He can tie his shoes and drive a truck, but strip him of all comfort—ALL COMFORT— and he will cut up his neighbor's children, rather than go a day without novelty groceries. In 1901 ice cream wasn't invented yet. In 2001 a twelve year old boy killed as many children he could see in fifteen minutes. Once in a lifetime would have been a very sad tragedy. Once a month could have been corrected with the discriminate slaughter of our modern economy. Once a week is human insanity. Ice cream... Murder.. Gee, I wonder what twisted, freak mother tucks you in at night, future fella.

We are all nuts. I am trying to save what sanity I have left for my children. I need to write about why I think it's all cuckoo. You still don't understand the positive good of home school, and every quarter expect a report on her progress. What? Can't you read the paper? She didn't kill anybody. Is that not good enough? Can't that be progress? No? It's queer that Daddy should want them beside him. He's going nowhere because he knows our world cannot and will not even try to protect his children. This realization has bored deep into his psyche. It will have its effect on evolution. God future fella, I doubt you got even one fertile sperm left in a million. Psychologically it's ruined, and probably wise enough to commit suicide before ramming into her greedy egg. I hear that's the way the dinosaurs went. Polluted themselves to the point of their own lizard sperm getting smart enough to quit.

I believe in the wonder of my daughters. I believe in the spring robin, the blue sky, the chance in a lifetime to be alive. I believe in the naturalness of all things. It's true, I even believe in the beauty of man. I believe in hope future fella. You better hope too. For without my belief, you do not exist.

I am the last living artist in Oswego, America. I am not afraid to believe in the truth.

Spring cleaning on West Seventh Street. So much to do. Just one lifetime to do it in. To the teahouse then, for it's annual wash and burn. An oily rotten, wreck of an old tool shed I rebuilt for joy to the protests of my family. At first there was an over-populated ant colony eating the wood hollow. A billion ants delivering everything to their queen, herself the size of a well fed mouse. The previous owners, now dead, used the shed to save everything! And everything stunk from the rot the first morning I broke off the door. I knew then that I would preserve Mr. Reynold's closet workshop at any cost. I would be the one to keep his original, innocent intentions. Certainly he didn't dream about tools all those long, quiet afternoons in the shed. Whether he knew it or not, he was wondering about the life everlasting.

My first act of demolition was poisoning the ants. No more sweet air for their tiny spiracles to take in. Ha!

Then I pulled out the rot and restructured the foundation by hammering a steel pole through the floor, eight feet into ground. I laid shingles to cover the hole in the roof that rain water, ants and time made. I built a floor on top of the dirt, and sometimes I sit in the teahouse on summer mornings with my coffee. A tall oak tree hangs its tired massive limbs just enough feet above my chair to crush me during a strong wind. Oswego is known for its strong wind. It blows from the west. In the west I built a small reminder of the East I once strove to become.

What is the East? I have lived these last few months in the Northern East. Oswego Siberia, where the Laptev Sea meets the frozen tundra. Life became frigid, sad, and agonizingly repetitive. Even the glow from the glorious Northern Lights was dull and depressed me. I kept a fire lit all day and night, and went crazy. A man will howl at the moon if left alone too long. This was not the East I fell in love with as a youth. There wasn't even a moon to bark at. I decided to make my move to the hot, wet green of Singapore.

With my small pack and my wild eyes I left the earth's natural prison.

Oh what misery I suffered in its frozen hell. What self pity! The men were wild. Each did something very bad to end up there. I followed the banks of the Lena to the Aldan, eating only snow and reindeer scat until I reached the mountains and the first human village. There I begged the women for scraps until I regained the strength in my arms to work for my own food again. I lived and worked in the village for several weeks until the morning I saw the spring fox gobble up the chickadee.

That day a small sun rose for the first time, and I got a memory of joy. I left the village taking the lumber roads through the Miklav Forest, over conifer hills, and some happier declines all the way to the Sea of Okhotsk. It wasn't so bad with a sun to rise each morning, a loaf of bread, and traveling men to share their voices with mine.

I bought passage on the first freighter heading south to Singapore. That is when my knowledge fell apart. I can't find Singapore. Even after searching for five minutes on my tiny plastic globe. Guess what? I say Singapore does not exist. My fingernails exist. I pick at them and pull off each one. Sometimes I go too low and pull off some skin. Blood. There's Singapore! No, that's Bangkok. And I should laugh at the sound of that. Because it *is* funny. The seven a.m. sun rises in the east over Hank's house and I have more snot in my sinus than salt water in the South China Sea. I am a man. "Don't shoot I am a man." That was printed on my bright orange hunting license holder strapped across my back. I never shot a Chinese pheasant. The Adirondack Mountains have wild peacocks living too high up for my hope to climb. Peacock makes me laugh. Mindoro, Panay, Sulu Sea. Still no Singapore. I don't care how many foreign ships dock there with sailors taking pictures. Bandar Seri Begawan. What is that you smart ass? It's called "playing globe with a black ocean". It could be a world of men or one with just black cats. Then no twilight cruise through the Spratly Balabac Strait. Instead a "feed us our dinner now, Ron, or we'll jump on your head and chomp out your eyeballs".

Where are we going? Oh yes, to a Singapore that does not exist. Got it! I was wrong. At the southern tip of the Malay Peninsula, near the equator. Now wonder what every eleven year old boy, born at exactly 3:35 p.m. on February 8th, is doing in the city of Singapore. That's knowledge. Try the same thing with an eleven year old skunk. Are there even skunks in Singapore? That is knowledge. I'm on a freighter. What's a freighter? Now build one, from the up to the ground, all by yourself. That is knowledge.

I hate knowledge. Knowledge is for men and men are woe faces and rollbellies. I hate wonder because it begins at knowledge, then takes a freighter to the mouth of the Ganges, only to be swallowed by a little Indian girl praying with her mouth open for Rama to get her a toy. I like pretend. Children pretend. I like children because I can trust them to hate knowledge almost as much as I do.

I live in a small house in the backyard of my mind. A grown man must kill knowledge. No one knows a thing, and the book we find to know we know, doesn't know what the lice is dreaming, so it doesn't know either. I can wonder if the lice is dreaming about a dandruff dinner. But that's just silly. I can pretend that the lice will wear a pretty dress and go out to the best hair restaurant in the city. Or it can stay home and sing a song about its favorite pore to bore into.

What are the Nicobar Islands doing without a king? This morning I dub myself Monsoon King of the Nicobars. Me and my bamboo broom sweep out the dust in the brain. Just before the rains come I get a horrible itch on top of my head. Knowledge is a man promising himself last night to write down all he knows about the East. He wants to give an exotic flare to his writing that is dull, pompous, and dull. The man doesn't know what he is. He doesn't know what a daffodil is either. One doesn't have to sit cross-legged to know the overwhelming no-no of knowing. Oh how lucky I am! Oh, how lucky the Monsoon King of the Nicobars! Sweep out the dust. Welcome the spring. Go get a job.

Tomorrow is Easter. Can't get a job on Easter Sunday, so this after-noon I shall continue the writing thing.

I am in love. Nothing matters. Life is lucky. I am glad I got the special opportunity to walk along the river with my beloved. I take nothing I write seriously. That is important to remember. I am creating a very small book about nothing. I know it's nothing and that makes me hap-py. I am a man sleeping in the arms of his lover. My belly hangs slightly over my jeans. I get mad when the porch wood rots. I hate home repair until it's finished and then it's okay.

Spring is bearing down its cheer upon me. I will find work and step in line. I need the money. Who was Rimbaud? I have to read his book. All I know about him is what Henry Miller wrote in *Time of the Assassins*. Carrying around the equivalent of twenty-five thousand dollars worth of gold in his belt. What does that mean? Why is Rimbaud sought after? Do we think we have something in common with him? I guess we do. Everyone in written history had a dirty ass thirty minutes out of the shower. Whether a rain shower, or snow shower, or even a very sterile, hot bathtub shower. Every one has a stinky ass, and that is why I never take personal triumphs too seriously.

I don't mind being ripped off. I sleep with the most beautiful woman in Oswego. You can have my money. I will rub her thighs. I am not afraid of getting old. I look forward to it. Do I fear death? I don't believe in it. I can't understand it. I do not foresee it. When it comes, it won't give any warning. No first hand accounts published on the subject. Unless that is what *A Season In Hell* is all about. Impossible. No hell but life. No heaven, either.

A wonderful, cleansing nap and walk we had today. It seemed every-one was outdoors, airing out their rot. The river has been emptying all the melt into the lake. The Oswego river flows north. Today southern water flows and mixes with my blood.

A great day. A better night! I want to renew all old friendships. I want my friends again. I want to be free all afternoon to lay in the grass. I want to have a picnic. I love food. I have been away for quite some time—so internal and lonely was I.

I have children. I am an artist. All the dreams of my youth are coming true. I might even go so far to say I enjoy making my home Oswego.

How nice it would be to have humble friends in our lives once again. Any takers? I'm open for offers. I had three friends who lived here long ago. They were just passing through. At that happy time we had no need of money. Just enough for rent and meals together. Until? I don't know what happened—and I don't think they know either, but sure enough, each got his call to depart. Had to go some place in the world. Any place besides Oswego. Too quiet here to get concrete feedback on their hopes and dreams. So they moved away. I don't blame them. Still, youth is so stupid. Always wants to run to prove to no one how great it can become. And where does it go? To New York City! Ughh! Then ten years steadily dodging a longstanding, sincere friendship for the promise of new ones to form on the East side, in box 38. You live in West box 127, and have the key to prove it! And $2200.00 to give away each month to a faceless landlord who lets you live there and climb her crooked staircase. "Box 38, allow me the pleasure of introducing box 127 to you. Box 127, meet box 38. Now you two, shake hands and run back to your boxes!" New York has a quiet too. The kind of quiet to keep an army of analysts extremely busy. I am a friend who has been open and the same for thirty-four years. I'll be sixty with the same dreams. All I want is my families' laughter to be shared and appreciated by others not related to us. Please, are there any takers?

Today I forgive my old friends their transgressions. They didn't want to abandon me. They went away like Rimbaud to find riches for prestige and freedom. It was minimum wage and an over-demanding friend like Ron which drove them away. My dream of ten years ago was to be here today playing flag football with children in the park. What crazy ambitions! What fruitless aspirations! When will old friends finally prove to their invisible Lords the value of their serfdom? At what hour exactly does a man become satisfied with his toil? How many humiliating times must his ears get boxed, and his deepest pride peed on again and again to realize there is no pleasing anyone but himself?

I have my invisible lords. I am just a stupid peasant too. I don't mind going nowhere if I can only be of some use.

I am a good house picker-upper. Actually, rarely do I clean with a wet rag. I pick things up and put them away. I can give the appearance of clean.

I am a good father.

I am a good husband.

I am a loving master to the house pets.

I am a great success in anything I do besides house repair and keeping a job. I am a good artist, but in Oswego, that's like saying you're a good doctor without patients, a busy plumber without a truck, A swell floor-mopper and wall-washer at the power plant, without being a card-carrying member of the Capitalist Pig Party.

Every window I look out of I see a truck. Every truck I see once cost more than the house I live in. I am good at so many things. The one thing I am awful at is making money. I get too worried, but only because I am trapped in Oswego. At the North Pole I wouldn't care, as long as there was plenty of blubber oil available. In fact I could divert all energy into sustenance living. But not in Oswego, surrounded by money. A truck out my window with a decal on the bumper. "Pheasants Forever". Now transpose the driver onto the plains of central Africa, wearing nothing but jeans four sizes larger than his original waist. What will eat him first if not a flock of starving pheasants?

I am going to write my book within a book. I will write a primer for artists—a book of reference. I feel useful. I will make enough money, provided I can convince a money-faced publisher of the huge potential market. For that to happen, all present university professors must die. And then it's open season for my book's promotion. Target market: artistic American-speaking students world-wide. I predict the book being sold to exactly four universities, and by the year 2030, seventeen people will have read it from cover to cover. I joke with my wife that I don't expect to make a penny from my efforts, but that posterity will award our children and their children enough money for a day's supply of oatmeal. I joke although the death of art is so very real.

Book For Artists

You are right. Every one else is wrong. As much as you need people, they must be cast out. If you can't get to a canoe, swim out to sea as far as you can swim before cramping. Turn around. If the shore cannot be seen, and you are the only human being floating, count yourself very unlucky to be the only living artist in your community.

It's not fair and there is no helping you. You might be rewarded, and you might not. The strongest people in the world are artists. They're just not the brightest. Start treading water.

When you feel the cramps, and you will feel the cramps, climb out of bed in the morning and pity yourself. Do this before the army gets up. No one, not even those who love you the most will tolerate your hope for long.

You might get a big break. But only if you make it worthwhile to somebody who is worth something. Real art is always a generation or two before recognition. But then it's only the life of the artist that gets recognized. It means that nobody comes to help when you're drowning. Not because they hate you. They just don't want to have the kind of fun you're having being an artist. *Not that kind of fun!*

Poverty and degradation aren't your friends. Not at all. But they will tolerate you, as long as you don't tease them. In a hundred years your relationship with suffering becomes some of the most romantic music in history. Your life becomes an art. What you produced with pain and suffering, people now want to have. Calendars are made with colorful or nostalgic examples of your life and works, a specific one starring each month. The supreme mockery. Even the richest overlord loves a good story about sacrifice. I don't know why. Maybe it brings him back to moments in time when his life had meaning. Before money. Patrons of the arts? Never. No such thing. They are mockers of art. But isn't that obvious? Whoever is in possession of a Van Gogh now should be shot on the spot where Van Gogh shot himself. That I even know of Van Gogh in Oswego should be reason enough for my hanging. That the people I know know Van Gogh is proof of imminent Armageddon. Because they are not artists, but will give the dirty prick Van Gogh both thumbs up for life and work well done. Which means, and it should give you the desire to immediately swim out to sea as far as you can, that no one will ever care about your work, and, unless you starve yourself, have all night conversations with God or Beelzebub, while getting progressively skinnier and brain dead—until you give in to the pressure to want to drown yourself, your work will not be appreciated even by your own mother in your lifetime. I don't care how many colorful cartoons you have finished in your studio! You will never be an artist unless you suffer immensely, die, and wait a half century.

A great American painter of the 21st century must do without peanut butter and solid, lasting friendships. He might even refuse to talk to anyone for the next thirty years. He will eat, shit, and sleep his art on canvas. It won't matter until that magical day he decides to swallow fire while slicing off his own head. Then I promise, the human world would not let his grandchildren starve. That is how to become a well-received painter.

The writer is so much worse off. Grammar makes it more difficult for a man to fake it. Abstract writing has no blues and greens to decorate a room. Frame the following words and hang them on the dining room wall:

Sea fish bit hairy ass of bunk-a-bunk
dinner dish scrape plate a lot—got
quiet at da camp a moonlight—might
get the boys to diddle the girls
diddle the girls, diddle the girls...

What is one to say about crap like that?

The off-writer won't receive a penny in this life or the afterlife unless he can fill a fat book with a plot about diddling the girls, and a sub-plot about an evil pet cemetery, which in itself carries a risky theme about a lawyer acting like a hero. And still, this won't get him rich enough to eat with his art until he promotes his embarrassing words of work to the wrong man who happens to be the right guy to get him money.

He should just stick with the bad poetry, break his back, and be found dead in his room with a rabbit's genitals hanging from his mouth. A billionaire's grandson will buy the original manuscript for twenty million dollars.

"Sea fish bit hairy ass of bunk-a-bunk." It has quite a ring to it, eh? I'm telling you it does. I will tell you what you have to like. I represent all the representatives of American Letters. Every other one likes 2% milk on *Special K* for breakfast. Over half of the winning writers in America are university professors. Good grammar, a better promoter, enough degrees on the wall to prove how clever he is. Or be modest with no degrees showing. Just take the money and grow a fat tummy. Tenure and vacation, and another book to add to his collection of himself. The sunniest summer days out mowing the lawn. How can he not believe in the work he does when it pays so well?

Polyp! My beautiful wife just said "polyp". She was referring to obstructions she would have to feel for in my anus if I went for the job that requires a finger in it before getting hired. "I could have you do it" I told her. "You can get the doctor to show you what to do."

"You mean look for polyps?" she asked.

Oh my beauty, my best friend... Yes! God damn I just love our sweet potential to death! She is more of the artist than I will ever be. Stick to the nameless work Ron. Make enough walnut burgers to serve three. Your mother-in-law comes over. Offer her yours without telling. Cover the pan on the stove and if anyone asks where yours is—point to the covered pan on the stove. Nameless art. Write letters to friends and lovers, and once in a while, to family. Bleed your joy and pain all over the pages. Place in the envelope a small painting you did to the music, and a picture of your funny face. That's art. Work like a work dog at it for the rest of your life. Spend every waking moment you can going about the real business of art. Art cannot have a name or a price tag. Art can and should feed the artist. No artist deserves a stranger's finger up his ass. An artist became an artist more than anything because of his aloneness. He wanted to be left alone. He is frightened of a world he did not create. Uh-oh. I'm repeating myself. First no-no of art. Always progress. Forward!

Today, going to the bank for the absolute last bit of cash in our name, I stumbled upon a bank purse lying on the pavement next to our car. I picked it up. Oooh it was fat. "This is from God." I thought. "Oh what a funny trick." I'm sure it would have contained enough cash to take care of us for at least a couple months. Bury it in the yard for rent and food, and a little spending cash for fun—I'm telling you, just a little!

What do I do? You know what I do. This is a book for artists. I don't care whose money it is. If I were anyone else, I would take it and hide it immediately. Even if I was honest and religious I would take it. A man cornered must steal. He needs only to *feel* trapped. But I knew this trick. I have been out searching for lost money on the ground before. When that desperation begins, the money soon follows. Either I get a job or win a million dollars. I start trusting in invisibles again. I no longer worry myself over trivial matters... Money being the king triviality. Beneath my angsty exterior a calm breeze ensues. A trusting calm. Whom do I trust? Nothing human. That money was for the taking, and I didn't take it. I didn't even open the deposit purse to count it, or look to see who was looking. I walked the purse back to the bank entrance and handed it to the first man walking out. I knew it was his. Don't ask me how I knew. But I knew, and I know what God was up to.

Coincidence? No. One thing is for certain. No man in Oswego loses a bank purse on a sunny spring afternoon.

I don't recommend this behavior for anyone. It's money. If you find it on the ground, take it. Unless you enjoy suffering.

Art is easy. Anyone can make art. Art to be made is not the art I want to have. I am suffering for this book. That is art. Not only am I suffering, but my family must endure the growing pains of my creation. To understand the word suffering one must not take the money he is reduced to begging for. One must also write a book he thinks is ca-ca, and wipe his ass with it when he's finished. It's true. That must be the final aspiration for every pure work of art. How can I make the aspiring artist understand that everything he paints or writes is a piece of crap?

It is all crap.

That is the first rule of art. There is no second rule without living and dying following the law of the first. So I won't tell you. I will feel it in you. You can ask me. No matter how good you are at expressing yourself, there is no way to articulate suffering. Believe me when I tell you how often I have tried. So suffer and sing and crap out one explosion after the other. You are an artist when you realize whatever you create is sludge. Other creations are no less a work of art. But only the artist is art.

Make sense?

I hear the gladness of the bird off my balcony. My baby coos beside the breast of my loving friend. We are such wild, careless dreamers. April began in our bedroom. The past is death. The future is murder. The energy circulating throughout one human hand could feed and clothe and warm a planet of suffering creatures.

But who cares?

Dog obedience is tonight. My daughter and I have been taking our quickly excitable dog to Auburn for the past two weeks to get learnin'. He's a smart dog. A loving dog. A good family dog. Yet he needs to be around other dogs. I drive Rachelle to Auburn because I love her immensely, and she needs to be around other kids. If necessary, I would drive her to Pennsylvania once a week for class. I believe in a life taken to its extreme side of nonsense. *For love.* I truly don't give a damn about my own petty desires if to satisfy them means limiting the passions of the ones I love the most. I am a fake and a fool. But I know I love better than anything else I do. My talent is giving me. It is the reason I have a beautiful, wise princess for a wife, sensitive children, and very careful pets. There are nights I lean back in the hard chair of our poverty and feel like the other son of God—not the poor bastard who suffered the cross, but the first son, the eldest, the legitimate one who got all the neat stuff along with Dad's true blessing.

Lately I've been overwhelmed with worry for my little girl. Something odd is happening to her—there's a change in her behavior, very slight, but noticeable to such a sensitive fellow like myself. I can't tell if it's the right change. I am worried for her.

From out of the blue, over the span of a season, she's developed a passion for the pop/rock band 'Nsync. I must make it clear to the reader that before this recent mild mental disturbance, my daughter knew virtually nothing about the strip bar America with its smoky room full of drunk hoods and mascara bar flies. She was growing up Italian in a small Appenine Mountain village. Dad was a cook in a hotel restaurant. He asked the village strong man if he could work nights instead of days, so he could teach his daughter without daily interruption. The village leader said, "What, is our school not good enough for a cook?"

"No Sinor," said the man.

"Yes. You can work nights. But you can amount to nothing more than a line cook for the tourists. Comprende?"

"Si. Sinor."

And that is how he kept her world quiet and happy, without the shame of carelessness that cast shadows over the other children.

'Nsync is not the problem. Music is never wrong. In fact, for an eleven year old, they're safe enough, as long as she can keep the French Kiss out of her Barbie play.

I don't expect anyone to understand why I do the things I do. But I am her father. And the word "father" alone brings more of a world to my mind than any American I know would allow himself to believe. I am her father. I want nothing else to happen to me besides peaceful children who are able to give and receive love. I am her father, and that truth is the center of the universe until she graduates from my care.

There can be no half way with the children. There is a pretending out there in America. A huge pretend play game happening. The parents are telling the world how much they love their kids. They are saying this in the same breath they use to shout at them. American parents are selfish, hungry monsters with tunnel vision. The word "guidance" means nothing to them. How could it? When they were children getting ready to make children, each was assigned a guidance counselor. What was that? These weren't orphaned boys and girls, were they? To be sure, the counselor was neurotic enough, and neglected her own spawn during their formative years. She wanted a job, a career, a field. She wanted to play the game. She became a guidance counselor. She had children and sent them to be taught by another teacher. Everyone sent the kids somewhere else to someone else to teach their open minds life's lessons. So why shouldn't she? She was deserving. Where was her special present? She wa-wanted her special present!

I believe that's three or four generations now of insanity allowed, actually recommended, and sometimes forced. Schools hire guidance counselors. I often wonder if mom can remember back to those precious, few minutes when she pushed out something alive and very fragile.

I wish my guidance counselor told me to learn a trade, develop an easy sense of humor, don't go to college, cook my own food, wash my own clothes, make enough money to teach the kids myself, and don't dare have kids if I plan to play the crazy games my parents and their parents played.

I would say the parents of America rarely meet the children even halfway. Actually, some just throw them away. How can a father allow his child pass through a metal detector to go to school? Today Daddy drops his baby girl off in the school parking lot, hoping that while he's off playing the game, she doesn't get teased or shot. He might pray every night that she won't get pregnant, or take drugs or shoot someone herself. Yet Dad will push her out of the car anyway, every day, and drive away. Not to see her again until later that night, when it's time to feed her and turn out the light in the barn which he calls a safe and loving home for her. One day she'll become Farmer Brown to her own little pigs. That's modern living, oink. No matter how well daddy and mommy disguise the truth. Oink-oink. They raise their children for slaughter. Loving parents may work very hard to get them into the right barn. But after all, it's never their best. And it's always bacon for breakfast. Oinky-aloinky—boink-a-boink!

You don't believe me? Why? How could you not? What do you need? What does Daddy need? What does all the damned human world need?

More money, perpetual security, progress, and newer, cleaner things to look at.

Oh that's right, I almost forgot. Gas, electric, garbage, mortgage, please god, anything, everything, wheels and a good paying job! A new computer, a better dinner, three accounts at the bank, clothes when we want them, new boots twice a year, a new car, an old car, nothing more that what the poor guy couldn't get while teaching the kids himself.

What I mean is so obviously scary. Let's brace ourselves for this one. *There is nothing that cannot be got at a walk.* For every thing received, some thing will be taken away. Newton's laws? Universal wisdom? More about dog obedience in a moment. I'm on target now. I think that I am on to something.

Recently our family has lived with very little money. Still, we have eaten well and even paid some of the bills. Heat, electric and phone. I possess books to help teach my daughter, and hot water to wash the babies' diapers. It's true, you have no heart. Americans have gone on a rampage killing sensitivity. Like zombies of the movies—becoming that imagined horror show without needing a nuclear fallout to jump start the undead. You have no heart. You can afford everything I can. I am sitting in a Morris chair. I have running water. I even ate a bowl of cereal this morning. And, I am teaching my own children. I am spending entire days beside my wife. Not because I am lucky, or fortunate, or even wise. I know what love is. I have a heart. Now I know it's your plan to eat it. Good god, you're the zombie, aren't you? Run!

Both my wife and I feel the lack in our lives without friends. We need you to come back from the dead. You left a thousand years ago, but by some heroic feat, I alone will get some of you to come back. My wife needs friends she can talk to. She wants to picnic with you and your children. But not if you intend to eat out our hearts, instead of these delicious jelly sandwiches we've prepared.

You have no heart. Why are you working away from the family? Why are you putting your children in school? Are you playing Russian Roulette with their spirits? Yes! You do not understand what a child is. You don't know your husband. You never loved your wife. You diddled her. She diddled you. Then you got the product of your screw. And now no one even diddles anymore. Everyone eats hearts.

I make fifty times less than you. But you do not multiply your life fifty times greater than mine. Do you have fifty more chairs? Fifty more hot water heaters? Fifty more automobiles? Fifty more children? You cannot have a heart. You must be reading this the way you go to the bathroom, or shave your face or your legs. I know everyone is a failed parent as soon as the child steps into an industrial room at the tender age of four or five. What important work are you doing that justifies being excused from the responsibility of raising your own?

I have one window in front of me. And you cannot possibly look out of fifty in front of you. So you must be living overkill. Where is your dog obedience class being held tonight? Forget that. Where is your parental obedience class?

Are you an important chef? Where is your daughter at 11:00 a.m.? Are you an intelligent manager? Where is your son while you manage more money? You have so much stuff, but never fifty times more than what the poet down the street has. All the children are becoming indifferent, apathetic, unsure. Nature or nurture? You, the monster without a heart, are a lone Skinner box concealing macaroni and cheese for dinner and a trigger with the safety off. Take the lid off the box so the kid can shoot his friends and eat their hearts. Oh small joys! He didn't finish his macaroni and cheese! There's a little pile left, pushed to the side of his paper plate. You're going to finish it for him, aren't you? You can have his life and eat it too. And as usual, drag your stuffed ass back to work!

Oh piddlepiss. The truth is too painful for me too. Where was I before bringing all the children into my loving care? Loving care. Hmm. That's right, 'Nsync.

They are fine millionaire boys, I am sure. I could write another hundred pages about pop music, and the laying out of our children for the sexual molestation of America with horns to climb over. I wanted to talk about Radio Disney, and the magic machine that turns ten year old girls into aspiring pole dancers. There is enough wrong to write about forever. But I am in charge of publishing. And I don't have any money. I have wasted my time in writing these letters to semi-erect lap dogs.

This is the last book the poet writes about why everything is screwy. If you're not near crazy after a walk through your town in America, then there is no hope for you. I cannot be bothered anymore to scratch my head thinking up delicate ways to scold.

I will continue to write. I will always write. However, from now on I must choose my subjects more wisely. Today is April 20, 2001. I am thirty-four years old. I got a call back last night for a job. I am going to cook French fries again.

Ten dollars an hour. It is my trade. Amazing how these tiny cures of money temporarily rig us up until the next blow-out.

Misanthropic Love Letters

An Open Letter to friend and family...

I surrender. I must go on record. I begin my true career today. My spirit down-sized itself into a fickle, indecisive, pot-bellied embarrassment. Now I am stuck in internal revolution. When I am through and all the manias on the inside are hung on the outside, then I will have erased doubt, denial, melancholia, fear... What or whom do I have to fear? All the animals laugh at human melodrama. I swear everything human that is not connected to love is melodrama and useless.

I am not useless. I am a child.

Look here friends, family, all strangers alive today, and those living tomorrow. I am through playing the sad game. I want to live the life I was born to live. I cannot wait for security in order to practice happiness. I do not wish to pursue happiness. It's here! At my writing table. The same table I set my meals upon. The table from where I teach. The table in the kitchen of my home.

As downright stupid and confused that I was at twenty, at least I had the foresight to know I would be ready to write "professionally" by my thirty-fifth birthday. Thereafter, I would keep no job that would steer me away from my true desire. I have done horse and mule work to keep the artist in me alive. I purposely hacked at all financial opportunity because I could never imagine any other life for me besides that of the poor artist.

For the time being, (and I pray that I can summon the courage to make it forever) my indentured servitude is over. Now at thirty-four years of age desire is shooting out of every pore at a screaming boil. Freedom! Poverty! Yes! For the rest of my life I would like that my government mark me out as one of the impoverished. Frankly I believe that its mark of poverty is a king's income for a sane man.

Because I am a father and a husband, I realize that I will never join that degraded class of poor which turns out the brilliance of Hamsuns, Van Goghs, and Dostievskys. I want to do my part providing the necessaries for my family. Therefore I foresee several more degrading jobs popping up in the future. I write this letter hoping that someday I can be employed by you or someone you know. I am a fantastic cook. I can create all sorts of delicious goodies for the gourmet. I am also quite handy around the house. Home repair. I prefer electrical work to fine carpentry. In fact I am pretty good at anything which can be finally hidden behind a professional job. I can paint the inside and outside of homes. Not too well, but much cheaper than you'd pay someone else to do it just as poorly.

What I really want is to sell my paintings. While the writing is in progress I plan to paint for relaxation as well as keep the creative juices flowing. I use mostly acrylic and sometimes watercolor. I'm good enough. That is to say, I am a living artist, and whatever I do today should be of some interest to posterity. I will charge twenty-five dollars plus shipping and handling for each finished work. I will take commissions. Presently I am painting a goldfish in a busy underwater scene. When it is finished I will have spent approximately eight hours working on it. You can see what a measly hourly wage this will make. A little over three dollars an hour. Yet it's such a sweeter life than sweeping a stranger's floors to get my butter.

There are those who think my business will fail miserably. I am positive that it will! But not trying is wrong living, and who wants to be guilty of *that*!?

"The primary thing is this, that whatever money is given me constitutes a mortgage on the future, my future as a writer. Making water colors is so much play for me; it gives me a release. In other words, it keeps me happy, enthusiastic and alive, and to be happy, enthusiastic and alive is a prerequisite for the artist."—Henry Miller

The point is I won't go another year suffering for illusions which others may have of me. (A path I have foolishly followed for most of my adult life.) I am not a sole provider. I am a father, a friend, an honest, loving, incredibly cheerful, desperately creative and funny man. I want coffee in the morning, hot, delicious food for dinner, rent paid, and time. You can help me achieve my first three objectives by offering to purchase one of my books or paintings. Time is up to me. I could make the most of it with your financial, or at the very least, moral support.

One more quote before singing off... It should set the droning, one hundred page tone of bitterness for the remainder of this book. Erica Jong wrote the following about Miller, but it works too for all of us lazeabout, good-for-nothing, artsy-fartsy types:

"The New York that Henry left in March of 1930 was nowhere as fraught as the New York of today, but it still bore certain similarities. In New York it was a dishonor to be an unknown writer; in Paris one could write écrivain on one's passport and hold one's head high. In Paris it was assumed (it still is today) that an author had to have time, leisure, talk, solitude, stimulation. In New York it was, and still is, assumed that unless you fill up your time with appointments, you are a bum."

So be it. But I must warn you that I did not set the stage for this play, although I share the guilt of every actor playing in it. Help if you can, or decide to breeze alone through this one safe life never to support a fallen man unless he's prepared to give you back some proof of financial success. Invest in paper clips but never individual men. The return is slight compared to the trillions already in degradation circulation. My hand holds a blank sheet of worthless paper. Sometimes I write words on it. Sometimes I fill it with colors of joy and light. It's not plastic or perishable. It won't make much money. But it shouldn't make me broke either. It's time now to make an exchange to benefit humankind. Neither of us will get much out of it, but one of us will get some money to buy food.

Hello. I am a writer. I am finished as a man. That's enough. But I need something to do. So, the rest of this book is a silent scream of agony to prove to myself the obvious. I will not torture my wife any longer. I am a loafer, a vagabond, a hobo of the spirit. I am nothing. I am a loser of the first rank.

A man is an idea. An idea comes from man. Man is his own idea about himself. Leave me, love me. I have nothing to do with anyone from this world. I am a writer. So you can read what I write and then you can go to hell.

This cry-baby versus man crap has my insides twisting and squeezing. I don't want to be crazy. If I don't give up now, I might do myself lots of damage. That possibility was not in the initial plan, since I remember being born to be alive. Yet because I am alive, here today, in modern America, I cannot truly exist as a man. Therefore I have decided to live the life of a man vicariously, through my own image of myself. And I shall write to prove that I am a writer, as well as a living, breathing, human entity who hates and loves himself on equal par.

Actually I probably hate better.

I can hate myself often enough to begin to wonder what exactly is the matter with me. Why live through another night if tomorrow is the first day to rid the world for good its many human shows of blunder? Why the stubborn, insane desire to want to write about hate, as it's happening, and with no end in sight?

Who would agree with me that hate is now necessary to survival? The life-force fueled by hatred? Where? Among the animals? No. People are crazy. Animals don't hate. People have made me crazy because they hate, and I am a people who hates. Anyway, this short book will help me get through the worst of it. The hate that is. Better to hate hard than be saved lightly. Better to hate than play eternal hopscotch with the holy scripture of your choice. Do you think that your boss, your bank, your landlord, your creditors love you? No. They hate you. They despise you. Play these circle games all day long, every day until you die with people who hate you very much. And when night falls and you're alone in the dark, take those precious seconds left before sleep to turn into yourself. Oh no! Where are you? Not there. Not there either. Search all you want and find nothing because there is no you. Man, woman, animal, flesh, organs, bones? Who says so? You? What is you? Can't sleep? Good. Because everyone hates you. So it's best to watch your back. Take a walk outside. Look up into the starry sky. Tell me what star that is—no, that one! The one you cannot see without a telescope. Quick now, tell me its exact distance from the tip of your tongue. What gases make up it's light? Can a guinea pig survive floating in its orbit if there was a alfalfa pellet to snatch every five revolutions? Answer these questions correctly and then you will be ready to travel back inside yourself to discover what it is you are!

Am I a father, a husband, a care giver to house pets? Our guinea pig has difficulty breathing. She's been laid up for a week in a small cage pissing on herself. Any other night, I would stop what I was doing to clean her cage. Not tonight. She must suffer. I am a caged pig too. Full of misery and death, but above all, suffering. I didn't create it. I have no love for it. In fact, I am ready to destroy it. I could kill a Peruvian grandmother patrolling these hills at twilight for us terrified, little pigs. Damn right I would leap up and sink my fangs into her wrinkled neck skin. You can bet I'd slurp the blood out of her jugular, just for the hope of finding myself. Tonight it's eat or be eaten, no matter what the pretty face disguise we slip on.

Where the hell am I? What country is this? Who are these queer inhabitants? The problem is that I have lived like a minister for the past ten years. I should be a murderer and get paid well enough to put food on the table. Or at least a thief sneaking up from behind and stabbing you in the leg for a few dollars. Why not? Have I missed out on something? Is this a perfect world? Is it even a good one? Murder happens and then there's breakfast. Whoever thought to stop eating in order to stop murder? Has that kind of love ever been attained? The truth is that the two or three people in the world who know how to love like that would not stay alive for long if anyone got wind of their idea. I know the truth gets cut by the human censors. If the humans found truth standing vulnerable alone somewhere, they most certainly would unleash their total ferocity upon it.

Most of humanity today, right now, tonight, is murder, rape, and funny fart jokes. My life has been ten years of filtering out the filth of humanity in order to protect my child. I've made all their rotten brain piss pass through me, first. An infected, thick sewage being pressed through my sensitive China cap. This has saved my oldest daughter from premature aging. Yet during this near fanatical process of sheltering her, I have clogged up my heart and soul beyond repair. Wonder, vision, truth, beauty? Human words. The poet's hope, the painter's dream, and the suicide's proof that it's all just pretty lies told to ignorant, happy babies. The trick is to shelter your young just the perfect amount, so they don't grow up hating like you do.

Last night I upset my wife with a phrase I read out loud from my writing. She said I would never say, "sure as shit," in real, everyday conversation. She's right. Not in the real life I have with her. No, of course not. Unfortunately this life, this human life, expects me to be several mes before getting tucked into bed at night. She also said that my writing is angry. Too angry.

We fought for over an hour, made up with a glass of wine, perused our wide open hopes and dreams, and afterwards sat down to watch Hollywood's latest R rated movie. The words "fuck, bitch, and pussy," and a steady stream of innuendo about fuck, bitch, and pussy. Repeatedly throughout two hours of fuck, bitch and pussy, bullets splashed in and out of people's blood streams, humans stabbed and got stabbed by humans, and gorgeous actors and actresses pretended to fuck each other like hairy dogs pretending to be human.

I write, "sure as shit" and my writing becomes material set up special for the criminally insane.

I am frozen in this life. I am an artist in America. I could be a factory worker, or the wealthy owner of three car dealerships, and the same sad, stunted life would envelope me. That means I haven't changed a god-damn thing with my writing. Effort is frustrated. It is wiser to paint the casing pink than write a chapter about nothing, even if the latter saves your sanity. My mother-in-law told me that her niece married a millionaire. And then she said if a girl marries for love, why not fall in love with someone who is rich? That would be the smartest thing to do, right?

Yes. She's right. Money is everything in America. Money and bigness. If you have a lot of money, you have a big house, a big car, or maybe a small car, but it's bigger because it cost a bundle. Big is big money in America. If it is this way everywhere in the world then I think that I want to die. Hope tells me that you, my only reader, are a small thing with few wants and a little money. *Multum un parvo.* Much in little. Are you big? Yes? Then you are a filthy, dirty beggar I think. If I were an honest man, I would have the god-sanctioned right to do to you what I did to the squirrel crossing the street. But I am not an honest man. This is what I need to prove to you. I am less than zero. But if I think that nullity of myself, and the title of this book includes the word *misanthrope*, then you can probably guess about how high up the place is where I hold my opinion of you.

I intend to write a living book. However, in order for it to come alive, I must hate the very skin off of you. But I am writing it for your love too, even if I don't like either of us. I hope we will grow together and the same to appreciate this book. It is the year 2056. Anyone hear me? Fifty-five years ago I got infected with hate, and I wrote about it from a wasteland. Did it do anyone good? I don't care because now I am dead. I got to say what had to be said, and now I am dead.

Letter of Resignation to all Future Employers:

I am becoming more and more interested in objects, scenes, places which are dilapidated. I am attracted to things run down, broken,
and decaying. I am associating cleanliness with loneliness, strength
and power with confusion, neurosis, and utter despair. I am finding
out that America is a spoiled child, and I have no sympathy for her. I
know that the child will grow into something monstrous and equally
harmful, to one day neglect her own children, but with an increased
estrangement, molestation, violence. And healing will altogether cease.
And understanding will die.

America is rich, fabulously rich. Rich and glamorous. So rich and
refined that her toilets are palaces where shit never stinks. Her kitchens
full and well-equipped with the finest foods, yet nothing is cooking.
Her parlors are stunning, but empty of personality, and no one comes
to call because she is terrified of her neighbors—all of them.

No one is content. It is not important to be. A good thing is security;
a bad thing is drug addiction. The drug addicts are the ones who fail
marvelously. Non-entities. There is no other way. Happiness is truly
dead until a man finds a large sum of money. Art is for the college
bred, and the college bred are making art with computers. No one is
painting original works of art, besides maybe the preschoolers, and that
happens in between TV time, but only if there is nothing else to do,
and mommy and daddy have temporarily slipped through the clutch
of modernity.

No one is stopping to eat and drink. Unknown purpose, plastic
goal. And in the spastic rush to make a living, nothing is left standing. Strangers are trampled. Loved ones destroyed. Houses gutted...
Houses which never were homes. For the American house is built of
old plaster or new sheetrock, and after all, just a flat facade to hang a
meaningless painting on. One brushed by a great artist of course, but
the beholder sees nothing, feels nothing... The walls are up. They will

fall and be built again, and again. Unknown purpose, plastic goal... Dementia. Nothing is allowed to die. It better be breathing or back away! The young get younger and the old won't age. To stop means to be destroyed, by yourself and your illusions. To let on that you may be ill is one step closer to suicide. No one denies tomorrow. Nobody gets old. No time to rest. No death. Unknown purpose, plastic goal...

I write my resignation to all employers, past, present, and future. I am finished with your colossal despair, your anxieties and petty fears, your impossible hope. Why hope? You predict no end. Always I hear the words "tomorrow" and "more", but no one is listening to the reality of no tomorrows. Each day I get more and more confused, more desperate, unyielding. Shall I accept this fate? You put me in a box and I am slowly suffocating. I am a trapped toad made house pet. This is my death box. I will go mad hoping for life, for freedom. My big eyes will watch and hope, waiting for that precious second when the lid lets in a stream of light, and for an instant I will hope again. The child will call out, "Mommy, my toad looks sick!" So what? The lid will come down. The lights go out. Eventually I will hope until I croak, after several thousand more lightning bouts of depression, anxiety and fear over the near impossibility of setting myself free.

At a time in my life when I should feel rich with joy, wanting to be married, wanting to remain alive, desiring happiness..., I find myself instead becoming increasingly angry, disturbed, upset, separate. Your common ideals, your status quo, your worship of no-nonsense, your whole persona, infuriates me! I can hop, but how far? I am locked up in a shoe box. The hopeful thought that brings temporary relief is that once I was told these walls are paper thin. But all my teachers are dead. So is my belief. I find it more difficult these days to believe a word they wrote. I have no more living belief.

Presently I am employed and sick in the noodle. Something is amiss, I know not what. Maybe I detest work. Maybe my passion for loafing is too great. Maybe I am too smart, and know that I am waiting in line like so many pounds of meat with legs in the way. I fall into a special category of men unknown even to myself. No one can label me, therefore I have promise.

My dear employers, what does all of this have to do with you?

Listen, you being the money, spending the money... You even owning the responsibility to share the money, you living a whole lifetime of money, it would be impossible for money not to be your end. However, loving money and being American means that you don't give a damn about the artist—the writer, the painter, the candlestick maker. By graciously employing him, by putting him into a position where he does not belong, you unwittingly show your contempt for his spirit. You might swear that you are doing him a favor. Money is the common need, is it not? You think that he can support a loving family with the paycheck that you supply. He can write in his spare time. And if he times life perfectly, someday his work will be found in supermarket checkout aisles across the nation. What a fine piece of work! The towering obstacles in his way! Finally! The time has come for his sun, his moments of clarity, light, joy! Maybe even a fortune. Because of your generous support the artist was able to endure despite all roads (besides yours) being closed to him. Is it something like that? No. You dirty old man. Art can only be perverted by you.

Listen, art is not a trade. One cannot make it on command. Nor is it ever a hobby, to pick up and begin again whenever time allows it. One thing for certain, art is always the result of bad timing. The artist is whim incarnate. He is, because he has to be, whether or not time allows for it. Herein lies all of his madness. Time and poverty. Good friends to the artist. However, a couple bitter enemies to the man refusing to be the artist. The plumber knows a trade. Time is money and money isn't poverty. The artist knows poverty. The man-in-the-artist can respect poverty and even appreciate it to a degree. But in times of weakness thinks that he could do very well with what the god damn plumber has. And the man-in-the-artist is haunted by his own reoccurring desire to take the limits of time and detonate an infinite explosion inside of it. How can two physically equal, yet morally and spiritually opposite mammalian types play the same game of life, expecting the same results? Both live in the same town, perhaps the same house, and yet the space of an ocean exists between them.

What is a man? Is he a plumber? Yes? What code of living has he set for himself? Is he fed up with an ugly, mad world? Does he search for beauty in a toilet bowl? Does he find beauty there? Where does he get his mental nourishment? The daily news? The classic rock station? Is he peaceful, content, or a revolutionary plumber? Are his ideas plentiful? Does he put them into action? Is he in love? Does he give a damn? Why does he break his back? Why won't he stop? Why isn't anyone alive? Does he want to be happy? Onward. Yes, onward. Always today and tomorrow. Today there is a sink to fix; tomorrow, a sewer pipe.

He's growing old. Now he is old. There will be no more growing. He is fine right where he is. Today he is as hard as a rock. Tomorrow he is a petrified street elbow. And he will have it no other way because he is dedicated.

At an employee meeting not long ago, my boss addressed his final words to me. "Ron, don't you have anything to say? Any criticisms, ideas?" I said nothing. Just shook my head.

All he wanted were new ideas for lunch salads and veal tenderloin. For him the question was simple enough, direct, even needful in a business that relies upon customer titillation to make money make money. However to me it rang of blasphemy. And it was—from the artist's point-of-view. Questions pertaining to business make my nerves snap, crackle, pop! Sorry boss, I haven't any menu ideas. Nor have I a special presentation to give to veal, none to color your money anyway. No preparation dreams about filet mignon, bluefish, flounder, lobster tail... I am sympathetic towards the plight of these beasts, but I have no passion for, nor any desire to cook them for money. So, ironically, I thought that this time it was I who was ripping off the boss and not the other way around. Humph, imagine that!

After the meeting, while walking along the river, I considered the possibility of writing a letter to my boss, explaining to him my own ideas about cooking. My mind was so clear. Surely I could win him over, earn his trust, if nothing more. I would tell him that the only real cooking is what is frying in the pan at home. Sustenance. I cook to eat and eat to live. How strange a labor it is cooking for the paying customer. Cooking behind closed doors no less. Cooking food that I would eat only if I were starving. But I will gladly touch it, trim it, flame it, stir it, spice it, flip it, for eight dollars an hour. Ouch! I might kill it myself for ten bucks. For thirty dollars I would set fire to old zoo animals and drag their smoking carcasses back undercover of night. For forty I swear to God I'd be ready to defrost frozen corpses if asked of me, and there was a pension forthcoming.

I would explain to him how in one sense I am following quietly in the footsteps of great union brats and spoiled children. I will not clean up my room, but I will gladly drain my parents for all they have, or my boss, or the government, or God... It's the American way. That is how things get done around here. Give me more for less! That's my motto. If you want me on the broiler, then I expect eight-fifty an hour. If I am to order fish, then make it nine dollars. Hell, for a modest salary I will even manage the slaughter house. If you desire a silent partner, I am prepared to spend every waking moment with you. Provided that you make me rich.

What am I going to do? This is your racket, boss. I would like for you to do the best that you can. Begin by firing me. Or at least offer me a salaried dishwasher position. That is something which I can do cheerfully. I just don't think cooking this way is my thing anymore.

What do I want then? Maybe I should put the same question to you boss. How can you create the sweet life for yourself without having to deal with the likes of me? You don't want a hero. You want roux, buerre blanc, piccata, Madiera; you want a pinch of scallions here, a dash of salt there, capers on the salmon, red onion in the salad. You may need all these things because your future depends upon them. But me? My future will depend on nothing.

What are you going to do about that, eh? Tough to find and keep good employees. It's better to take on all tasks alone. But then that wouldn't get you rich enough quick enough. So you're forced to take small risks many times. You hire a workforce of poor, dreamy artists. It pays off in the end. It always pays off. Otherwise you wouldn't be in business and I could struggle proudly the rest of my life without your money whip to keep me in bondage.

Lately I fear my ideas. I don't dare put them through the final test. I live the life of the worst type of hypocrite. This makes me a true non-believer. To end up at the same place everyday without contentment means to fail, miserably. What is worse than to fail without ever trying? I cannot say that I am running into walls consciously, because I have been asleep. I am forming habits which, as time passes, are becoming very hard to break. Like the current job which I despise but come back to everyday, religiously. Worst of all, I fear that if I quit and never came back, I would still form the same habits, just in a different habitat.

Presently I am in the process of inflating my ego. I am testing its elasticity. Someday I will burst like a balloon, and then I may very well see for the first time the smile on a human face, the grass, the stars, the living scenery that I once placed my dead self in like a paper doll. I say that I am working up to that point. It may take a while; yes, it may take a very, very long time.

In the mean time what can I do? What a question! I can dig ditches of course. I can work the register at a fast food joint. I could go for broke and earn my doctorate. America needs more psychiatrists, more surgeons, more professors, more nuclear physicists, more veterinarians. I can even run, dance, skip, or juggle for the right price. But I don't want all that! And there is no way to describe exactly what it is that I do want. I seek the invisible "what," the illusive "it". The it that is untouchable, unthinkable, untranslatable. I can say this about the *it*, and it is a fact. Money is not one of *its* by-products. In *its* realm there is nothing to lose and nothing to gain—a world where one must dedicate his life to *its* vaporous instability.

Meanwhile I remain priceless. I can neither be bought nor sold. This is all that I can do to separate my life from yours. So often I have muffled my spirit to make excuses for you, to cry, to laugh, to lie for you. Nevermore. It is high time that I check out of this asylum. I was crazy. My life was not good while I was with you. I took an extended vacation in your dream. But your dream is insane. So long. I am drifting out of it.

I cannot expect myself to work for the boss anymore. I know too much or too little. Either way I have been forewarned. There is a voice inside me which calls out, "Everything is screwy! Breakout before you become a permanent, lifetime worker in America. They will get you if you don't leave now! The odds are very good that once you cross their threshold, you're stuck for life. Once inside you'll be bombarded with overtime hours, vacations, pay raises, Christmas bonus'... Even a slight murmur of protest shall provoke the display of a fat portfolio of what their wages have built: a family, close, bosom friends, a never-shrinking better living to content themselves with. Abandon ship! Run away! Go back to from where you came. You can't possibly be wooed by all of this stuff. Can you?

Can you?

Very good question Mr. Throop. A question which has held you in limbo for so long.

I can't believe it.

Well Jesus, Ron, look for yourself. It's such a cozy, seemingly content and overflowing place.

Dear future employers, I write to you the voice of an angry and confused man. I write to you for negatively for positive reinforcement. I write to be reminded that I am human. That I am positively human. I express my humanity with the written word in order to avoid the great modern American heart-melt. I know where I must begin. The earth being contaminated, the earth destroyed, children still being born to die unfulfilled, unhappy... What does anyone want with that? Fame? Fortune? Half-fame, a quarter fortune? A fearful life pretending freedom?

By declining every offer that is made to me, I create meaningful, positive action. I do not want your offers. They distort me. I do not want your money. I do not want the be-all and end-all of the corrupt American mind. To join you means to give up so much, beginning with my sanity. Relinquish all chance for peace, tranquility, serenity? No way. I quit! And down the road, if I make the mistake to join up once more, I will quit again. And again. And again. I must make this constant quitting so much seasoning of my destiny. It is part of my plan to create an identity virtually unknown to the American mob. I'll remind you of it each passing day with my life to contact as a guide. Listen here you greedy boss of bondage present and bondage future... I quit! I quit! I quit!

Phew. A piece of my peace being made, I leave you now to your own end.

When can we get together and go shopping for a hand-held King James Edition pocket Bible? This is paradise. I should love it here. But mankind has amounted to just too many full grown bodies all of which put together, house barely a small crumb of spiritual freedom. Not long ago our representative of the good life came to a fork in the road. One path was the quiet, contemplative existence. The other was the same thing with lots of yummy cookies to eat. He chose the one with the cookies. Every one followed. Some distant long dead relative of mine, the black sheep of his family, the bum without property, the lazy husband, the no good son of a bitch, rotten cousin, smelly-assed idiot, stood at the fork in the road of life, waiting expectantly for the spoon.

Now it's money and stupidity because it's $55.69 for the pocket bible. I want to go with you to the store and purchase one. Then I want to take you by the hand to the land where babies starve, stand beside you in the cold room where the stiff body of a child lies holding flowers. I want to give you a peek at the world where our new pocket calculator gets shoved thirty inches up the colon of the man who thinks he knows Jesus. I want you to see for yourself what a tremendously useless thing the human being has become. If he did nothing more than what he was doing up to approximately 500 years ago, the earth might have been saved from the homicidal silliness of mankind. You can say technology polluted the world thus far. But I say it's the people's cookie farts bloating the atmosphere.

June 22, 2001. On the other side of Addis Ababa, three pregnant mothers are too weak to even beg for food. Their big eyes watch potential rice balls walking by, but all hope is lost, and each will die soon enough. Last night at the drive thru, they gave my dog two biscuits, one green and one purple. I think I will dedicate this book to all the children even if most of them are crazy. But I feel that if one or two can be reached immediately, the trees might decide to take nourishment into their limbs this year and forgo their recent decision to dry up so to choke us to death. At present, a welcome summer rain falls hard on my garden. Food is the last thing anybody needs. Mr. raccoon is too fat to waddle across the street safely. Cars are riding over its head. Not a turkey buzzard in sight. Not for days or weeks. The raccoon rots to the bone. Nothing is hungry here. Over there? Yes. Across the ocean many are starving. From here the statistics might appear gruesome. An African proverb: When an old person dies, a library is burned to the ground. An American nonchalance: When an old person dies we are afraid for a few hours after breakfast, sad on and off, before dinner, and then giddy when the lawyer comes over to give us presents with dessert.

In Africa old people have eyes that no American could look into without having his guts turn around once inside himself. In America old people have eyes that would want to strip an African naked, tear away all flesh of dignity, love, security, hope—then lay it down on a busy road, to roll over its head with steel cars and trucks. The children must not care too much about the old people because the old people want to be children. They play dress-up like children. They finish up their lives wanting to play like children. Yet when they're old and too weak to walk or feed themselves, the children are grown-up and almost old themselves, wanting to start play some time soon. In America it's something quite similar to kicking the aged in the face until death. And when that's over and done with, we slap the dirt off our hands and then get back to work. The old teach the young to be indifferent towards death. As if our babies couldn't see the line of road kills littering our freeways, our highways, our thruways, our countless ways to get away. That deer's head is hanging on by a thread! Is that a whole possum or an organ pancake with blood syrup? Daddy, why is that African man sitting cross-legged on the side of the road, gobbling up a mutilated raccoon? My tummy hurts, Daddy! Please stop the car. My tummy hurts, and you don't care at all about the murder of my playthings.

Affluence and swimming pools. Everyone here has nothing to say. Yet the silence is not wise. It's stupid. The look on their faces is a dumb one of fear. Fear a-plenty. Fear of losing the affluence and swimming pool. I say buy alpacas, a girl and a boy, and go broke all day long with the birds. We are sad, frowning beasts of unnecessary burden suffering from lifelong joy constipation. Giono writes for

Bobi: "Youth and joy is a passion for the useless." That means live and die for a jar of hardened peanut butter.

I reside on the corner of living death, number seventy-two, where the sweeping never ends. Adventure is over. Death happened yesterday. Everybody went to heaven without saying goodbye. Then heaven kicked out the selfish brats. I want to throttle little boys for being born too alive for idiot parents to guide them.

It is time to write a book of morals, of principles, of destiny. It sounds queer, I know. Time to live some other philosophy besides "I have a rotten hole in my porch that needs to be fixed." Listen to me. Mark my words. All the mothers and fathers are dead beat, apathetic, girl men and boy women. They are dumb bullies walking tall in an Internet schoolyard made expressly for television's empty fake life. For purity to reign, for the sake of our mental health and happiness, America must cease creation altogether. It makes nothing worthwhile. Only more apathetic androgynies with the curiosity and wonder that befalls wet cement blocks.

Now we know how the mob rule of democracy breaks a healthy mind. No thoughts beyond going to the post office, to Florida, out to lunch, the cleaners, on a lawnmower. It's the death of spirit and personality. I can't believe how ungoofy the grown-ups are. I sit down on the porch of suburbia, drink from an aluminum can and watch the neighbors swarm about me. Not one of them is silly enough to notice. The plastic silliness of the world engulfs them. It is an enormous obviousness that is staggering. One must gyrate a goofy hump dance with the dog, whistle his own made-up tunes, ask unanswerable, nonsense questions to no one, just to light a tiny spark of happiness. Freaking Christ, we need to be silly or die!

No. Instead one drinks scotch or tries yoga, and then watercolors, and then health food, and then screams out "why me?' while his uninvited guest cancer gobbles up entropy cells. It's all too serious. Everyone needs a loud laughing at. The neighbor sets up his sprinkler with such a sad face. The plants would rather wither away and die than be quenched by such unendurable sorrow. Every woman in America between the ages of twenty-two and fifty-two must either turn all-out lesbian or band together to laugh together in packs at one man standing naked holding a toothbrush. American men are nothing but excellent material for Pakistani comedians. I asked my daughter to count the obese people yesterday. Granted we were at an ice cream stand, but I bet similar results at a water fun theme park.

There will never be a revolution. Just look at what we are dealing with! When life is this sterile, potential revolutionaries become soy milk drinkers. Where are the mad ones? The hermits with a sense of humor and human? The craziest crazy of all is that such insanity can take itself so seriously. I don't know one person as healthy as myself. I don't look up to any living man. I look down at dried up dead worms on my walk to get orange juice. In a world consisting of billions of like creatures, how can it be that the future of humankind is all up to me?

I am going to go out on a limb and say insanity is the disease. Everything in America is now a mind disease. There is no more room for good physical health because our fat brains have taken over. The fall cannot be prevented. Now we are falling. Jump off the limb because they're going to cut down the tree anyway. Daddy's got a wallet stuffed with cash so the tree-cutters must come. Daddy doesn't mind if the tree-cutter is a boy half his age with a plastic phone to his ear. He's all decked out in fashionable shorts and cloth belt, white sneakers, and moosed hair. Daddy's got money and that's all that matters. Even if in some cultures a man would die from shame if he could not complete these natural tasks alone. That is not the point. Today the ancient tree gets put down with paper money taken from the paternal wallet.

I am going to write. I am writing now. It is inevitable. I've been pushing it off for so long. America wants that I go crazy and soil myself. I swear that I have never met another poet. The closest I've come to finding one agrees with me that the sky is falling, and then rushes home to mommy, smokes a bowl in his bedroom, and gets rocked to sleep by late-night cable TV.

I am going to start the revolution. Gather all ye rosebuds now you sloppy piglets, crush them between your fast food hamburger and chew. Soon Ronnie boy's gonna walk by dropping death onto your pot-bellies.

I could kill. The apathy is total now. The slaves are eating their breakfasts. There is nothing that can stop me from hating you. My cat struts through the tall grass with a dead bird in his mouth. Oh that proud animal doesn't need my store-bought bag of urinary tract kibbles. I'm going to get you first! Did you think I would just wait for the cancer to eat me? Or for the President to bomb me? Or for the

CEO to pollute my lungs? I say America should stop breathing. And it will. This is the beginning.

My wife is envious of the old lady who's in charge of the community garden. I wonder if she knows she's living and sleeping with the man who will watch the old woman burn at the stake, while he chews on one of her asparagus spears. I am a fat, humming high voltage wire. I want the nuclear power plant enveloped in flames. I want foreign fighter jets to spray bullets at my home. I want disaster to wake me up enough to kill. To gather my daughters up in my arms and run. I won't wait for the judgment that will never come. I want everyone to start believing in their local flora and fauna more than in their own, fellow human beings.

Poetry is dead. I believe that life is dead.

Whoever reads my book, know that I know you are dead.

I want to hold her hand and cry.

I have never met a man I would want to imitate. I must be the last human being alive who does not accept logic.

I do not believe there is a man who struggles to complete himself like I do. No other bodies in the park grass lying around like beggars waiting for poetry. Even the women, who could be our last, and greatest poets, are content to remain a male waste product recycled into farm animal key holders, crafted for the next generation of men to hang their tiny, insignificant glories upon.

Men, ha! There's a book out on the shelf, a bestseller, entitled Being a Man. That's also a popular phrase these days used with the hope that nobody sees the man stripping off his lace underwear and standing in front of the mirror with those bony knees quivering. There's a chapter on John F. Kennedy. As if he was a man! A shit father, a cheating husband, a masturbating girl-boy, sticking his finger in his ass and smelling the finger. I want all men to emasculate themselves. He was President? A martyr? For whom? The Alabama negro? What, you don't think he smirked every time his piss drunk father said that word?

His contemporary, Fidel Castro, was, and is more of a man. Hail Fidel! Still, just a smidgen less the baby boy than JFK. All world leaders need and want to be spanked. It's the truth. Fidel dreamed of being a baseball player. John Kennedy thought Robert Frost was a poet. "Ict bin Berliner" The Berliners should have set him on fire and tinkled warm piss over his ashes.

We are bonkers. 100% careful to the edge of madness, and dying of cancer before getting the bright idea to live first, and then die. Stand apart from the world as it turns now. Stand on Mars to watch. Stand in your own front yard. Open your mouth and stand there not making a sound. Nothing is here because of you. You stand alone without any truth. People never talk to people like they do to dogs and cats. God pity the human beings.

At work the country music station plays. It's been torturing me. Some of the cooks know the refrains. They talk the words instead of singing them. The sky is black and three mile high thunder clouds billow out of the stratosphere. If I knew there would be this much death of spirit when I was nine, I would have made many, many tiny steps away from men. By this time I would be lost in a forest of heaven on earth. The cooks are like plumbers. They have no creation dreams. They put things together and listen to the commercials on the radio. "It would be a pity if you don't shop at Honda City." After our children kill us for the highest irony of all—reanimating their souls— I hope they make pee-pee in our mouths.

I want to quit my job as punishment for their constant displays of apathy and inertia. That has always been the bane of my desire. I would rather live and die the way God wanted me to, but my stomach turns sick inside while watching them, and I can't stay still long enough to save for myself a quiet, uneventful, uninterrupted, sweet, ecstatic life.

My friend called last night. I told him to be nineteen again or die. He'll never kill himself. I could give him a loaded pistol and he would watch TV and forget that he was in possession of instant-death. He must call himself back to the gray thoughts and gray days. No one ever exchanges money. No things. Always people, friendship and love, in our nostalgic dreams of the past.

This is not esoteric writing. My friend is like everyone else. A money slave with the real freedom of mad joy lurking several miles deep down in the chasm of his true mind. But his life remains to be a taco sandwich and a long, nightmarish sleep on a cot rocking over the edge of the chasm. Finally mankind has freedom of movement, of sunshine and water without too much disease and death. So he watches TV with this never before known freedom. My friend would not kill himself even if I mailed him some deadly pills with a note attached that said, "Eat us and die instantly". So my equally good advice was to become nineteen again. So far he has not raised children to love and adore. His father bails him out of trouble. From a little friend's point-of-view he will always be thirteen. I told him to eat when he gets hungry, have enough money for beer and cigarettes, and meet me at the tubes at seven-thirty. We'll crawl inside and talk about girls and feel free because we can finally talk about what we want to do with the girls.

Last Friday I put up a sign for the wait staff. "Please donate to my friend who might end his life soon." Twenty-three cents went into the bucket. I want them all to be set on fire.

These wasted suicides won't even do the job the right way. In the forest or out on the ocean. They want to be discovered and buried properly. "Please don't forget my note." I don't know of any suicides that happened the way I would kill myself. That selfish bastard still has a cellular phone and pumps gas into his shiny silver car. "What about my couch?" he says to let me know that I will never see his suicide come to fruition. He doesn't know how to love. Won't do anything for love. Wants money so he can fuck. Love is dead. It will be love when it's a leap off a speeding train in pitch darkness. If you won't walk deep into the forest to kill yourself... If you don't have that sensibility to cut out your bowels before a squirrel who won't tell anybody, then all you want to do with life is fuck it.

God! Excluding my wife and children, I don't even have a friend! We are now afraid to talk to each other. Man to man? Pat, my dear friend of our precious youth, you have become an androgynous money slave ass-sniffer! You have the balls of a girl-snake, the greed of hyena, the raving love and illuminating shows of life everlasting that a sloth expresses to an aluminum can. I can never be the friend I was at thirteen. A friend of yours now would have to drag you into a forest and serve you an Amanita muscaria pie.

This truly is the living death. I told my wife and my mother that I'm going to screw a strip of wood into the wall to hang my pans. "No, no. You'll rush it, and we want it to look nice." Women are not made to know pain. I am ready to take over the world to establish my kingdom, and yet I allow myself embarrassment over the decoration of a wall. They don't see the world dying. They don't see the marvelous rebirth of humanity. They see perfect walls for no one to look at. I see the sky falling and hear all our babies screaming for their mothers.

Buck and Barney are the two cooks who keep my ten dollars an hour secure for the time being. Buck has been cooking for twenty-three years. Barney for seven. They're both idiots, but Barney is also an asshole. Buck was offered two dollars more than minimum wage to work the busiest line in Oswego. Seven-fifty an hour to cut through five ribs, broil two gallons of scallops, ten pounds of fish, grill burgers, steaks, and chicken, make marks on all roasted steaks and chops, non-stop for five hours, falling behind, getting ahead, but mostly staying behind, and then mop up the mess on the floor afterwards. Buck didn't show up for work last night. Time to join him. Here's the letter I wrote to my managers, Ted and Barney.

Dear management,

It's time to leave for good. Twelve times is a charm.

I'll make this resignation short and slightly bitter. I can't give overtly lax management the pleasure of me keeping quiet.

This restaurant sucks bitter and I know why. I'd rather go broke standing upright than play "Neurological Breakdown" night after night for greedy monkeys. So I leave with some final thoughts for Ted and Barney. Take the remarks seriously because I only write what I know.

Ted, you suck, through and through. You are the worst kind of manager. You think that cutting an ounce off a steak is good management. You are just the bosses' mouth. So, you have aspired in a lifetime to becoming the mouth of a crazy man. Boss is Mr. Potter from It's a Wonderful Life, and you are Mr. Potter's wheel chair pusher. You play around with a man's wage. If I were Buck, I would consider shoving a handful of my wage up your ass.

You are whatever you desire to be. A good father? A quiet man? A sexy dancer? Outside of work I wish you an ecstatic life. I don't know, perhaps you put on a gracious mask upon leaving the restaurant. Maybe out whistling behind the wheel in your 4X4, you imagine yourself to be Harry Bailey, or Ernie, the happy cabby. Imagine what you want, because imagination is all we got left. I imagine that if I dressed up my dog Beany in a collar and shoes, he'd manage the restaurant better than you. I bet I could train him to not shit on the floor during service. I would like to say the same for you. But you're untrainable. Not housebroken. Not only do you ca-ca the joint, but you leave everyone else's shit there to stink it up too!

The restaurant is filthy. That could be forgiven if it kept its cheer. It's just not a cheerful place to work anymore. Everyone is unhappy. Even the bus boys and dishwashers have an opinion of disgust.

A suggestion of choice for you, if you so desire to become a better human being, and therefore a smarter manager... Quit the restaurant business immediately, or clear those god damn cigarette butts off the parking lot! Get to work you laze-about, you sniff ass! Stop stuffing your face with bread and butter chunks, and teach your employees to trust at least half of your poor decisions.

Hello Barney. I gave Ted more than he deserves. My intention was to focus on you, since you'll be struggling in this crappy business for the rest of your life. This is criticism you'll appreciate in ten years. But now you're too arrogant to appreciate a good spanking. Arrogant with Golden Award margarine! Absolutely ridiculous!

I told you the first week I was hired back that your employees can only be as good as the manager. In this type of business anything good starts at the top. I have been at this restaurant long enough to develop a smart sense of the good and the bad—for this restaurant. I also worked at the Captain's Corner with you Barney, long enough to know how inexperienced you were at management. You had no understanding of proper training, consistency, scheduling, cleanliness, food handling...In fact, you had no qualifications to manage. So this restaurant hired you to manage its kitchen. Like Ted, you think money is management. The plumbers at the Captain's Corner gave you that disease. They were working with plastic pipe and out-gas of glue—not glorious food that needs to be handled lovingly by inspired cooks. I tell you, now is the time to be humble and learn.

As a sous chef, Jeff Bellow worked twice as hard as you. One has to live the kitchen to head the kitchen. If it means being in at 9:00 a.m. to teach an employee the "right way," then you do it. For your own sanity. Presently, you're not the right stuff for management. In the cover letter to my resume, I wrote that I needed to work in a well-managed establishment. Neither you nor Ted are making the right moves. So I go, happily in the right as usual, but broke again for sure.

You're a good enough cook. I'll give you that. However, you need to develop a love for the food you prepare. And stop talking French! Christ, the French would bury your face in merde if they knew what you were doing to their food. Golden Award! Might as well piss in the sauté and save yourself a lemon.

I've enjoyed working beside you during the busy. When I was making mucho bucks as my last chef's assistant dupe, I had to go off salary time and again because I couldn't look the other guys in the face. I worked like a madman, but when crunch time came, all of our brains were melting—not just mine. The discrepancy in pay was not deserved. Damn ownership and management, forever playing money master to wage slaves.

It would do you some good to sweep the parking lot. Even the good lard knows you can't get a dishwasher to do it.

Outside of work, in a more mellow world, I hope we can meet with a handshake and a couple laughs. I believe I helped you out where and when I could. Now it's time for you to save your own ass.

Good fortune to you and your little girl.

Adios Ted. Talk to you cowboys in the next life.

George Bailey

I'm locked up in the teahouse. The rain is heavy. Wind too. I feel the energy to write another eighty pages. But as usual I will write two or three pages worth of mock-enlightened rant, and call it a day.

Last night while waiting in a parking lot in the rank and filth of dirty, soiled, and brown Auburn, NY, two eight-year-old boys took turns throwing a concrete rock into a rain puddle. Wonderful I thought! Innocence. Real joy. Oh, but it wasn't long before I convinced myself that in ten years both of these boys would be insane. In twenty years, criminally insane. In thirty years, homicidally insane. In forty years, practically insane. In fifty, barely lifting a golf ball off the delicate mowed grasses of insanity. Irrigated grass. Technological grass. In sixty years both boys would possess a bleeding, cancerous gash in the prostate. One of them would talk of nothing but his open sores and the dumb dot-head doctors who insist on operating. The other boy would get plowed over by a tractor trailer because he drank two scotches at the club instead of cuddling up in bed with his dying wife.

I am thirty-four years old, sane enough, and as wise as I will ever be. There's not a positive goal to aspire to in a country where all the children are insane.

I am overflowing. The creative spirit is tickling and teasing me. It goads me to write what I cannot write, because if I wrote it, I would no longer be human. So I had better stop writing for people.

There.

I am writing for goats. I don't want to pretend that I am an intelligent human. I'm not even a smart goat. If I wrote in goatspeak for eighty pages or so, maybe I could find a goat that would eat my book. Every pasteurized, homogenized house on this street should have a goat in the yard. And now that the children are insane it's high time for their bleating goats to explode.

My happiness is awake. It was asleep underground but now it is awake. Although still underground. I want all of you to feel the gladness I feel while my wife and I cuddle with the children in bed. I am so far down below that even your sewers cannot reach me. No one can see me. And if you light a match to get a better look, your face will explode.

Can you smell hot homemade pancakes served on a white plate? Can you taste the maple syrup and salted butter melting over the top? In late September the clouds carry the first cold rain that will help you forget the Roman-ness of summer. Time to hibernate like the animals. My writing must have some feelings you share when wondering about the bliss of nostalgia. This particular letter must be a feel of gray clouds moving over your hands while you lie down in the grass for the last time this year. Soon the true cold and wet, and then snow. Spring is newborn up until the age of equally ravenous and stupid adolescence. Summer is manhood, womanhood. Fall is the present of whatever you are. And winter is all about remembering the bummer of mortality... Life is one such year, and then it's over. Just like that.

I hate America because it has stalked my imagination day and night and attempted murder on my sense of adventure. A listless waiting. A small rise and fall in the chest. One eye might open for a second, when no one is looking. This is the new frontier? This space? This emptiness? Fill in the void here? You stupid, overtly pleasant numbskulls! Adjust your lives this instant to continue the rightful evolution of our species. Think about where the day should go when you are alive! No death. No unhappiness. No more bottomless brain sludge in an acid lake. It's been twenty-five years since I have spoken with an enlightened human being. We were lying down in the soft grass tossing a stick back and forth. The clouds passed overhead while time passed away. I want all of you to change course by tomorrow! Become the overflowing reservoir you were born to be. An Alpine lake, too deep to measure, and water pure enough to drink and breathe if you are a fish. I don't think that I will ever get through to you. You are a target I hit, round after round, but cannot penetrate.

This teahouse is my only material treasure. My anger will cease and my love for humanity flower the first morning I prefer to brew tea and not count money. In my dream of last night there was satellite TV hooked up in the basement. I have read Suzuki's plea to the western man. I know that if his books were stacked up beside a box of stale vanilla wafers, the western man would blankly flip through the pages looking for pictures, while eating the cookies. If his wife was beside herself with anger, screaming out her final "No!," he would take the wafers to the living room, lay down on the sofa, channel surf, and chew. If he had the choice of Suzuki or death, he'd sneak the box of wafers down into the basement and munch and munch and munch for however long it took death to pass over him.

The life in me has never been this ready to release itself. I feel a total desperation, but the only positive action I can dream up is a new plan to quit my job. When I was young I could take a bottle and a friend to get the madness off my chest. Today it's just madness that doesn't go away. Unavoidable masochism. I chew flat stones instead of stale wafers, in a pretend show to stay a step or two away from men.

I need one other person to be as daffy as me. Just one, do you understand? Then we could make our bitter points heard to the walking cadavers of the earth. Are there even two people out there brave enough to share their mad, post-modern personalities? Will anyone play concrete rock with me? It's not only very unlucky to be socially sane, but to be so is the mark of the highest insanity. The socially sane shop for furniture. One important aspiration of the socially sane is to get through life with just a moderate intake of alcohol. Another is a painless death. Social sanity means never having to fall down drunk in front of your children, unless you can get lucky, and die drunk. Controlled decision-making. Silent dreaming. Extremely controlled dreaming and silent decision-making. Secret dreaming. Underground dreaming. Dream awake, however be prepared to utter a sober "please" and "thank you" upon each human encounter. Watch the boys drop a rock into the rain puddle. Shhh! Wait and hope and dream that there will come a wonderful day when your brain decides to pick up that rock and drop it in the puddle again. Meanwhile, while silently dreaming, ask, "What are we having for dinner?" Wait a moment for an answer. Be patient. One never needs to demand an answer. It will most certainly come. Social sanity must always be polite. Time will get its chance to tie those little boys up into a life of constant, silent, agonizing dreaming. Time waits well. So do the socially sane. They are consummate waiters. Always on purpose.

I think Janie was teething the day the war began. I am at war with America. Come get me.

Afraid of death. Terrified of living without coffee. Consumers continuing movement after having every organ sucked out of their bodies and the bodies stuffed with purchases! I am a man trapped in the culture of no culture. These rows of American flags protect materials. Imagine what the flags are covering... Behind that flag's door is a pot-belly drinking soda on the couch. He would shit his pants if an armed-to-the-toe, sandaled Arab walked into the room. Box cutters? Americans were overtaken by box cutters? The caged poodles in the hold of the plane were ready to leap through the floor and tear at the hijacker's flesh, but no man was ready to risk his life to save his life. Jesus, whenever Jesse James held up a stage, he made sure there were several robbers with him, and plenty of guns too. If not, the women passengers, petticoats and all, would jump down off the stage at full gallop, and ferociously scratch out eyeballs to prevent assault and robbery. But these guys had box cutters. Box cutters!

Flags and more flags. We need bigger flags for bigger houses. What a warning to the world! "Bomb us with our own planes and you just see how many flags we can buy!" Now the terrorists back East, burrowing in the sand, have a sense of humor. This moment their leaders are sitting down around a campfire, giggling and toasting their luck with tin cups of warmed goat's milk.

My wife and I admit that I must be careful what I write. Too many stupid people in the world. She fears for our safety. No fear-struck tiny editor mind would publish this book in America anyway, so she shouldn't worry. She can worry the day I address all of my manuscripts to Pakistan.

Is it over? Is the war over? A "Don't Tread On Me Flag" is popular at market today because it's different. A fine symbol for revolution with an autumnal Winnie-the-pooh flag waving below. Got to prove to our neighbors that we are patriotic and incurably tasteless. Beany Babies for sale down a rural American road, and when church lets out up the street, I swear to God that not one of those flesh blobs looks human. Stunted human moles, young and old with flab roles. No man walking down the steps, tall, strong, proud, fierce. Everyone into a new car. Even the rectory hangs it's token flag. Next to the Monsignor's satellite dish!

Kenneth Patchen wrote about the war in 1940. Hell's images for pompous literati to slice open their wrists with. But no one who mattered read it. The killers never read. Ferocious dogs and their mad, continuous barking. The indifferent cold murder of children and the elderly. The running and hiding behind walls to rape twelve year old girls. Lynching. Tying up negroes and Chinamen to trees and snapping rubber bands around their constricting testicles. Stopping along the highway to rob a service station. Setting up camp on a riverbank southwest of Detroit. The relentless bombing from the skies, bullet holes, bleeding... The masses cannot understand. Their children will go to school to recite The Pledge of Allegiance. I must nip that insanity in the bud. It is my intent to poison their little minds with the truth, for someday they will be grown-up enough to kill. I must teach them now, in innocence, the value of life, of every life, human, skunk and stinky Arab.

At the dinner table I have told my daughter that war can be creative. If America dropped baskets of fruit over terrorist compounds, I would rave about being a patriot and wave my flag out in the yard, on my car, out my ear. I'd take it to bed with me. Baskets of fruit, toy horses, lemonade packets, toilet paper, dog bones... War is hell, but only from lack of imagination. Drop sacks of body odor, a billion dollar bills, false teeth by the thousands. Strap a couple billionaires to gigantic fresh-water fish and drop them with a surprising message of devotion to humanity.

Why the billionaires? Because they are the ones the evil doers want. Tie Bill Gates to a mother salmon fat with eggs, ride him and the poor fish five miles into the sky, tie a note to his wrist that reads, "I think that you starving sand niggers smell" in Arabic, or whatever language those dirty beggars speak nowadays, and drop him, the fish, a bright light, and a parachute over the bleak and wide desert of human sadness and poverty.

I say seize his assets, and those of anyone else who would allow decorative crafts into their homes. Seize everything made of money and convert it all into silly bombs. We must retaliate with laughter. Terrorize the world with laughter!

But I am through with war. It doesn't exist. I said Janie was teething the day the war began. She's still teething and it's over. Finished forever. No more human wars. They're too funny. Historically speaking human blood wrought from war is funny. It is entertainment. It's still Thanksgiving in November and beer picnics on Memorial day even if a Johnny's head was sliced off in 1863 or 1943 or 2003. It never matters. I want very much for this book to blow some fresh air into our children. I want to empower each child with the vision of becoming a remarkably better parent than what exists today. I write for the children although I don't want the children to read what I write. It is a book for when they grow up. If I finish it, they will grow up by the year 2020. If I don't finish it, all the babies presently cutting teeth will have their brains blown out impersonally by whichever President you elect. My finished book is all about teaching the children music and sewing, cooking with love, and building shelters for safety and never decorative deception. It is teaching them sanity. Because right now, at present, the parents cannot differentiate between sane or insane. I need to shine some light on the darkness coming. Truthfully, there is no danger that your local lettuce-nibbling backyard rabbit hasn't felt a thousand times already. Still, we tend to make our imaginary monsters massive, ferocious, and unmerciful, even if they are not real. American monsters at their most violent and murderous, are really just crying new born babies with sore gums.

I loathe American Democracy. It sucks. I think we need a king of America. A successful revolution would crown a king. A king would spare us another four hundred years of cancerous madness. But what would happen to the poets? Well, he would have to wipe them out of course. I mean the four or five who foolishly kept writing the truth. The rest of the pretties, the laureates and the university professors— they could keep writing the safe crap that buys things, whether medium-sized boats, new cars, or self-esteem. It might please the king. Only in times of near disaster would it matter to me that I had a silver tongue. Then I'd speak up knowing that my throat would be cut by the king if I did not.

Yesterday, on the way to my sister's new house, I drove the car across a bridge built over an ancient river. Down below, along its southern bank was the timeless village of Lashojas. Autumn's blaze was full, singing praises of Indian summer. Canoes paddled up to docks where the children gathered to play. Husbands and wives were out walking, dreaming, of their golden day and the last still night before the cold winds blow.

"This is the real world," I whispered to my wife who was nursing our baby in the backseat.

"What?" she asked. The broken muffler drowned out my talk.

Then I said, "Canoes," as if expecting her to see all that I saw of the invisible village during those few seconds spent speeding over the bridge. She saw. She knows. We have a baby. We cry. We feel.

Lashojas had a king. Not a mayor. Not a chief. No governor, no supervisor. The king had the power of the village's strongest man, balanced beside the weakness of its most sensitive woman. The people sat at council. It mattered what they said, so the king could make his best decision, which was unanimously accepted. How could his decisions not be pure? Each utterance was true, every action needful, all no-action religiously necessary. Lashojas had a warrior-king. Without him, there would be no Lashojas.

Were they free?

More free than any freedom anyone has ever imagined.

More free than a United States Citizen?

Well, if freedom meant a safer place for human fear and apathy to reign, then no, the men and women of Lashojas were not free. Freedom was not a word in their vocabulary, nor was it ever a sign to motion. The people called themselves "trees with legs." The king had all rights to hurricane or calm summer days. Yet he never ruled on whim. Nor did he need to conceal automatic weapons beneath his pillow. He kept no army besides devoted trees with legs, all of whom had unyielding, equal ambition to raise sane and healthy children. There was no nuclear missile ready in silo to annihilate the neighbor village, nation, or planet. No prisons that could comfortably fit a walking tree with legs.

When human evil came to Lashojas, the king killed it with his bare hands. Then he cut it up and fished using tiny cut chunks of its flesh as bait.

The United States has a president. It has freedom too. Freedom that is well defined, which doesn't make a difference because its people are caged singing parakeets, not walking trees. When the President says, "kill," the parakeets clump together and trill "kill." When the President says, "Good parakeets," the parakeets coo and cuddle up in flannel pajamas. They are proud of being caged birds. And why not? They have the biggest cages, bursting surpluses of parakeet food, shiny parakeet cars and trucks to wash and wax by their immaculately clean water bottles. When the President says "everything is evil," the parakeets coo. When the President says "Have a good time," the parakeets take off to Disney World, warbling and wondering, only to crash into walking trees and explode. When the President says time to kill again, the parakeets go shopping. They praise their god who is the parakeet with all the stuff. Their president is a money god.

No parakeet will trust another parakeet. Mother and father parakeets are waiting for the President to appear on TV. The baby parakeets are staring into the mirror. They are singing "me, me, me, me, me." The President is on. The President sings.

"Hey wait a second!" says the want-to-be walking tree parakeet. "He's not singing to us from a cage. He's a thousand miles away safe in a steel mansion with many bullet-proof rooms. He has servant parakeets, a free car and all the gourmet seeds he can eat. He flies in leisure through the most ominous skies because the parakeet air force protects his wing. La! La!" The lone parakeet is startled by his own, emerging voice. "La! La! Who the hell does that President parakeet think he is bossing? La-la-da-dent-ta-da! President of the parakeets my eye! I have every right to be the President of me!" The parakeet with the new voice sings out to his fellow caged birds. They cannot hear. They drown out the new voice of the parakeet with a flood of their combined singing. They watch their President on the TV. They sing songs about their President. They pick out the best seeds in the dish. They buy parakeet toilet paper and sing "freedom" and "God bless America" because their President told them to.

The lone parakeet flies off to Montana, buys a used cage and carries it in his beak to a remote woods.

Meanwhile the entire population of the United States of Parakeets minus one rebel, caged bird, has their necks broken and feathers plucked personally by the king of Lashojas. That night he orders his cooks to prepare a grand feast to mark the change of season, and initiate another walking tree.

Even if I had the originality to access entry into the minds of future man, and they bought fifty of my books a month to keep my grandchildren free from toil, what good would that befall my family if their memories of grandfather were of a broken, and defeated man? Especially if all they ever wanted was a toy?

To continue on this course means to be too poor to give them a plastic bag to play with during a visit. I couldn't even find one of those last night to shut out the freezing cold draft above the sill! My wife said, "Well, we'd have to go to the grocery store to get one of those!" Then she laughed. I laughed. In twenty years, neither of us will be laughing.

The spiritual meltdown of America. Yes of course! But what good is showing them if in return they cannot provide a chicken to braise in my pot every Sunday? I am spent. I want so badly to leap over to the other side. I want the opportunity to make the money I see being burned all around me. My daughter is selling candy bars. She put $22.00 into the 4-H piggy-bank this month. I made no money for my family. No money. Not even for food. Nada. What's worse is that I am completely indifferent about getting a job.

I believe I have the right to steal for food and rent. Yet I won't even imagine the opportunity! Total and absolute slave mentality. They got me! It's a Saturday morning of the 21st century. I possess heaven's eternal right to demand two percent of the millionaire's income. A lousy two percent! That feeds the family, and delivers a toy or two for the children this Christmas. Why not? No millionaire earns his fortune, not working the way I have over the years. Five dollars an hour. Ten, fifteen, even fifty an hour and there's nothing waiting for us besides cancer and heart disease. Only a persistent, insanely determined few can get to the million. They should be the most unlucky in a healthy society, and raided right now for a fair distribution of their dough. It's a lie to say that anyone has ever earned that kind of money. It just isn't true.

How many thousands of years philosophers grappled with the mysteries of life! Some in robes, most in rags, a few stark naked, but all in need of a bath. And for what? For more unsolvable mysteries! Fate, spirit, wealth, happiness, law, morality... No. This morning I stopped believing in morality. I launch internal mind spit at anyone who practices morality. My neighbor has enough to share with me. Money, not morality. I can take him by the throat and demand fairness, compassion, humility, and money, good god, yes... Money! Demand a position beside him at the office to prove to the world that I can squeeze a dollar from innocent blood as well as the next guy. If he doesn't budge, I'll take his money or his life—whichever I can get to first.

Aeons of thinking philosophy, arranging philosophy to fit a philosophy. And what is there now? An infinite number of paths leading to money. And still only one lonely road into the soul. Ten thousand years of practiced thought. So what? For this? Through every age, every epoch, all laws made by kings or legislators had to be broken by real philosophers. Then the philosophers were hung, or stretched, or tarred and feathered to death for breaking the law. Over time truth came to despise real philosophy because it could never amass an army before all of its soldiers got killed off. America, the modern empire, enforces its laws at the bottom in order to protect the top. It doesn't matter if the bottom mass is a million times that of the top. The bottom can be that huge, that massive, but the law would never allow one lucky man to crawl out from under it. That might make the top drop another fifty bucks. So today laws are made to break the philosopher long before he can summon the courage to break them himself.

The philosopher is trespassing in America. He might walk tall, but get caught on the treated lawn of the millionaire, and off to prison, or a fine, or no job, or divorce, or "here's fifty more channels for free, you human embarrassment! Be entertained and be thankful! If we catch you farting around this property again, you will be shot dead."

In America the philosopher is anathema, the millionaire admired, the middle class, the envy of themselves, and the poor, always deserving to be envied and admired, someday. Truth is anathema. And each philosopher accuses the other of seeking a pension and not the truth. Correct! There is no truth after a man watches his second car commercial.

Who or what do you think these new and popular terrorists want? America? Do you really believe that? Yes you do. The reason for the recent flag proliferation. But I tell you, and telling you I know lessens my odds for a healthy dinner this week... Still, I tell you anyway. Listen. The terrorists want our millionaires. And yet we refuse to hand them over. There will be no more terrorism if we drop ten in the desert right now, freeze their assets, no—take their assets and bake money pies with them. Drop them and their pies to feed the hungry. Give up our millionaires to the terrorists! That's what they want, and if anyone actually listened to their desperate plea to America, we might achieve a better understanding. Perhaps even take a step closer to morality.

Why did the World Trade Center have to be so god damn big in the first place? Could not the business smarm of this nation conduct the rape of our planet from underground? All of this is the fault of a cocky architect. A wiser Joe would have built Rape Central as close to the center of the earth as possible. How many companies upstairs do you think practiced honest, caring, business acts of love and devotion to their clients, employees, and the unrecognized gazillions of other sentient beings occupying planet earth? Each greedy business had its crooked fingers pushed up deep inside some poor man's ass while busily cutting back another species to extinction. I'm sure of it. And so are you. But we're entertained too well to think about those things. Too painful, especially before, during, and after such a delicious and filling supper.

And the other terrorist target...Tell the truth. How many murders do you think the Pentagon has been accomplice to? And don't you dare say that there is any such thing as necessary murder! My guess is, since the birth of our nation, that office, or its equivalent, has killed more or less about two million people. That's a very rough guess. The exact number can probably be determined, depending on your willingness to trespass onto its well-guarded estate. Just don't get caught, or they'll shoot you dead.

Tell me, what is Al-Qaeda? What does it stand for? Does it mean "bomb and burn innocent bodies?" Should we murder Timothy McVeigh's entire family; grandpas, grandmas, ma, pa, sister, brother, etcetera, and a few more thousand relations not by blood? According to this government's recent logic, oh absolutely! Actually, following its broken line of reasoning, we should bomb strategic pieces of this nation off the map. These lands were McVeigh's temporary hideout, were they not? If the FBI didn't catch him, Mr. President could have had Florida decimated, if he guessed that's where evil Timmy was hiding out.

But I despise myself for giving the murderers of the world my time and effort. Right now, undercover in America, every man, woman and child is perpetuating murder. Jesus, I'm sorry but it must be true. If I don't hear another dissenting opinion soon, I'll go mad. If there was just one other sane human being to talk to, I don't think my argument would get far enough to reach its inevitable conclusion of retribution. Just one more philosopher to explain my position to, for him to agree or disagree, but more importantly, for both of us to go out after talking and find a recreation less demanding than "round up" and "execution".

Give the terrorists the millionaires! Just don't give them the millionaire's money. They can have the men and women who make money their mission. They can shake each one over the sand, to death if they want to, and find nothing besides pale faces and eyes staring wide open. Without money, money cannot be made. Good riddance to the millionaire, I say. Bad news for the terrorists.

The real terrorists, the true "evil-doers' are the millionaires and any government that supports millionairism. It's the truth. Why should I explain it to men who refuse to think like men any longer? Real terror is obeying laws made against your conscience, and every law that has ever been made without my permission has gone against my conscience. I am so embarrassed to be an American. I am terrified to be an American. I fear my own country, like my countrymen pretend to fear planes being hijacked and steered into billion dollar buildings. I could squeeze an Arab until his eyes popped out. I am not frightened by this man, his bombs, nor his belief. I could take on any human being who challenged my heart's desire. Our government is no human being. It shares the same ideals as a terrorist organization, just on a more massive, near infinite scale. It is greater than Allah, than Yahweh, than it's own Jesus Christ, and the most terrifying truth is that *it knows!* And speaks murderous gibberish with a lunatic's zeal. It has purposely made itself master of a weak belief, built from fear, and lasting only because it is supported by nuclear missiles. Behind its present unlimited power the helpless American dogs play about without a care in the world. They are shit-sniffers who won't change a thing until the morning their food bowls aren't full.

But the real bonding strength of our country comes from the millionaire. What he represents to the shit sniffers is a lifelong, hope that the bones to come will get bigger and bigger. He is master. He decides which paths the loyal dogs will take. The terrorist dogs need his bones too. They need even more. Like an SUV and a rocket-launcher. These poor Arab dogs are no different from us. Just a touch more envious because of their poverty. They just want what every dog-brained citizen of the United States of Fatstomachs wants. And a rocket launcher. Hmmn. Where can a poor Arab dog get one of those?

From Grandma next door?

No.

From Lenny your best friend?

No.

From 99% of the shit-sniffing dogs in America?

No!

From the millionaires?

Should I write "yes?" Or should I beat you into the corner with a rolled up newspaper?

Meeting together, somewhere lost in a forest, I could give any millionaire smaller than me, a black eye and push down to the ground. And I know that terrorism would cease to exist if I knocked enough of these shorter scumbags into the dirt. The universal jihad of truth instructs us to turn on our masters, to upset our yummy food bowls, and go straight for the jugular.

But what about America? Why do I fear the country as a symbol more than the entire store of pot-bellied men who inhabit it?

Because as long as nuclear weapons exist, America cannot be beaten. Power is top dog. I can't imagine that a significant number of men live within these borders who would dare rise up to eliminate the bombs. Not even for the sake of their children. The fathers accept both nuclear bombs and millionaires. The fathers follow the millionaires. The fathers look the other way while their children are beaten with a stick by the millionaires. Even if all men were once themselves children and dreamers, it is only children, small children, very small children, the children before their mothers and father's wrong teaching... Only these small, helpless puppy humans, most still waiting to be born, can be trained to triumph over power.

Why?

Because in America, even the wide-eyed toddlers want to become millionaires!

So who will help these tiny babies?

Well, I am struggling to do my part. What are you doing Mr. and

Mrs. Fatlapdog?

Babble babble babble. I am not strong. I have not the strength to take on a country. My neighbor could say "Boo!" and I'd jump, then run, then hide. I am an American. I am over two. I guess I want to be a millionaire also. Yes, maybe it's time to admit defeat. You and I, from the beginning of time, and until the end, are the greatest cowards that have ever existed under stars in the night sky.

Time now to write my letter of application. I want the CEO job.

Generic Letter of Application For CEO Job

Today I shared a loaf of stale bread with my dog while my wife ate frozen shit on a shingle. If we decide to pay our bills and not buy food, tomorrow's dinner will be less and much worse. I want to eat and share a warm bed. I want to get excited over the purchase of a small toy this Christmas season for my new baby girl. My oldest daughter would like some good books and a reading light. She already has a library card, but we are not so certain that electricity will be in flow come December. And my wife? All she wants is my happiness. And a little money.

Therefore I want the CEO job. It will make me happy. I want it and will get it because I am smarter than the boob who is presently in control. Coincidentally, I want to rip off people and wear a sharp suit too. I want to make the company a million unearned dollars right now, not tomorrow, not even tonight. Now! I want to strip all company employees of dignity, and stamp my name on their paychecks. I want to enslave human beings and have a parking place reserved for me. I want to join you guys. Let the Board of Directors vote me into power. I think if the majority of investors get this letter, then the job is in the bag.

Here's what I want. $26,000/year, weekends off, and two week's paid vacation. I'll work hard for fifty or sixty hours each week. I will do this without a company plane, or car, or estate bought special for me. In fact I want no fringe benefits besides free coffee and a private bathroom.

There, I just saved the company a million dollars, and nobody got fired besides the single human piece of waste who was running the show yesterday. In the next minute I will sign a document that will save the company fifteen million dollars.

I, Ron Throop, expect not a dime of retirement money. No severance pay. Nada. Zip. If I don't do the job, please fire me, and get someone who can do it better for cheaper.

Signed: Ronald J. Throop   Date: Recently

Okay. So what is it we are selling? Dog food? No problem. Now that I am at the same pay as a veteran factory worker, we will be able to slash our prices and beat every competitor. I see here that your product design sucks. Well, the company is in luck. My wife is an excellent graphic artist. She will have the consumer believe he is buying a five pound bag of sugar cereal for breakfast. I might persuade her to do that for a mere compliment. Now you can fire half the advertising team. Another two million saved.

There. I just made our dog food number one in America, and this quarter's profits will break an earnings record. I don't ever expect a raise, so no conservative investor need fear a sudden growth spurt in my swimming pool.

Or are we selling cotton swabs? Same thing. I got a plan to screw over the Texas farmer good and proper. Next season he will be begging our buyers to stop by his field before crossing the border to Mexico. The crazy chiquitas down there work all day for fifty cents and a promise. You don't think I got the stomach for that? Oh I know some countries where the armless and legless disabled will role our cotton balls between their teeth and tongues for just one glass of clean water.

I will save you millions on the sale of whatever bauble, big or small, which you presently dangle in front of the dreamy eyes of fellow, zombie-struck human beings. You name the product—telephones, natural gas, electricity, garage door openers, ceramic bowls, toilet paper, giant, blood-dripping, cut-open stomach stink slaughterhouses... I am your cheapest and smartest choice. I am a marvel. Not only am I young, fit, and prepared to play along for the rest of my life at your cheat of humankind, but I am also quite good looking. So there's more money saved on advertising. Send over a film crew on my Saturday off. They can catch my wife and I warming up on top of a box of your crackers, or next to one of your checkered chair pillows. If it's nail clippers, just dub a row of them dancing across the screen and we'll be the leading seller of nail clippers by nightfall. I promise I won't charge a penny for that kind of service. My wife will probably expect some small compensation. Perhaps a new dress.

I am not kidding. I am so in earnest that it frightens me. I will represent your jigsaw puzzles, alarm clocks, tiny painted clown crafts, cheese spread, diaper pins, ant traps, playing cards, trucks, cars, paper plates, lawn mowers, screw guns, fence posts, television, DVD, VCR, rubber wire, jelly jars... On and on and on, and I will take the first offer, no matter what embarrassing trifle it is that you spend the better part of your lives trying to sell to everyone. Oyster crackers? I love them! I'll do anything to keep them profitable and in circulation. But I will not die for them. And neither will the overpaid moron who is presently ripping you off as CEO.

It would be foolish business to not even try me. There are two or three jackasses fired every day. Their stories are on the front page, and honest naive people feel the crunch in their retirement portfolio because that smiling white-toothed bastard had the board of directors sign him over a tremendous retirement package of goodies. Why should the board care? They still keep their jobs and their tremendous packages-to-be. Americans give lip service to the free market economy. What specialty do these top nips possess that any base-level nip couldn't develop simply out of real need for a job? Organizational skills? Public relations? A librarian or dog groomer could make the same, or better, decisions just as cleanly. It cannot matter because it's always figures, and never people. Merge the telephone mogul with the asphalt shingle and paper-clip robber-baron, fire six thousand people all suffering the possession of a car payment they can't afford, rearrange this department, add a secretary there, don't empty that trash basket until next Thursday, fly all the executives on the same plane, crash the plane, save two more billion...

You are afraid, aren't you? I might be in earnest. Then your competitor hires me, gets really rich, and you and your buddies lose the timeshare on that piece of ocean in the Caribbean. No, how could I trust you to share my letter with those people who matter? So when I send this application, I'll make sure to send a copy to a union worker or shareholder meeting loudmouth. I need a job, and I think that my simple solutions to your company's massive overhead might achieve some backers. If I am persistent I may even get the support from your volatile army of wage slaves who just got canned in a CEO supported sweeping up and downsizing of human dignity. That won't get me the job I need, but it will definitely piss off enough people to make a difference. If religiously persistent, I can provide for my wife and children. I might consider taking the CEO position of the company dedicated to sweeping up and clearing out the rotten millionaires and billionaires of the world. For as long as there is a man out there making a million dollars a year, in a forty hour work week, there will always be the man whose back breaks to make that man the million dollars. There is not a rich man out there, even in weak moments of benevolence and good will to men, who would refrain from anonymously whipping another human being to the ground in order to make more money for himself. All rich people partake in a massacre of the human soul. It cannot be helped. It will always be this way as long as there are words like "cell phone," "conduit," and "airplane" used to scramble and pollute the brains of the insignificant ones. (The millionaire's money runners).

We are all daffy. Now let's use this silliness to our advantage. Hire me. Simply for the worldwide positive disturbance I will create. Could it mean more profits? You betcha! On the cover of the nation's newspapers: "Time Warner/AOL Hires Throop To Do It's Raping." Or "Purina Bags New CEO Living Closer to the Bone Than the Average American Dog."

To hire me would show the world that your company has a regular guy to push its regular products on the regular consumer. Profits would certainly matter to me. I would want to keep my job. Why would I piss off your blood-thirsty mob of shareholders? It's either dividends or death for the lot of them. That the majority have allowed its executives to prance all over the earth creating and destroying like Indian gods is most certainly the bane of capitalism, and will forever remain a clueless mystery to me. Granny with her sixty shares invested should know exactly what the executive ordered for lunch. If she knew it was a bowl of lobster bisque with garnish of caviar, and a 20% tip was left on top of that, with her money... Well then, you might see granny get just ticked off enough to join in a hostile takeover and cutting up of the CEO.

Moreover, if hired, I promise to keep track of all expenditures. I intend to save the company money at every juncture. That means when we plan to buy out Chunky Tuna, Inc., and break the news to its top men over lunch, I'll make egg salad that day, bake the bread, and do all the dishes by myself.

Granny will appreciate that. She will rally behind me. I will get elected. All the stockholders will praise the company for such sound, honest decision making. Twenty-six thousand, weekends off, and two weeks paid vacation. I might even consider taking the job as a volunteer, provided your product is life-giving, or even somewhat necessary to sustain life. I would, however, expect home-cooked, free meals for my family, more nutritionally and aesthetically satisfying than shit-on-a-shingle.

Please consider an interview. I am ready for my fair share. I am also quite confident that my presence will only strengthen the goofy machine that is your company—always so serious about nothing really besides making more money. Let me in and I promise to do just that!

Let's go!

The eyes inside focus in on three to four chores at a time. I walk into a room and immediately bombard my time as if I not only wanted to kill it, but blow it to smithereens. What truly needs to be finished before the snow falls? In 1800, December moonlight was bright enough reason for father and son to shingle a roof. In 2001 the same moon shines, and so much activity is meaningless because it is unnecessary. No father son team tackling the weather, keeping mom safe for hasty puddings. Plenty of fathers and sons still, but all of them up late, alone somewhere, picking their asses. I wake up to notice the difference between midnight roofing work to keep the snow's weight from caving in the rafters and killing the family, and the cold, moonlit night when I admit to myself that I am afraid of the dark. I live my life in a trance. I don't know it until I wake up. And then what do I do? I take out the garbage while thinking about the dirty dishes, the load of laundry, the dust balls, the whining dog.

The brain mellows itself enough to see the tree, but never the leaves. The day it sees the infinite maddening colors of leaves and not the tree, man will have aspired to his first awakening. Finally he will have forgotten that he has a brain.

There are a few crazies out there seeing the leaves today. But you and me? We'll be content to suck in our guts while standing before the full-length mirror. Okay boys, now let's curse out the fat jelly below the chin. The hairy stomach, the man-breasts, the flab arms, the heavy neck, the hunchback, the chicken legs. Hate our physiques. Despise and deplore its mental store above. And nobody sit down to eat another cookie before cleaning up that mess in the garage!

After 1930 "neurosis" was the catch word for the American intellectual dwerb. Nowadays it's neuroschizophrenia. My only life accomplishment which I hope to make manifest in my children is the murder and meticulous clean-up of neuro-schizophrenia.

I am crazy because I want to paint with acrylics and teach my children the art of being alive? Yes. That is fine with me because I will live longer, which means that more cakes will get baked. I will kill time often enough to see the leaves. And why not always remain crazy if they already expect it of me? Unless I am not crazy enough. Then I better watch out, or they will certainly carve me up to fit neatly in some obscure corner of their neuro-schizophrenic scheme. Become a car mechanic or business lawyer, aspire to chefdom, manager, the pitiful CEO, force-fed an artificial, insatiable desire to know more than him or her, be smarter, quicker, wittier, funnier, and get money to afford three shampoos in the tub, and a fifty thousand dollar car that rusts.

Oh no. Not me. I'll get crazier if I have to. Keep ty-typing away. Tip-tip-tipitit-ding! I'll walk up to my seventy-year old typewriter, ready to begin my unending string of letters to you, to them, to silent comrades dead or unborn, and I'll bang-bang at the keys to keep me from banging bullets into you, to them, to nonexistent comrades unborn or dead. I guess perfect sanity was the bright autumn day when this typewriter was handed over to me. Hand-delivered out of a train at the station during a short period in my life when I fell in love with being crazy. A few pennies, a borrowed home, a man! A crazy one, that's for sure. But a man! Hot-diggedy dog! A man! Poor. Comfortable. Uncomfortable. Crazy. As sane as a bird. Wild and ordinary, with holes in my shoes and a starving heart.

It was all me. I wanted to be crazy. I consciously became callous, cruel, and loopy just to temporarily live the life of an artist. What's new? Here I am again.

My daughter is in the process of writing a diary for the young girl whose parents died in the World Trade Center attack. She is a born writer who will one day make a difference in her world. I have to wait until the year 2100. Only then will I get the respect of the post-consumers. Isn't it true, though, that if I was never born there would be no 2100? Does that sound crazy? No? How about this?

Snickle-pickle-put-a-pan-

ping-struck-a-dan-dan

Folapolapontickle!

Letter to the couple who came for dinner last Saturday

Dear Shannon and Bill,

I want to take this time out in my busy day to write down my thoughts to you both. What I am thinking and what my voice utters are so diametrically opposed to one another, that it's quite a wonder sometimes how I can get my thoughts to agree with the mouth to say "feed me."

More than anything I am sorry that I did not mention what mattered to me most last Saturday during our little dinner get-together. Oh I've been plagued all week with guilt and self-disgust for not divulging my true personality. At the time I think I was more concerned that you liked me. I didn't want to give the impression that I was a social retard, even though I most certainly am. What I really wanted to do was pee in your wine glasses. I knew immediately upon your arrival that the night was going to be angst and despair. That we would die or go to sleep. I realized how much I hated myself for not being true to everyone I meet.

Well Shannon, you're a secretary and Bill is a car salesman. I am a hack writer temporarily unemployed as a line cook, and my wife is your boss at the office. Not one of us is proud to be human.

Civilized? Yes, painfully so. Civilized to the power of googol and speeding faster toward the last straw of civilization. Peeing in your cup was the final act. At least from this house. Maybe my letter will re-civilize me. Do you think? No, it will only increase the strength of my cowardice. Bill will never see me again. But my wife must co-work beside you, Shannon, everyday to talk about television shows, popular movies, your promiscuous teenage daughters, Bill's new raise at the job... If I send this letter, she might never speak to me again. But I can't worry about that. To stand through another torture like last Saturday night would finish me off for good. Absolutely necessary that I nip this in the bud right away.

Did you like the dinner? I cooked for five hours. I prayed that every-

thing went well so we would open up like children do. That's what the
wine was for. But we never open up quite like flowers, do we? More like
four green garbage dumpsters and each one of us a child carefully dropping his dog's bagged shit inside. What was it we talked about for the
first five minutes while uncorking our tiny nightmares? The ride over.
The damn construction and the detour you had to take. Bill actually
seemed to be put out. He didn't want to come. But he's supposed to
love his wife. And me mine. It isn't enough that you girls are together
five days a week. Bill made you go to his friend's house last month. He
brought along a twelve pack of beer, and had one helluva time. The
boys got drunk. The girls talked about curtains, until the husband's
monosyllabic conversation switched to sex. Then even the table got
excited and shook for a few seconds. But that was it. Everybody went
back inside themselves. Bill wiggled the keys, and before long you were
back home checking on the kids in bed while Bill puked up his pizza
and beer in the downstairs toilet.

Oh I know Bill hates me. My dinner made him suspect. American
men don't whip up a hollandaise out of nowhere. Before I took your
coats I should have mentioned where I thought the night was heading,
that I've been through this before, that I could only allow two successful destinations for the evening—a hide-and-seek game after dinner, or
hopeful talk about revolution, personal and/or nation-wide.

But I was guilty. Caught in the game that we're all presently losing. I
cooked all day. I didn't draw, paint, or play. I didn't dream. I had to impress you. "We have so much good food to eat," I probably told myself.
"I must cook and artfully arrange their dinner. Then they will like me
and see that I am alive."

Wrong! No more. Next time it's hide-and-seek. Or we can all sit down
at the table and draw a picture for our kids. Crayons! Could you imagine? Oh no, of course you can't. Yours was the last dinner party that
this house will ever see. I won't allow another tragic story about a new
bathroom to my table again! Ceramic tile or hardwood? It won't matter
if I have to take a pee. Marie will pull me aside and whisper, 'Did you
pee in the wine again?' And I'll give her a playful, guilty look. She will
lovingly slap me on the shoulder, and we'll tell the other couple to run
outside now and play, while we do the dishes for the absolute last time!

It has to be this way or more letters. I am not ready to go down such
a frustrated and lonesome path. I actually fell asleep last Saturday night
forgetting to kiss my wife. I don't mean kiss her, and then turn out

the light either. You know what I mean. God, the heat we can create, but instead give up these nights to fashion and society! Shannon, you remember Bill, the first time, the second time... The time he pressed his body against you and the thrill of your heart, the excitement, the dreaming and hoping was a pleasure/pain that held your fragile belly in a vice. Those were the moments of true security. Not money, not job, not dinner. Hungry for sex, for love, for care of another human being. That's the hunger for life taking on a new form. We lust for life as children. We live again when our bodies take shape. We call that youth as we grow older and invite another couple over for dinner. Then we think to ourselves what's gone is gone forever and hell is another Saturday night getting ready to step into our shiny car for a drive over to the home of a couple we will never have the strength to know again how we knew them in the golden days of youth.

Now look at us. Saturday night at the Throop's! God awful. We could promise that next time we meet in the woods out back of your house. There at the path leading in, in the dark... Me with two bottles in a bag and Bill pointing the way to the big rocks where we'll build our fire, pass the wine, and talk and laugh again like we did when we were still near wild and fearful of each other's sex.

Yes! Next time we can concentrate on getting to know each other again. No hardwood floors. No curtains at K-Mart. The night shall be a romp through the forest of our youthful dreams. I'll kick your ass Bill if you go near my wife. Shannon looks great! Her cheeks flushed yesterday when she talked to her friends about you. Go for her and I'll work on mine. We will catch the girls in the dark, stop where we haven't been in years, build a small fire, and talk about our hopes and dreams. Is it cold? Do you even notice? Hold her hand. I'll hold hers in mine. I will give her my coat, and I'll give up these Saturday nights for the rest of my life to live each one in fantastic hope like I did when I was a boy. Like you did before this rotten, hopeless dinner, and the thousand before that... They must end. Most certainly they will happen over and over again in an agonizing sameness, unless we summon the necessary courage to destroy them.

You are both invited next week to search alongside my wife and I for our true hearts. Otherwise, stay out of my life until my wife knows me again how I wanted to be known before the first fainting kiss.

Hello Pat,

Look! A letter! It must feel so good to get mail that doesn't beg for your money. It must feel like Christmas receiving correspondence addressed to "No-man's-land, USA."

I don't know why I write. No particular reason. My next book will contain many letters; maybe I just want to add your name to the bunch. Years ago I used to write to Tony when life was pretend and Tony was *The Pretender*. Now I haven't the desire to get in touch with that fakealot. You, however, are human, and two eyes that will look upon my pile of crap, even if only in brief moments of personal desperation.

The truth being told, I need another human being to fondle my thoughts. Marie hears so much dirt in a day that it's a wonder she can give me a second look without following it with a violent kick in the crotch. I need to write letters. I'm tired of writing to nobody. I am sick of a world that refuses to write to save itself from spiritual slaughter. We need more letters! Why bother opening the mailbox? Who's getting a present? It's junk mail or anthrax, and just the appropriate amount of bills to keep you and your neighbor enslaved for a lifetime. There is not enough open speculation about the expected stability of people's brains. Look what I see. The whole lot of us walk around like Goofy with his pants down. Our viewers already expect from us the most outrageous acts of stupidity. But to expose our ugly genitals while being so stupid? Pornographic. Demented. Just too much perversion for this poor man to bare.

Speaking of bears... Are there any lumbering by your window in the north country? Is one trying to read over your shoulder right now? Do you think he would agree with my bit about Goofy, if he was dumb enough to read?

Look Pat, they hand out literacy by the millions, but never expect any of us to use it properly. They demand articulation, but really all they want is to hear us say the word, "articulation," so every one in the room can know each other's limits, and talk incessantly about the kind of every day drama a squirrel would piss on, if he could sit still for five minutes and take into his tiny squirrel skull such a relentless banter of meaninglessness. Pick your words recklessly mi amigo, and put them into letters. No one is interesting enough for a conversation. I say make a man read what's on your mind, even if all you ever think about is shit. We all admit that in person we don't listen to a word the other person says. Don't bother to say anything. Write it down! Then he is forced to read. Write it all down, even the bowel movements of your everyday life. Wait for the biographers or the staff psychiatrists to write out explanations for you.

This week I plan to write to a couple credit card companies. I want to offer them a rate they can't refuse. It's time for the poor man to fight these birds. With power? No! Letters. More letters. Open, angry demanding letters. No pussyfooting, "please can we meet on common ground?" letters. What have we done in the past about our insurmountable debt? We pay the bill. It comes, and we pay it. Now some other naked Goofy searching for his trousers is sending anthrax poison through the mail. I think that he just wants to punish his creditors. Too bad, he thinks, that the mailman, and every other average Joe in Nincompoopville is left wide open to death. Every one is vulnerable because death is inevitable. Who is innocent? It wouldn't matter because death is never fair. The man sending death-by-mailman might be death itself. But who would believe that unless the President said it was true? Believe in God, in Jesus, but don't believe in death. Absolutely absurd to think it could come dressed up in man's clothes. Most of us are certain it will never come at all. Death never hits us until it does. I say there would be no fear if death was obvious and expected. If it was real, like a man, and all at once sat down at every table in America.

Meanwhile, we have all been smeared with the kind of evil the President decries. What are we to do as Americans if, after thorough investigation, these deadly letters are being sent by reindeer from the Seattle Zoo? Or from teens who broke into a laboratory a couple months ago, and stole a box with some "neat shit" in it? Or what if it's a man named Ahmad Pakistan who has been living in Iowa for six years just waiting for his chance to kill people? What difference does it make to God? All humanity over twelve years of age is already plagued with the virus that mistrusts living and ignores death. Even the poor reindeer in the zoo. Like the rest of us, he expects his special dinner on Sunday too. Only death will prevent him from getting it. But who really understands this? It's getting worse each passing day. All the Goofys want their new, special thing. A Volkswagen Bug, ice skates, salvation... Has anyone considered the nineteen lives lost, the nineteen "evil" lives, in the September 11th drama? You can bet that God has. Who thinks about the 20 million Russian lives lost during WWI? Only some professor trying to make a point. But out of that human tragedy we got better TV. Video biographies of Lenin, Trotsky, and a mad Joseph Stalin, whose deeds made even Hitler think, "Wow, can't beat that!" What interesting viewing! Today this new world media touts it's recent 3000 dead statistic as if it just counted jelly beans in a jar, and I'm supposed to be shocked because Tom Brokav got a sheet of death dust in the mail? I say good riddance to the sleeping animals. My dear friend, it's time to wake up and live, even if for just a very short time. But be careful! Humans everywhere prey on other humans, and if that was an unfair beginning, it's a justified end. What does it matter that we, as biological phenomena, could live strong, healthy, vibrant lives for two centuries or more? We're lucky to get in as many years as we do dressed as presidents and pedophiles. Still, it's a weak life that embraces its father's legacy of "follow the rules sons and daughters. No matter what the horrors of humanity show you... Always follow the rules!"

Last week I watched a show on TV entitled "Hitler's Women." The commercials in between were all about choosing the right financial advisor, or buying the best SUV, and I thought that any Jewish man alive today with a link to the Holocaust possessed divine right to explode a bomb in the building where that film was being broadcast. Was his grandfather humiliated, robbed, beaten, deprived of food and water, and then set on fire so that the owner of the television station, and all the people connected to it, could make a vile living feeding on the murder of eleven million human beings? The people at home, including myself would get their just desserts too. Why not? How could such once unimaginable horror be born again into our imaginations as "before bedtime entertainment?" It's a fucking shock to the system just to think about that insanity for five minutes.

But we no longer invite ourselves into our true thoughts. Therefore rarely are we shocked, even for five minutes. I don't think a shock could shock us, not ten thousand volts, or even our own heads cut off and thrown rolling across the street. Does it matter? Shocked or not shocked, three thousand murdered, or a show about bunnies, and yet the commercials still come. The economy grows or slows, the money either comes or goes, children lose their fingers and toes. The commercials still air on time and always on purpose.

Happy Day! So how is the job treating you? Remind me never to get political again. The sad truth is, however, that life and living itself must get politcal if its going to boil down to crying out against the boiling of human beings. Extremist. Dangerous. I'm on the wrong side and at both extremes of the political spectrum. Either way my color is dark and unhappy. I cannot trust a single soul.

My dear Pat, you called last night to tell me once again about your financial predicament. Don't do that anymore. You are poor, broke, down without a dime, but this does not prevent you from having a pot belly and cable TV. Anyway I don't care. Not until you join the ranks. Not until you are ready to cast blame. My father called up a few hours ago to ask me for Christmas suggestions. He's going shopping at the Mall tomorrow. This has got to stop. I am a grown man. On the other side of the world America is bombing children. Bodies are being ripped open, bombs are falling, blood is spurting out of holes shot through human bone and skin, and running into sewage drains. Bombs are raining on the desert and in the street. Everyone on that side of the planet is screaming. What could I possibly want? What do I dare need?

Jesus Christ, is there a sensitive man I can talk to?

My old friend, you are the bottom dreaming of the top. But your top is my bottom, and I don't know a single soul alive who thinks like me. Now I think I can tell my Dad what I want for Christmas.

I would like some teeth of a murdered Afghan child. I want to wrap them in a handkerchief to lay beneath your granddaughter's pillow. I want the tooth fairy to hover lightly above the murdered Afghan child who lies inside your grandchild in bed, sleeping and dreaming on her pillow.

And Dad, wouldn't it be swell if all of America had to run outside tonight screaming in the pouring rain? Wouldn't it be great to know that by tomorrow the world would have collapsed and all the wrong was gone for good? That too. I want that too.

I don't know if Border's has that, or JC Penny, or Kinney shoes. You might have to go to Awareness.com, but by the time you get online the whole world might be dead. And really, who would know or care as long as we preserved in our brains the hopeful thought of shopping today?

This letter has become another one of my anger bombs. Please make

this stop. Teach me soon Pat, before I go nuts, the art about not giving
a good god damn.
 Goonnite.
 Ronald

Letter to The Credit Store, Inc.:

Hi,

You don't know me because I haven't a face. This morning I want to put one on so whoever you are will know me, and we might become great friends spending lavishly together for the rest of our lives.

Twelve years ago I got a credit card while attending college. Five hundred dollars credit was quite a sum to the boy who had not a penny in his pocket. Nor a job. Nor any intention of ever getting a job. I took it eagerly, (show me any nineteen-year-old without means who would not), and spent every dollar allowed on gas money, cigarettes, chips, soda, and beer all the way to New Orleans and back.

I am sure that then I had every intention of paying my debt. However, a year later, after graduation, I was cooking my meals on a wood stove and trying to stay alive without money. So you can see I was unable to pay the monthly balance. Interest added up by the hour while I ignored every single bill that came to my table. Any heat in winter depended upon my own two hands, so I decided not to make money-making a priority because my infant daughter needed wood on the fire and constant giving moments of loving attention. I am proud to say that for quite some time I was able to chop, stack, and burn my fuel without earning a dime.

Years passed. I lived from check to check, or from week to week without a check. I moved my home over twenty times, and was even homeless a couple Aprils in a row. My initial credit card company finally gave up on me. They sold my account, writing me off as a bad debt. Tax savings for them, and a new human poker chip for an upstart garage company to gamble with.

Fortunately I was in the right frame of mind to not give them the chance to make a profit by me, at least not without my consent. I too wanted a piece of the action. But the new company never sent a penny my way. Only more letters demanding money.

Year after year I was sold to many different companies, probably for some ridiculously low sum, and each company not losing a penny on my bad debt because the IRS was, and is, a WASP mafia-like organization of government worshiping, half people with no self-respect. Then last year I was caught off guard. I answered the phone.

It was your company calling.

You wanted the sum I spent in New Orleans, plus nearly double the principle in interest. I wanted to please my wife. Like the fool I am and shall always be, I agreed to your terms, forgetting that I had every right to hang up the telephone. Guilty about money spent twelve years ago, I was getting older, more set in my ways, and leaning further toward the open arms of the middle classes. I wanted to mow my lawn, eat my meat, drag my bones about the house like a two-week old battery-powered toy, and pay all outstanding debts, eventually. At the time I never thought about who I was paying. Who had begging rights to my money? Was it you? But you were not my initial lenders. You were the parasitic worm of man, the lowest of the low, exceptional human cheater, better than the best thief at tying up and ripping off members of your own species. I realized this the moment I hung up the phone. I was caught. Cornered by middle class conscience, self duress persuaded my player to surrender his piece in the Capitalistic Extortion Guilt Game.

Oh well. The fool and someone else's money.

I paid the debt with a little extra to spare.

Now I want my extra back.

My last bill says I have a credit balance of $12.02. You can choose not to pay in full. However, there is a minimum charge of $.59 and an annual interest rate of 20.07%. If I am not in receipt of at least the minimum payment by December 21, 2001, there will be a delinquency charge of $35.00 added to your account. If you do not want to be written off as a delinquent by a delinquent, I would suggest sending the money right on time.

I am doing business as "Ron Throop's Credit Emporium" and your company is my first customer. After reviewing your economic history I regret to inform you that your credit limit is set at $12.02. So no card will be issued.

You will receive a bill each month for as long as you are in debt to me. Your account number is 12345-6789.

Any questions? Call me. You already have every number ever associated with my name.

P.S. This is how I calculate your average daily balance. First I figure a portion of the 55,000 years of pent-up, sado/masochistic debt, and divide that by the cost of a discount camera, and five pound can of cheap coffee bought on credit at a thrift store. Then I take the beginning balance of a very cheap Christ, Zoroaster, Mohammed, Buddha, five hundred and twenty-two Hindu deities, add an endless slew of new, meaningless purchases, multiply that ending balance by the zero lifetime spent calculating credit and debit, inhale a deep breath of that infinite emptiness, and blow it into a big green plastic bag. I quickly tie up the ends of the bag, walk out into my backyard with a spade and my new big balloon, dig a deep hole, drop the big balloon in, cover the hole, and firmly pack the very cheap dirt down over it. Then I lay the spade on the grass beside my toes, pull my jeans down around my ankles, and piss a hot stream of urine all over your money grave. This gives me the "average daily balance," and a very powerful sense of lifetime security.

P.P.S. I think I shall charge you an annual fee of $45.00 beginning January 1, 2002.

P.P.P.S. This communication is from a debt collector.

Pleasure doing business with you, you usurious scum of the earth.

Ron Throop

Letter to Mr. Ahmed Kuschbash, an Old Afghan Man Watching His Grandbabies Explode

You don't know me but I am a citizen of the United States. Your country is being bombed by my leader's followers and I don't care. I'm too worried about getting a job. Anyway, what special prize would I get for wondering about the safety of your family? So you see, I can't worry. The President said not to worry. He said America is fighting a crusade against evil. To tell the truth I also find some solace in the green flashes and thick, hot smoke choking your insignificant nation. It's interesting and, I confess, even a bit soothing to my spirit. My television won't show your son's intestines hanging out of his barely breathing body. I think that's because our journalists would chew on a hot sandwich with curly fries rather than tell the truth.

I don't care because I can't, not because I would, even if I could. I am an American scum, a coward, a hideabout. This winter I'll most certainly pay taxes on time to have my road paved next year and your grandchildren blown apart tomorrow. I am not alone. All of my American brethren are cowards too. As long as the money comes, and the video, and the new car—we will hand money over to the war machine, the evil crusaders, the sick fundamentalist white, black, and blue preachers who run the country now. Thanksgiving is in two weeks and I think we'd eat you dirty people if the President told us too, and ordered his generals to wrap you up in plastic mesh bags like headless Tom Turkeys.

Mr. Kuschbash, I understand that you just turned seventy-nine years old. Congratulations on your long life. Hopefully upon reading this, you still have warm blood in circulation. Or has one of our bombs already speckled your cave walls red? Do you like dying for no cause? Were you retired? No, you could not possibly understand what that word means. You're still milking a single goat and will every morning until a United States soldier fires a bullet through your head for speaking in tongues. You should see how the little old men and women of America sympathize with your present plight! As long as the retirement check comes in the mail, the typical senior citizen does not care a new set of teeth if a troop of soldiers just forced you to swallow your own big toe. Would you care about them if you had shuffleboard, golf, a proud array of cheap pretty things to look at, and lavender-scented sheets to lie down upon? Yes you would. But you're an ancient religion that Americans cannot for the life of them understand, even though they've been given the power to think freely. Americans are spoiled dogs. Loyal pets to the machine. Dedicated in equal proportion to the amount of hamburger chunks tossed to them.

I must admit that I am no better. Yes, I am young and against everything, but I also have my own babies, and do not intend to raise a finger to help you old man. I fear that something bad might befall my family. I fear my government, but not in the same way that you fear it. In this country, a soldier cannot pull a man out of his home and shoot him dead in the street. Not here in America! No, the sneaky rats of our government would have the flag wavers do it to him first. My own neighbors, the mob of men and women who need Afghan children to die so their hearts can glow warm with brotherhood. No, if I show the slightest mark of dissent, their gentle ways, their hearts overflowing with glorious thoughts of brotherhood, will break into my house, rape my wife, call my oldest daughter a sand-nigger loving toad, and surely stone me to death. I see what bombing your country does to them. It fills them with purchasing power. They're hopping up and down, joyfully waiting for Saturday's tip to the shopping mall. Every single one of these monsters I see about town will remain silent until our government says that the war is over. Translated into the Afghan tongue that means literally "get a good look at your friend's head today, Mr. Kuschbash, for tomorrow it's faceless history".

It is the mob mentality of my neighbors, the living dead, waiting for their chance at shuffleboard and medicated living; they are the guilty ones. God says so. Any real poet says so. Yet both are forced into quiet for fear of their lives. Yes Mr. Kuschbash, it's true. America would blow it's own God out of the sky if it stood in the way of their right to be ignorant and lazy. My street's representative to God has an American flag waving from his porch roof and satellite dish attached to his steeple. He must also appreciate very much the green flashes ripping across night sky!

I understand that you had nothing to do with crashing jet liners into very tall buildings. But I promise you that I am the only one here who understands that much. My countrymen would disagree, because the President says you have to die else the price of gasoline and airline tickets will rise by twelve percent. That's all the reason anyone here needs to want proof that you are dead.

Dear Mr. Kuschbash, are you still reading? Or did you crawl out of your cave to milk the goat, pump some water, or do whatever poor, luckless chore you must do to survive? I understand. My President publicly swears that you're a violent madman. He vows to kill you and everyone. I know he is sexually, religiously, and ferociously frustrated. And he is also true evil. He and everyone else in the world knows that your only utensil is a scratched, aluminum spoon. And no doubt old man, you have the superpower to pop out our eyeballs and fling them with that spoon.

Finished? Yes of course you are! Might as well enjoy what night you have left, do whatever it is you funny-looking ragamuffins do for enjoyment, play a game with a long stick, smile your toothless hopes and dreams for one more night, because tomorrow you're dead waste!

Anyway, what I want to know is this... What would you do if the American war machine accidentally left behind a B-52 bomber outside your cave? Inside the cockpit you'll find a little instructional manual written in Arabic. It contains information needed to fly it, and mechanically unlatch the big hatch in the hull so you can drop shiny yellow bombs and matching colored food parcels on the harmless village of your choice. What would you do with such a gift? Would you follow through with its original, satanic intentions? Not likely. I think instead, you'd set up housekeeping in the plane, divide the food out evenly among your family and friends, and let the goat nibble on the shiny yellow bombs. I would wait for your reply to tell me if my assumption is right, but your head and body will be separate by morning. Oh well.

Here's a fact about those shiny yellow bombs. Did you know that our barely literate military pilots name each one before dropping it on your children? Here in America we watch the TV news every night, every single lonely night, just night after night after night, and many more nights to come until the final night comes, about the same time at night when you walk outside to milk your goat. There's a video of a pilot smiling as he writes "from NYC fire department" across one. They personalize the bombs. It's funny business to Americans. All of us put a smile on before killing your families from thirty thousand feet up in the Afghan sky. Each one of these baby killers would shit himself in your sandbox if forced to explain his cowardly behavior to you face to face. I know the anger boiling inside your soul. I know that you will want revenge if you survive an attack. I know that if you were a few decades younger, you would become tomorrow's terrorist, and offer your life up to the nearest demagogue with a semi-feasible plan. An eye for an eye, correct? I would do the same. Who in God's whole creation would not?

These news videos fill me with dread. But I will forget about you Mr. Kuschbash just minutes after I turn off the television. I promised my daughter creme bruleé for dessert tonight. This morning I watched my wife get out of bed, and was aroused by her beauty. The moment she stepped into the shower, three maybe four American bombs erased the village on the other side of that mountain. Your village is next Ahmed. I am sorry that no one will be left to buy a bag of your goat's milk. But as far as I can tell, I am the only one who is sorry in America.

But to be completely honest... If I had only goat's milk to bake in my custard, and my government began bombing you so that cow's milk would come back to my kitchen, and the TV news anchor man said, "Don't worry! We'll never show you a dead Afghan child. Just pretty green flashes and objects exploding on the ground which we're told were trucks carrying fuel to Afghan tanks. Either that or water jugs being pulled by Afghan mules..." If I could get these conditions to insure a sweet and silky custard, I too would not care a beating heart about you Mr. Kuschbash. That's the truth. And absolutely universal outside of Afghanistan!

I just got into the family bed and snuggled up in my sheets to watch my beautiful baby dream. She's nine months old and fully enjoying her free and happy existence. My wife stepped out of a hot shower and one American bomb just blew your neighbor's cave up into dust and blood. You heard the screams. Did you think that terrorists lived there? You thought that Omar and his two shy daughters weaved blankets all day to sell at market. Not anymore. America said it will kill anyone with the name Omar. Then it said it will kill anyone who weaves blankets. It's not a crusade against the evil ones. No. It's a massacre of the different. It is the hot winds of destruction sent by the foul breath of human nature. The pretending innocents sit down to eat a bowl of custard. They won't partake in the slaughter of humanity, directly. They just eat dessert and complain a little bit while the Kuschbash population is erased from existence.

The sun is rising in the east where America digs for you a hot smoking tomb Mr. Kuschbash.

I am sorry for you old man. But in this age of distrust and paranoia, I promise to forever remain more sorry for myself.

Good luck!

Ron Throop. An American coward.

Letter of Application to the United States Election Committee From the Rama Party:

Dear sirs and maybe one madam (who wants to be a sir),

Hi, my name is Ron Throop and I am running for the office of President in the year 2004. I am curious to know what preparations I must take in order to get my party on the ticket. Is there a total number of signatures I will need? How many? Any specific clauses (besides the obvious ones) which keep all honest and sincere people from trying to become President? When can I start campaigning? Please send a reply as soon as possible.

I will be fully endorsed by the Ramas. Enclosed please find my party's official description and mission statement.

Thank you for your time.

Ronald J. Throop

The Rama Party

Under cover of night, Rama brought Lakshmana and Sita with him to his mountain retreat. He wasn't ready to be king. Scandal would erupt in his father's palace if Rama accepted power too hastily. He believed that time in exile would help cleanse his spirit and strengthen his resolve. Time and sacrifice he thought would cement the trust of the people.

Rama lived a peaceful existence on the mountain, loved by his perfect bride Sita, and loved and counseled by Lakshmana, his loyal half brother. His days were simple and wonderful until the morning the many-headed, lunatic monster, Ravana, stole Sita from Rama. Then the epic story of the quest for Sita begins. Flying monkeys, wise vultures, voluptuous evil deities dancing a test by temptation, secret worlds within our world, battles being fought, lost and won with bravery and meaningful death—always without smart bombs, machine guns, biological weapons, and land mines to act as a kind of appetizer to the threat of total annihilation which neither Rama nor Ravana could pull out of their immortal stockpile...Those were the days of man. As ancient as India and probably older.

We suggest to anyone who is thinking about joining the party to read *The Ramayana* to learn more about our hopes and fears, and our wiser solution to the present-day American crisis. We believe that success will come, but only after a total majority reads our story. For time is the maker of all miracles, and time is one thing the Rama Party has in abundance. We desire that each individual American nurture his natural right to dream all day from under a tree in an ancient forest. We believe that American freedom should consist of lying down most of the day dressed in loose, colorful clothing. All ideals, all morals are born out of that perfect hour while reading aloud the tales of Rama and Sita to our loved ones. The whole forest is alive with joy. The wild monkeys leap and laugh high up in the canopy. All days from now on are to be this sleepy and innocent.

In 2004, or 2008, if conditions are ripe (and if Rama is old enough), we will put our representative up for Presidential election.

Rama is dead but Ron Throop is not. In order for him to accept the highest office in government, he must be elected by a 99% majority. At present Ron is our only member. The party doubts very much that America, in its current loathsome condition, could spit forth another man or woman to share with Ron his romantic ideal for the presidency. Although he alone can save the country from disaster, no one has yet been willing to follow his path of thought to find out how. (If you or someone you know is a Lakshmana, please write to our candidate as soon as possible. He needs a sane and strong running mate to help with the hunting and seemingly endless wood chopping).

Rama left his kingdom. If elected President of the United States, Ron Throop promises also to leave. He will go into hiding immediately. He has already made his plans for an arduous climb up an unknown wooded mountain. All decisions of state will be made from a small, modest hut he will build singlehandedly. Aside from signing or vetoing only those bills delivered to him via a trusted messenger, he will do very little in the ways of governing. No sound will be made to the public, nor to the hired representatives of the public who make noise and more noise, with unjust intentions to pollute the public always. Because our candidate refuses to pollute the public, he will have no intercourse with the other two branches of government.

No domestic policy. No foreign policy.

In fact, no man or country is invited to dinner, unless he or it agrees to hike up the mountain alone to meet the President.

We of the Rama Party believe like Thoreau that the state which governs least, governs best. Our new president will not employ a secret service to lock up his retreat in constant surveillance. Once every day he will meet with his cabinet for a walk and talk about the state of the nation. Each member will have a cabin too, and a family there to love and interact with after advising the President. The cabinet will live in cabins, the only appropriate abode for members of all governing bodies.

Throughout his term, policy cannot waver, even in the likely event that a rogue nation vows cannibalistic jihad until every last American has been eaten. Ron will keep good to his promise to do nothing.

Assassination attempts are inevitable. The party knows that the killer must be smarter than both the President and his messenger to ever get near enough to murder. Still, any successful assassination would be honored by the party. We hope the killer would choose to remain on the mountain to finish his victim's term.

Meanwhile the President shall not be concerned over such trifling matters as self preservation. There's a country to love and look after. How will the common man refrain from paranoia if his own President does not feel safe? Ron will accept the job after receiving 99% of the vote. No need to justify spending the people's money protecting his skin from the radical wing of the 1%. The job pays too well to care. We strongly believe that a President should expect to die for his country. No one should protect him if he cannot protect himself. Therefore, only warriors need apply. If the President-elect is not prepared to defend the country all by his lonesome, then too bad for the entire country. Rama was an expert bowman. Ron will know how to shoulder his bazooka like a pro.

The job pays well, but our candidate expects no monetary salary. He will live on donations of food and fuel for the length of his term.

Remember, no domestic and foreign policy. All governing consists in the guise of whatever paper reaches his office for signature. No Brownie troops to meet with on Thursday morning. No Chinese Premier to happily shake hands with today and tomorrow threaten with nuclear tough talk.

Ron knows that it's the world's children who have their faces blown off in a war. Therefore he will forever be aggressively against it. A Secretary of War will be chosen to keep in touch with the death-wielding generals in times of hostility and unrepairable conflict. In the unlikely chance that war is declared, our President, holding tightly to his bazooka, must be the first to charge the enemy. If a draft becomes necessary, it will call for all propertied, married men, over the age of forty-five, who bought a new car at least once in their lives. Our party knows what is needful to perpetuate god's animals on earth, and it's not the miracle of money making money. The money hoarders never make good soldiers. So they get sent down to the front lines first. Ron believes in saving America's youth for procreation. He knows that all wars yesterday and today are provoked by the rich and powerful. Ron says that the old rich men are too fat and comfortable to ever make a worthwhile country anyway. So each one shall stand behind his President and wait for the call to charge.

Four years of doing absolutely nothing! Letting the country go. The Executive Branch of the United States Government acting like the part time babysitter it should be, and putting on no new masks! The money we could save! The example the President would set! Nothing ever before like it. Not even George Washington. "A New Precedent by Your President!"—That could be our motto. Or we might prefer the following one: "Cloud-hidden Whereabouts Unknown". Give us a party for our platform and we promise never to show our candidate in the public eye.

In 2004 or 2008, it's Ron Throop and the Ramas.

If he gets one other vote it might be enough to set America on a winning path.

I want to write this down while the fear is still fresh.

I live along the windy shores of Lake Ontario. We have nothing of any value to bomb besides a nuclear power plant and my home. It's dark just before dawn. Moments ago I heard a large plane flying low in the sky. I stepped outside my front door into the frosty air and felt the plane crashing into the power plant. I imagined the split second and the overwhelming power of explosion liquefy my body, my house, my family. We blew into space. We melted into nothing.

Fear is crazy. Being a man unable to defend against an explosion larger than a firecracker is insanity. How can I protect my body? What strength has a single man against the machine that pretends to ask his opinion before taking its revenge upon the world? Nobody has asked me for my yea or nay on the subject of war. Nor have I personally put my representative into a seat in the federal government. There is no one whom I would want to represent me other than my close, personal friend Pat. Yet he has no intention of running for office.

So I am unrepresented.

Who is?

Dangerous question.

In a nation of 300 million, I would probably be close to the mark to say that about five thousand are represented. If it's a hundred thousand, it's still not enough. Even a hundred million counted for is not America—at least not the ideal which the present king and queenies pay such horseshit lip service to.

We have three branches of government. Let us attempt to find one honest soul.

The Executive

No. Every one knows that the President is a spoiled rich kid, playing with toys, and a partisan boobie who can only hire other partisan boobies if he's not going to be contradicted while telling lies. So the President, his cabinet, and all secretarial and janitorial positions made at the

White House are partisan liars, and brutal too if they assist in the murder of a single human being. They will become honest citizens the day the President publicly admits that he is the leader of a mass murdering, profiteering organization of clean-shaven, blood-thirsty baboons.

The Judicial

Appointed by presidents. They get to pick the cases that they want to hear. Almost madness. Doesn't that say enough? There are nine of them, in addition to an army of secretaries and janitors.

The Legislative

The Senate. Two people to represent a state. There are eighteen million people in my state. If we all ate the exact same dinner last night, I would be satisfied with my representative. Impossible. And he shall be a immoral thief to boot the moment he steps into a car not bought and paid for by his own sweat and struggle.

The House. Opportunistic thieves who don't dare campaign for the secretarial and janitorial vote. Tend to wait for the local union leader, or big business representative to give a donation.

This is why America is not free. It says that we are free to voice an opinion. But in a life or death situation, which cannot be a more final and necessary situation to voice an opinion, we can speak up, but it won't do a bit of good, and it might even kill us. If the king and queenies of America want to kill, they most certainly will. We have the freedom to talk and the shackles to stay put, but for the sake of our lives, never raise a threatening finger.

I think the American government acting as a blind, ravenous cancer is going to kill as many civilians as Hitler, Stalin, and the man most responsible for the Armenian genocide. I am certain of this because our President has already used the word "evil" and "crusade" on public television. Wow! Those are pretty strong words! The king and queenies of America are going to kill every single one of us eventually. Of that I am certain too.

It's bound to happen. If it isn't America, it will be China. If not China, Jamaica... Nowhere are people free. If America is the freest nation, and it can wreck total destruction upon the weaker nation of its choice, how are we to trust other nations with equally destructive powers, yet leaders who admittedly crack the whip to keep their people down?

My god, I say trust China first. Where do we see their government presently spending billions of dollars dropping bombs on children? A billion people, who will admit that they are subjugated by a minuscule few, and yet I bet that they are more loyal to their repressive government than Mr. Patriotic American waving his fifty dollar plastic flag, simply because the Chinaman knows damn well that he is not free. The wise Chinese is lied to, admits he is lied to, and lives his unfree life while regularly filtering truth out of lies. But he knows that alone he cannot defeat a government of nuclear weapons. So why for the life of self and family would he even try?

Same in America. Here is propaganda. Here they hang flags on the front porch, and then sit down on the steps to drink their delicious gourmet coffees. Why organize to fight the monster? It's gourmet coffee!

The fear we need to save our souls is enemy planes enjoying cruising altitudes in our airspace. We need to be humbled. We need to be bombed daily so that we can feel again. Never have we been so needful of a forced occupation of our lands. Hasn't happened yet in United States history, although I am sure it would do a great deal of good for American and especially world preservation.

A revolution in America will never come from within. We are a nation of spoiled puppies driving cars to and from our overflowing food bowls. A million people could not rise up against the government its forefathers created. We praise the latter and then ourselves for realizing the success of their experiment. Madness. They made a monster. They nurtured the monster. Guilty from the start, they fed their hideous creation with money pies wrought from slavery. Only white men with property enjoyed personal, ridiculous ideas of freedom. A woman lived and died beside her husband, to be named in the end "His Wife" on her tombstone. There was no freedom then for the majority. Some freedoms today, but even the smallest freedom must be paid for. By blood? No. More money! Today the greatest freedom Americans wish to uphold is the freedom to make money. There is no freedom guaranteed to not make money, hence all men enslaved to a life of not creating their own lives. Hence, hence, NO FREEDOM!

How easy for our leaders to put down a revolt! America has engorged itself way beyond the most imaginative idea of God's wrath thought up by the typical eighteenth century human brain. There might be a judgment day, but the leaders of nuclear nations are the only ones currently in power to initiate it. In America the President has the nuclear power to prevent any threat of civil war. There is no target too small or too big. A hundred million might organize by telephone. But they're dead before a manifesto can be written up. More than anything the President fears his own head getting hung on a post. Each night while in bed, he peruses his personal survival itinerary with crackers and tea, tucked snugly beside Mrs. President under a fluffy down comforter. Fellow Americans, how many nuclear warheads does it take to wipe out life in North America? You don't know? I promise you the general knows. Which general? Pick any one of those mini-satans having brunch with the President this morning. How can we be certain that the two of them have not already constructed a special, secret plan to murder every single one of us?

All of this distrust is brushed off as paranoia. Of course it is! It must be paranoia because there is no day left to debate after the morning of "ouch, my face is melting off my skull..." There can be no proof of it not being paranoia until after everyone is dead.

Ambition is dangerous. There does not exist one world leader who has inwardly freed himself from maniacal ambition. America, in its present, pretend democracy, cannot stray too far away from its idea of the worst evil in the universe. Our President does not meet my standard of manhood. Nor does Prime Minister Gumbai ruling the little known African nation that America nukes tomorrow because Gumbai is evil and the American president wants to go on crusade and kill people.

When a leader starts talking about God, evil, crusade, and bombing missions all in one breath, it's time for a people to welcome the forceful footprint of another culture onto their lands.

God, would it be that bad for us to lose? How bad was it in France during the German occupation? Was there music? Was there dancing? Was there wine flowing? There weren't nuclear weapons. That's some good times, eh? What would be left for the occupation to occupy after a nuclear drop-off? Hitler, a French family, eleven million unfortunate Europeans, and all the people in the world would have disintegrated. It takes a lot less pent-up evil to press a button and annihilate whole populations. It's impersonal. Which makes such a terror that much more likely. Now that it is easier to kill, it's easier to kill, understand?

I think that I might be patriotic enough to volunteer my body to the resistance if there ever was an occupation of America. Just for something to do besides "obey and pay," until I'm dead and even buried in money. Although first I would need to convince myself that after the war this government would be much improved. That is to say, just a touch less embarrassing and hypocritical. Oh yes, and I should expect that all the nation's top dogs be rounded up and brought to the newly instated World Children's Court. There they would be tried and convicted by the universal judge which existed before the dinosaurs, and hasn't left since. All leaders guilty of just one violent crime against any human being would be publicly tickled to death, disemboweled, stuffed, and put on perpetual parade around the earth.

Wow. What are the chances? In such a world, I would become 100% patriotic American.

Parents of America force-feed fear into their children, killing any hope for natural freedoms to grow. What happened to wisdom? It used to be something that grew with age. Right from wrong? The children know it. They always have. What child gives a damn about your good deeds, professional acumen, loving demeanor, or whatever lie it is that you pretend all day long while knowing, Jesus Christ, *knowing* that man's world is a push button away from extinction? You think little Charlie will ever get anything finished properly when tomorrow his tiny face will be smashed in, and his skull cracked, because you, yes you, only you, you sick, twisted ghoul, allowed for this demonocracy to break into your home and take him, without so much as a murmur of complaint. Coward! Name all the armaments stockpiled in the United States Armed Forces. Do it now you imbecile, you shit father, you embarrassing human being! I want the exact number and names of every baby killer that you buy with tax money. Do it! Find out! Do it, you dog! I want the name of the soldier who would walk into my home, by rule of the President. I keep a list now, on my refrigerator. I intend to scribble out each name until the last baby killer is dead and buried. My God why has our power to protect the children vanished? The amount of fear each of us possess in one brain cell, is so tightly wound and compact, that if unraveled, would stretch 600 miles all the way to the White House with a "Please don't kill me" sign hanging at the end. You are a taker. You do not give what the universe gave to parents of all species. Instinct of self-perpetuation. Here you are at the end of your life leaving the children little notes of death signed by you and your lawyer. Money, a house, maybe a stamp collection for junior and his bride. But never wisdom. Priceless wisdom. The only needful protection to pass on to loved ones.

And now, seated in a cozy house chair, you think that you're protecting the family. You little piece of nothing. You fearful little pig in space. I am so sick of what you make humanity. You want that I too am as fearful of living as you? Respect one man today and protect your own child's life. How do you respect man? You give him this hate of yourself as your last expression of neighborly love.

Meanwhile, acquiesce while your brutal leaders bully ten conventionally armed Arab nations united against us. Play with the kids on the floor that you just washed and waxed while the U.S. Kingdom of Madmen piss off another Chinese nation, or rub the wrong way a volatile despotically armed Russia. I promise there will be nothing to look forward to besides a tiny state-of-the-art nuclear warhead seeking out your child's left eyeball. Tomorrow Pakistan will have one of those. Our trigger-happy leaders already have a hundred. If just one exists, God's law of inevitability says it most certainly will get used.

The end of the world?

A sure bet.

We can try to organize and revitalize a nation of strong-backed mothers and fathers. But first one strong man must make a beginning. It would be a miracle coming. Just one man to protect his child. Not God, not nation. One Man! He alone would make a beginning. The miracle is that if and when he made his move, he would actually be supported by enough neighbors to make even a dent of difference. Without the name Mr. WalMart, or Mr. Fordcar, or Mr. Dollar store, it would take more than a miracle to jumpstart a nation of deadbeats tucking their fear in at night. Who would be so foolish to invest time and money in a man who has nothing but a beginning? What if to begin, he hijacks a plane with feather pillows and a loud threat, and flies the plane into a building of nuclear missile engineers? What if that was his beginning? I think it could be a very rational beginning. The irrationality of it all, the miracle transcending rational thought is that there even exists one man left in America to make a beginning.

Progress is so slow.

Geez, maybe it might be smart for America to lead in the fight for a one world nation. It has the power now. Why not use it wisely? Make each nation an equal entity with equal vote. What is the United States, Italy, Iraq, Taiwan, besides a constant reminder to humanity that it still has not aspired to human? What is the vision for humanity anyway? Is our evolution to be so slow that we will have run out of time before ever realizing our true potential?

Yes it is. Painfully slow. Retarded. Almost brought to a complete halt. Look what damage America presently inflicts on the world, and it cannot even get to one man! It bombs an entire nation looking for one man. It bombs from above and is afraid. It bombs undercover of night. It cannot get to the one man. Americans at home are afraid. Yet swear that they felt anger after their buildings burned.

No.

When a man is truly angry and seething with vengeful thoughts, he does not wait for the government to clear a path for his wrath to walk down. A man would leave today for Afghanistan. If I was the father of a daughter who was slain in the World Trade Center collapse, I would see to it myself that anyone connected to her murderers was tortured and burned before my eyes. At least I know I would die trying. Avenging the death of a loved one. I believe Americans have forgotten all of their god-given rights. I know they have forgotten their god. As I write this some families of the dead are suing the government for a bigger compensation check. Consumer cannibalism.

I dare one man to be successful at anger. I dare myself more and more each day.

It is futile. Nothing could be more hopeless and self-destructive.

Just hearing a plane buzz overhead in the sky brings constant reminder to the American man of how small, how little, how tiny, how weak in mind and spirit and heart he is, and always will be until the end, which will be a very bitter story, I'm afraid.

A day later...

There are zombies in the midst. There are slow-walking, groaning cadavers everywhere. The city streets our mobbed with death. The countryside breeds zombies on the farm.

I am almost to the edge. I've been running and hiding and running. I know the end is near—for me and the zombies. Still, they follow me day after day, and into some nights. What is the matter with us? We must escape. We have to find safe hiding. The river jungles of the Amazon? A frozen cave at the top of the Mount Marcy?

I live in the central Middle Class Mountains, where the zombies have their strongest hold. I constantly change daily routines in order to disguise my life from thems. At night I go out looking for trouble. I don't know why. I feel the need, but it's like a human siren sounding off, and they rush at me from every angle. I can tear the head off one or two, to give myself a narrow escape. What good is that? Ten more leap into view. All night I run without any place to run to.

I think that I might be alone. Perhaps the zombies have at this moment begun chewing up my friends and family. If I don't see life exhibiting itself immediately, if in a whole day I cannot differentiate between cold death and lively action, then I think I might end life myself, before the zombies can take their first nibble of my flesh. So far it's a narrow escape. Just be careful. I might sign my next letter in zombie.

Dear Middle Classes,

Several years ago in New York City I spent an entire month of autumn nights hiding out in my friend Beth's loft dreaming, and refusing to come down until I could be coaxed with coffee or food. The safest pattern—with the least possible human interaction. One evening in particular I lay awake flipping through pages of *The Wandering Jew* when Beth came home with her gay older brother, Sam. She knew I wouldn't come down from my high bed to socialize, so my true whereabouts were not revealed.

"Where's Ron?" Sam asked, as if he was wondering about the cat.

"Probably out walking."

"That guy is weird," he said. "He has such a strange sense of being."

"That's Ron. So, what do you want to get Mom for her birthday?"

For my sake she changed the subject. Then climbed into the loft to get her money, winked at me, and left with her brother to go shopping. Maybe mom got a cookbook or a pretty candle stand. Three years earlier she got a gay son out of the closet. Which was fine provided he didn't hide in people's lofts or do peculiar and freakish things like read wisdom books, or walk for the pleasure of walking. No. A few years back she was forced to contend with a new outlook on life. Her son was queer. Not strange. Not weird. In fact he made a lot of money despite his queer condition. He bought furniture for his condo. He bought a stereo, a plane ticket, a wardrobe. He bought the Sunday paper, and actually read most of it too! And he played a very good game of tennis, even for a man with his man-loving desires.

Anyway, their mom loved Sam. After all, he was still her only son. Truly, it didn't matter what he had sex with as long as he kept quiet about it whenever she brought Dad along for a visit. Not necessary to have frequent reminders that their son was gay. What business was it of theirs? He drove a nice car. He dressed nice. He was a high paid accountant with an established firm in New York—the grayest, most dismal exciting city in the world. Soon she came to think that her son's life was actually quite exotic, not at all immoral, indecent, or degenerate, like she used to think. She loved her son. So what if he was gay? He was an upstanding member of the community. And he always remembered her birthday on time.

Up in the loft, I lay back on the pillow and let his careless words play over and over again in my mind. I was crushed. I got the impression that everyone thought of me in this light. The village idiot. The eccentric loafer. The poor dreamer. Maybe I had the wrong idea. Maybe I was strange. Maybe I was weird to the point of being judged asylum ready by my peers. I hadn't a penny to my name. I had a child to support. I was living off the kindness of my friends. I was high over the thought of a free egg breakfast with coffee. I was euphoric and then deeply depressed. I felt free, yet at the same time a prisoner of my own quietness. How long would my welcome last? Was I going too far down?

Then it occurred to me in a flash, thank God, that, like Beth's mom, I too was being put on. I was part of the problem. I let the gay brother Sam put me on. I recalled that not long ago, Beth brought me over to his apartment to watch one of his gay movies. It starred a man with a thick mustache dressed in a blue and white striped, fuzzy bathrobe, playing with himself. The doorbell rang. A thirty-year-old man pretending to be a fifteen year old paper boy handed the paper to the man. The mustached man asked the boy what he expected for a tip. The boy said that he would very much like to suck on the mustached man's penis. And then, as expected, the two men acted out their parts while all our children's dreams and fairy tales burst into flames and died.

Middle class morality. A complaint of Eliza Doolittle's father. My sole complaint of humanity from up in the loft on those terrifying fall nights, and to this very day. Sam is not alone. We are all liars to the soul. Sam dressed up like his heterosexual good provider Dad. But with all the apparent smart looks of money, he could not disguise his screaming desire to blow the man with the mustache. He was gay, everyone knew that for sure. But only his sister and I knew now that he was a gay pervert. A minor reality, but a huge realization which set me back on the path soon enough. My sanity was saved once again by juxtaposing the secret life of a degenerate dreg from the middle classes with my wide open desire to be in the class of no class.

Liars to the soul.

Liars to each other.

Beth's poor gay brother Sam. My poor friend Beth. My poor self, barely able to make out the truth wandering around among dreams in clouds behind the transparent jiggling jelly I won't dare leap into and squeeze myself through. I pretend to try. But I am just another bona fide member of the middle classes. We are the world's spiritual losers. Count on us to always put a million dollars to good use. I would buy more useless books to read, and perhaps a small lake to read them by. Sam would buy a new and improved video collection—some with actual fifteen year old boys sucking and fucking. One would buy a car, a business, a summer camp... One would put it in the bank. But which one would take the million dollars and blow his nose into it? Who exactly would break this newly acquired fortune down into a million separate dollar bills and side his house with the money pile? Who would roast a marshmallow sandwich over the coals of the bonfire made of a million dollars and some sticks of wood?

Millions, maybe billions of us, so similar, so forever the same. One life of mass similarity. Degenerate dregs. We've come to think perversion is freedom. The sensors allow "mother-fa-er" over the radio waves, because freedom sings rap songs about "big black asses." Rape is the middle class. Race is the middle class. The middle class is ninety percent sad and masturbation, and always a different movie about new and improved ways to murder and rape. The middle class immoral? The middle class degenerate? Sure, the middle class goes poopy and smells its fingers. The middle class flosses and feels clean. It is home for the homeless soul, the helpless, always careful, and cheerfully idiotic. Sure its children are insane, and the parents are children, two times nuts over. Pretending freedom out of a plastic shopping bag. Steel pipes beat against our heads, an order for prescription drugs, and waiting in line without complaint. No complaints. Don't ever complain! Always wonder what they will think of you. Be polite, mock your neighbor politely behind his back, love until you're bored of loving, and buy an exercise bike to heat up loins that aren't used unless walking to and from your parked car.

Here's a question for you—

How many pairs of shoes does it take to protect the delicate feet of the middle classes? I don't know how the hell they wear them out without walking! They don't walk. Nothing ever gets worn out before the next purchase! It's all about a little bit of more money, isn't it? Aren't we dumb like death as soon as we open up our mouths? What do we have to say? What important news is there to relate? Do we even know what it is we are talking about? Who remembers getting through our last conversation? Steel pipes beating our heads into the ground, and we still try to fix our hair with bloody fingers. I cannot stand the moral degeneracy of our no-culture! I've spent too much time alone with the precious words of the life-givers. The few who pointed to the light, died, and then left me the legacy of "hate for a change".

I do not respect any living creature that accepts money. I love those that need it. Love them enough to swing a steel bat against their skulls. We need a good movie. Tonight in the city, there are four or five more gay paper boys getting home from school, laying down on the carpet and blowing their male dogs. Gay is middle class. Not gay is middle class. Black and white can share or not share their cookies in the middle class. The rich and the poor are non-existent in the middle class. Channel seven is the all-class channel. Still, in three seconds exactly, every person in America in front of a television will laugh a careful middle class laugh. Not one middle class cat or dog will laugh until a steel bat splits their master's skull. And then it's a wild dog and cat dance of death to the middle class.

City, country, farm, or any life medium which includes the electronic cash register, to never pull an egg out of a chicken's vent, to believe that two cars are better than one, to get a damn good job, to think about a raise in your check and a rise in your pants while watching the handsome people on the screen, in your own private living room, doing it perfectly together while you and the misses and the kids who are old enough sneak into a room alone and play alone, with yourselves alone, to not rate your holidays "S" for "Sad, middle class audiences only", to swear you only live once, and make sure there's never more than two piles of laundry on the floor...

God dammit, I want my rightful place in society! You should see my shoes! I can't afford another pair. America wants to shove both of these worn-torn things up my ass. I am alone now. Poverty is not glorious when you're alone, smothered to near death by the middle classes. What do I have to do? Stop at the little store after work in my sharp suit and galoshes to pick up cat food? Is that it? Oh I know my wife hates me. My daughters ridicule me. I know what I look like to a young MAN, before my position in life rallies up to mash his spirit. I am picking up cat food. Oh and when I get home you just see how almost wealthy I can get! I got the newspaper right here, and on my lap there's my best friend the dog who gets people food overflowing in his silver bowl thank you very much. My socks cost more than Ron Throop's last seven dinners, and I got twelve more pair clean and folded in the closet.

I make 56 a year, and I live in a house with 2200 square feet of internal weeping space. My buddy at work has three kids and one bathroom. That's an idiot for you. Hell you're all idiots! I think I haven't had an honest conversation since I was eighteen years old. But that didn't come easy either, even with a joint and six pack of beer. You're afraid of me and I'm simply terrified of you. I won't help anyone. I love money, although I pretend to love my wife. Neither of us will move a god damn muscle to make our children proud. They're in control anyway. My fifteen year old is on the pill and laughs at my hair. She lost her innocence the day I stopped loving her, which was any day I thought about the 56 a year. I like to peek inside the fridge when I'm not hungry. Sometimes I pick up a book just to put it back down. The sun comes up. I don't see it. And I don't give a shit about the moon. The whole earth is when I wake up and turn in frantic circles around and around a pretend sun, and I got nothing to show of my existence—not even a real, honest to good, fruit or vegetable I grew and preserved myself.

I got the cat food. I don't care about the night. Truthfully and honestly I have never in my life wondered out loud. I see the young girls on the TV and I want to do to my wife what I did to the young girls on the TV. But I don't plan to do it with love because the only thing I love and revere is money and I worship it in ungodly repetition. Every Tuesday and Friday night I walk through the door with a bag of cat food. That's it, and that's easy.

I'm tired. I am always so tired. I am going to bed tired and waking up tired. The world is turning closer to Christmas. But sit on the moon and see if you can guess what crap the middle class sets under the tree this year.

I have to keep hate alive. Although I can't stand for it any longer. I stink of hate. I wallow in it. I acquire more strength from it. Sometimes I get the desire to join the other side or die. To know and understand, but most importantly, *believe* in quiet, non-eruptive emotions as long as everything seems okay. I pretend to want to be through hating things that were never good enough to love in the first place. I imagine that patience will get me to my essence, eventually, and show me who or what it is I truly am. I always thought hate was a good path to be on for this type of mental excursion. And it is, if you can handle the sometimes fantastic condition hate puts you in. For anyone who has ever hated as well as I do must know it is himself, his lying, sick and dying self, whom he hates the most, the utmost most.

Am I capable of finding love in this deep, blinding darkness? Love of myself, of me, mine? Love of me? I should ask myself this instead... Is hate a negativity that must be avoided in order to love?

No! Absolutely not. Hate is a needful and necessary form of expression. More so than ever in the age of monster technology and aggressive fearyourownneighbor-ism. You must first understand that hate is not the opposite of love. It works beside love. For example, one hates to show how much one loves. Don't get confused. Hate is not racism. Hate is not genocide. Hate is not hunger. Serious problems do not arise because of hate, (besides poverty). No, bad things happen because stupidity brazenly squatted on love's territory the morning love woke up weak and radiant, and forgetting to defend herself.

Yet stupidity is only partly responsible for what hate gets blamed for. Power is the brains and stupidity is its strong arm. Power protects and perpetuates stupidity. It uses stupidity to get what it wants. The powerful want you to think that hate is the cause of evil. No. Power fooled love into thinking that stupidity was a-okay, even kinda cute, harmless.

Then stupidity usurped love's fertile ground to plant the seeds of evil. Stupidity takes evil for nourishment. Stupidity needs evil to live. Power and stupidity are the reasons for evil. Hate needs God, even if hate wants to open up God with a knife for being such a complete failure to humanity. Why did God fail to maintain a world where hate could protect its love? Hate hates genocide. Hate hates nuclear weapons. Hate hates Hitler, Stalin, American presidents 1 through 79. But what hate hates most is an apathetic, loveless, and hateless America. Hate promised love that it would expose the power behind a stupidity nourished by evil. Too many billions of people have not expressed the hate needed to check power's seemingly endless rise. There's too much talk about Jesus's love, but nothing about his hate. Sure Jesus turned the other cheek. He'd do it again and again, for quite some time too. But then one day he'd have to become a man. People without hate. They call it love. They mean Jesus. Clumps of stupid people. Ignorant cows, chewing, and allowing power the open gate freedom to feed, clothe and shelter stupidity. Contrary to the belief code set by power, hate wants to feed the world. Hate would wash our faces clean of racism. Hate would want to stuff the potential beauty of mankind down the nation's throat. Hate would demand that a fair God reign in our hearts and in our children's hearts. Hate would not want to kill, but needs to clearly show power that hate is prepared to die for its cause. This makes hate a very dangerous threat to power's domains. Hate knows that without hate, humanity can kiss its ass goodbye! Hate knows this hate is a stronger love for mankind. No matter how stupid hate believes most of us are, hate has hope that one man, one woman can believe in a beginning.

It will be a very long winter of hate. I could set myself free and join up in the ranks of the powerful and stupid. I could hire myself out to the action news team and with a smile give nightly accounts of murder and death-by-mishap. No. I prefer my lonely, self-appointed role as hate's philosopher, prophet, and artist. The people's living concerns will not be mine. Besides, I hate the people. They do not aspire to my ideal of man: to hate for love to reign. I want freedom for every human being. I desire to persevere with hate. I can hate a man because a badger will never be as stupid as a man. This is the philosopher writing. Obviously we are doomed, but not because a family of squirrels are nestled together tonight in a warm bed of dead leaves... This is the prophet calling out to deaf ears. And I shall paint the whole bloody picture of humanities' annihilation by power and stupidity! This is the elusive, struggling artist whose life I will give my own life to nurture.

This morning my visiting stepfather tossed me the want-ads. I reached for the front page instead. There was a picture taken at the India-Pakistan border where the routine changing of the guard continues at a time when all life might end. Another awakening. These bearded, colorful men, soldiers dressed in traditional attire, traditionally preparing to eliminate the planet earth, but not one of them thinking that tonight, whether he acts or not, a starving, innocent child will get traditionally stabbed until dead. There was a huge crowd sitting on a hill overlooking the demonstration. Beyond them was a sky stuffed with a hundred gray clouds, heavy, pregnant, and ready to break water. I concentrated on the fantastic changing colors of the sky. I did not think about the impending human doom, nor did I recall the empty feeling doom brings while doing some usual chore like brushing my teeth. No picture came to mind showing what happens to a child's face after picking up a live grenade. The sky was snow gray and the trees behind the soldiers were going darker green with the setting sun. To hell with human beings I thought. Straight to hell with them. They cannot represent true life any longer. They only get in the way. I saw beauty in the background of a picture fraught with human animals. It was sent over the wire for the world's editors to print as shock material, yet I saw nothing that they wanted me to see. I saw stark green living, breathing trees. I saw an old, wise sky going to sleep day after day for a billion years, with or without the changing of the guard, the mass of humanity, or myself.

Tonight, in this chilled twilight, while the winter sun sets over my frozen backyard, I have made a very big decision. The sun will continue to rise everyday to the ax-wielding stupidity of mankind. That same sun sets on my small, hopeful intentions, and I know that I am as right as I will ever be. Because I desire to give this piece of my thoughts to you, the invisible reader, I know that I must be a loving human being. I might write angrily and carelessly. That cannot be helped. It is the way my machine works when it is pushed up against a wall. It fights back screaming. And I know the chances are better for victory if you hate your enemy, and aren't goaded to fight by cowardice and fear, like the typical soldier. I will die first by hate, because it's good to make the attempt to clear out all that you hate. And then I will die for love. Because after your best shot of hate, that is all there is left.

Philosopher, prophet, artist? Yes. But also father, husband, friend, teacher, student, wanderer, homebody, and divinity. What do I really care what you or posterity thinks? This is my fight. I shall not let my love be bullied by the brutal, careless whims of a stupid mankind. I understand death. I accept it whenever it happens to me. The knowledge of its inevitable finality is responsible for the howl while I write. I am one man who launches hates' minor attack on the human world. I am also a fool who knows that he must attempt to preserve the reality of the universe, the unmanned part of the universe, all by his lonesome...

Tonight I became an insect watching from a green tree getting darker with the setting sun. I am only a very small thing. But I hold the fight of many unrecognized nations. I represent the non-human world of poets, most women, animals, insects, fish, all trees, all plants, all life that does not line up each new sunrise prepared to kill, without also being damn well ready to eat their kill. I cannot go the rest of my life ignoring stupidity. Even as a lowly insect, I know that I am smarter than all of man's nations. And I know it would behoove quite a few species that I became just as powerful as all of man's nations.

Two thousand-thirty-five years ago Christ was born in the land without snow. He was a dark-haired baby who didn't wear diapers. Christ was a baby and all babies live peace. Besides hitting his mother when he wanted her to play with him, he was very peaceful. Kings brought the divine child presents, not one of them a small plastic toy phone. A variety of presents, but not one that a child would want to play with. Frankincense and Mir? Don't ask. Just receive and smile, smile and receive, and make sure the gifts are big enough not to get lodged in your new savior's throat.

This Christmas more than one person will drive forty miles to purchase a popular candle holder. When my oldest daughter was very young, she was taught to give nothing besides love and attention, and occasional crayon drawings of devotion. Slowly, gradually, over the past couple years, Santa Claus has left her heart. It is only a matter of time before Christmas makes her deeply and hopelessly frazzled like the rest of us.

I am out of the kind of work that writes you a check for the holidays. Joy has left my body. I have no way of knowing if I will ever be able to help support this family financially. And because of the money problem, I start to wonder if I am husband or father, or anything good at all. Money is the sickness of our hearts. It is the sole cause of any depression that exists where no tragedy has occurred. Because of money I did something yesterday that I thought I would never do. I went out peddling my books all over three counties. I had to ask my wife to take off from work. I borrowed a car. It had an American flag attached out the back window waving "I am tasteless" to all and sundry on a cold, bright December morning.

I drove to every bookstore and library in Central New York. By the end of the day I sold to three stores and involuntarily donated one set to a library. I walked up to the head librarian embracing my precious books. He received me quite cordially. I expected him to escort me over to the money box and pay me for my efforts. Patiently I waited while he talked about the lack of arts and culture in the Mohawk Valley. "One bookstore," he complained, "in a county of 250,000. Can you believe it?" Yes I thought, but here, let me put my hand out again, palm up, and hope that you get the hint. Nothing. Instead he stepped into his office and came out grasping the local swap sheet, suggesting that I advertise my books with the used cars. Then he offered me a book signing, but recanted, saying that in the past those only worked well with children's book authors. Then I imagined that he would prefer to ram the heel of his boot against my skull rather than pay me the paltry sum necessary to justify my existence as a writer. Culture or no culture. I should have killed him on the spot and fished through the petty cash box myself.

Now the thought of peddling my own books was and is a personal nightmare. Total desperation made me do it. Man will succumb to anything when the money is tight enough to cheat his own children. Except work at a dollar store. No. I won't do that. So what if an offer has already been made...? No. I will very calmly open up an artery before dehumanizing my existence at a dollar store.

After a day driving in and around Syracuse New York, I discovered the worst hole in all of the world to raise a sane family. You drive around for a full morning in it, penniless, in a borrowed car and see for yourself what an incurably sick and twisted, groaning hell of a city it is. Two of the bookstores on my list of ten were abandoned. Two more sold only pornography. Two were consignment, and the second one of these wouldn't take my books unless he could get the whole set for fifteen cents.

Yesterday I lived the life of a traveling salesman in America. Except I was selling a product which I made myself. Of course one couldn't eat my product—strike one. Nor was it something quite like holly leaf wrapping paper sold at a huge profit for charity. Strike two. Encyclopedias might have brought better luck, if I went door-to-door with the volumes I researched, wrote and published myself. Strike three and out. Actually lying prone in a basement beside a gassed Willy Loman.

A few years ago my chef left the restaurant business to peddle oyster crackers for an upstart company. Up before dawn, he drove his car over two hundred miles every day except Sunday. Boxes of light, airy oyster crackers stacked to the ceiling in the back seat. He peddled throughout a retail world that he convinced himself was in sufficient need of better oyster crackers. The best oyster crackers. In fact, over time, he couldn't understand how restaurants stayed in business without his delicious oyster crackers in stock.

Once he got me to try them, while he stood at my side waiting for affirmation. Holy God, the blind arrogance of delusion! Every time he said "oyster cracker" I envisioned spiraling rounds of slow-motion bullets busting out the back of my skull. His behavior was beyond delusional. It was insane, maniacal—an oyster cracker... Jesus Christ! Yet I played along, chewing for his benefit, although at the time I felt like striking him down and stuffing his mouth full of oyster crackers. He wanted to sell them to everyone. He was preaching the Word about oyster crackers. Each book that I wrote and got published, no matter what value its content, was written with the dreams that appear while walking alone at night in fear of death. I collaborated and created with the body which houses my soul. It was all that I had then, and all I have now. For $12.95 I will share its story with you. That's all the Word I know.

You say sure? As long as it's told over a bowl of steaming hot seafood chowder? Fine. Just try to ignore the steady stream of bullets drilling holes into my head. Promise me you'll crush those crackers quickly and take the soup onto your lap. I'm spilling blood.

Why this staunch, masochistic refusal to become equally excited over my own creations? How can man live a whole life never to stand up and lustily sing his own praises? Even if he foolishly sings to some greater power beyond him... It has got to be more stimulating than worshiping oyster crackers, right? I mean, how could my old boss become the apostle of a dry cracker company without having committed suicide yet? Hasn't he already gone way beyond the point of just considering it? Unless the crackers are laced with enough extra preservatives to fool the rest of us into thinking that he lives, I tell you that he must be dead already. A soul must die each moment an oyster cracker gets believed in.

To tell the truth, I hate my books. I despise them. I hate the product that I wanted to sell yesterday, during a weak moment when I thought my children needed toys for Christmas.

Privately, however, I intend to sing my praises while the rest of mankind watches me bleed. But I won't be singing for your money. I will sing, but know that I know it's not what I write into books that makes me praise-worthy. I am 100% man. I am a man. My blood heats up my wonder and desire. I can be squeezed until warm blood spurts out of my pours. But I will continue to sing while bleeding. I believe that every man's blood is my own blood. And every man should sing the song of watching it flow. I am singing for me and for you, even if I know that you, if given the choice, would choose a low-sodium oyster cracker over the intactness of my blood and its systems. Translated into easy, easy easy...

You suck
my blood.
But would rather have an oyster cracker.

Now tonight I am a hack. This is the end of the book, and the fifth time I promised myself openly in a book to bury the anger in a deep hole and write something beautiful for once. I lied. It is impossible for me to concentrate on the beautiful. I know where I live. These are my own eyes and I cannot play "pretty picture" with them, no matter how perfectly glorious the world would be if I could lie to myself more frequently.

There is a young man named Gangsta Williams being tried tonight for the murder of a seventeen-year-old girl. He shot her in the face and blood poured out. She died while the blood flowed out of her skull. I live forty miles away from the murder scene. I live a million miles away from humanity.

I appreciate your human murder. It is necessary and good for me this evening. It makes me right. It makes me feel good to remember, without much effort, that America is just a smelly hole I drop my garbage into.

Yes of course Gangsta is a piece of human ca-ca. I would like to watch his face clawed apart, eyeball to eyeball, by the mother of the child who was slain. But I was thinking about Germany today. I asked my daughter to imagine what a German Christmas was like. We were thinking of warm strudel and kugen, a hundred mountain villages each with its token butcher and steeple, Heidi and her Grandfather on skies... I thought about the glorious humanity thriving in a German village before Jesus and the Nazis. Sure it was imaginary, but so was the hydrogen bomb, once. Nothing will ever become something without first imagination, and then belief. The former is a healthy recreation for a childlike mind. But belief is the reckless preservation-in-motion of both angels and devils.

Life in the village was busy and wonderful. It looked best during a heavy snowfall. There was a bakery, a butcher's block, and wooden toys for sale in every shop window. Now I've decided to place Gangsta in the village I dream about. Presently he's pointing a pistol in the face of one of Hans Friedaflach's daughters. She's more astonished than frightened. "Dis koonnnot hopin' heera." She's right. Here comes Hans skiing down the mountain just in time to catch Gangsta before he pulls the trigger. Hans takes a second to survey the scene, then he takes Gangsta by the eyeballs and kills him.

I want to take Gangsta by the eyeballs and kill him too. Don't you? Won't you?

Liars! Wasted sperm! Rotten eggs! You allow for it. You let this happen. Now lay back in your easy chair and whistle "live and let live," while Gangsta plans and executes the murder of *your* little girl.

Today I picked up my daughter's book about German Americans. There was a picture of a man who was tarred and feathered for not supporting the war bond drive of 1917. The caption underneath the picture also told about another man who was beaten to death in prison for not wanting to volunteer with the Allied cause, to cross the ocean, to butcher his cousins, aunts, and uncles in Germany. On the page opposite there was a short article about the German internment during World War II. All proof of American criminal behavior that I had no previous knowledge of. In America the lies are hitting us the moment we are born. The truth is more fluff to stuff into our pillow cases. In America truth makes for very comfortable and cozy drool catchers.

I told my daughter that we should start looking at the world as if living in an imaginary time before Bismarck and the Holocaust. In the village of forest fairy tales, fear of God and trembling desires, the bright white nights of lighter living with moonbeams...

1862. Now that's a year to be alive in Germany! Especially at Christmas, and in the mountains, where the snow falls heavy without a sound, where the cholera and poison gas can't get in by airplane or autotrain. It's Christmas, 1862, and tonight is the one night out of the year for all Christians to feel safe and nearly immortal. They are safe with their savior Jesus Christ keeping watch over his domains.

The family stands around the piano singing carols. Nobody is faking. All are rosy-cheeked and glad, and actually faithfully believing in their god.

Tonight back home in America, Gangsta William's got talked about on the TV News. Gangsta was a bad boy. A very bad boy. Yet Gangsta, on his worst day, could not hold a loaded automatic weapon to the anchorman who covered the story from a downtown courtroom.

Gangsta was smiling. The anchorman was serious. Gangsta looked into the camera and snickered. The anchorman kept to the story, looking very grave. I am no longer human because the anchorman did not laugh an uproarious laugh in the face of a man named "Gangsta". I have ascended into the blue azure beyond human because the anchorman got paid by other human beings to tell the murderer's story. I am seated beside lord god our savior, I might even suggest the two of us play cards tonight, because I don't dare look to mankind for any cheering up.

He'll play. I'm told that if I win, I get to choose how we punish Gangsta.

I won. Lord god our savior let me win I think. So I have decided to push a serrated knife into Gangsta's belly, and probably his mother and father's belly too, for the bigger crime of stupidity, which they have obviously committed. Actually, any hurtful crime brought before lord god our savior and myself, from this day forward, is inexcusable, and punishable by a thousand screaming deaths. Who dares to carry stupidity and its murder so pretentiously into our kingdoms?

Tonight, just a few hours before Christmas I realize that a huge mistake has been made. I was accidentally born a human. I don't know what I was supposed to be, but it was not human. Maybe hyena. I am always laughing in the face of man. Anyway, I have become ferule. I am almost wild. Look at me. I forgo all my human rights and expect to be hunted, tortured, and killed for my tainted meat by midnight. But this smarter, more wild animal already knows that you fearful bedwetters will make a legal season first, to give me a sporting good chance to escape.

I look human. I smell human. I may even act a bit human, sometimes. But I am not human. I am a semi-wild animal. Once, long ago, my pack defended itself to preserve itself. There wasn't any evil. Only hunger. But that was a time before I was born, a life which I had no control over. Now the pack is not related in any way other than by species. Pack became country soon after the survival instinct became unnecessary. Small packs need not roam, hunt, nor play anymore. Leadership is dead. True leadership. The kind which defends without question the lives of its individual members. My country does not assume responsibility for me, my wife, my daughters, my dog. No pack leader. Hence, Gangsta. His own mother would let him fry. But the state protects him. Gangsta blew the face off of a young girl. He doesn't know what a man is. So he must die, right now. No questions. No arguments. All life outside of man agrees with me. Gangsta must die immediately. Immediately I tell you. No justice. No court. No humane treatment. The moment the young girl's face was blown away, a rock should have been picked up by the nearest pack member and used to pound a hole into Gangsta's head.

Here is the end. I promise. It is time to finish up the hate letters to my fellow man. I have to play Santa tonight.

Listen. Gangsta is evil but the anchorman was serious. He refused to laugh out loud, while silently watching his imagination cut up Gangsta into thirty smaller pieces.

Gangsta.

Gangsta.

Gangsta. And now I am over the edge. I prefer to make myself wild. There is my mountain cave, a pine forest, bright star lit skies, and a moon to laugh out loud to. I stalk the mountains high above the village, always on the lookout for a sour piece of human flesh.

The end.

Gangsta will go to prison where life is insane, and he will be fed well, with other jolly thieves and rapists. The anchorman will drive home to his children with lots of money for presents and popcorn. He wants the wife to watch him on TV at eleven. She knows his routine. No voice of protest. No video shot of his declaring, "Stop please, I can't do this anymore." She already knows, by repetition, that her anchorman husband will not provide one honest opinion. It's the news. It can lie anytime, but it cannot have an opinion. She knows this. Once there existed the faint hope in her heart that she would watch her husband behead a Gangsta with the point of his fountain pen. No. That hope and pride died together the same night, during his first assignment of a hit and run. He got good at keeping a straight face anytime evil bent him over to shove a truncheon up his ass. Now she waits for sleep. At eleven-thirty she can go to sleep. Though presently she expects to frown the perpetual frown that she's been frowning behind her sad heart for years. He will say "Gangsta" without laughing an uproarious laugh. He will say, "shooting death," and then it's possibly three more decades of heavy sobs into her pillow. He will say, "Gangsta" again, and if her mood doesn't improve tonight, then surely she'll be dead by morning. He says "downtown courtroom," and quite unexpectedly she livens up. Suddenly, she and I, and everyone else who's feeling a little bit wild these days, are out roaming the earth together again, in packs, tearing the flesh off any beast who stalks our territory with the intent, *just the intent*, of doing harm to our children. On the third and final "Gangsta," she bursts out laughing, leaps up from the couch, and in a giggling frenzy, runs into the kitchen, out the back door, around and around the house, and then back into the living room, doubled-over, laughing and laughing while the anchorman scolds her for not being the least bit sensitive to such an important issue. She's laughing in his face, screaming "coward" and "Gangsta" in between breaths of hysterical laughter.

Now I am laughing.

Tonight began as a German Christmas in my mind. I turned on the TV to see a thing that amused me very much. I laughed an uproarious laugh at the infinity of life which happens every second all around me, and although I did not give one bit of it permission to be so wrong, by it I can recognize the absurdity of a life not lived on my own condition. This life is absurd. I don't think humanity can survive another minute without becoming ferule. Not here in America anyway. I live here. I should know. Tonight I escaped out the side door, and ran across the street into the woods. I think it might be a good thing to stay here until everyone goes away. Far, far away. But who really knows? Tomorrow I might sneak back into the house expecting dinner, a bed, or maybe just a stomach wrenching laughter at the face of a Gangsta, a TV anchorman, or you. Personally I think humanity should be ousted from the pack. Gangsta doesn't matter. Neither do you. Not to time. Not to dogs. Never to God. Do you think that I think you're one to decide, pisseltit?

www.ingramcontent.com/pod-product-compliance
Lightning Source LLC
Chambersburg PA
CBHW050434290526
45786CB00006B/2028